CLIO'S LIVES
BIOGRAPHIES AND AUTOBIOGRAPHIES
OF HISTORIANS

CLIO'S LIVES

BIOGRAPHIES AND AUTOBIOGRAPHIES
OF HISTORIANS

EDITED BY DOUG MUNRO
AND JOHN G. REID

Published by ANU Press
The Australian National University
Acton ACT 2601, Australia
Email: anupress@anu.edu.au
This title is also available online at press.anu.edu.au

National Library of Australia Cataloguing-in-Publication entry

Title: Clio's lives : biographies and autobiographies
          of historians / editors: Doug Munro ;
          John G. Reid.

ISBN: 9781760461430 (paperback) 9781760461447 (ebook)

Subjects: Historians--North America--Biography.
          Historians--Australia--Biography.
          Authorship in literature--North America--Biography.
          Authorship in literature--Australia--Biography.

Other Creators/Contributors:
          Munro, Doug, editor.
          Reid, John G. (John Graham), 1948- editor.

All rights reserved. No part of this publication may be reproduced, stored in a retrieval system or transmitted in any form or by any means, electronic, mechanical, photocopying or otherwise, without the prior permission of the publisher.

The ANU.Lives Series in Biography is an initiative of the National Centre of Biography at The Australian National University, ncb.anu.edu.au.

Cover design and layout by ANU Press. Cover image adapted from *Clio, the Muse of History* by Artemisia Gentileschi, 1632.

This edition © 2017 ANU Press

This volume is affectionately dedicated to the memory of

Geoffrey Bolton (1931–2015)

Geoffrey Bolton was an enthusiastic participant in the project from which this volume arose, and in the workshop at which his and the other essays were initially presented. An accomplished biographer, with four book-length biographies to his credit reaching back as far as 1958, he was also one of the finest Australian historians of an exceptionally productive generation of scholars. His presence was a highlight at the workshop. Despite deteriorating health, his characteristic combination of erudition and affability was undiminished. All of us were deeply privileged by his participation and, in sadly bidding him *ave atque vale*, we acknowledge gratefully the magnitude of his contribution to this and so many other scholarly endeavours.

Contents

Acknowledgements ix

List of Contributors. xi

1. Introduction 1
   Doug Munro and John G. Reid

Autobiographies of Historians

2. Writing History/Writing about Yourself: What's the Difference? . .17
   Sheila Fitzpatrick

3. Walvin, Fitzpatrick and Rickard: Three Autobiographies
   of Childhood and Coming of Age 39
   Doug Munro and Geoffrey Gray

4. The Female Gaze: Australian Women Historians'
   Autobiographies. 65
   Ann Moyal

Nation-Defining Authors

5. 'A gigantic confession of life': Autobiography, 'National
   Awakening' and the Invention of Manning Clark 81
   Mark McKenna

6. Ceci n'est pas Ramsay Cook: A Biographical
   Reconnaissance. 103
   Donald Wright

Discipline-Defining Authors

7. Intersecting and Contrasting Lives: G.M. Trevelyan
   and Lytton Strachey 137
   Alastair MacLachlan

8. An Ingrained Activist: The Early Years of Raphael Samuel 173
   Sophie Scott-Brown

9. Pursuing the Antipodean: Bernard Smith, Identity
and History..199
   Sheridan Palmer

Collective Biography

10. Australian Historians Networking, 1914–1973 227
    Geoffrey Bolton

11. Country and Kin Calling? Keith Hancock, the National
    Dictionary Collaboration, and the Promotion of Life Writing
    in Australia..247
    Melanie Nolan

12. Imperial Women: Collective Biography, Gender
    and Yale-trained Historians..........................273
    John G. Reid

13. Concluding Reflections..............................301
    Barbara Caine

Index 307

Acknowledgements

This book had its origins in 2011, in a proposal by the two co-editors for a panel session at the then forthcoming 2015 Congress of the International Committee of Historical Sciences in Jinan, to be entitled 'Biographies and Autobiographies of Historians: Their Historiographical Importance'. It turned out for the better that our proposal did not make the cut for the congress. We promptly turned to Professor Melanie Nolan – one of the proposed Jinan panelists – to see if the National Centre for Biography (NCB) at The Australian National University (ANU) would be willing to host a workshop based on the idea of the panel but expanded to become a more ambitious undertaking with a published collection of essays now to be the ultimate goal. She responded graciously and positively, and the intensive two-day workshop in Canberra on 4–5 July 2015 proved to be a firm foundation for the book. By common consent, it was a memorable gathering. The participants gelled and the exchange of ideas flowed back and forth.

Accordingly, we are very grateful to Melanie and all at the NCB – and especially Karen Ciuffetelli, who took care of key organisational matters – for being our hosts at the workshop. A number of ANU scholars attended and contributed notably to the discussions; in particular, Malcolm Allbrook, Frank Bongiorno and Chris Wallace were kind enough to chair sessions. Ann Curthoys and Stuart Macintyre were unable to attend the workshop, but provided behind-the-scenes support. We also thank Tom Griffiths, who presented a paper on Eleanor Dark that could not appear in the collection because it was already committed elsewhere, but that added greatly to the workshop.[1] Funding support came from the NCB itself, and from the Gorsebrook Research Institute of Saint Mary's University (Halifax, Nova Scotia).

---

1   Tom Griffiths, 'The Timeless Land: Eleanor Dark', in Griffiths, *The Art of Time Travel: Historians and their Craft* (Melbourne: Black Inc., 2016), 16–41.

As the collection made its way from workshop to book, we again received valued support from a number of quarters. As we have noted in the dedication, the presence of Geoffrey Bolton was a highlight of the workshop, and we are very grateful to Carol Bolton for giving us the editorial freedom to prepare his now posthumous essay for publication. For helpful comments on the collection and on the specific essays, we thank warmly the two peer reviews and the members of the Editorial Board of the ANU.Lives Series in Biography. As editors, of course, we are deeply grateful to all of the contributing authors, not only for their fine essays but also for being receptive to our suggestions and dealing with them so expeditiously. An especial role was kindly taken by Barbara Caine, who provided the closing commentary at the workshop and then also contributed the Concluding Reflections to the book.

Finally, the publication process through ANU Press was smooth and expeditious, and we especially thank Geoff Hunt for his expert copy-editing.

Our profound gratitude to one and all!

Doug Munro
John G. Reid

List of Contributors

Geoffrey Bolton (1931–2015) was a prolific and versatile historian and biographer. In a long and distinguished career, he held chairs of history at the University of Western Australia, Murdoch University, the University of Queensland and Edith Cowan University, and also served as foundation director of the Australian Studies Centre in London. His work for the *Australian Dictionary of Biography* included the authorship of 94 entries. A recent publication in his honour is *A Historian for All Seasons: Essays for Geoffrey Bolton*, edited by Stuart Macintyre, Lenore Layman and Jenny Gregory (Monash University Publishing, 2017).

Barbara Caine is Professor of History and Head of the School of Philosophical and Historical Inquiry at the University of Sydney. She has worked extensively on historical biography and on the importance of individual lives in writing history. Her publications include *Destined to be Wives* (Oxford University Press, 1986); *Bombay to Bloomsbury: A Biography of the Strachey Family* (Oxford University Press, 2005); and *Biography and History* (Palgrave Macmillan, 2010). She is currently writing a history of women's autobiography.

Sheila Fitzpatrick is Professor of History at the University of Sydney and Distinguished Service Professor Emerita of the University of Chicago. Her recent books include two memoirs, *My Father's Daughter: Memories of an Australian childhood* (Melbourne University Press, 2010) and *A Spy in the Archives* (Melbourne University Press, 2014), a monograph, *On Stalin's Team: The Years of Living Dangerously in Soviet Politics* (Princeton University Press and Melbourne University Press, 2015) and a book on her late husband's experiences as a displaced person in Germany in the 1940s, *Mischka's War: A European odyssey of the 1940s* (Melbourne University Press, 2017).

Geoffrey Gray is an Adjunct Professor of History at the University of Queensland. He is author of *A Cautious Silence: The Politics of Australian Anthropology* (Aboriginal Studies Press, 2007); *Abrogating Responsibility: Vesteys Anthropology and the future of Aboriginal people* (Australian Scholarly Publishing, 2015); and co-editor (with Doug Munro and Christine Winter) of a special issue of the *Journal of Historical Biography*, 16 (2014) on the theme 'Telling Academic Lives'. He is presently a Chief Investigator on the ARC Linkage Grant, 'Serving our Country: Aboriginal and Torres Strait Islander People in the Defence of Australia'.

Mark McKenna is Professor of History at the University of Sydney. He has published widely in biography, the history of Australian republicanism and Indigenous history. *An Eye for Eternity*, his biography of the Australian historian Manning Clark, won five national awards including the 2012 Prime Minister's Prize for Non-Fiction. His most recent book is *From the Edge: Australia's Lost Histories* (Miegunyah Press, 2016).

Alastair MacLachlan is an Adjunct Professor at the Humanities Research Centre and the Research School of the Humanities and Arts at The Australian National University. A pupil of Sir John Plumb and an early modernist by training, he has written on the British Marxist historians and is completing a dual biography of Trevelyan and Strachey, *The Pedestal and the Keyhole*. His most recent publication in the field is 'Becoming National? G. M. Trevelyan: The Dilemmas of a Liberal (Inter)nationalist, 1900–1945', *Humanities Research*, 19:1 (2013), 32–43 (special issue on 'Nationalism and Biography', co-edited by Jonathan Herne and Christian Wicke).

Ann Moyal, AM, LittD (ANU), Hon DLitt (Syd), FAHA, is a historian of Australian science, a biographer and an autobiographer. The author of many books and papers, she has conducted research and some teaching in a number of Australian universities. She founded the Independent Scholars Association of Australia in 1995 and is a member of the Emeritus Fellowship at The Australian National University.

Doug Munro is an Adjunct Professor of History at the University of Queensland. Previously a historian of the Pacific Islands, he has become more interested in auto/biography and in telling academic lives. He has written on such diverse historians as George Rudé, G.R. Elton and J.W. Davidson, and has co-edited two previous books for ANU Press – *Scholars at War: Australasian Social Scientists, 1939–1945* (with Geoffrey Gray and

Christine Winter, 2012), and *Bearing Witness: Essays in Honour of Brij V. Lal* (with Jack Corbett, 2017). He is currently writing a history of the New Zealand Opera Company, 1954–1971.

Melanie Nolan is Professor of History, Director of the National Centre of Biography and General Editor of the *Australian Dictionary of Biography* at The Australian National University. She has published extensively on Australasian history; *Kin: A Collective Biography of a New Zealand Working-Class Family* (Canterbury University Press, 2005) won the 2006 ARANZ Ian Wards Prize and was shortlisted for the 2007 Ernest Scott Prize. She co-edited, with Christine Fernon, *The* ADB*'s Story* (ANU E Press, 2013) and chairs the editorial committee of ANU Press's series in biography, ANU.Lives. She is currently working on a survey of biography and history.

Sheridan Palmer is an independent art historian, curator and an Honorary Fellow at the University of Melbourne. Her interests are in Australian and European art from the twentieth century to the present, with an emphasis on the lives of artists and art historians. She has published *Centre of the Periphery: Three European Art Historians in Melbourne* (Australian Scholarly Publishing, 2008) and more recently *Hegel's Owl: The Life of Bernard Smith* (Power Publications, 2016). She is currently co-editing with Rex Butler *Antipodean Perspectives: Selected Writings of Bernard Smith* (Monash University Publishing) and researching post-war modernism.

John G. Reid is Professor of History at Saint Mary's University, Halifax, Nova Scotia. His research areas include early modern north-eastern North America, the history of higher education, and sport history. The author of *Viola Florence Barnes, 1885–1979: A Historian's Biography* (University of Toronto Press, 2005), his editorial publications include *Britain's Oceanic Empire: Atlantic and Indian Ocean Worlds, c.1550–1850* (Cambridge University Press, 2012; co-edited with H.V. Bowen and Elizabeth Mancke). He is a former co-editor of *Acadiensis: Journal of the History of the Atlantic Region*, and is currently researching the history of cricket in Nova Scotia to 1914.

Sophie Scott-Brown gained her PhD in modern history from The Australian National University in 2015. Her research uses lives to illuminate contemporary British and Australian intellectual history. Previous work has included the first biographical portrait of British historian Raphael Samuel (*The Histories of Raphael Samuel: A Portrait of a People's Historian*, ANU Press, 2017), and histories of Australian readers' encounters with English writers. She is currently working on a study of the life and work of Anglo-Australian anthropologist Phyllis Kaberry.

Donald Wright is Professor of Political Science at the University of New Brunswick. His research interests include biography, historiography, and the politics of memory. He is the author of *The Professionalization of History in English Canada* (University of Toronto Press, 2005), and *Donald Creighton: A Life in History* (University of Toronto Press, 2015), a finalist for the 2017 Canada Prize for best book in the humanities and social sciences. He is now writing a biography of Canadian historian and public intellectual Ramsay Cook (1931–2016).

1

Introduction

Doug Munro and John G. Reid

This volume of essays was inspired by the increasing though still-limited body of scholarship connecting the writing of history directly with the lives of those who write it, and the contributions were initially presented as papers at an intensive workshop held at The Australian National University in July 2015. While the writing of historians' lives by themselves or others is not new in itself – Edward Gibbon's *Memoirs of My Life and Writings*, for example, appeared posthumously in 1796 – considerable discussion flowed during the 1980s and 1990s from the publication of Pierre Nora's *Essais d'ego-histoire*.[1] The extent of subsequent developments is demonstrated in the seminal work in the English language – Jeremy Popkin's *History, Historians, & Autobiography* – where the significant increase in historians' autobiographies and associated discussion of the genre becomes evident.[2]

The early years of the twenty-first century have seen additional perspectives developed. The editors of a 2014 special issue of the *Journal of Historical Biography*, entitled 'Telling Academic Lives', offered a paradox: 'we contend that, because the historians analysed here are at times flawed, selfish or narrow-minded individuals, they are ideally suited

---

1   Pierre Nora, ed., *Essais d'ego-histoire* (Paris: Gallimard, 1987); see also Jeremy D. Popkin, *History, Historians, & Autobiography* (Chicago/London: University of Chicago Press, 2005), 74–5.
2   Popkin, *History, Historians, & Autobiography*. A monograph-length study on biographies of historians has yet to appear, but see Doug Munro, 'Biographies of Historians – or, The Cliographer's Craft', *Australian Historical Studies*, 43:1 (2012), 11–27, doi.org/10.1080/1031461X.2011.640694.

to make a case for the humane: flawless and lifeless they are not, but human they are'.³ History, therefore, was an essentially humane pursuit, incompletely understood except through exploration of the characteristics of the historian either through autobiography or by authors who are themselves historians. For Jaume Aurell in 2016, specifically examining historians' autobiographies, such works may be read moreover as 'cultural artifacts that convey their authors' theoretical perspectives on their lives and profession', and as 'privileged sources of intellectual history and, more specifically, of historiographical inquiry'.⁴

Thus, Nora's invitation to historians to make their own formation part of their historical study, and so to blur the distinction between objectivity and subjectivity, has continued to resonate during an era in which historians have long put aside pretensions of being objective. But the degree to which subjectivity is integral to historical practice remains an area of active debate. While this discussion has particular significance in the area of historians' autobiographies, it also bears on the wider significance of biography as an underpinning to historiographical understanding. Accordingly, the contribution made by this book is to examine the ways in which biography and autobiography can enhance historiographical understanding in four principal areas, and to conduct a reconnaissance in each.

The opening section is devoted specifically to historians' autobiographies, considered especially in a context of gender-based analysis. As the Australian historian Ken Inglis once observed, '[a] lot of history is concealed autobiography',⁵ a point that Sheila Fitzpatrick addresses in the opening contribution to the collection. Taking her own experience as historian and autobiographer as a point of departure, Fitzpatrick argues that the nature of history as an artistic pursuit ensures that there is a 'personal subtext' to historical writing that complicates not only the task of the autobiographer but also that of the biographer writing about the life of a person to whom they are personally close. This touches on questions of 'truth' and accuracy. Fitzpatrick takes up Philippe Lejeune's injunction that writers of autobiography have a pact with their readership to get it

---

3   Geoffrey Gray, Doug Munro and Christine Winter, 'Editors' Introduction: Telling Academic Lives', *Journal of Historical Biography*, 16 (Autumn 2014), 2.
4   Jaume Aurell, *Theoretical Perspectives on Historians' Autobiographies: From Documentation to Intervention* (New York/London: Routledge, 2016), 1–2.
5   K.S. Inglis, *This is the ABC: The Australian Broadcasting Corporation, 1932–1983* (Melbourne: Melbourne University Press, 1983), 1.

right, insofar as they are able.[6] As she notes in her first autobiography, there is the question of honesty: 'But honesty is another can of worms: what do we mean by it?'[7]

There are those who insist that autobiography is a form of creative writing, a selective account that deploys techniques of the novelist – what to highlight, what to downplay, what to omit altogether, and which themes to develop. When writing autobiography, an author – historian or not – may indeed leave things out for many reasons, though without necessarily leading to serious distortions of the overall picture. Conversely, there are also cases when an autobiographer will draw attention to the certainty of alternative interpretations of the same event.[8] Yet historians, when engaging in strict historical analysis, must also be selective, in the interests of maintaining relevance to a given question or for the sake of concise and focused exposition. Historians, moreover, adopt literary devices of many kinds, even in the chaste context of monographs or scholarly articles. It is true that the range of reasons for selectivity may extend further for an autobiographer than for a historian writing as such. There may be omissions in deference to the sensibilities of immediate family or in the face of even stronger constraints – as in the case, as noted by Sheila Fitzpatrick in this volume, of A.J.P. Taylor's *A Personal History*, which omitted any mention of his second wife in the light of her threat of legal action if she were brought into the picture.[9] In short, autobiography is not – and it cannot be – the whole, entire, unvarnished truth, but neither is it a fictional genre. And, as a context within which to understand an author's analytical work, it can be intensely revealing.

Accordingly, Doug Munro and Geoffrey Gray, in a comparative study of three accounts by historians of their formative years, note the increasingly revelatory nature of historians' memoirs generally and go on to discuss the overlap between family histories and autobiographies of childhood as well as teasing out many of the dominant themes of the

---

6   Philippe Lejeune, *Le pacte autobiographique* (Paris: Seuil, 1975).
7   Sheila Fitzpatrick, *My Father's Daughter: Memories of an Australian Childhood* (Melbourne: Melbourne University Press, 2010), 5.
8   See, for example, David Lamb, ed., *Just Beyond Reach: Peter Noel Lamb: Selected Memoirs* (Sydney: Rankin, 2003), 66, 77–8. The former page reference reads, 'anything I write about family dynamics runs the risk of being seen as partial, incomplete, arbitrary, misleading, inaccurate or worse – memory clouded with emotion is a problematic archive to be mined – so I won't even try to apologise in advance for my selection of "facts."'
9   See A.J.P. Taylor, *A Personal History* (London: Hamish Hamilton, 1983), x; Adam Sisman, *A.J.P. Taylor: A Biography* (London: Sinclair-Stevenson, 1994), 397.

subgenre.[10] They also identify the increasing tendency of autobiographies of childhood, and historians' memoirs generally, to adopt the methods of conventional monographs – although often lacking in the trappings of footnotes, bibliographies and index. Notwithstanding variability in quality, historians' autobiographies are now normally the products of careful deliberation and research, which their authors approach and execute as they would any other piece of serious historical writing. This is in contrast with, say, the earlier autobiographies of male Australian historians where there is some, but not much, internal evidence of them having an archival basis rather than being written from memory.[11] Munro and Gray's message is that historians' autobiographies of the better sort represent serious scholarship and ought to be so regarded.

Finally in this section, Ann Moyal examines autobiographical writing by women historians in Australia over an extended period of two centuries, placing special emphasis on the distinctively gendered elements of autobiographies by such historians as Jill Ker Conway and Sheila Fitzpatrick, as well as her own autobiographical work. Moyal situates these works within a wider Australian tradition of women's autobiographies that – by contrast with the 'personal odysseys of pioneering endeavour' that suffused male autobiography – were 'franker, relational, concerned with childhood, people and places, some masquerading as regional or local history'. They were often adjudged by male critics to be trivial, but Moyal shows how they collectively represented a unique cultural influence, and also how by the 1980s women's autobiographies, notably those by historians, came to embody 'an emerging awareness of the advent of professional careers'. While not all of the historians considered in this section of the book are women – John Rickard and James Walvin are the exceptions –

---

10   Jill Roe, *Our Fathers Cleared the Bush: Remembering Eyre Peninsula* (Adelaide: Wakefield Press, 2016) also illustrates the indeterminate boundaries and the extent to which autobiography is a mixed genre, the author using her own experiences and those of her family to introduce aspects of a regional story while explicitly deploying her training as a historian to contextualise and historicise.

11   G.V. Portus, *Happy Highways* (Melbourne: Melbourne University Press, 1953); W.K. Hancock, *Country and Calling* (London: Faber & Faber, 1954); Hancock, *Professing History* (Sydney: Sydney University Press, 1975); Paul Hasluck, *Mucking About: An Autobiography* (Melbourne: Melbourne University Press, 1977); Fred Alexander, *On Campus and Off: Reminiscences of the First Professor of Modern History at the University of Western Australia, 1916–1986* (Perth: University of Western Australia Press, 1987); Russel Ward, *A Radical Life: The Autobiography of Russel Ward* (Melbourne: Macmillan, 1988); Manning Clark, *The Puzzles of Childhood* (Ringwood: Viking, 1989); Clark, *The Quest for Grace* (Ringwood: Viking, 1990); Clark, *A Historian's Apprenticeship* (Melbourne: Melbourne University Press, 1992). One never knows: in an email, Geoffrey Gray suggested to us that Hasluck often made the claim that he wrote from memory, including the writing of *Mucking About* – but 'with a file at his elbow'.

nevertheless, the three essays, taken together, offer confirmation of the value of gender-based analysis of historians' autobiographies and of the distinctness of women's autobiographical writing.

Moyal's chapter also underlines the sheer prevalence of historians' autobiographies by Australian women. By Moyal's count, 13 Australian women historians have, between them, written 23 book-length autobiographies – a number that probably rivals those by counterparts in the rest of the world combined.[12] Arguing, indeed, that Australian historians, both men and women, are the world's most productive at the autobiographer's art, Jeremy Popkin suggested a convergence of reasons for this proliferation.[13] In Popkin's view, these autobiographies are often of high literary quality and are recognised as having made 'an important contribution to their society's overall tradition of first-person writing'. The autobiographers are often prominent historians who are well integrated into the country's intellectual and national life, and so have cultural authority. The cumulative effect is to impart to historians' autobiographies a respectability and legitimacy that encourages imitators. As Popkin says, one can now 'speak of a genuine corpus of historians' autobiographies, as opposed to a few isolated individual initiatives',[14] and the genre is

---

12   Autobiographies by non-Australian women historians include Nechama Tec, *Dry Tears: The Story of a Lost Childhood* (Westport, CT: Wildcat, 1982); Carolyn Steedman, *Landscape for a Good Woman: A Story of Two Lives* (London: Virago, 1986); Lucy S. Dawidowicz, *From that Place and Time: A Memoir, 1938–1947* (New York: W.W. Norton, 1989); Annie Kriegel, *Ce que j'ai cru comprendre* (Paris: Robert Laffont, 1991); Arlette Farge, *Le goût de l'archive* (Paris: Seuil, 1989); Susan Groag Bell, *Between Worlds: In Czechoslovakia, England, and America* (New York: E.P. Dutton, 1991); Deirdre McCloskey, *Crossing: A Memoir* (Chicago: Chicago University Press, 1999), doi.org/10.7208/chicago/9780226556727.001.0001; Régine Pernoud, *Villa Paradis: Souvenirs* (Paris: Stock, 1994); Lousa Passerini, *Autobiography of a Generation, Italy, 1968* (Hanover, NH: University Press of New England, 1996); Maria Tippett, *Becoming Myself: A Memoir* (Toronto: Stoddart, 1996); Jenifer Hart, *Ask Me No More: An Autobiography* (London: Peter Halban, 1998); Elisabeth Roudinesco, *Généalogies* (Paris: Fayard, 2002); Sheila Rowbotham, *Remembering the Sixties* (New York: Verso, 2002); Gerda Lerner, *Fireweed: A Political Autobiography* (Philadelphia: Temple University Press, 2002); Lerner, *Living with History/Making Social Change* (Chapel Hill: University of North Carolina Press, 2009), doi.org/10.5149/9780807887868_lerner; Antonia Fraser, *Must You Go? My Life with Harold Pinter* (London: Weidenfeld & Nicolson, 2010); Fraser, *My History: A Memoir of Growing Up* (London: Weidenfeld & Nicolson, 2015). There are also several collections of autobiographical essays by women – such as Eileen Boris and Nupur Chaudhuri, eds, *Voices of Women Historians: The Personal, the Political, the Professional* (Bloomington: Indiana University Press, 1999) – as well as numerous stand-alone journal articles.
13   Jeremy D. Popkin, 'Ego-histoire Down Under: Australian Historian-Autobiographers', *Australian Historical Studies*, 38:129 (2007), 107, doi.org/10.1080/10314610708601234.
14   Ibid., 106. Biographical study of Australian historians also shows no sign of abating, as instanced by the recent publication of Tom Griffiths, *The Art of Time Travel: Historians and their Craft* (Melbourne: Black Inc., 2016).

propelling itself forward under its own momentum. The autobiographies have often, Popkin adds, made an important contribution to national debates, not least on the recurring question of national identity.

This latter point also connects with the essays in the book's second section – one on an Australian historian, one on a Canadian – which focus on historians who have taken a crucial role in articulating and explaining national senses of identity. Mark McKenna's examination of the autobiographical writings of the profoundly influential Australian historian Manning Clark shows that these works represented 'the final expression of Clark's fictive historical style' and can be read as 'allegories of [Australian] national awakening'. Thus, Clark engaged in a form of self-invention through the telling of stories both about himself and about the emergence of the modern nation. Donald Wright, meanwhile, examines the early life of the Canadian historian Ramsay Cook, finding there the elements of the outlook of a historian very different from Clark, but who nevertheless grappled with comparable currents of national emergence – centrally concerned in this case with the development of a bilingual and multicultural Canada during the 1960s and 1970s, and the resulting need to attend to minority rights and to explain French-speaking to English-speaking Canada. The interrogation of the history of each national experience by each respective historian was profoundly influenced by personal formation and evolution, and each historian in turn conceptualised uniquely influential interpretive patterns in the understanding of Australia and Canada as national societies. And, therefore, both McKenna and Wright engage deeply with the relationship between analysis and imagination both in the lives of their subjects and in their own practice of the biographer's art.

Part of this grappling with questions of national emergence involved the portrayal of a very public figure, notably in the case of Manning Clark as a partisan for the cause of the Australian Labor Party. In turn, it entailed questions of self-definition, and in this respect Clark made much of pivotal moments in his life. One of these was walking through the streets of Bonn in November 1938, the morning after *Kristallnacht*. Viewing the broken glass and contemplating the violence, said Clark, affected his outlook on life – only that Clark was in England at the time, arriving in Bonn a fortnight later. Instead, he had appropriated his wife Dymphna's account of the immediate aftermath of *Kristallnacht*. For the sake of a good story and the moral that went with it, he continued to place himself among the broken glass, even when he knew this to be untrue. He was knowingly in contravention of the autobiographer's pact that he tell the truth and be accurate.

One of the biographical issues raised by comparison of the two chapters was famously addressed in Samuel Johnson's dismissive comment on Oliver Goldsmith's treatment of the life of Thomas Parnell: 'nobody can write the life of a man, but those who have eat and drunk and lived in social intercourse with him'.[15] It can, of course, cut both ways. McKenna did not know Manning Clark, but – via Clark's massive archive, through interviews, and in communication with Dymphna – he probably ended up 'knowing' his subject better than all but Clark's closest associates.[16] Wright, by contrast, has interviewed Ramsay Cook, who preferred to stay at arm's-length. Biographers, moreover, are only likely to have known their subjects for a phase of their lives, usually in the latter stages. Adam Sisman mentioned this with regard to Hugh Trevor-Roper. There were two Trevor-Ropers, with the younger firebrand being quenched by an older, mellower version, and it is this later persona that comes out more strongly in Sisman's account. Sisman himself recognises that he 'may have been influenced by feelings of loyalty, affection and gratitude' to a man he only got to know in his softer twilight years.[17] Such caveats apart, it is surely doubtful whether any biographer would claim it a *disadvantage* to have known his or her subject. With the unexpected death of Ramsay Cook in July 2016, Wright experienced a sense of personal loss as well as being deprived of a key source.[18] McKenna, on the other hand, has different sentiments with regard to his own subject. Given Manning Clark's desire to control the narrative of his life and his intolerance of criticism, he probably would have disliked reading *An Eye for Eternity*, and McKenna notes that 'when it comes to writing Clark's life, I'd rather him dead than alive'.[19] All the same, to have known Clark at some point in his life might well have been useful to his biographer.

---

15   John Wilson Croker, ed., *Boswell's Life of Johnson: Including their Tour to the Hebrides* (London: John Murray, 1848), 235.
16   On Clark's archive, see Mark McKenna, *An Eye for Eternity: The Life of Manning Clark* (Melbourne: Miegunyah Press, 2011), ch. 2. McKenna was given unimpeded access to the Clark Papers by Clark's eldest son and literary executor, Sebastian Clark.
17   Adam Sisman, *Hugh Trevor-Roper: The Biography* (London: Weidenfeld & Nicolson, 2010), xvi.
18   See Don Wright, 'Ramsay Cook, 1931–2016: Scholar and Friend', activehistory.ca/2016/07/ramsay-cook-1931-2016-an-obituary (accessed 17 October 2016).
19   McKenna, *An Eye for Eternity*, 23. The other major biography is Brian Matthews, *Manning Clark: A Life* (Sydney: Allen & Unwin, 2008). See also Doug Munro, '"How Illuminating It Has Been": Matthews, McKenna, and their Biographies of Manning Clark', in Philip Payton, ed., *Emigrants and Historians: Essays in Honour of Eric Richards* (Adelaide: Wakefield Press, 2016), 98–131.

The third section turns to the biographical study of historians who exerted a major influence on the definition and emergence of the discipline of history. Alastair MacLachlan's study of the intersecting lives and careers of G.M. Trevelyan and Lytton Strachey underlines how, in the context of the development of professionalised history, two historians who shared social and intellectual influences in nineteenth-century England could move in contrasting directions. While Trevelyan ultimately became part of the academic mainstream at Cambridge, and politically well-connected, Strachey remained as 'an irritating gadfly – and a supercilious intellectual' in the eyes of formal historians.

Ironically, Strachey is the better known of the two, largely thanks to their divergent personalities and despite the efforts of Trevelyan's biographer, David Cannadine.[20] Whereas Trevelyan was a high-minded model of rectitude, Strachey moved in the free-thinking Bloomsbury circle, which makes for better copy. Strachey's higher profile also owes something to films such as *Carrington* (1995) and to a lesser extent *Al sur de Granada* (2003). Far more influential is Michael Holroyd's 'full-frontal' biography of Strachey, which was a circuit-breaker in that it exponentially expanded the licence of biography to expose and disclose, and to venture into the realms of what had previously been considered off-limits and purely private.[21] The result would have horrified Trevelyan, who wrote an unrevealing autobiography and laudatory biographies, most notably his Garibaldi trilogy. Trevelyan had to have conquering heroes (and vanquished villains) to write about, in the same way as Strachey needed hero-figures to debunk. Ultimately, for MacLachlan, 'history is written with ideas and philosophies as well as with words', and to explain the movement of Strachey and Trevelyan from friendship to antipathy requires the biographer's engagement with 'their families, backgrounds, lifestyles, assumptions, moments and milieus'.

Studying the early years of a much later and very different British historian, Sophie Scott-Brown also probes these biographical elements in emphasising the emergence of Raphael Samuel as an organiser – in a political sense and in the development of his intellectualism. For Scott-Brown, it is important to recognise that 'thinking is a fundamentally social activity',

---

20   David Cannadine, *G. M. Trevelyan: A Life in History* (London: HarperCollins, 1992); and more recently Laura Trevelyan, *A Very British Family: The Trevelyans and their World* (London: I.B. Tauris, 2006).
21   Michael Holroyd, *Lytton Strachey: A Critical Biography* (2 vols; London: Heinemann, 1967–8).

and that Samuel's early life shows that values and skills are inseparable. The young communist activist moved on to become the central figure in the efforts of the History Workshop movement to democratise the writing and dissemination of history, and Scott-Brown defines the importance of Samuel's 'distinctive form of applied intelligence', which provides insight into the political approach of the Workshop as well as into Raphael Samuel's own 'complexity as an individual thinker'. The essay also provides an implicit reminder that matters of reputation lie at the heart of biography. Historians typically have short 'shelf lives'; their writings are soon overtaken and readily forgotten by the next generation of practitioners. Samuel died as recently as 1996 and despite his being the subject of several journal articles, he may already be entering that liminal phase of being remembered or else forgotten. Scott-Brown's analysis of the linkage of intellect and biography goes far to establishing that distinctiveness in Samuel's life and work that will continue to be recognised for its influence on the discipline of history.

Finally in this section, Sheridan Palmer connects the search for identity of Bernard Smith, the eminent Australian art historian, with the sense of anonymity that stemmed from being an illegitimate child and a fostered ward of the state. Smith emerged as a scholar fiercely committed not only to subverting uncritical views of Australian culture but also to the establishment of an Antipodean identity and of the country's cultural autonomy. Smith was thus comparable in some respects with Manning Clark who, in his different way, was also deeply involved in addressing such concerns.[22] Yet Smith also shared with Raphael Samuel the crucial influence of Marxism, never surrendering his 'Marxist humanism', or – as he himself put it towards the end of his life – his ability as 'a utopian communist' to believe in a future characterised by human progress. As an intellectual and in his influence on history as a discipline, however, Smith was especially noteworthy for his deployment of the skills and sensitivities of the art historian to trace the emergence of an 'Antipodean psyche' and to frame antipodeanism by disentangling 'the historical, scientific, cultural and political forces that moulded Australian art and its modern cultural identity'. His often polemical but always historiographically sophisticated challenge to imperial forms of cultural hegemony was a defining element in the emergence of modern Australian cultural history.

---

22 See also Sheridan Palmer, *Hegel's Owl: The Life of Bernard Smith* (Sydney: Power Publications, 2016).

The fourth and final group of essays deals with collective biography. While having some affinities with histories of the historical profession – such as Peter Novick's study of the fate of the 'noble dream' of objectivity among US historians, Donald Wright's analysis of the professionalisation of the discipline in English Canada, or Tamson Pietsch's examination of the British academic world in the era of settler colonialism[23] – collective biographical studies nevertheless have a different and distinctive goal. They are characterised primarily by their focus on the intertwining of the lives of historians brought together by networks of varying kinds – whether, in terms of the essays in this section, those in a formative era of Australian historiography, those associated with a scholarly endeavour such as the *Australian Dictionary of Biography* (*ADB*), or those associated with an approach to US colonial history embraced by the 'imperial school' at Yale – but are frequently disparate in personal, social or gender-related background. While having the additional value of placing individuals in wider historiographical and institutional contexts, such studies more importantly define the impact on the lives of multiple individuals of their professional and other interactions.

Thus, Geoffrey Bolton's study of the networking that underpinned the emergence of a professionalised body of historians in Australia spans the era from the founding of state universities to the establishment of the Australian Historical Association in 1973. The role of Oxford connections, notably through Balliol College, is examined, as is that of post–Second World War growth that stimulated the desire for a specifically disciplinary organisation through which networks could be formalised. Bolton draws attention to the role of the School of History at the University of Melbourne. Under the leadership of R.M. Crawford, the Melbourne history school was regarded as the finest in the land from the mid-1940s through to the mid-1960s, and strategically placed to

---

23   Peter Novick, *That Noble Dream: The 'Objectivity Question' and the American Historical Profession* (Cambridge: Cambridge University Press, 1988), doi.org/10.1017/CBO9780511816345; Donald Wright, *The Professionalization of History in English Canada* (Toronto: University of Toronto Press, 2005); Tamson Pietsch, *Empire of Scholars: Universities, Networks, and the British Academic World, 1850–1939* (Manchester: Manchester University Press, 2013), doi.org/10.7228/manchester/9780719085024.001.0001. There are also histories of history departments, notably William Palmer, *From Gentleman's Club to Professional Body: The Evolution of the History Department in the United States, 1840–1980* (Charleston, SC: BookSurge Publishing, 2008).

exercise patronage and exclusion.²⁴ Women had little place in the scheme of things before 1973. It was only in the 1970s that a younger generation of female historians began consciously to organise their own networks that sought to avert the constraints of reliance on male patronage – especially as innovative fields developed in areas such as women's history and Indigenous history. Bolton's chapter provides a solid basis for further exploration of his theme, informed by his insistence on the dynamism of 'the conversations that enabled communication among historians from both the newer and the older fields of historical endeavour'.

The interaction of older and newer directions of enquiry is also central to Melanie Nolan's examination of the evolution of Australian biographical writing in the context of the role of the *ADB*, including consideration of the historians who have been contributing authors and of its biographies of historians. The *ADB* began under the influence of W.K. Hancock at The Australian National University. Hancock exerted a profound personal influence on the project, but also worked in close association with the leading historians of his era. One of his earliest initiatives was to call a major, four-day conference in 1957, which brought together academic and non-academic historians from all parts of Australia, with the twin goals being 'to gauge the state of Australian history and to begin a conversation among Australian historians'.²⁵ From the first, therefore, the *ADB* was not just an indispensable work of reference but also a living project, thriving on the interchanges among diverse historical authors whose lives and careers were profoundly influenced by their participation in this collective enterprise. Not surprisingly, the result was an evolutionary process that linked the *ADB* with broader currents in history and biography. These included the increasing prominence of biographies of women, in a sophisticated gender-related context, as well as the conspicuous development of an interest on the part of both male and female historians in writing about their families in a way that melded biography and autobiography. Within the academy, Nolan concludes, historians have tended recently to return to

---

24   See also Fay Anderson, *An Historian's Life: Max Crawford and the Politics of Academic Freedom* (Melbourne: Melbourne University Press, 2005); Geoffrey Bolton, 'The Problem of History', The Kenneth Binns Lecture, given at the conference, 'An Open Book: Research, Imagination and the Pursuit of Knowledge', National Library of Australia, 29 April–1 May 2005, www.nla.gov.au/professor-geoffrey-bolton/the-problem-of-history (accessed 31 December 2015).
25   Melanie Nolan, '"Insufficiently Engineered": A Dictionary Designed to Stand the Test of Time', in Melanie Nolan and Christine Fernon, eds, *The ADB's Story* (Canberra: ANU E Press, 2013), 16.

the genre of biography 'to write about themselves and/or other historians', on the principle that 'how, and in what circumstances in all its fullness, one writes helps to understand the history that a historian constructs'.

Finally, John G. Reid seeks to define the explanatory power of collective biography in reference to a group of aspiring and established women historians in the United States in the first half of the twentieth century. The so-called 'imperial school' at Yale has been credited by some historians with providing a nurturing intellectual space for women doctoral students, and collective biographical analysis reveals some truth in this assertion, although also important limitations. The unquestioned leader of this grouping of historians was Charles McLean Andrews, who had come to Yale from a short sojourn at Johns Hopkins but also a much longer one at Bryn Mawr, where he became accustomed to supervising the work of women graduate students. While Andrews was no radical in gender terms, the evidence suggests that at Yale, female graduate students in the US colonial field did believe that they benefited from an environment in which their work was valued both by mentors and in the context of their own networks. The women were characterised by a degree of social diversity – showing that their Yale careers had profound biographical significance – although those who attained their doctoral degrees gravitated disproportionately to faculty positions in women's colleges. This in itself showed, of course, that important constraints remained. Yale provided, the essay concludes, 'a fragile ecology' within which women from varying social backgrounds could pursue their scholarship and even aspire to 'life patterns that allowed for the balances between employment and research and between career and family to become negotiable, though always within limits'.

In all of these areas, therefore, this book links biography and autobiography with broader intellectual and social currents that influenced historians and their discipline. The goals of the collection include not only bringing forward the substantive findings of the contributing authors but defining their combined significance and identifying productive directions for future research. Barbara Caine's reflective concluding chapter addresses these wider questions, and underlines the inseparability of biography and autobiography from historical understanding in the context of the evolving historiographies of the early to mid-twenty-first century. Indeed, Caine identifies the emerging focus on the lives of historians as nothing less than 'a new way of writing the history of history, both as a discipline and as a profession'. Purely institutional or methodological approaches thus give way to studies informed by 'the impact of particular forms of family life and education, of personal outlook, and especially of social networks on the work of historians'. While challenges inevitably arise from acknowledging the role in historical writing of imagination and indeed of personal myth-making by the historian, nevertheless Caine is confident – as expressed in a phrase that we are happy to make the conclusion of this Introduction, as well as ultimately of the book as a whole – that the currently 'wide and ever-growing interest in historians' autobiography and biography will fundamentally change the ways in which we see, think about and write history'.

Autobiographies of Historians

2

Writing History/Writing about Yourself: What's the Difference?[1]

Sheila Fitzpatrick

According to Philippe Lejeune, writers of autobiography implicitly sign a pact with the reader to tell the truth, or at least the truth as they know it, about themselves.[2] That is, primarily a subjective truth. As for facts, the expectation is presumably that autobiographers will convey the facts as they know or remember them, but without a necessary obligation to check their memory through documentary or other research. There is no autobiographer's commitment to objectivity, rather the contrary. The autobiographical truth is, by definition, a subjective one.

Historians do not have an explicit pact, and the theoretical assault of the past 20–30 years on objectivity as a historians' goal, as well as the rise of oral history and memory studies, have muddied the waters. However, I think most historians (at least outside the cultural field) would assume that their task is to 'get the story right', implying an obligation of factual accuracy based on careful research in archives and other primary sources, which are referenced in such a way as to allow others to check their accuracy. Cultural historians are partial exceptions, since they may be after somewhat

---

1   Part of this chapter draws on a short essay, 'Demoyte's Grey Suit: Writing Memoirs, Writing History', published in *Australian Book Review*, 362 (June–July 2014), 26–30, which was itself an abridged version of my Ward Lecture, 'Writing Memoirs, Writing History', delivered at the University of Sydney on 27 March 2014.
2   Philippe Lejeune, *Le pacte autobiographique* (Paris: Seuil, 1975).

different goals, such as recovering forgotten 'voices', or analysing how historical events have been remembered and mythologised, represented in different contexts and by different groups. The obligation of accuracy here must be accuracy of reproduction and representation. Historians who focus on memory are perhaps the least committed to the positivist goal of 'getting it right', since a certain relativism about the actual past is built in to the exploration of ways people remember it. This same relativism, however, tends to incline them towards a stance of detachment rather than advocacy.

This essay will offer an account of the problems and issues that arose when I, being a historian by trade, started writing autobiography but continued to write history. Whether I am writing as an autobiographer or as a historian is a moot point; I hope historians will not find it too self-indulgent. The main question to be pursued is how the experience changed my stance on and understanding of the objectivity/subjectivity discussion. I will conclude with an examination of territory that I find still trickier than writing about my own life, namely: writing, as a historian, about the life of someone close to me, to whom I feel a strong commitment of loyalty.

As I was taught in the history department of the University of Melbourne in the 1950s, the historian's task was to strive for objectivity. We were like scientific experimenters, not letting anything contaminate our experimental data. Full objectivity was, of course, not realisable, but it was a goal to which one needed to get as close as possible. The personal and the partisan were biases and distortions that would prevent you getting at 'truth'. If you wanted to offer a subjective view (so the conventional wisdom went), write literature or propaganda, not history. Nevertheless, the Melbourne approach to history, at least in my time, was not inimical to the idea of the writing of history as an art or craft rather than a science. I encountered social science imperatives for the first time on arriving in the United States in the 1970s, and for a while attempted to satisfy them and suppress the literary impulses that came more naturally to me.

For a long time, I was a true believer in the objective approach to writing history, primarily because I found myself working in America during the Cold War as a historian of the Soviet Union. With Soviet historians writing blatantly biased accounts of their own history (their work going through censorship to make sure they got the bias right), and American scholars writing pretty blatantly biased accounts of 'the empire of evil' from their side, the only possible stance seemed defiant objectivity, or the refusal to take sides. Of course, it was a stance that got me into trouble with both sides. The attitude in US Sovietology in the 1970s was that if you were not unmistakably 'anti-Soviet', you must be pro. The Soviets were even more insistent on this dichotomy, and moreover added their own Marxist rider that the claim to be objective was in itself a political stance of non-sympathy with the Soviet Union. They called people like me 'so-called objective bourgeois historians'. At least that was a better category than the other one available to non-communist foreigner historians of the Soviet Union: 'bourgeois falsifiers'.

By the 1990s, the Cold War was over, more or less, and within the historical profession, objectivity was getting a bad name and subjectivity was getting interesting. The moment I remember becoming aware of this trend was when I moved to the University of Chicago in 1990 and gave a talk to the department on my work, giving my usual critique of politicised history in the Soviet context, and our black and feminist historians glared at me and said: *What's wrong with politicised history?* I saw that the issue of advocacy history was a bit more complicated than I had thought, but I still did not want to write it myself. Objectivity and detachment might, I conceded, be considered an emotional (subjective) choice like any other for historians, but, if so, it was my choice.[3] Feeling detached came naturally to me (and not just as a historian), so I was going to stick with it.

There were lots of problems of bias and selectivity surrounding the published and even the archival materials I worked with as a Soviet historian. Thus, I added a highly developed scepticism about the reliability of sources and alleged facts to my temperamental stance of detachment. My historical subjects, I found, often did their best to mislead and hide their real selves and purposes from me. That is particularly true of political history, which I tackled obliquely in my first book,[4] and have recently returned to with *On Stalin's Team: The Years of Living Dangerously in Soviet*

---

3   See the interesting discussion in Paul White, 'The Emotional Economy of Science: Introduction', *Isis*, 100:4 (2009), 792–7, doi.org/10.1086/652019, and the articles that follow.
4   Sheila Fitzpatrick, *The Commissariat of Enlightenment: Soviet Organization of Education and the Arts under Lunacharsky, October 1917–1921* (London: Cambridge University Press, 1970). One of the subthemes of this book was the post-revolutionary discovery by the new Bolshevik leaders of the importance of institutional interest in politics, once you are running the state and not just planning revolution.

Politics.[5] Stalin was a great self-mystifier with a talent not only of fashioning himself for history but also of fashioning his archive for historians. But it's true of any kind of history about people who left records. They give you an account of what they did and why they did it, but that account is spun for the audience and the record; the trick is to find out what they actually did and why (to the extent this is knowable) they really did it. Perhaps I go too far in my suspicious approach to all statements of motive (one of my books is called *Tear off the Masks*);[6] while I am not a Marxist historian, I think it is one of the things I picked up early on from Marx, the great unmasker. Stalin picked it up too, and he certainly took suspicion to an extreme. The objects of his suspicion included historians who insisted on scrabbling in archives without a fixed conviction about what they were going to find there. He called them 'archive rats'.[7]

Stalin was proud of not letting people pull the wool over his eyes. He particularly prided himself on knowing that whenever a bureaucracy asks for money, its people are lying about their actual resources and exaggerating their needs. This is something historians should remember, too. Institutional archives – that is, the records of government bureaucracies – are basically telling the story *from the institution's point of view*. Their aim is self-justification, often in complex turf wars with other institutions, not the gathering of objective and reliable data for the use of future historians. The same applies, *a fortiori*, to personal archives, even if not everyone is so upfront about it as Manning Clark, who (as Mark McKenna has told us)[8] left explanatory notes and cross-references for the biographers' guidance in his papers. As a historian, you should never have a happy relationship of trust with your sources and the data they offer you. Your sources and your data are all, in the nature of things, biased.

Given my favoured stance of detachment and my well-honed scepticism about source bias, I seemed the last person who ought to be writing memoir or autobiography. In fact, it did not occur to me to do so until in 2006 Louise Adler of Melbourne University Press heard me give a short talk on

---

5   Sheila Fitzpatrick, *On Stalin's Team: The Years of Living Dangerously in Soviet Politics* (Princeton and Melbourne: Princeton University Press and Melbourne University Press, 2015), doi.org/10.1515/9781400874217.
6   Sheila Fitzpatrick, *Tear off the Masks! Identity and Imposture in Twentieth-Century Russia* (Princeton: Princeton University Press, 2005).
7   I.V. Stalin, 'O nekotorykh voprosakh istorii bol'shevizma' (1931), in J.V. Stalin, *Sochineniia*, vol. 13 (Moscow: Gosudarstvennoe izdatel'stvo politicheskoi literatury, 1951), 96.
8   Mark McKenna, *An Eye for Eternity: The Life of Manning Clark* (Melbourne: Miegunyah Press, 2011), 28–34.

my father (the radical historian Brian Fitzpatrick), and suggested I write a memoir about him. I thought that might be not only an interesting but also a useful thing to do, given that I had not really managed to come to terms with him in the four decades since his death, just stopped thinking about him. So I did a trial run in a 'Diary' essay for the *London Review of Books*,[9] and when people wrote in to say they recognised him, that he had become a living person to them, I was hooked. I thought of it initially purely as a memoir of my father.

When writing his autobiography, A.J.P. Taylor said nothing about his second marriage, in deference to the objections of his second wife, who had made it clear that any mention of her in the book would almost certainly result in legal proceedings. It did, as Taylor acknowledged, result in 'some odd gaps', which he might not have countenanced had he been writing a biography of, say, Lord Beaverbrook.[10] In fact, it is tempting to do things like omitting a marriage you do not like to remember. But as I got deeper into the business of writing autobiography, I decided that would be cheating. I also decided that in some special circumstances, you are allowed to cheat, though preferably with some warning to the reader (which Taylor gives) that a personal censor has been at work. My methodology in writing *My Father's Daughter*[11] was more or less that of a historian, despite the fact that I was basically interested in conveying personality and relationships, which had not been a primary endeavour (or at least not recognised as such) in any of my historical works.

I started by writing down everything I could remember about my childhood under chapter headings, not looking anything up, treating my memory as a primary source that I was transcribing. Then I expanded my source base as in any other historical research project: reading the documents, doing oral history to check my memory against others', trying to square and check the various accounts. My approach was so much that of a historian that I even included a bibliography and list of archival sources at the end. Still, I was startled by the discrepancies of the various oral accounts and documents, and even more by the fact that things that I subjectively believed – *knew* – to be really important in my life had somehow not made it into the historical record. I saw that if I had

---

9   Sheila Fitzpatrick, 'Diary', *London Review of Books*, 8 February 2007.
10   A.J.P. Taylor, *A Personal History* (London: Hamish Hamilton, 1983), x.
11   Sheila Fitzpatrick, *My Father's Daughter: Memories of an Australian Childhood* (Melbourne: Melbourne University Press, 2010).

been another historian working just with that record – that is, without my own memory and sense of the 'truth' about my life – that historian would have (from my point of view) got it wrong.[12] At that point, I had a sudden fear that perhaps I would never be able to write history again. If a historian who was not me could not get my life right without my help, how was I going to get Stalin right, even leaving aside the fact that he, the great mystifier, was consciously out to hinder me?

Then there was the awkward question of my memory, used by me as a primary source. If it is part of historians' Hippocratic Oath not to trust their sources, why am I trusting this one? But then, as a memoirist, what choice do I have? What you remember and what you believe to be the truth about your life are impossible to separate. One can, of course, argue that the genre of memoir allows for more detachment than autobiography; perhaps here the implicit pact (à la Lejeune) is to tell a story about yourself and your times that is based on personal memories, but only those memories that are deemed relevant to the times experienced – in other words, something less than full disclosure as far as personal life is concerned. In any case, memory is the basic source in both genres. So how do we accommodate that basic scepticism about sources that, as a historian, I have been preaching?

There is only so much scepticism that memoirists can deploy about their own memory. To be sure, you can play around at the margins, as I did in *My Father's Daughter*, telling readers where my memory of events was contested by other people's memories (for example, the 'hate Sheila' campaign at school, vividly remembered by me, but denied by my schoolfriends),[13] or had been found to be inaccurate (the song I remembered my friend Camilla Maxwell singing in 1958, which turned out not to have been written until two years later).[14] But basically you have made a pact to tell the truth about yourself and your life, and your memory is the only access you have to that. So my memory misdated Camilla's song, and on top of that I passed the false memory on to her, making two mistaken witnesses – but that does not mean the singing of the song and the emotions associated with it did not happen.

---

12 For more on this, see Sheila Fitzpatrick, 'Can You Write a History of Yourself? Thoughts of a Historian Turned Memoirist', *Griffith Review*, 33 (2011), 1–7. See also Sheila Fitzpatrick, 'Getting Personal: On Subjectivity in Historical Practice', in Alf Lüdtke and Sebastian Jobs, eds, *Unsettling History* (Frankfurt a/M: Campus Verlag, 2010), 85–99.
13 See *My Father's Daughter*, 112.
14 See *My Father's Daughter*, 188–9.

2. WRITING HISTORY/WRITING ABOUT YOURSELF

As a memoirist, in distinction to a historian, you are pledged to tell the emotional truth rather than the strictly factual one, a subjective rather than an objective truth.

When I started that first memoir, I envisaged it as a detached work written with a light touch – a good likeness of my father, warts and all, catching the essence of his quirky personality. It was not my plan to go deep in self-revelation; I initially saw myself as outside the painting, like the portraitist, or at least with my own individuality muted and camouflaged. It did not work out that way. I had not gone far before I realised that you do not make a portrait of your father without stirring up all sorts of emotions – love, pity, disappointment, resentment, regret – and without offering an involuntary self-portrait as well. The way I structured the memoir was a progression from the father as the small child's hero to the teenager's discovery that the hero had feet of clay. You would hope that after adolescence came some kind of reconciliation or happy medium, but, in my case, my father died suddenly with us unreconciled. So that had to be part of the story; the light, detached touch would not work. Writing this part of the book made me cry, and I realised with a certain alarm that I wanted to make the reader cry, too.

That is an aim that I would never have admitted as a historian. If I examine my work, however, especially the social history, I see that often I was indeed trying to move my readers, even to make them cry, but that I generally did this in a voice other than my own, via quotation. In another age, historians were bolder. The key quotation I used to convey my sense of the pathos of revolution in my first (dissertation-based) book, *The Commissariat of Enlightenment*, was from Thomas Carlyle's *French Revolution*, describing Robespierre going to his execution wearing the sky-blue coat he had had made for the Festival of the Supreme Being: 'O Reader, can thy hard heart hold out against that?' is how Carlyle ends.[15] I do not think I could have got away with writing something like that in my own voice in an Oxford DPhil thesis in 1969.

My father, Brian Fitzpatrick, was a Carlyle man at heart; as a teenager, I came to dread his purple passages, usually written when drunk. He is known as a radical economic historian specialising in British imperialism in Australia and the Australian labour movement, but if you look at

---

15 Thomas Carlyle, *The French Revolution: A History* (2 vols; London: J.M. Dent & Sons, 1955; first published 1837), vol. 2, 359.

his later work – *The Australian People*[16] and, particularly, *The Australian Commonwealth*[17] – you can see that he was way ahead of his time in introducing not just his civil liberties/human rights concerns but also putting *himself* into his history. Before he wrote his histories, however, he wrote an autobiographical novel, *The Colonials*.[18] It includes lots of great social history about the home front in the Melbourne suburb of Moonee Ponds during the First World War, but the key thing in it is the portrait of his father, written ostensibly from the standpoint of an omniscient narrator but actually from that of the 14-year-old son, the stand-in for the author's younger self. The son is infuriated by his father, critical of him, but he also feels a great, almost crippling, pity for him and his disappointments. The literary progenitor for that particular emotional combination is Edmund Gosse's *Father and Son* (1907), a favourite novel of my father's.[19] As a 14-year-old, I shared his liking for it, which pleased him. Probably his identification with the son was so great that it did not strike him that I might see not only the son but also the father in him.

My father's intrusion of the personal in *The Australian Commonwealth* was a source of embarrassment to me as an adolescent, when it came out; now I tend to see that element as a virtue. But I myself have been fairly scrupulous in separating my personal writing from the historical. In the 1990s, when the Soviet Union collapsed and its archives opened, I did a lot of interesting archival work on questions of social and cultural history of the 1960s, but when it came to writing it up as academic history there were problems. I had a strong irrational feeling that once we got to the moment of my arrival in the Soviet Union – 'when I came in', in the autumn of 1966 – it stopped being history, and therefore could only be written (by me) as memoir. But at that point I was not interested in writing memoirs. 'Bring in the subjective element,' colleagues and publishers said, 'it's OK now, it's even fashionable'. I did not want to do it. Apart from perhaps reminding me of my youthful embarrassment at *The Australian Commonwealth*, it apparently violated my personal sense of genre. If I am in it, it is got to be a memoir. The sole exception to this is a curious little piece I wrote on the absoluteness of truth, once you were

---

16 Brian Fitzpatrick, *The Australian People, 1788–1945* (Melbourne: Melbourne University Press, 1946).
17 Brian Fitzpatrick, *The Australian Commonwealth: A Picture of the Community, 1901–1955* (Melbourne: F.W. Cheshire, 1956).
18 Brian Fitzpatrick, *The Colonials*, with introduction by David Fitzpatrick (Melbourne: Miegunyah Press, 2013).
19 Edmund Gosse, *Father and Son: A Study of Two Temperaments* (London: Heinemann, 1907).

looking from the old Soviet Union, based on my interactions with the 'truth-telling' journal of the 1960s, *Novy mir* – territory I returned to later in my *Spy in the Archives* memoir.[20]

My dislike of putting myself in, however, did not mean that my scholarly historical books had no personal subtext. It is not true of all my books, but it is true of some, and I gather from my fellow historian Jonathan Steinberg that this is not unusual.[21] It does not necessarily imply a prejudgement of the meaning of the events, so much as a kind of emotional disposition with regard to them. These particular topics of historical enquiry connected in some way to personal concerns of mine, and that was part of the reason I was interested in them. In *The Commissariat of Enlightenment*, for example, the subtext was whether it was morally acceptable for intellectuals to work with power, which meant making compromises but also getting things done (as the Commissar, Lunacharsky, did in the Soviet Union), or rather to maintain the stance of perpetual opposition and, by implication, moral superiority favoured in the Soviet Union by many members of the intelligentsia and, in Australia, by my father.

By the time I was born, my father had put away his autobiographical novel and his original family along with it; apart from one brother, he seemed to have ditched Moonee Ponds, claiming – to my shock as a child – that he could not remember all his sisters' names. I did not see how anyone could forget something like that, and I still cannot. In the novel, he treats the sisters with sympathy, but he compacts the five of them into two. That seems to me almost as incomprehensible as forgetting their names. This reaction suggests that autobiographical fiction is not a possible genre for me. However tenuous the notion of a fact may be, I am apparently hardwired with the idea you have to stick with them. For me, the fun of telling the story, whether history or memoir, is partly finding a story that make sense within the constraints of the known 'facts', which so often and annoyingly get in the way of our best interpretations.

---

20   Sheila Fitzpatrick, 'A Short History of Truth and Lies in the Soviet Union from Stalin to Khrushchev', in Belinda Davies, Thomas Lindenberger and Michael Wildt, eds, *Alltag, Erfahrung, Eigensinn. Historische-Antropologische Erkundungen* (Frankfurt a/M: Campus Verlag, 2008), 91–104. See also Fitzpatrick, *A Spy in the Archives* (subtitle for British edition *A Memoir of Cold War Russia*) (Melbourne: Melbourne University Press, 2013; London: I.B. Tauris, 2014), 220, 245–6.
21   When he was at Cambridge, Steinberg (now at the University of Pennsylvania) ran a seminar in which historians were invited to talk about the personal subtext of well-known works – and many knew exactly what was meant, and were willing to reveal it. Personal communication from Steinberg.

Having written one memoir that veered off into autobiography, I sat down to write another, *A Spy in the Archives*,[22] telling myself that this time it would stay as a memoir, with a light, detached tone, and also with lots of local colour. The subject was Moscow in the late 1960s. This was a subject that I apparently could not write about as a historian, but which had provided me with the subtext of at least one book, *Everyday Stalinism*, which, although its subject was the 1930s, was in conception strongly informed by my firsthand astonishment in the late 1960s at the manifold discomforts and inconveniences of everyday post-Stalinism.[23] This time I had more fully shed my historian persona than with *My Father's Daughter* (no bibliography or list of sources here). There is one chapter in *A Spy in the Archives* – the *Novy mir* one – that could be read more or less as it stands as cultural history (or at least the kind of cultural history, common in scholarship on the Soviet Union, that also has an element of personal testimony).[24] Otherwise, I have attempted to recreate the times only from the very specific point of view of a resident foreigner. In the Soviet Union, the marking and special status of foreigners was extraordinarily strong, meaning that it was difficult, even in regard to people one knew intimately, to be sure how the world looked to them when you, the foreigner, were not present to skew the data.

In the event, *A Spy in the Archives* did not veer as much into autobiography as *My Father's Daughter*, but it veered a bit. For one thing, Igor Sats, my Soviet adoptive father, became a central character; it became a book bringing Igor back to life. Igor was an old spy, as he liked to boast – meaning a field reconnaissance person in the Second World War, not a KGB man – and the KGB gave both of us a certain amount of trouble about our friendship. But that is not the main reason *A Spy in the Archives* has that title. In the Cold War 1960s, the Soviets thought all foreigners who did research on their history, politics, society and culture were likely to be spies; among historians, the most suspect were the very small group, including me, working on post-1917 topics. I, in addition, came directly

---

22 Fitzpatrick, *A Spy in the Archives*.
23 Sheila Fitzpatrick, *Everyday Stalinism. Ordinary Life in Extraordinary Times: Soviet Russia in the 1930s* (London/New York: Oxford University Press, 2000). If I moved my 1960s observations back into the past, several novelists have used this book as a basis for their fictions about the 1950s – they include Francis Spufford, *Red Plenty* (London: Faber & Faber, 2010), who acknowledges the debt on p. 363 – or, in even more recent times, Tom Rob Smith, author of *Child 44* (London: Simon & Schuster, 2015), as stated in interview with Kate Evans on 'Books & The Arts', Radio National, 16 March 2015.
24 Fitzpatrick, *A Spy in the Archives*, ch. 6.

from St Antony's in Oxford, which was constantly attacked in the Soviet press as a 'spy college'; its fellows, including my DPhil supervisor, did in fact have close connections with British intelligence. We – the 20 British exchange postgraduate students in Moscow in my year – were all obsessed by spying (it was the age of Philby and the Cambridge Four);[25] however, given my topic and my St Antony's affiliation, I was probably more worried than most about being 'unmasked' as a spy and expelled. They did unmask me in the end, as I relate in the book,[26] but fortunately did not realise that the author of the article they regarded as the 'next thing to spying' was me, actually in the Soviet Union at the time, because the article was written under my maiden name with initials and they thought the author was a man. But apart from the adventure aspect, this spy business left a mark on me. From the Soviet point of view, any foreigner who burrowed away trying to find out their secrets (as I was doing in their archives), was 'objectively' – that is, in the overall scheme of things – a capitalist spy, regardless of whether they were on any intelligence service's payroll. I knew I was not on anyone's payroll and I did not feel like a capitalist. But I am not sure that under interrogation I could have denied with any conviction that I was essentially a spy.

Stalin would have had no doubts about the matter. All historians who put data above ideology were 'archive rats' and, if they were foreign, they were spies, it was absolutely clear. Stalin and his team was my next project, a historical one again, archive-based though written for a popular audience. I approached it with my normal sense of detachment (which can also be read as a God's-eye view implying moral superiority)[27] and a specific determination to avoid pushing any political agenda (not that I was conscious of having one). But I did bring one personal conceit to the work, undoubtedly inspired by my Moscow memoir and the Moscow memories they had revived. This was to imagine myself as a spy in Stalin's camp, using the intelligence tactic he most feared – planting a spy among his closest associates to get the inside story.

---

25   The two defectors of the early 1950s, diplomats Donald Maclean and Guy Burgess; Kim Philby, who defected in 1963; and the art historian Anthony Blunt.
26   Fitzpatrick, *A Spy in the Archives*, 281–2.
27   When I read Sarkar's (approving) reference to 'the passionless voice of superiority' of the impartial historian in Dipesh Chakrabarty's recent *The Calling of History: Sir Jadunath Sarkar and his Empire of Truth* (Chicago: University of Chicago Press, 2015), 96, doi.org/10.7208/chicago/9780226240244.001.0001, I had an uncomfortable sense of hearing myself when young. Admittedly Sarkar glossed this as superiority to the biases of temporal and spatial location.

My book, *On Stalin's Team*, is not a Stalin biography, but rather a collective biography of Stalin and his team – the dozen or so men who over a period of 30 years were closest to him (Molotov, Kaganovich, Khrushchev, Beria among them).[28] It is not conventional political history, more like an ethnography of a ruling group, focusing on strategies for coping, surviving and advancing in the world of what Montefiore called Stalin's 'court'. The team's wives and children are in there too, and I use memoirs quite heavily as well as political archives. I am essentially applying to the top political elite the techniques I used to describe the everyday practices of ordinary people in my earlier social history books.[29] This is the first big historical work I had written since finishing the *Spy in the Archives* memoir in 2013. The question as I started writing was whether, and how, the experience of writing memoirs was going to change things. I read around in the theoretical literature on objectivity, and the point that impressed me most was Thomas Nagel's:[30] to the extent that objectivity is a 'view from nowhere', it is a contradiction in terms. If one thinks in terms of portrait painting, the painter might think she was approaching her subject with an open mind (without a 'point of view'), but he was undoubtedly proposing to paint him not only at a particular point in space and time but *from* one. In other words, he was somewhere in physical relation to his subject as he painted, not nowhere. That brings me back to Stalin. If my view of Stalin cannot be from nowhere, where is it from?

I puzzled about that for a long time. The way the point-of-view question was always posed in Soviet history during the Cold War was 'for' or 'against': are you writing a pro-Stalin book or an anti-Stalin one? Undoubtedly, my private feelings about Stalin are more anti than pro, but it goes against all my instincts to take either of those two positions. There are people who think that if you are writing about one of the twentieth century's great 'evil-doers', showing up the depth and breadth of his evil is the sum of what you should do. That is a great task for a prosecutor but not, to my mind for a historian – or at least not for me as a historian. I want to understand the people I write about, how their minds work, why they think they do the things that they do, what they see as their

---

28 Fitzpatrick, *On Stalin's Team*.
29 Sheila Fitzpatrick, *Stalin's Peasants: Resistance and Survival in the Russian Village after Collectivization* (New York: Oxford University Press, 1994); Fitzpatrick, *Everyday Stalinism: Ordinary Life in Extraordinary Times*.
30 Thomas Nagel, *The View from Nowhere* (New York: Oxford University Press, 1986).

options. That is not what a prosecutor does, or, for that matter, a counsel for the defence. So I cannot make either of the basic Cold War positions my starting point.

Leon Trotsky and Isaac Deutscher wrote their Stalin biographies from Trotsky's standpoint, that of a political opponent defeated by someone he saw as a mediocrity.[31] The Russian Dmitri Volkogonov, formed in Soviet times as a military historian with a deep respect for Stalin, wrote his biography in the spirit of disillusionment generated by the collapse of the Soviet Union and discrediting of its value system.[32] The Russian writer Alexander Solzhenitsyn (in his novel *First Circle*) and the American political scientist Robert Tucker in his Stalin biography were both trying to understand the man who had made them personally suffer – in Solzhenitsyn's case by sending him to Gulag, in Tucker's by preventing him from marrying his Russian fiancée at the end of the 1940s.[33] But, unlike some of my other books, *Stalin's Team* has no personal subtext – unless I deceive myself, which of course is always possible. Stalin and I do not have a personal connection. Even my conceit of being a spy in his Kremlin does not extend to a fantasy of personal contact. If I try, in imagination, to put us in the same time and space, all that happens is that I melt away as fast as I can before he notices me, which is what I used to do back in the old days in the Soviet Union if there was a KGB man around. If they do not know you, my thinking was, you are in less danger of being pulled into one of their tricky schemes.

Still, that does not get me off the hook about having if not a point of view in the metaphorical sense, at least a vantage point for observation of Stalin. Am I defying Thomas Nagel and trying to capture a view from nowhere? I was afraid I might be, with *Stalin's Team*, but after a while I decided I was off the hook. I *have* chosen an angle of vision in the book. It is from within the team – setting up my easel among his close associates, mixing with them all at the office and the dacha. I found this a very interesting perspective, and quite different from any of the usual ones. It is

---

31 Leon Trotsky, *Stalin: An Appraisal of the Man and his Influence*, trans. Charles Malamuth (New York: Grosset & Dunlap, 1941); Isaac Deutscher, *Stalin: A Political Biography* (New York: Oxford University Press, 1949).
32 Dmitri Volkogonov, *Stalin: Triumph and Tragedy*, trans. Harold Shukman (London: Weidenfeld & Nicolson, 1991; first published in Russian in 1989).
33 Alexander Solzhenitsyn, *The First Circle* (New York: Harper & Row, 1968); Robert C. Tucker, *Stalin as Revolutionary, 1879–1929: A Study in History and Personality* (New York: Norton, 1973); Tucker, *Stalin in Power: The Revolutionary from Above, 1928–1941* (New York: Norton, 1990).

not Stalin's own point of view on himself, because the team, viewing him with a mixture of fear and admiration, could never fully rid themselves of the sense that they were his potential victims. But it is not the familiar *victims*' point of view either, because the members of the team, along with Stalin, were big-time perpetrators, more or less convinced that the various types of repression they executed were justified and necessary, even if, being less bold than Stalin, they might not have thought them up themselves. The team has double vision, as perpetrators and victims simultaneously, which makes a nice vantage point for the historian.

For all that, I have to admit that Stalin has left his mark on me, as perhaps the subjects of portraits often do on their painters. In the past, when I analysed political processes (not my main activity, but it occasionally happened), I tended to do so very much in my father's voice – not necessarily his opinions but his tone, which was the slightly ironic one of someone who loves the political game but is only in a marginal way a player, with no party loyalties. My father was my real-life reference point for political process, and he revelled in the political fight (nothing pleased him more than being heckled at public meetings and prevailing over the heckler), but bore little malice towards his opponents and, in any case, was rarely in a position to take revenge on them. Not so Stalin, though he, too, loved the political fight, and missed it once he had effectively closed down all possibilities of open opposition. Stalin was an arch-Machiavellian, a pastmaster at intrigue who was also ruthless (a quality completely alien to my father who, like me, tended to see the pathos of things). Stalin could, at times, view his own activities with detachment, even amusement, but he also had a naturally suspicious nature and a serious interest in vengeance. He almost invariably attributed the basest motives to those around him, especially his opponents.

It was just recently, three or four months after finishing the book, that I noticed something that might be called Stalin's revenge on me, namely that I had begun to analyse political situations in Stalin's super-tough-minded way, like a chess-player with a relentless interest in maximising outcomes and no concern about casualties. Fortunately, this remained a private and abstract activity. Occasionally, however, it has proved useful. The case came up recently of a displaced person from the Soviet Union with a shady past who reached Australia after the war and immediately, bafflingly, retracted his earlier statements that he had not fought for the

Soviet Army or been a Communist Party member.³⁴ Channelling my father, I had no idea why he did this, unless it was an unlikely attack of conscience, but channelling Stalin (as I involuntarily did), I knew exactly what the man was after: as an ex-Soviet citizen used to dealing with security agencies and looking for a protector in his new environment, he was putting up his hand to attract the attention of the Australian Security Intelligence Organisation (ASIO) so that he could be taken under their protection as an expert informant on communism. The only problem was that ASIO did not understand the signal, so he was deported.

This story comes out of my current historical project (jointly undertaken with Mark Edele) on displaced persons (DPs) after the Second World War. Apart from the matter of occasional prompts from Stalin's ghosts, this has no evident personal or memoir dimension, being absolutely straightforward transnational social history. The project, funded by the Australian Research Council (ARC), charts the experiences of refugees displaced from the Soviet Union during or at the end of the war, with particular attention to the redefinition of 'displaced persons' as victims of communism rather than victims of war and fascism (the Allies' and international organisations' initial conception), the importance for success as a DP of clearly articulated anti-communism (in gaining selection by a host country for resettlement), and the impact on the burgeoning Cold War discourse on communism of their arrival in the late 1940s and early 1950s.³⁵ This was the largest lot of non-British immigrants of alien cultural heritage and irretrievably foreign languages Australia had ever absorbed. The study is based on multiarchival, multilingual research. The questions and approach are those of a social historian, in this case with a sociopolitical slant from the Cold War material. I am nowhere in this picture, not even as a spy in someone's camp (as with the Stalin book), no axe to grind, no roots aspect (no ancestors from this group, or indeed anything but boring Anglo-Celtic stock).

But wait: is it really so straightforward? Actually, I do have an interest, although it is a hidden one. My late husband, the physicist Michael (Misha) Danos, was a DP from Riga (which had recently and unwillingly been incorporated into the Soviet Union, along with the rest of the

---

34   The case is in Ruth Balint's unpublished paper, 'Story-telling in Occupied Europe: Displaced Persons and the International Refugee Organisation, 1947–1952', and the discussion occurred at a conference on 'The Holocaust and the Soviet Union', organised by John Goldlust in Melbourne on 27–28 May 2015.
35   Edele and I are the editors of a special issue of *History Australia* on this topic: 12:2 (2015).

Baltic region) in Germany after the Second World War. He did not come to Australia, like the cohort I am studying, but one of his closest friends (one of my interviewees) did, and lived there the rest of his life, irritating me on my occasional visits with Misha in the 1990s by purporting to be an expert on all things Australian, and vehement critic of all things pertaining to the Australian left. I did not acknowledge his expertise, even though I had lived abroad for most of the half century he had lived here, and resented being told what to think about my own country by a foreigner who spoke with an accent (a truly Australian attitude surfacing). I also resented his criticisms of my father as a quintessential Australian leftist deluded about the communist world outside, and particularly his demand that I endorse these criticisms, by way of what the Soviets used to call self-criticism on my own and my father's behalf. Regardless of whether or not I agreed with them (which up to a point I did), I was not about to admit it to him: it was a question of loyalty.

You may say I set aside the demands of loyalty when I wrote the 'warts and all' memoir, *My Father's Daughter*. Yes, but only up to a point. I was prepared to put in the warts in my own terms, in order to convey the man in all his complexity and contradictions, but I probably would not have written, or at least published, the book if, in the end, I had not reached a kind of reconciliation with my father that enabled me to celebrate him. But, of course, it was a worry for me: there is a long discussion in the book of loyalty and whether the particular notions of loyalty my father instilled in me justified my approach.[36] The same went for my mother, against whom I had quite strong grievances from the past: I managed to work my way through them well enough to make several reviewers of the book more sympathetic to her than they thought I was, which I count as a success.

I had already discovered with *My Father's Daughter* that when you write memoirs, you can make the dead alive for readers who did not know them, as well as those who did. That was an important discovery for me; I remember the keen sense of having acquired a new power, to raise people from the dead. The concept came from the carol 'The Seven Joys of Mary',[37] and I recognise a certain hubris in appropriating it. But it was with that in mind that I took the first step towards writing *A Spy in*

---

36 Fitzpatrick, *My Father's Daughter*, 85–6, 253.
37 'The very next blessing that Mary had / It was the blessing of five / To think her little Jesus / Could make the dead alive.'

the Archives, which was to write another 'Diary' piece on my late Soviet friend Igor Sats for the *London Review of Books*.[38] Just as they were going to press, one of the editors emailed that he was fascinated by Igor, and did I not have a photo from the 1960s I could scan so that he could see what he looked like. They published that photo, which the *London Review of Books* rarely does, and I was tremendously pleased: another of the people I loved raised from the dead. So if I could do this for my father and Igor, how much more reason to do it for Misha, I thought. Moreover, I knew, as a historian, that I had the raw material for a wonderful book on his life as a DP in the box of family correspondence, diaries and photographs left to me when he died.

That book on Misha as a DP was a parallel project to the ARC-funded scholarly study of DPs who came to Australia.[39] It was a labour of love, involving hard practical work deciphering handwriting in German (and whatever other language he and his polyglot mother felt like writing to each other in), which was something new for me. German was Misha's best language, but not mine. When I wrote my two memoirs, I hoped that readers would appreciate my father and Igor (as well as my mother and Muscovite Irina, who are also major characters), and I think that in general they did. I would have been disconcerted to provoke a strongly negative reaction to any of them. As for my self-portrayal, I did not set out to make myself unlikeable, but I did not feel outraged when a few reviewers thought I was: I felt they had a right, and that it was not incompatible with my purposes. I had meant to give the readers the information to form their own judgement.

But the Misha book was another story. If I wrote about him, I wanted readers to like him. I may even have wanted them to love him, or at least to see why I did. That presented me with the subjectivity/objectivity problem in the sharpest form. On the face of it, the objectivity problem might seem less, in that I was not a participant in the events I describe in the book, since I did not even meet Misha until 40 years later. In fact, however, it was more acute because I felt the demands of loyalty more strongly. I am not sure that, in writing this book, I would have been prepared to go wherever my data took me, if it seemed to diminish Misha. I certainly would not have been prepared to change my opinion of my subject in the process of writing.

---

38 Fitzpatrick, 'A Spy in the Archives', *London Review of Books*, 2 December 2010, 3–8.
39 *Mischka's War: A European Odyssey of the 1940s* (Melbourne: Melbourne University Press, 2017).

Mischka's War, the title of the book, in itself is a demonstration of the fine line I am walking. Mischka is not what I called my husband; to me, he was Misha. But to his family, even in my time, he was either Mike or Mischka, the last being what he was usually called in Germany after the war. There is a whole saga to be written about his names (Misha, Mikelis, and other variants) and which was the 'real' one; a question he would never answer. He introduced himself to me (in America) as Mike, then he told me he was often called Mischka, and I then renamed him Misha, which turned out to be what his family called him in his childhood in Riga. Using 'Mischka' in the title is a way of distancing myself. But at the same time, I decided, after some internal argument, to use the more personal of the two introductions to the book, which I drafted some years ago, and to allow myself to enter the story as the researcher (whose relationship to the subject is, of course, known) in quest of information and answers to questions.[40]

Writing about the life of someone close to you raises all sorts of difficult questions. I will finish this essay by drawing attention to one of them: whether it is legitimate to use your subject as case study when making a broader historical argument or scholarly intervention. I did something like this once, about my father, when I wrote an (archive-based!) article on what he knew and could know of the world outside Australia in that era (the 1930s to 1950s) when Australia really was cut off and access to information, apart from that obtained firsthand by travel, was seriously constrained.[41] Reading his papers, as well as the published work, I realised very vividly the constraints on him from lack of access to reliable information about the outside world and his attempts to remedy and compensate. I saw that only some parts of the outside world were real or relevant to him, like a globe with only some regions lighted up, constituting a kind of personal epistemological geography, and, moreover, that these lighted-up regions were known to him primarily through a finite list of favoured interpreters or authorities. This interested me initially as an insight into my father, but I also thought it an interesting way to think about Australians in the whole period before the 'tyranny of distance' was mitigated by plane

---

40 Something similar is done by Mark Roseman in *The Past in Hiding* (London: Allen Lane, 2000), although he was not related to his subject, a Holocaust survivor.
41 'Brian Fitzpatrick and the World Outside Australia', in Stuart Macintyre and Sheila Fitzpatrick, eds, *Against the Grain: Brian Fitzpatrick and Manning Clark in Australian History and Politics* (Melbourne: Melbourne University Press, 2007), 37–69.

travel and the internet.⁴² You could see my essay as a kind of tentative intervention in scholarly debate on Australian intellectual history, with my father as case study; although if this had been its primary purpose I would no doubt have published it elsewhere.

A few years later, in a similar vein, I wrote an article on Misha for a transnational memory volume emphasising his dislike of being classified by ethnicity or nationality, or indeed in terms of any broader category other than theoretical physicist.⁴³ This involved both an assertion of individuality and a reaction against the categories imposed on DPs by occupation authorities and international organisations, which could determine their fate but were also simplifications of a complex situation (as in the case of Misha's nationality/ethnicity) or straight-out misrepresentations. This set me thinking about the ambiguities of national/ethnic identity in Eastern/Central Europe in the mid-twentieth century, and could have been the basis of a scholarly intervention in debate on the topic. But again, I would have published it elsewhere and written it up somewhat differently if this had been the primary purpose. I did not feel any real uneasiness about either of these two publications.

But, recently, I did something dodgier. I had to write an article for a special issue of a scholarly journal on DPs, and the due date was too early for me to finish the Paris and Moscow components of my archival work on that topic. So I thought, what source base can I use that I have basically mastered? The answer was the Danos papers,⁴⁴ supplemented by archival resources of the International Refugee Organization and the United Nations Relief and Rehabilitation Administration, as well as the National Archives of Australia. But in this essay I did not use the Danos materials primarily to illuminate the lives and individual personalities of Misha and his mother, whose correspondence in the DP period was my backbone source. While acknowledging my personal connection to the subject, I used these materials to make an intervention in the historians' debates about DPs. My argument was that, contrary to much of the

---

42 Geoffrey Blainey's phrase in *The Tyranny of Distance: How Distance Shaped Australia's History* (Melbourne: Sun Books, 1966).
43 Sheila Fitzpatrick, 'A World War II Odyssey: Michael Danos, en route from Riga to New York', in Desley Deacon, Penny Russell and Angela Woollacott, eds, *Transnational Lives: Biographies of Global Modernity, 1700–Present* (Basingstoke: Palgrave Macmillan, 2010), 252–62.
44 These include the personal papers still in my possession, plus the Musings from the 1990s, which I have already deposited along with his physics papers with the Michael Danos Papers in the archives of the University of Chicago.

literature and memoirs that present DPs purely as pawns of fate, DPs actually exercised agency in many ways, a range of which I illustrated on the basis of case studies of Misha, his mother, and a Latvian friend of his who ended up in Australia.⁴⁵ In short, this was an instrumental use of Misha, and I am not sure whether I should have done it. These are not doubts about the essay's professional legitimacy but about something more like moral appropriateness. There was nothing substantive in the article that would have disturbed Misha, and he would almost certainly have agreed with the argument and thought it worth making. I am fairly sure that he would not have objected to my writing the book about his DP experiences, would even have welcomed it. But, given his resistance to categorisation, he might have felt differently about a case study in which he was firmly put in the category of DP. Did I cross a line? Does it make it any better that the peer reviewer for the journal not only liked the argument but also took a great fancy to Misha *as an individual personality*, and sent a message wanting to know more about him? That reaction came as a relief to me, and almost felt like a justification. But an uneasiness remains.

I have outlined the various twists and turns of my parallel but sometimes intersecting lives as a historian and a memoirist. Along the way, my sense of the distance between these two endeavours has narrowed. I see them in some ways as contradictory, but that does not particularly bother me: life is full of contradictions. The process has made me more self-aware than I was earlier about what I am doing when I write, which is probably a good thing, and certainly intellectually interesting, at least to me. Above all, it has made me see myself as first and foremost a writer whose writing happens to be based on historical research, rather than as a researcher for whom writing is just the medium for presenting historical findings. But a historian-writer is probably what I always wanted to be; I did not particularly enjoy the effort in my early years in America to remake myself as a social scientist. I do not really believe in history as a science, even allowing for the fact that, in the light of chaos theory, real-life natural science is a lot less law-bound and predictive than social scientists and humanists tend to think.⁴⁶ In my judgement, historical knowledge is not in any important sense cumulative. Historians can make no predictions,

---

45   Sheila Fitzpatrick, '"Determined to Get On": Some Displaced Persons on the Way to a Future', *History Australia*, 12:2 (2015), 102–23.
46   See Michael Danos, 'Chaostheorie und Geschichte', *Geschichte und Gesellschaft*, 30:2 (2004), 325–38 (posthumous publication prepared by SF).

except about probabilities, and history has no laws. It makes sense to me to see historians as practising a craft, using a particular kind of raw material, and governed, like all crafts, by various conventions about their preparation and use. The writing of history can also be seen as an art, in which our storytelling is shaped (within the conventions of our craft) by aesthetic considerations. It is in that capacity, I think, that it comes closest to the writing of autobiography, which can scarcely be regarded as a distinct craft and is certainly not a science. Clio, the historian's patron saint, was a muse in Greek mythology, and seven of the other eight muses personified various arts. Her emblem was an open scroll of parchment. Back in the days before objectivity and subjectivity became concepts, she probably would have been as happy writing her own history on the scroll as that of the Greeks.

3

Walvin, Fitzpatrick and Rickard: Three Autobiographies of Childhood and Coming of Age

Doug Munro and Geoffrey Gray

Once a comparatively rare beast, historians' autobiographies are becoming prevalent to the point of being commonplace. Since the 1980s, such works have crystallised into a genre and have become a historiographic growth area. Limiting the head count to monograph-length works, a dozen historians' memoirs were published in the 1970s, rising to three dozen in the 1980s, five dozen in the 1990s, and the contributions continue apace.[1] Once on the fringes of the historical enterprise, historians' memoirs are now edging closer to centre stage. Increasing frequency has lent respectability. There remain significant pockets of resistance, the usual canards being that autobiography is inescapably egotistical, self-indulgent and narcissistic. Nonetheless, the genre is rapidly gaining acceptance and being treated seriously – and not simply historians' autobiographies but autobiography by academics generally. Almost without exception, historians' autobiographies contain a chapter or chapters on childhood and coming of age. In parallel with the increasing prevalence of historians' autobiographies, a subgenre devoted to the childhoods through to the

---

1   The figures, which are conservative, are taken from Jeremy D. Popkin, *History, Historians, & Autobiography* (Chicago/London: University of Chicago Press, 2005), 307–22, whose bibliography lists 381 historians' autobiographies in the English, French and to a lesser extent German languages, of which over 160 are book-length autobiographies, depending on how they are counted.

young adulthoods of historians has also become a growth area. We are concerned in this chapter with three such works: Sheila Fitzpatrick's *My Father's Daughter* (2010); John Rickard's *An Imperial Affair* (2013); and James Walvin's *Different Times* (2014).[2]

The authors are of the same generation, born within eight years of each other, and spent their careers in the academy. All have safely passed their three score and 10 years and are still actively publishing, especially Fitzpatrick and Walvin. Rickard and Fitzpatrick were born in Melbourne, in 1935 and 1941 respectively; the fact that two of the texts are by Australians reflects the Australian over-representation of historians' memoirs, including those of childhood. After an earlier career in the theatre, Rickard became a historian of Australia at Monash University. Fitzpatrick, by contrast, carved out a formidable reputation as a historian of modern Russia, mostly at the University of Chicago. Walvin, by contrast again, was born in 1942 in Failsworth, in the Greater Manchester industrial belt. Based at the University of York (UK), Walvin's research interests are many, and the overlap between life and work is evident in *Different Times*. The historian of childhood now writes about his own childhood; the historian of Victorian values discusses mid-twentieth-century working-class values; the historian of transatlantic slavery (Walvin's speciality) talks about working conditions in the Lancashire cotton mills and hat factories; and the historian of soccer includes a chapter on his beloved Manchester United and the Munich air disaster of 1958.

---

2   Sheila Fitzpatrick, *My Father's Daughter: Memories of an Australian Childhood* (Melbourne: Melbourne University Press, 2010); John Rickard, *An Imperial Affair: Portrait of an Australian Marriage* (Melbourne: Monash University Publishing, 2013); James Walvin, *Different Times: Growing up in Post-War England* (York: Algie Books, 2014). Other historians' autobiographies of childhood include A.L. Rowse, *A Cornish Childhood* (London: Jonathan Cape, 1942); Donald Horne, *The Education of Young Donald* (Sydney: Angus & Robertson, 1967); Richard Cobb, *Still Life: Sketches from a Tunbridge Wells Childhood* (London: Chatto & Windus, 1983); Amirah Inglis, *Amirah: An Un-Australian Childhood* (Melbourne: Heinemann, 1983); Bernard Smith, *The Boy Adeodatus: The Portrait of a Lucky Young Bastard* (Ringwood: Allen Lane, 1984); Ronald Fraser, *In Search of a Past: The Manor House, Amnersfield, 1933–1945* (London: Verso, 1984); Manning Clark, *The Puzzles of Childhood* (Ringwood: Viking, 1989); Kathleen Fitzpatrick, *Solid Bluestone Foundation and Other Memories of a Melbourne Childhood, 1908–1928* (Melbourne: Macmillan, 1989); Jill Ker Conway, *The Road from Coorain* (London: Heinemann, 1989); Sydney Checkland, *Voices Across the Water: An Anglo-Canadian Boyhood* (Aberdeen: University of Aberdeen Press, 1989); Robert Allen Rutland, *A Boyhood in the Dustbowl, 1926–1934* (Niwot: University Press of Colorado, 1996); Peter Gay, *My German Question: Growing Up in Nazi Berlin* (New Haven/London: Yale University Press, 1998); John Molony, *Luther's Pine: An Autobiography* (Canberra: Pandanus Books, 2004); Helga Griffin, *Sing Me that Lovely Song Again …* (Canberra: Pandanus Books, 2006); Joachim Fest, *Not Me: Memoirs of a German Childhood* (London: Atlantic Books, 2012); Arnold J. Bauer, *Time's Shadow: Remembering a Family Farm in Kansas* (Lawrence: University of Kansas Press, 2012).

Contextualising

It is in the nature of autobiography to be about 'other things' and 'other people' as well as being a depiction of the autobiographer's life, with the result that several types of content will coexist within a given autobiography. The back cover blurb describes *An Imperial Affair* as '[p]art biography, part autobiography, part social history'. It is also partly an autobiography of childhood, partly a family history and, as the subtitle goes, a 'portrait of an Australian marriage'. *My Father's Daughter* could be characterised as part autobiography, part family history (and also the portrait of her parents' marriage), part biography of her father, and in part an exploration of memory.[3] The essential point is that childhood memoirs can be positioned at various points along a conceptual continuum, with autobiography at the one end and family history at the other. *An Imperial Affair* is located at the far end of the spectrum, focusing on Rickard's parents, Philip and Pearl.[4] It contains relatively little direct autobiography, and thus presents a useful contrast for the purposes of discussion.

The three books are family histories as well as being childhood autobiographies. Individuals are almost always brought up in families, which is another ways of saying that there are no exact boundaries between a memoir of childhood and a family history. All families have secrets, or at least things they wish concealed from the outside world; these hidden dimensions can be used as a vehicle for introducing each book. Rickard's father Philip started work in 1926 at the Stores and Accounting Branch of the recently formed RAAF, rising to the rank of Group Captain. His duties involved numerous postings at home and abroad, which meant relocating his family or else being separated for extended periods. Handsome and personable, Philip needed female companionship, resulting in two affairs. Pearl was understandably devastated, especially on the second occasion, but to avoid scandal and disgrace, not to mention the effect on the children, they patched up their marriage. He ends by quoting the lines in a James McAuley poem: 'they were good people, / They cared for us and loved us' (p. 146).

---

3   Equally difficult to categorise are Biff Ward, *In My Mother's Hands: A Disturbing Memoir of Family Life* (Sydney: Allen & Unwin, 2014); Jim Davidson, *A Führer for a Father: The Domestic Face of Colonialism* (Sydney: NewSouth Publishing, 2017).
4   Pearl initially called herself Mildred. For the sake of simplicity, we refer to her as Pearl, irrespective of what time in her life.

There is also an affair in *Different Times*, one that was staged inside the family home. Shortly after Walvin's birth in 1942, his father (aged 32) was diagnosed with tuberculosis and spent his remaining dozen years coughing up his lungs and painfully wasting away. Across the road lived Joe Eyre, his best friend from childhood days. Joe had his own cross to bear, from the physical and psychological effects of mistreatment in Japanese POW camps. Joe visited his old friend on a daily basis and at some point he and Emma Walvin began a furtive relationship – resulting in Ian (b. 1952), who was the spitting image of his father. On this occasion, there was no recrimination, although tittering went on among neighbours and relatives. More than 20 years later, Walvin asked Jack (his father's elder brother) 'about the whole saga of Joe, Mum and the baby. Without a hint of disapproval, Jack simply said that our father knew, and didn't mind' (pp. 68–9). In a further twist to the tale, Emma Walvin and Joe Eyre never married, although they had plenty of opportunity. Joe was clearly in love with Emma, but he never proposed and she married someone else. The reason is clear enough to Walvin – namely, Joe's commitment to his own mother, the only person who had never given up hope for his safe return from the war. Joe's own wife had left him for another man during his absence and he 'resolved to care for the one woman who *had* stuck by him through the bleakest of times, and whose daily prayers had somehow worked. As long as his frail mother lived, Joe could not commit himself to another woman', and so he lost his opportunity (p. 68): 'I was her son before I loved you,' as the lines in Verdi's opera *Il Trovatore* go, 'I cannot abandon her now.'

There is nothing so dramatic in *My Father's Daughter*. Sheila is the daughter of the radical Australian historian and civil libertarian Brian Fitzpatrick (1905–65). There was one outright affair (pp. 51–3) and he had numerous girlfriends, platonic or otherwise, which naturally upset his wife Doff. Sheila also 'started to find Brian's girlfriends seriously irritating' (p. 106).[5] This was not the only dynamic making for an uncomfortable home life. Dominating the household was Brian's heavy drinking, which ate into the family finances and prevented him getting an academic appointment

---

5 An account by one of 'Brian's girls', in reality a protégée, is by Beverley Kingston, 'Brian Fitzpatrick's Graduate Student: A Memoir', in Stuart Macintyre and Sheila Fitzpatrick, eds, *Against the Grain: Brian Fitzpatrick and Manning Clark in Australian History and Politics* (Melbourne: Melbourne University Press, 2007), 88–96. See also Fitzpatrick, *My Father's Daughter*, 210.

and a secure income. Sheila was able to make her 'great escape' from what she frankly describes as an 'unhappy' family (pp. 2, 9) at age 15 when she enrolled at the University of Melbourne and lived in a residential college.

Doff's grievances with Brian and her not unjustified perception that he was the cause of her misery (pp. 17, 64) had a snowballing effect, with every new grievance piling upon the last. Bearing the brunt of her dissatisfaction was Sheila: 'My memory of my mother in these years was that life was unrelentingly hard on her, and she was unrelentingly hard on me' (p. 96). Sheila's close childhood relationship with Brian soured at adolescence when he became a repeated embarrassment to her, notably when his drunken personality took over from the sober one (pp. 105–6, 166), and it had hit 'rock bottom' when she made her 'second escape' and left for postgraduate work at Oxford. As a mark of her disapproval, she refused to answer Brian's letters when he offended her with one of his, and then suffered appalling shock and guilt when he suddenly died. There was eventual rapprochement, first with Brian's memory when Sheila returned to Australia after a 15-year absence, in 1979, and discovered that he 'had become part of the pantheon of the Left during the Whitlam era, it was an enormous relief to me; I had come to see him so strongly in pathetic terms, in terms of failure and futility' (p. 110). Reconciliation was also achieved with Doff. John Legge, the foundation professor of history at the recently created Monash University appointed Doff to a tutorship (having already rejected Brian for a position). Her confidence and self-esteem soared, her outlook on life changed, and by the 1990s she had abandoned 'a lifetime's practice in communicating grievance'. The metamorphosis of Doff and her changing relationship with Sheila are beautifully conveyed in the final pages of *My Father's Daughter*, where we get the definite sense that Sheila, finally, had also become her mother's daughter.

The theme of change

That there is change over time is a truism, especially in the context of the accelerating changes on all fronts in the eight decades since Rickard was born. Every autobiography deals with dissimilar times from the contemporary present, when circumstances were not the same and when people thought and acted differently. Whereas the theme of change over time is implicit in *My Father's Daughter*, it recurs in *Different Times*, as its very title suggests.[6] One motivation to write the book stemmed from Walvin's talking to his sons and grandson: 'they listen to my tales as if I were talking about a lost Amazonian tribe. It was utterly beyond their ken'.[7] Different times is also an underpinning theme in *An Imperial Affair*. It is also 'a portrait of a marriage' in much the same sense as is Nigel Nicolson's famous book of that title about his own parents,[8] and Rickard uses the story of his parents' marriage to illuminate:

> the larger story of Australia's role as a 'dominion' in the British Empire, which, although it had entered a terminal decline, still commanded the cultural allegiance of most Australians. My parents, like most middle-class folk then, took England and Empire as a given … Australia was a much smaller and more conformist society, with a population of a mere seven million, and although the War had exposed the irrelevance of Britain to our defence, the imperial connection remained fundamental to our sense of national identity … [World War I] was, as far as Australia was concerned, a British war in defence of empire (pp. 3, 7).

With Philip being in the air force, the forms and observances that tied Australians to loyalty to the reigning monarch were intensified in the case of the Rickard family.

The notion of the recent past being so different from the present is most pronounced in *Different Times*, which, as the back cover blurb states, 'weaves the personal details of one family's life into the broader story of the industrial north'. When Walvin was a youngster, his hometown of Failsworth was still dominated by the cotton industry. The characteristic chimneys of the cotton factories extended in every direction, an unrecognisably different landscape from today. Not simply the landscape but life itself was in the thrall of cotton. Although in terminal decline, cotton remained the greatest single employer, dominating the district,

---

6   Historians' autobiographies of childhood that make explicit comparisons between past and present are surprisingly rare. Even when their titles suggest a then-and-now approach, this does not turn out to be the case. See Paul Johnson, *The Vanished Landscape: A 1930s Childhood in the Potteries* (London: Weidenfeld & Nicolson, 2004). Those that make explicit contrasts include William H. McNeill and Ruth J. McNeill, *Summers Long Ago on Grandfather's Farm and in Grandmother's Kitchen* (Great Barrington, MA: Berkshire Publishing, 2009); Peter FitzSimons, *A Simpler Time: A Memoir of Love, Laughter, Loss and Billycarts* (Sydney: HarperCollins Publishers Australia, 2010).
7   James Walvin, email, 26 November 2014.
8   Nigel Nicolson, *Portrait of a Marriage: Vita Sackville-West and Harold Nicolson* (London: Weidenfeld & Nicolson, 1973, and numerous subsequent editions).

much like the coal mines and steel factories in other parts of Britain.[9] But the sites of labour that sustained life were also 'killing industries'. As well as the numerous-enough industrial accidents, respiratory diseases such as pneumoconiosis (from coal dust) killed miners and byssinosis (from the pervasive cotton fluff) saw off many cotton-factory workers (pp. 27–8, 73, 192). Walvin provides a salutary reminder that some of the conditions of labour associated with the nineteenth century persisted well into the twentieth century.

Family life

Childhood involves being part of a family. The Fitzpatrick and the Rickard households were described as being 'tight' or 'tightly knit' little families, but they mean two different things. The Fitzpatrick family was 'tight' in the sense of being 'close, crowded, tense, hard to breathe in', not to mention being hard-up (p. 9). The Rickards were 'tight' in the sense of being cohesive (p. 114). Their dynamics were quite different. They were marched in directions they did not want to go.

Doff Fitzpatrick's negativity cast a long shadow over the family, as did Brian's drinking (pp. 80–2). Both caused rifts between Sheila and her parents. The Rickards confronted an intruder of a different kind with the onset of Pearl's depressive episodes in the early 1950s followed by heart palpitations, which the doctors were unable to diagnose correctly, and eventual shock therapy for the depression. In delicate health until her death 10 years later, in 1962, Pearl endured more hospitalisations, lived in fear of a recurrence of depression and was then diagnosed with cancer of the bowel. Family life was anything but normal despite 'a sense of guarded determination to live a normal life' (p. 133). Rather, Pearl's ill-health was a brooding presence, intrusively and inescapably hovering over the family.

In the same way, the Walvins' home life was dominated by his father 'wasting away under the corrosion of tuberculosis' (p. 13). A stark childhood memory is his 'enfeebled' father coughing gouts of blood into the kitchen sink – the only sink in the house – whilst being physically supported by his wife (p. 39). This general scenario went on year in, year

---

9   Catherine Cookson's novel *Maggie Rowan* (London: Macdonald, 1954), ch. 1, compellingly portrays how a Tyneside coal-mining community was dominated at every level by living in the shadow of the pithead.

out, and Emma was left with a 'pervading sense that there was no way out of the cycle' (p. 48). She was the breadwinner and responsible for the upbringing of two small boys. Walvin recalls the 'unrelenting drudgery' that became part of his mother's daily life. There was never enough money. Midweek the money would run out, and often too the food had run out or was running low, so that 'there was nothing to do but wait for the next pay packet, or hope for a gift or a loan from a relative or friend' (p. 48). The food itself was unappetising and unwholesome, dominated by Spam and potatoes.

It was only the kindness of friends and especially of relatives that enabled the Walvins to get through. Whereas the Rickards and the Fitzpatricks were essentially nuclear families, the Walvins were more an extended family. During their childhood, the two Walvin boys were in the care or spent time with their maternal grandparents (p. 39), which took some of the strain off their mother. The grandparents helped out by buying shoes and clothing for the children, they chipped in with financial help, and they took the boys to soccer matches and for seaside holidays at Blackpool.[10] But they also gave more than material assistance; the moral support provided an emotional 'safety net' (pp. 82, 201).

The charity of friends and wider family were expressions of working-class solidarity, but as Walvin points out the tight-knit working-class communities of Greater Manchester were essentially 'local' – that is, bound by a narrow locality – and based on nearby institutions such as 'workplaces, shops, places of worship, drink and entertainment, and schools' (p. 97). There is no nostalgia in his account, only a vision of a largely unlamented world, inhabited by the crooked timber of humanity, which nonetheless had it good points, foremost of which was a sense of responsibility to others. Help and even salvation could come from unexpected quarters. When Ian was having difficulties with his uncaring stepfather, a couple with whom the family had very little contact enabled him to escape a difficult domestic situation by taking him in as a boarder (pp. 96–7, 188). The short and simple annals of the poor make for depressing reading.

---

10 Seaside holidays were a national institution. During their stay in England in the late 1930s, the Rickards also went on seaside holidays, but at respectable Bournemouth rather than the more-distant and downmarket Blackpool (*An Imperial Affair*, 40).

Walvin's working-class background has shaped the historian he became, as evidenced by two of his books on nineteenth-century British social history. Not only has he written about seaside holidays, which he so enjoyed in his youth, but about childhood itself, and both books are to some extent concealed autobiography.[11] Much of the content of *A Child's World* corresponds to childhood experiences of his own. *A Child's World* is not only informed by the events of his own upbringing but is overwhelmingly about impoverished children, as he once was.

Sexuality

The greater willingness of contemporary autobiographers to relate more intimate detail is another indication of living in 'different times'. The same authors who might, say, 40 years ago, have been circumspect are now less restrained and move with the spirit of a more candid age. Nonetheless, Rickard, Walvin and Fitzpatrick tell markedly different tales of sexual awakening and early experiences.

When he was well into his teens, Rickard's father introduced him 'to something called "the facts of life"'. That such a highly sexed man should feel so awkward and embarrassed by his fatherly duty speaks volumes about the reticences of the age. 'You'll soon get interested in girls', he explained, a statement that struck Rickard as both 'faintly indecent' and 'highly unlikely' (pp. 113–14). If the penny does not drop, it does so 14 pages later when Rickard relates his first homosexual relationship. His parents suspect what is going on and he is outed; in what must have been an excruciating experience for all concerned, Philip and Pearl suddenly confront him, framed by the doorway to his bedroom, 'leaning forward a little, yet careful not to step into my room, as if somehow respecting my privacy while even intruding on it' (pp. 128–9). As Rickard explains elsewhere, 'for me the 1950s was a sex-free zone. Not of course that I wasn't thinking and fantasising about sex but, given the social mores of the time and my own family background, I had great difficulty coming to terms with my sexuality'.[12]

---

11   James Walvin, *Beside the Seaside: A Social History of the Popular Seaside Holiday* (London: Allen Lane, 1978); Walvin, *A Child's World: A Social History of English Childhood, 1800–1914* (Harmondsworth: Penguin Books, 1982).
12   John Rickard, 'Sydney: The Class of '51', *Australian Historical Studies*, 27:109 (1997), 176, doi.org/10.1080/10314619708596052.

Walvin is equally frank in describing the lack of sexual knowledge and experience of his generation of teenagers, who went to single-sex schools where sex education was off limits. Neither were such matters discussed in family circles. There was, nonetheless, a fascination with all things sexual. Adolescent males had a rampant interest in this great unknown and would swap coarse stories, but that was pretty much the extent of it: they were 'innocents in an age of innocence' (p. 130). The height of his experience, if it can be called that, came at dancing lessons, which provided the 'fleeting opportunity to hold a girl in my arms. One girl was especially busty, and holding her close, in the last waltz, was an early experience of sexual bliss' (p. 108).

Fitzpatrick was more liberated. Living in Women's College, an affiliated residential college of the University of Melbourne, gave scope for sexual expression that would have been out of the question had she remained at home. An early entrant to university, aged 16, her new milieu was liberating in more ways than one:

> In this new world, remarkably, there were people like me; I was not [the] oddity [that I felt myself to be at high school]. I had friends, even a boyfriend. Away from home, I could forget the old dragging undertone of uneasiness, the everyday worry of what unpleasantness might turn up next (p. 128).

It also involved swapping stories with fellow students-in-residence about what awful parents they had.

It went from good to better. To solve her shyness, she had boyfriends and for the first two years was always holding someone's hand. There was a practical as well as a romantic reason – her short-sightedness presented initial difficulties in finding her way around (p. 127). There was also the discovery of sex, which was enjoyable 'both in and of itself and as a way of being close to someone', and it is difficult to imagine these days that earnest discussions within Women's College on the morality of premarital sex would be the case (p. 144). Her first serious relationship started in her second year, but neither she nor her partner was interested in marriage – in Fitzpatrick's case because she 'was afraid of suffering [Doff's] dreadful fate and being deprived not only of a career but of all possibility of happiness and enjoyment in life' (p. 148). There were other complicated relationships. What stands out is the frankness with which they are related, without being unfair to the other person.[13]

Music and sport

In referring to the late 1950s 'tug of war for the cultural soul of Britain', Walvin laments the consequent polarisation of opinion and taste. There was a high-browed culture represented by so-called serious literature and classical music as opposed to a popular culture of comics, trashy novels and pop music: 'What was it going to be? Bill Haley or Barbirolli? *The Brains Trust* or ITV?' There was also a widespread feeling that high culture, such as orchestral music, and sport were oppositional:

> From the first I thought much of the debate oddly unnecessary. Why did it have to be one or the other? Why couldn't we settle for a new kind of cultural pluralism that allowed people to pick and choose as they saw fit. Was it so odd to like the Hallé [Orchestra] *and* Manchester United? (p. 133).

Rickard and Fitzpatrick did not embrace cultural pluralism to the same extent. The subject of sport never comes up in *An Imperial Affair*, in contrast to Rickard's discussions of his parents' musical interests and his own involvement in the theatre. For her part, Fitzpatrick gave up sport altogether when she went to university 'and, having become an intellectual snob, looked down on it, especially hockey' (p. 117). Walvin, by contrast, is passionate about soccer and Manchester United – a devotion that remains undiminished, and has led him to writing books on the subject.[14]

Thus, *Different Times* includes an entire chapter on soccer, culminating in the Munich air disaster of 1958. The 23 fatalities included eight Manchester United players, the famous Busby Babes. It was not the first such soccer disaster nor the most serious, but it hit home hard: older

---

13 See also Peter Nicholls, 'Sheila Fitzpatrick as an Australian Teenager', in Golfo Alexapoulos, Julie Hessler and Kiril Tomoff, eds, *Writing the Stalin Era: Sheila Fitzpatrick and Soviet Historiography* (Basingstoke: Palgrave Macmillan, 2011), 197–202.
14 James Walvin, *The People's Game: A Social History of British Football* (London: Allen Lane, 1975); Walvin, *Football and the Decline of Britain* (Basingstoke: Macmillan, 1986), doi.org/10.1007/978-1-349-18196-4.

people averred that it felt even worse than the Blitz.[15] The mood of misery in Manchester following the Munich air disaster is caught by Walvin, who was witness to the city's reactions. The hearses proceeded from Manchester airport to Old Trafford, and '[d]espite the bad weather and the time (it was almost midnight), huge crowds turned out to line the streets to pay their silent respects. The misery of it all lingered over the city like one of its infamous dark skies, and simply wouldn't go away' (p. 156). What also has not gone away, different times or not, is the behaviour of supporters – 'the raw adult vulgarity, and … football's amazing ability to transform normal folk into demented ranters' (p. 149).

The three memoirists are in greater accord when it comes to music. It should hardly surprise that classical music continues to play a significant part in all of their lives. They were brought up at a transitional time when the radio and the gramophone represented the only switch on–switch off home entertainment, so people still had to make their own amusements, and learning a musical instrument was more in evidence than today. Despite straitened family circumstances, Fitzpatrick learned the violin from the age of five or six (just as her brother learned the piano) and received enormous encouragement from Brian, himself a lover of Beethoven (pp. 74–6). She was talented, but her approach was akin to that of her schoolwork in that she could do well with insufficient effort. Her involvement in music and playing in various orchestras was a significant part in Fitzpatrick's early life. Reflecting on her adolescent violin playing, Fitzpatrick saw it as 'quite separate from the family; that must have been one of its advantages' (p. 91). She put the violin aside at the onset of university studies. There was a brief resurgence of interest in music a few years later (p. 180), but only in later years, following a bereavement, did Fitzpatrick resume active musicianship in chamber music, mainly quartets.[16]

Neither Walvin nor Rickard had such intense encounters with music, but it was still a presence. Philip Rickard was a church organist and it was music that brought him and Pearl together (p. 6). Music remained 'part of the family culture' throughout their marriage: there was a ritual of sherry and music before dinner (p. 115), and they were at the heart of the church

---

15 Less than eight-and-a-half years earlier, an aircraft carrying the Italian champions Torino crashed with total loss of life, and again it took a full decade to rebuild the team. Paul Dietschy, 'The Superga Disaster and the Death of the "great Torino"', *Soccer & Society*, 5:2 (2004), 298–310, doi.org/10.1080/1466097042000235272.
16 The original version of *My Father's Daughter* contained a separate chapter on music.

choir when they finally settled in Sydney. They were also avid concert- and theatre-goers (pp. 38–9) and they instilled in Rickard a love of classical music. Although never a choirboy, the Anglican Church was and remains important for Rickard, who has written a history of his parish church in North Melbourne.[17] When his voice broke, he was encouraged to take singing lessons. Later, as an actor-singer in London, he harboured ambitions for opera and lieder. More to the point, 'it was the world of theatre, always a site for cultural subversion, that offered the real [sexual] freedom I had been groping towards all along. There I came to realise that the temptation I had been resisting was in fact, for me, the truth to be embraced'.[18] He only ceased his 'raffish career' in theatre in 1971, when appointed to a lectureship at Monash University.[19]

Walvin's musical experiences began at the age of six when he joined the local Anglican parish. Neither parent was Anglican, or musical, but Walvin was attracted to St John's because its Sunday school offered social activities and 'a range of instruction' (p. 108). There, his singing was noted by the choir mistress and he was inducted into the choir. He had the singular good fortune that a First World War veteran liked his singing voice and gave him hours of tuition. Rickard was also a choirboy and he also took singing lessons (p. 115), but these activities had a lesser effect than they did on Walvin, for whom St John's was an important part of his growing up. It had two long-term effects on Walvin. One was to provide 'an early apprenticeship for a career which required me to sing for my supper in front of students and the public' (p. 108). Second, and despite losing his faith, he acknowledges that:

> the Church of England left its fingerprints all over me. Its rituals, its calendar, its hymns and liturgy, all and more remain embedded deep in my brain. Today, there are times when I feel I am one of a dying breed of Anglican survivors. In recent years I have attended funerals where the only people in church who seemed to know the hymns, prayers and protocols were me, the minister and the organist (p. 112).

---

17 John Rickard, *An Assemblage of Decent Men and Women: A History of the Anglican Parish of St Mary's North Melbourne 1853–2000* (Melbourne: St Mary's Anglican Church, North Melbourne, 2008).
18 Rickard, 'Sydney: The Class of '51', 176.
19 Rickard has written a number of academic articles on the theatre: '"A Fine Song and Dance!": Manning Clark's History – The Musical', *Victorian Historical Journal*, 59:3–4 (1988), 3–20; '*The Boys in the Band* Revisited', *Meanjin*, 52:4 (1993), 661–6; 'The Melbourne Theatre Scene: A Personal Perspective', in Seamus O'Hanlon and Tanja Luckins, eds, *Go! Melbourne in the Sixties* (Melbourne: Circa, 2005), 17–30.

Self-representation

The three memoirists represent their selves in quite different ways. Rickard, for the most part, remains a shadowy figure in a text which, after all, is a portrait of his parents' marriage. He is the little boy in the background, who occasionally emerges to recall an event; to accentuate the obscurity, he sometimes refers to himself as 'John', rather than by a pronoun. Only in his final year at school, followed by his tertiary education, his involvement in the theatre and sexual awakening does he emerge as a more rounded individual.

Walvin presents himself as curious and self-motivated, characteristics that coexisted with a sceptical attitude and a strain of indignation, making him a 'prickly teenager' with 'an abrasive, bolshie view of the world' (pp. 45–6, 82). He finally lost his religious faith at the age of 17 after increasingly questioning the very worth of a God who had reduced his family and those around them to such dire circumstances (p. 111). The ultimate break was a result of the vicar's enthusiastic endorsement of capital punishment, although Walvin suggests that this was the occasion rather than the cause. Walvin also bristled during the 1959 election campaign when Prime Minister Harold Macmillan used the phrase, 'You've never had it so good', which he later realised was broadly correct, but at the time it seemed a 'sneering insult' (pp. 168–9). He also admits that the English class system 'irritated me immensely' (p. 163).

Misgivings were also directed at the British Empire. The qualms initially centred on his grandparents:

> What had this great empire done for them, or for my relatives and our neighbours? My grandparents lived simple, often impoverished, lives with little to show for a hard week's work except a couple of shillings deposited in the holidays savings club, and the few pennies set aside in the local burial club. Their meagre pleasures seemed a poor reward for their part in an imperial success story (p. 80).

But there was more to it. Walvin came to dislike the chauvinism and the insularity that stemmed from Britain being an imperial power. The 'demonology of foreigners' and the prevailing notion that 'abroad is beastly' were part of his environment (pp. 79, 138, 141, 181). Funnily enough, he had a treasured collection of Biggles books, those empire-affirming texts *par excellence* (p. 115). The circuit-breaker was a summer exchange scheme organised by his school, which had him off to France for a month to live with a French family. He returned a confirmed Francophile and, as a 14-year-old, was now openly questioning the prevailing assumptions that lands across the sea were a combination of 'dangerous locations, untrustworthy foreigners, foul local weather, [and] unspeakable food' (p. 135). He acknowledges that he must 'have become an irritating adolescent challenge to relatives and friends, not merely because of normal teenage awkwardness, but through my inquisitive and doubting presence' (p. 141). Some of Walvin's attitudes were a product of his particular working-class upbringing and others were a reaction against it.

Fitzpatrick presents herself with a searing and uncompromising honesty: 'As a historian I have always taken pride in putting in what I discovered … It would have been nice to have left some things out [about myself], but I found myself unable to do so' (p. 5). It cannot be easy to write positively about an unhappy upbringing, but there are times when there is an element of the self-lacerating: 'Cynicism and pessimism were a cherished part of my chosen persona at university' (p. 127); 'I had not yet outlived my adolescent habit of sulking and was prone to moodiness' (p. 145); she refers to her 'habit of not hiding from people things that might hurt them' (p. 183); and she applies the words 'insouciant' and 'insouciance' to herself (pp. 123, 135). It is little wonder that few people write their autobiographies of childhood given how painful the requisite honesty can be, both to self and to others.

Becoming historians

The decisions of the three authors to embark on careers as academic historians involved, in varying proportions, a mix of inner urges and opportunity, deliberation and chance. There were other choices: Fitzpatrick had music; Rickard's first career was in the theatre; and Walvin might have ended up a schoolteacher but for the opening up of undergraduate places at the 'redbrick universities' in the late 1960s. In that way, numerous working-class adolescents had the opportunity of a university education that would otherwise have been beyond reach.

Neither Fitzpatrick nor Rickard particularly liked their time at secondary school. Rickard finished his schooling at Knox Grammar, a private school on Sydney's North Shore, at the time of a philistine headmaster. But two or three good teachers on the staff (although not the history teacher) gave him the idea of going to the University of Sydney where he enrolled for an Arts/Law degree. It was the family expectation that he would go to university and, although Philip hoped he would enrol in engineering as he would have liked for himself, he had no problem with his son doing Arts/Law. As runner up in the Shell arts scholarship in 1956, he spent a year at Oxford but does not indicate his course of study. Nor does he say how he became a historian, apart from indicating that history was his real interest (pp. 120–2). Nowhere mentioned in *An Imperial Affair* is that Rickard did a potted PPE (Philosophy, Politics & Economics) course at Oxford, for which he received a diploma. Returning to a job in Australia with Shell, he drifted into theatre to get away from corporate life, and remained in acting for 10 years. A friend arranged an introduction to meet John Legge, the history professor at Monash University, and Rickard embarked on an MA thesis. What started as 'initially something to interest me' then became a PhD thesis with a supporting scholarship, and eventually he was offered a lectureship in the Monash history department in 1971. This was at a time when Australian universities were still expanding, but only barely in the Monash history department. He described himself to us as 'the last expansionary appointment' in the department.[20]

Neither does Walvin make an extended statement on the steps along the way to becoming a historian, but he provides numerous clues. His was not a promising start given that he twice failed his 11-plus examinations, an iniquitous system whereby 11-year-olds were 'sorted into educational sheep and goats' (pp. 119–20). Instead of enrolling in a grammar school he was consigned to a technical school and might have withered on the vine but for an enlightened headmaster, who steered the brighter students into academic subjects, and 'a handful of committed teachers' who inspired and enthused (p. 130). Another was being able to escape the impossible conditions for study at home by toddling across the road and working in Joe Eyre's front room (pp. 3, 48, 80, 183). Equally important, the Manchester Central Library was a 'home away from home' as a secondary school student, and became 'his favourite place in the whole of Manchester (apart, that is, from Old Trafford)' (pp. 33–4). He was already showing considerable motivation and self-discipline in being able to work on his own (pp. 65, 116) and he describes the Central Library as where his 'real education took place' (p. 130): 'In the end,' he writes, 'my secondary school suited me well, and what shaped my teenage education were books,

---

20   John Rickard, telephone interview, 28 June 2015.

Manchester Central Library and a few devoted schoolmasters' (p. 120). The school and the library in Manchester also meant that Walvin started to experience worlds beyond the intensely localised environment of his upbringing. Interestingly, Walvin mentions that his mother's 'pervasive culture of hard work' together with the need for punctuality in his first paid job as a newspaper delivery boy 'helped establish a pattern of work that became a permanent feature of my working life' (pp. 159–60).

But what prevailed on the studious Walvin to become a historian and not something else? He is under no doubt that talking to Second World War veterans, from his mid-teens, kindled his interest, beginning with discussions with Joe Eyre over endless cups of tea in his front room (p. 11):

> Initially they were all reluctant to talk to me – an awkward but curious teenager – about their experiences, but eventually they spoke up, sparking what became my lifelong curiosity about history … I must have been cheeky and insensitive: an inquisitive teenager firing questions at older men about issues they were keen to forget and certainly didn't want to discuss (pp. x, 19).

As well as hearing about the horrors of their experiences, he was also exposed to their jingoistic and anti-foreigner attitudes (p. 135), but by this time he had returned from his first visit to France and rejected such sentiments. The Suez Crisis also contributed. Walvin could not understand the seemingly universal disparagement of Egyptians as well as the French:

> How could this welter of hostility to outsiders be explained? Perhaps all this had historical roots and perhaps the explanation lay in Britain's historical past? It wasn't clear at the time, but it now seems obvious: events were pushing me towards a more serious study of history (p. 146).

A further reinforcing influence, serendipitously, was a schoolteacher introducing him to films and novels, including Orwell's *The Road to Wigan Pier* (1937), and to the community studies of northern English cities that were being published in the late 1950s, along with a major sociological work – Richard Hoggart's classic, *The Uses of Literacy* (1957), which lamented the erosion of 'authentic' working-class culture (pp. 82–5).[21]

---

21   See N. Dennis, F. Henriques and C. Slaughter, *Coal is our Life: An Analysis of a Yorkshire Mining Village* (London: Eyre & Spottiswoode, 1956). Unbeknownst to Walvin, sociological studies of working-class London were also appearing. These are what Roy Porter was referring to when he described himself as being brought up in 'a stable if shabby [south London] working-class community completely undiscovered by sociologists': Porter, *London: A Social History* (paperback ed.; Cambridge, MA: Harvard University Press, 1998), xiii.

There were no guarantees that Walvin would go to university, which at that time was highly selective. He got no encouragement from his family or his wider environment to progress in that direction; any books in the house, such as his Biggles collection, were kept well out of sight (p. 115). As he puts it:

> [r]elatives clearly found my ideas and questions 'half-baked' (their favourite word for stupid) … acquired, they thought, either by reading too much or, more directly, by 'letting France go to your head' – my mother's way of dismissing my new habit of querying life at large (p. 141).
>
> My ideas were rejected as evidence of the dangers of education, and of reading too much. Grandma in particular seemed especially concerned about my reading habits. She even warned me directly: 'You mustn't read too much, our Jim. You'll get a brain tumour.' Her evidence for this amazing belief was the sad tale of a local boy who, having passed his 11+, promptly died of a brain tumour (p. 80).

Even then, a university education would have been out of the question had Walvin not won a State Scholarship and enrolled at the University College of North Staffordshire (now Keele University). It was a revelation, despite some initial social awkwardness. He was being paid to study; there were creature comforts, such as central heating and indoor lavatories; there was also a hitherto unimagined sexual freedom, even though students caught breaking the rules surrounding these matters were severely punished (especially the females). Walvin chose history over 'the intellectual desert of modern languages' (p. 197). Predictably enough, he began to distance himself from his background, not deliberately but because of sustained exposure to new influences.

The hardship of Walvin's childhood had moderated somewhat during his teens. Life became marginally easier in the 1950s and more noticeably so after 1957, as Macmillan had said (p. 170–3). More to the point, Walvin's schooling and his commitment to his studies provided a fulfilment that transcended his background – and it all turned out well in the end. While not minimising the hardship of 1940s northern England, the mellower tone of his later chapters suggest that his recounting the events has been filtered through the lens of subsequent experience.

There was always going to be a better chance that Fitzpatrick might become an academic historian, partly because Australia did not suffer the same hardships as did postwar United Kingdom. Neither was class such a barrier, resulting in a more egalitarian approach to making a career.

Having two intellectual parents, one of whom was an historian, was a good start, and Fitzpatrick did receive an acknowledgement in her father's book *The Australian Commonwealth* (1956) for her help with 'verifying and correcting' (p. 103). It was also a good start that Fitzpatrick was precociously gifted and entered the University of Melbourne aged 16. Having her fees paid and receiving an allowance by virtue of winning a Commonwealth Scholarship, she felt unaccustomedly well-off. It also helped that she lived in a residential college rather than having to continue enduring an unhappy home life. She was fortunate that she gained admission to Women's College, whose rules stipulated the entrants had to be at least 17. Fitzpatrick petitioned the head of the college to waive the rule, 'arguing that [she] needed to be removed from a difficult family environment' (p. 125). After a generally unhappy time at her high school, where brains were frowned upon, Fitzpatrick quickly found a support group of intellectually minded students.

Fitzpatrick followed a conventional path in becoming an historian. It started with getting increasingly interested in history and by associating more with the 'history crowd'. Brian's reputation as a historian was also useful (p. 135). By the start of her third year, she had given up thoughts of becoming a musician, deciding that it was too insecure a career. The Melbourne history department also played its part, by 'implicitly provid[ing] the standard against which [the units teaching her other subjects] – the English and Russian Departments, the Conservatorium – were judged and found wanting' (p. 151). Throughout, Fitzpatrick studied Russia, more by accident than by design, which provided a basis for her future career as a Russianist (pp. 133–4). Gaining a first-class honours degree in History and Music, she tutored in the history department for two-and-a-half years and published her first journal article (pp. 185–8), before departing for postgraduate study at Oxford University. Hers was, in a formal sense, a typical enough progression for a bright and aspiring student.[22]

---

22   Fitzpatrick recounts some of her experiences as a young historian in *A Spy in the Archives* (Melbourne: Melbourne University Press, 2013).

Motives and constraints

Historians typically pen their memoirs towards the end of a career or in retirement. They become their own biographers from a variety of motives, just as they become historians for many reasons. Unusually, *My Father's Daughter* stemmed from a publisher's offer; having heard Fitzpatrick give a talk about her father, Louise Adler of Melbourne University Publishing made the approach for a more extended treatment along the same lines.[23] Rickard's motivation was more personal; after finding a shoebox full of Philip's letters to Pearl, 'he began to feel the need, if only for my own sake, to unravel their story' (pp. vii, 1). Walvin, by contrast, was 'encouraged … by friends, who having heard me talk about the stories related here, urged me to write the book' (p. vii). He elaborated in an email, saying that he had 'wanted to write something about this for years – partly personal curiosity but mainly to record a way of life that has vanished'. There was 'also the matter of aging. I realized that unless I turned to this *soon*, I might never be able to do it – or lose the ability and evidence to make it possible'.[24] At quite another level, he was motived to write as a gesture of opposition to the elitism that typifies the autobiographies and the published letters of historians, which are overwhelmingly by the grandees and the 'toffs' of the profession.[25] He 'thought it right to write a humbler view – or at least from a humbler position' – another indication of fidelity to his working-class roots. It is by no means unusual for elderly historian memoirists from working- and middle-class backgrounds to 'to honor the lived worlds of their youth'.[26]

The question then turns on: what can decently be said about others; what ought to remain secret; what simply cannot be said? The three memoirists certainly take advantage of a climate of opinion that is more open to frankness and disclosure. Abuse narratives and explicit accounts of family tragedy are becoming commonplace. Death and disability narratives (pathographies), which often lay bare intimate details of bodily

---

23 The talk was turned into short memoir and published in the *London Review of Books*, 8 February 2007. A slightly longer version was later published as 'My Father's Daughter: A Memoir', in Macintyre and Fitzpatrick, *Against the Grain*, 163–9.
24 Walvin, email, 26 November 2014.
25 Walvin is referring to: A.J.P. Taylor, *A Personal History* (London: Hamish Hamilton, 1983); Richard Davenport-Hines and Adam Sisman, eds, *One Hundred Letters from Hugh Trevor-Roper* (Oxford: Oxford University Press, 2014).
26 See D.L. LeMahieu, '"Scholarship Boys" in Twilight: The Memoirs of Six Humanists in Post-Industrial Britain', *Journal of British Studies*, 53:4 (2014), 1011–31, doi.org/10.1017/jbr.2014.110.

malfunctionings and mental illness, have burgeoned over the past half century – an even greater growth area than historians' autobiographies has become.[27] The increasing popularity of reality TV programs is another indicator of widening boundaries, especially in its appeal to voyeurism. All the same, there are restraints, often self-imposed. Rickard and Fitzpatrick would have been unlikely to have embarked on their projects had their parents been alive. The impulse would be to leave their memories undisturbed. Rickard said as much when an interviewer 'asked him what he imagine[d] his parents might have thought of the book. I don't think he found answering this question difficult. His parents' generation valued its privacy; they would surely not have welcomed the exposure of their lives to public view'.[28] Whereas Rickard's sister was encouraging from the outset, it was not so straightforward for Walvin. Only when his brother Ian came to terms with his parentage and could talk about it openly did Walvin feel that his autobiography of childhood was a publishable prospect.[29]

Brief assessments

By what means do memoirists excavate and recall the past? There was that shoebox of letters from Rickard's father to his mother, miraculously preserved (the other side of the correspondence is missing). This started him on the project as well as making it possible. The letters form the empirical core but there were other letters, this time between parents and children and between siblings (pp. 125–6, 142). His parents kept diaries while in England in the mid to late 1930s. Pearl's diaries seem less extensive (pp. 27, 40, 44, 47). Philip's diaries were seemingly kept over a longer period and contain longer entries (pp. 41–7), and they were not necessarily a private affair; on at least one occasion, at the end of a 17-day motoring holiday, he typed up 'fifteen foolscap pages, which was designed not only as their own record, but to be circulated to their families in Australia' (p. 32). Finally, there are Rickard's own diaries, which he kept from the age of 15. The extent to which diaries can be misleading is

---

27 Anne Hunsacker Hawkins, *Reconstructing Illness: Studies in Pathography* (2nd ed.; West Lafayette: Purdue Research Foundation, 1999), 3.
28 Frank Bongiorno, 'Imperial Intimacies', review of *An Imperial Affair* by John Rickard, *Inside Story*, 19 September 2014, insidestory.org.au/imperial-intimacies (accessed 20 October 2014); see also Jeremy D. Popkin, 'Family Memoir and Self-Discovery', *Life Writing*, 12:2 (2015), 127–38, doi.org/10.1080/14484528.2015.1023925.
29 Walvin, email, 26 November 2014; Walvin, *Different Times*, 61.

indicated by Rickard's admission that his homosexuality was something he 'could only hint at' in his earlier diaries (p. 121). In addition, Rickard engaged in wider research and drew from his knowledge of Australian history. He also engaged in 'optical research' – the term coined by a biographer of Mary Queen of Scots who 'visited every conceivable castle, quagmire, byre or whatever associated with the Queen in three countries'[30] – as when he revisited Dubbo in New South Wales to gauge how the town, and more particularly the house, where he had lived almost 50 years earlier had changed (pp. 108–9).

At least two evidential points emerge from a reading of *An Imperial Affair*. One is the manner in which Rickard chews over the evidence, attempting to extract the last drop of meaning from a documentation that is rich in some respects but replete with omissions. The other concerns the limitations of memory, which itself is compounded by the gaps in the record. Rickard recalls a couple of dramatic incidents between his parents over Philip's infidelities (pp. 2–3, 100–1), but he was not in all places at all times. Besides, there is the fact of life for our authors that when they were growing up there were things were not said or done 'in front of the children' (p. 135). There was also the feeling that one's business was one's own, and if outsiders were to be kept in the dark on privacy grounds (p. 133), then so were the children. Rickard is sometimes left to remark that he has no memory of particular incidents (pp. 64, 94, 102). At one point, he mentions that 'beneath th[e] well ordered surface [of family life] there was an undertow of unhappiness which I have no memory of recognising' (p. 65). Indeed, he admits, as a young child, to having 'no inkling of what [his] mother was going through' when Pearl was taking treatment for her depressive disorder (p. 86). Rickard clearly discovered more about his parents from their letters than he ever would have imagined.

Different Times, by contrast, is not an archivally based book. Walvin had few, if any, written family records on which to draw. He did keep youthful diaries, long lost during one of several relocations. He was forced to write largely from memory, and there is always the problem in these circumstances as to what gets forgotten or misrepresented. As it is, he gives two examples of suddenly remembering long-forgotten events (pp. 89, 130). An important proviso is that his two brothers and an older cousin read

---

30   Antonia Fraser, 'Optical Research', in Mark Bostridge, ed., *Lives for Sale: Biographers' Tales* (London: Continuum, 2004), 113.

drafts and provided their own perspectives as well as making corrections. It would be useful to know the specifics and the extent of such inputs, just as it would the extent to which Rickard's sister's sometimes 'different perspectives' had on *An Imperial Marriage*.[31] Another qualification is that Walvin drew on his previous researches when giving historical context to matters such as tuberculosis, cotton, Hoggart and soccer. As with Rickard, there was the visiting of old haunts – 'a helpful jogger of memories' – and the use of family photos. The latter seemed inconsequential initially because they are atypical in the sense that everyone is attired in their Sunday best, in keeping with Emma Walvin's concern for outward appearances as the confirmation of respectability. As Walvin explains, the photos are 'both misleading and revealing. Though we looked nothing like that in normal, everyday life, our Whitsuntide appearance provides a telling insight into some of our mother's most cherished values' (pp. 51–2). But they turned out to be very useful, so more the pity that none appear in *Different Times*. Although it was not archivally based, Walvin's aim was to write a book 'that will stand or fall by the quality of the writing and how far it evokes a past time'.[32]

As well as recounting some of his own childhood, Walvin presents a remembrance of working-class life that locates his family within the broader story of the industrial north during the 1940s and 1950s. In doing so, he stresses that much of what his friends and family experienced was illustrative rather than exceptional. Joe Eyre's was 'a story in miniature' (p. 4) – he was 'one of untold legions who came home from the war harbouring hidden scars that troubled him to his dying days' (p. xi). He and his estranged wife were 'one tiny example of what was happening worldwide, as millions of people struggled to piece together lives shattered by warfare and upheaval' (p. 68). Walvin's father's illness and slow decline, awful though it was, was 'a common and familiar story' (p. 36). Many other women besides his mother 'were wrestling with similar circumstances' in the postwar years (p. 46). Eric Richards is an exact contemporary of Walvin

---

31 Inputs of siblings should not be underestimated. Gilbert Murray (1866–1957) regretted that his two elder brothers were 'no longer here to correct and amplify my record' when writing his own autobiography. Quoted in Francis West, 'A Broken Mirror: Gilbert Murray's Reflections on an Australian Childhood', in Christopher Stary, ed., *Gilbert Murray Reassessed* (Oxford: Oxford University Press, 2007), 33.
32 Walvin, email, 26 November 2014.

and he too grew up in working-class Britain. Also a grammar school boy who went to a red-brick university on a scholarship, Richards predicts that *Different Times* will become a primary document of its times.[33]

Fitzpatrick wrote the first draft of *My Father's Daughter* entirely from memory. She then compared her memory with her parents' papers in the National Library of Australia, and other family papers, talked to friends and family members, and checked other archival sources. She was horrified at the fragility of her memory: 'practically everything I remembered was slightly or significantly wrong, or at any rate contested by other accounts' (p. 6).[34] It would be more than useful to have had these itemised in footnotes, but Fitzpatrick does give numerous clues in the body of her text. The book she writes also bears the hallmarks of an essentially objectivist approach to history, in itself an offshoot of her study of Russian history where she had to steer between the shoals of the competing and polarised dominant interpretations.[35] She draws a distinction between 'honesty as emotional truth and honesty as factual accuracy' (p. 5) and says she is 'writing memoirs, not a history of my life' (p. 8). Fitzpatrick equates 'emotional truth' with what she remembers, as distinct from strict factual accuracy. Yet, in practice, she still writes very much as a historian and this concern with fidelity to fact and nuance is the major strength of *My Father's Daughter*.

Final remarks

This chapter is not intended as a cheerleading narrative about the bountiful virtues of historians' autobiographies. Their variations in quality preclude such a tactic. But we do feel that they ought to be more highly valued than they probably are at present, and childhood memoirs in particular. Historians' accounts of their childhood are often the best parts of their autobiographies. They are typically less inhibited and circumspect than the accounts of their careers. Once the memoir intrudes onto academic

---

33 Eric Richards, 'Emigrants and Migrants', in Philip Payton, ed., *Emigrants and Migrants: Essays in Honour of Eric Richards* (Adelaide: Wakefield Press, 2017), 142.
34 See also Sheila Fitzpatrick, 'Can You Write a History of Yourself: Thoughts of a Historian turned Memoirist', *Griffith Review*, 33 (2011), griffithreview.com/edition-33-such-is-life/can-you-write-a-history-of-yourself.
35 See Michael David-Fox, Peter Holquist and Alexander M. Martin, 'An Interview with Sheila Fitzpatrick', *Kritika*, 8:3 (2007), 479–86, doi.org/10.1353/kri.2007.0034; Fitzpatrick, 'Revisionism in Soviet History', *History & Theory*, 46 (2007), 77–91, doi.org/10.1111/j.1468-2303.2007.00429.x.

life there are, as Popkin observes, tacit rules surrounding the 'obligations to maintain the group's image in the eyes of outsiders', which lends a certain blandness to many historians' autobiographies.[36] Perhaps this is a common malaise for academic autobiographies generally, rather than being specific to historians. A.J.P. Taylor, as one of his biographers points out, 'did himself no [professional] favours' by writing an autobiography (*A Personal History*, 1983) that was inaccurate, spiteful and disparaging of others.[37] He broke all the unwritten rules. In writing memoirs of childhood, however, historians need not worry about professional censure of that sort and they typically have a frankness and freshness about them, although the sensibilities of family members may have some bearing on content. The problem with the genre is that one's childhood is the time of life where the written record is likely to be at its sparsest, and where memory is the principal source.

A more important consideration is that historians' autobiographies, whether of childhood or beyond, are becoming more monographic – in the sense of being research-based – as the three memoirists have demonstrated.[38] Neither do historians typically find the task of autobiography an easy one. Rickard hints as much in acknowledging the help of members of an academic life-writing group in Melbourne (p. vii), and this despite a comparable experience in writing about the dynamics of Alfred Deakin's family.[39] Of course, there are 'good' autobiographies and 'bad' autobiographies, just as there are 'good' monographs and 'bad' monographs. We doubt whether the three memoirists would regard their autobiographies as their most important work, but this is not to downplay their merits. Each book was a serious undertaking, involving all the historian's skills. They were written with a concern to 'get it right', or at least as accurately as could be managed. Is it not high time that historians' autobiographies of this sort receive the credit due to them as serious pieces of research?

---

36 Popkin, *History, Historians, & Autobiography*, 152.
37 Kathleen Burk, *Troublemaker: The Life and History of A.J.P. Taylor* (New Haven/London: Yale University Press, 2000), 365.
38 And generational family histories by historians even more so, because their authors are dealing in large part with events before they were born and are therefore dependent on archival sources: e.g. David Walker, *Not Dark Yet: A Personal History* (Sydney: Giramondo, 2011); Graeme Davison, *Lost Relations: Fortunes of my Family in Australia's Golden Age* (Sydney: Allen & Unwin, 2015).
39 John Rickard, *A Family Romance: The Deakins at Home* (Melbourne: Melbourne University Press, 1996).

4
The Female Gaze: Australian Women Historians' Autobiographies

Ann Moyal

A striking number of Australian women have ventured into the autobiographical genre. While a slew of immigrant men were producing their personal odysseys of pioneering endeavour and the exploration and appropriation of a new land in the nineteenth century, a regiment of women from diverse backgrounds began to record their remembered experiences and specific local responses to colonial life. The women's stories were very different. Franker, relational, concerned with childhood, people and places, some masquerading as regional or local history, in a strongly masculine society they were often judged as 'unimportant' or 'trivial' and not given publication at the time of writing. But they came to lay the foundation of 'a complementary culture' to male autobiography with its ongoing emphasis on national identity and image, and they have been judged by literary and historical scholars as a rich and unique reading experience.[1]

---

1   Joy Hooton, *Stories of Herself When Young: Autobiographies of Childhood by Australian Women* (Melbourne: Oxford University Press, 1990), Introduction. This source provides a rich study of Australian autobiography.

Turning to women historians in Australia, their contribution to the autobiographical genre across the twentieth century stands well within this tradition. The focus of their work remains strongly linked to reminiscences of childhood; to personal influences, relationships and places; and, by the 1980s, to an emerging awareness of the advent of professional careers. Yet, it is important to note that many decades before professional training for women became available, two earlier women strode the stage in linking their personal lives to national meaning. The first was the electoral reformer, prominent social commentator, journalist and writer in South Australia, Catherine Helen Spence, who in her *An Autobiography* published in 1910, at the age of 85, claimed firmly that her life and career had identified her 'with the evolution of South Australia from a province to an important state in the commonwealth', and ended with the strong words, 'by my writings and my spoken addresses, I showed that one woman had a steady grasp on politics and on sociology'.[2] The second woman was Dame Mary Gilmore – teacher, writer, influential commentator – who, in her two autobiographical works in 1934–35, *Old Days, Old Ways* and *More Recollections*, saw herself firmly as a 'tribal mother' in the contemporary male world and as 'the wise old woman with a unique understanding of the past'.[3]

Several decades later, the distinguished public figure Maie Casey, publishing her memoir *An Australian Story 1837–1907* in 1962, offered a different mode in representing her special connection to the country's historical past. Casey made her own childhood her autobiographical baseline, and worked backwards through her family history so as to situate it within the evolution of Australia. She used what she describes as 'a mixture of record and memory' in which, by means of research among historical documents and letters, family myth, and personal memory, she hoped to place and secure her own, her family's and her country's identities, and preserve them from disappearance.[4]

---

2   Catherine Helen Spence, *An Autobiography* (Adelaide: W. Thomas Printer, 1910), 100.
3   Mary Gilmore, *Old Days, Old Ways: A Book of Recollections* (Sydney: Angus & Robertson, 1934); Gilmore, *More Recollections* (Sydney: Angus & Robertson, 1935). W.H. Wilde, 'Gilmore, Dame Mary Jean (1865–1962), *Australian Dictionary of Biography*, National Centre of Biography, The Australian National University, adb.anu.edu.au/biography/gilmore-dame-mary-jean-6391/text10923, published first in hardcopy 1983 (accessed 10 August 2015).
4   Maie Casey, *An Australian Story, 1837–1907* (London: Michael Joseph, 1962); see also Hooton, *Stories of Herself When Young*, 71–3.

From a singularly different background, yet impelled by a kindred drive to capture and contain the true Australian essence, in this case of 'the humble workers of the outback', the populist historian Patsy Adam-Smith published her autobiographical *Hear the Train Blow* in 1964. Adam-Smith was brought up during the Depression in a railway fettler family as an adopted daughter, a biological fact she did not learn until her teens. The concept of social identity and recognition, united with her need for a personal sense of belonging and of historical remembrance, lay at the heart of her autobiography. Writing in a later edition, she affirmed: 'In some ways it is as though *we* never lived. There is no monument to the toilers of a land and they wouldn't expect it. But a nation will be poorer if it forgets them.'[5] Her book, rooted in the bush ethos and in the gusto and innovation of the workers, went into a number of editions and enjoyed wide acclaim. It also provided Adam-Smith with the background for her subsequent prolific output of popular Australian historical works (she published 32 books) for which she used manuscripts, oral history and memory in spreading and rehearsing her stories of the railways, ships, workers, Anzacs and prisoners of war.[6]

By the 1980s, trained Australian women historians, moved perhaps by the advances in feminist thinking of the 1970s, were turning to autobiography. Alexandra Hasluck, a graduate of the University of Western Australia, published her *Portrait in a Mirror* (1981). Hasluck had emerged as an independent historian from the late 1950s when the *Australian Dictionary of Biography* (*ADB*) recruited her to the first Western Australian Working Party. Her autobiography was a record as the wife of the politician, later historian, and Governor-General, Paul Hasluck, and of travel and encounters, but she paused to make some passing criticism of a tendency on the part of academic historians ('well-known' ones, she emphasised) to 'requote old errors' and 'retell old stories', without bothering to read new works. Yet this memoir by the first trained female historian proved to be less a reflection of self-endeavour and historical enquiry than a collective relational embrace. Looking into the mirror 'not

---

5 Patsy Adam-Smith, *Hear the Train Blow: Patsy Adam-Smith's Classic Autobiography of Growing Up in the Bush* (Melbourne: Nelson, 1987), 180 (emphasis added).
6 Adam-Smith's other autobiographical work is also an amalgam of mixed research involving the use of manuscripts, oral testimony and memory. See *There Was a Ship* (Adelaide: Rigby, 1967); *The Barcoo Salute* (Adelaide: Rigby, 1973); *When We Rode the Rails* (Sydney: Landsdown, 1983); *Goodbye Girlie* (Ringwood: Viking, 1994).

only does my own face look back at me,' she wrote, 'but also the faces of ancestors and contemporaries, all wanting to get into the picture: and I cannot keep them out'.[7]

In 1983, the University of Melbourne history graduate Amirah Inglis published *Amirah: An Un-Australian Childhood*, the personal story of her upbringing by Polish Jewish parents to be a communist and a non-religious Jew. An immigrant child and student in Melbourne balancing a deeply entrenched cultural heritage with a new egalitarian setting, her book reveals a complex search for identity between the inherited old world and a society that offered opportunity but also societal challenge. This book, too, made its focus on childhood, the family and girlhood, although at university in 1944, she records, 'it was impossible to avoid the discomforts of being a Jew', but, 'discovering the anti-Semitism of Karl Marx and of Australian trade unionists was', she wrote with candour, 'a miserable experience'.[8] Inglis's second autobiography published in 1995, *The Hammer & Sickle and the Washing Up*, frames her first marriage to the historian Ian Turner.[9] A decade later came the voice of another historian migrant, Helga Griffin, a long-time researcher for the *ADB*, drawn this time from a Turkish and German background and faced with a difficult acclimatisation begun in a prisoner-of-war camp. In her *Sing Me that Lovely Song Again …* , Griffin offered a detailed, penetrating and rigorously investigative account of her early challenges, her Catholic schooling and her emergence through childhood and university to meet her future husband, historian Jim Griffin. Through its many pages, however, it did not touch on her historian's life.[10]

In the early 1980s, a selection of Melbourne and Sydney women academic historians, together with professional colleagues from other disciplines, took on the task of describing their experiences and advancement in a male-structured world in *The Half-Open Door*, co-edited by University of Melbourne historian Patricia Grimshaw, and *Against the Odds*, co-edited

---

7   Alexandra Hasluck, *Portrait in a Mirror: An Autobiography* (Melbourne: Oxford University Press, 1981), 1. In 1978, Alexandra Hasluck, who had published eight historical books, became the first Dame in the highest rank of the Order of Australia for her services to literature. See Geoffrey Bolton, *Paul Hasluck: A Life* (Perth: UWA Publishing, 2014), 465.
8   Amirah Inglis, *Amirah: An Un-Australian Childhood* (Melbourne: Heinemann, 1983), 155.
9   Amirah Inglis, *The Hammer & Sickle and the Washing Up: Memories of an Australian Woman Communist* (Melbourne: Hyland House, 1983).
10 Helga Griffin, *Sing Me that Lovely Song Again …* (Canberra: Pandanus Books, 2006).

by University of Sydney historian Heather Radi.[11] Almost all the women in this scatter of anthropologists, historians, social scientists, scientists and educators were the first members of their families to attend university, and they show an emergent sense of female agency, a depiction of women who, having gained university degrees and taken steps on the academic or professional ladder, viewed themselves as representing, in Grimshaw's words, 'an alternative role model for Australian girls'.[12] Radi, who had been tutoring and researching her PhD at the University of Sydney during the mid-1960s, and then became a conspicuous feminist in the history field, set the tone:

> It took some time for me to grow into the work at the University in the sense of doing anything that others did not do as well or better, but I relished the independence which mother had wanted for me, and feared. … As my interests shifted firmly to Australian History, my experience as a woman and across class and culture was of recurring relevance for my work. I was emotionally ready for Germaine [Greer] and followed friends into the women's movement and began encouraging students to work in the area of women's history. I contributed a segment on women's history to the first women's history course taught at the University of Sydney and had the pleasure of having my recommendations on the inclusion of the study of migrants, Aborigines and women accepted for the Australian History option for HSC [Higher School Certificate] Modern History.[13]

The sense of agency is modest. The male paradigm of selfhood and its concern for 'understanding' and 'making a coherent system out of life' – as seen in Donald Horne's earlier *The Education of Young Donald*[14] – is absent from the women's more tentative narratives. While Horne presents his personal story firmly as 'sociography', the women place themselves in a scheme where their own sense of agency is still compromised but hopeful, their development again rooted largely in their relational pasts.

---

11 Patricia Grimshaw and Lynne Strahan, eds, *The Half-Open Door: Sixteen Australian Women Look at Professional Life and Achievement* (Sydney: Hale & Iremonger, 1982), 20; Madge Dawson and Heather Radi, eds, *Against the Odds: Fifteen Professional Women Reflect on their Lives & Careers* (Sydney: Hale & Iremonger, 1984).
12 Patricia Grimshaw, 'Introduction: Professional Women in Twentieth Century Australia', in Grimshaw and Strahan, *The Half-Open Door*, 9.
13 Heather Radi, 'Thanks Mum', in Dawson and Radi, *Against the Odds*, 185. In her chapter ('Thanks Mum', 170–85), Radi paid particular respect to her mother's contribution to her progress. It was a perspective many of the contributors to *The Half-Open Door* and *Against the Odds* shared.
14 Donald Horne, *The Education of Young Donald* (Sydney: Angus & Robertson, 1967).

The University of Melbourne historian Kathleen Fitzpatrick contributed to *The Half-Open Door*, but a year later published an autobiography up until her returning from Oxford University to Australia in 1928. It went into several editions and was judged 'a contribution to Australian letters'.[15] Essentially, it was a deep reflection on Fitzpatrick's childhood and girlhood among an extended family at her grandmother's house, 'Hughenden' in Victoria, and her education by Catholic nuns. Beautifully written in her maturity, it gathers remembrance into a social context but leaves her professional life, her ill-fated marriage to Brian Fitzpatrick and her historical writings aside. Fitzpatrick, nonetheless, was one of the very few privileged women to proceed from a degree at the University of Melbourne to Oxford in 1926, where she was affected strongly by the derisive treatment she received from her Oxford dons. Accordingly, she avoided a master's degree and the second-class honours degree she obtained from Oxford profoundly undermined her confidence and sense of self-worth. While she became a greatly admired member of the University of Melbourne's Department of History as a teacher and researcher, her own sense of agency remained conservative and she declined the opportunity of a professorship. 'I have always believed', she ends her chapter 'A Cloistered Life' in *The Half-Open Door*, 'that no one should be appointed to the highest academic rank unless he or she is either a profound and original thinker or a truly erudite person'.[16]

In sharp contrast, the Sydney historian Jill Ker Conway marked the arrival of a highly motivated historian and a forceful communicator who, with three books of memoir behind her, would come to dominate the Australian women's autobiographical scene. Her initial venture, *The Road from Coorain*, published in 1989, introduced a newly minted young historian from the University of Sydney in 1958, determinedly steering her path away from the provincialism of Australian life to a richer intellectual experience in the United States. Educated at a private girls' school in Sydney after a childhood in the parched Australian landscape of Hillston, New South Wales, she studied at the University of Sydney in the later 1950s and found the teaching of Australian history 'an exercise

---

15 Kathleen Fitzpatrick, *Solid Bluestone Foundations and Other Memories of a Melbourne Girlhood, 1908–1928* (Melbourne: Macmillan, 1983); *Solid Bluestone Foundations: Memories of an Australian Girlhood* (2nd ed.; Ringwood: Penguin Books, 1986); Fitzpatrick, *Solid Bluestone Foundations: And Other Memories of a Melbourne Girlhood, 1908–1928*, introduced by Susan Davies (Melbourne: Melbourne University Press, 1998).
16 Kathleen Fitzpatrick, 'A Cloistered Life', in Grimshaw and Strahan, *The Half-Open Door*, 133.

in frustration'. She shone in history but her rejection as a university medallist for the cadet corps of the Australian Department of External Affairs deeply marked her, and she dusted her feet of Australia and left the country for a research scholarship at Harvard. *The Road from Coorain* catches her awareness of the need to escape from the cultural attitudes of a patriarchal society that constrained clever women. The book, with its strong intellectual underlay, descriptive power and potent sense of female force, put Ker Conway on the Australian and American map.[17]

Her second autobiography, *True North* (1994), traces her scholarly evolution at Harvard, her marriage to the senior Canadian historian, John Conway, and their time at the University of Toronto where she became vice-principal. Already a broad scholar of American women, Ker Conway was sought out at the age of 39 to become the first woman president of Smith College, setting the stage for a dynamic period of growth at this then conservative women's institution. Her book *A Woman's Education* (2001) is in part a personal story but also a record of her successful administration at Smith College. Drawing on her own hard pastoral background, she wrote with spirit: 'I could learn what I needed to know to deal with almost any problem.' Candid, informing and interrogative, a certain solipsism, however, marks the narrative. Ker Conway herself took up American citizenship; however, for an Australian audience, her three memoirs – both in their recording and their genre – offer a key illustration of the pertinence of confident feminine thinking.[18]

There appears sometimes a work that, differing in perspective and evocative in character, claims a special place in our historiography. One such is historian Jan Bassett's *The Facing Island*. Drawing upon letters she had written to her since deceased grandmother Edie, a resident of Phillip Island in Port Phillip Bay, enabled Bassett to reconstruct her own life as a grandchild on the island. Interlacing chapters, meanwhile, introduced into the narrative the letters her grandmother had received when a girl from a young New Zealand soldier who, in August 1916, dropped a message in a bottle in Bass Strait on his route to the First World War. Relational and sociological in conveying these profoundly intergenerational recollections, Bassett also infuses her book with her own intellectual curiosity and

---

17   Jill Ker Conway, *The Road from Coorain: An Australian Memoir* (Adelaide and New York: Heinemann and Alfred A. Knopf, 1989), quotation from 184.
18   Jill Ker Conway, *True North: A Memoir* (London: Hutchinson, 1994); Ker Conway, *A Woman's Education* (New York: Knopf, 2001), 70.

passion for travel and with allusion to her historical researches on the lives and experiences of Australian war nurses across the twentieth century.[19] Throughout, her writing is tempered by the knowledge that she is facing death from cancer at the age of 46 and by her concern to make sense of her life. At one time a teacher of history at La Trobe University and a researcher at the University of Melbourne, she reflects, 'I have measured out my life in books', and concludes: 'I considered that I had served an apprenticeship as a historian and was ready to put my skills to further use. I had published a number of books, was working on another, and had plans for lots more.'[20] Jan Bassett died in 1999 without seeing her evocative personal story in print.

In surveying the reach of women historians' autobiographical writings in Australia, I have found great resonance and a distinctive connection between author and the craft of writing history in Inga Clendinnen's *Tiger's Eye*. Renowned historian of the Aztecs and Maya of Mexico, Clendinnen, a Melbourne academic, fell dangerously ill in her early 50s and, after a liver transplant, spent months of hospitalisation in which she endured what she calls 'unscheduled and surprising transformations'. Her description of her illnesses is a masterly section of her book. Trapped in her hospital cot at night, she drew her book's title from the remembrance of a tiger at the zoo, padding up and down with his indifferent sweeping gaze. He was, she found, the one animal who did not acknowledge he was in a cage, and his image and his searchlight eyes became her salvation.[21] Writing about her childhood, her insights sharp, she realised that 'the marshland between memory and invention is treacherous'.[22] But, caught up by chance, she was led to the journal of G.A. Robinson, Chief Protector of the Aborigines for Port Phillip District, conducting a journey on horseback in the early 1840s from Melbourne to Portland, and was restored, after illness, to the writing of history. It was her 'ticket in a bottle', and here lies the core of Clendinnen's compelling book.

---

19   Jan Bassett, *Guns and Brooches: Australian Army Nursing from the Boer War to the Gulf War* (Melbourne: Oxford University Press, 1992); Bassett, *The Oxford Illustrated Dictionary of Australian History* (Melbourne/New York: Oxford University Press, 1993); Bassett, ed., *As We Wave You Goodbye: Australian Women and War* (Melbourne: Oxford University Press, 1998).
20   Jan Bassett, *The Facing Island: A Personal History* (Melbourne: Melbourne University Press, 2002), 141. It was a characteristically aware and brave reflection.
21   Inga Clendinnen, *Tiger's Eye: A Memoir* (Melbourne: Text Publishing, 2000), 20–1, 192.
22   Ibid., 73.

Thereafter, as a historian, she put herself to know and interpret Robinson's journal of events and to recreate him sharply and empathetically on the page. It makes splendid reading. Committed and sympathetic in his dealings with the Aborigines, she writes, he 'contrived ways to live with the appalling, immutable fact of Aboriginal death'. Adjusting, he kept himself busy. 'Every night,' she probes, 'this burdened, driven man steals time from sleep to assemble his information, to fix the flux of experience, to assemble his information, to construct his self-exposing account of things.' Robinson is hopelessly divided. 'He picks up a skull and puts it in the van', she writes, and then he continues with his travels and general observations: 'From horror to banality in a breath.' But, as Clendinnen observes, 'the horror is preserved, and now it is there on record, for any of us to read'. 'It is possible', she sums up, 'that someone, some day, will read, and remember.' Complex, duplicitous, Robinson 'speaks to us and moves us still'. For Clendinnen, it was 'the miracle of history'. Blending personal agency and her deep 'immersion in the experiences and mind of a stranger dead long before I was born', it yielded a work that her publisher claimed as a 'triumph for the importance of history', and, for me, marked a major autobiographical thrust.[23]

My own role as an autobiographer also turned directly on 'encounters with history' and on historiography. But my first venture, *Breakfast with Beaverbrook: Memoirs of an Independent Woman* (1995), arose in part from a strong feminist conviction that women had appeared in contemporary Australian male memoirs exclusively as mistresses or wives, but, as I had enjoyed a historian's life, there seemed a good reason to present a new perspective. It was my good fortune as a history graduate from the University of Sydney on a scholarship in London to have an early encounter with the charismatic and powerful Max Aitken, Lord Beaverbrook, which became the centrepiece of my book. Beaverbrook, still the dominant press lord of the *Daily Express*, had during the 1950s purchased some of the key political papers of Great Britain including the Lloyd George and Lady Lloyd George Papers and the Curzon Papers, and the Bonar Law Papers earlier acquired by Will. At the age of 75 – to the great annoyance of academic historians – he had planned to keep them in his sole possession and become a historian.

---

23 The quotations concerning Robinson are in ibid., 191–218.

My appointment as his personal research assistant, with its life of glamour, excitement and tireless work, led to the publication in 1956 of the book *Men and Power*, which placed Lord Beaverbrook as a historian on the international stage.[24] He himself was a participant in history. A Canadian by birth and a Member of the House of Commons, he had been at the centre of manoeuvres in the British Parliament in 1916 to bring down Herbert Asquith and install Lloyd George in the Prime Minister's seat. His interest now lay in writing of the two critical last years of the First World War and the battle for power between the generals and the politicians. It was history of a gripping political kind and it became 'Our War'. My book provides a detailed account of the collaborative methodology, aided by the clever archivist Sheila Lambert (Mrs Elton, from her marriage to Tudor historian Geoffrey Elton), by which we worked.[25] But the critical point about this 'encounter with history' was the uniqueness of the man. Examined against the documents of the period, Lord Beaverbrook's firsthand knowledge of the players in those two vital years of war gave him a mastery over the documentary material that no other historian, working systematically through the records later, could hope to achieve. It was this combination that placed him in special command of this piece of British political history and, significantly, won him the acclaim of the historians of the ivory tower. Lord Beaverbrook died in 1964 and, despite the amazing range of his career, he wanted to be remembered for his books. *Breakfast with Beaverbrook* gave me the opportunity to illuminate the processes and outcomes of his historical work.

My second 'encounter with history' occurred when I returned to Australia in 1959 to help another distinguished but very different historian, Sir Keith Hancock, establish the *Australian Dictionary of Biography*. In his second autobiography, *Professing History* (1976), Hancock made oblique reference to an 'exhausting' quarrel in respect of the *Dictionary* as well as to another unrelated imbroglio, adding, 'Those stories had better not be told'.[26] But I was there, and had preserved the correspondence between Hancock and myself across the critical years of 1960–61 when the *ADB*'s relationship with the independent historian Malcolm Ellis was at its most

---

24 Lord Beaverbrook, *Men and Power, 1917–1918* (London: Hutchinson, 1956, and numerous subsequent editions).
25 Ann Moyal, *Breakfast with Beaverbrook: Memoirs of an Independent Woman* (Sydney: Hale & Iremonger, 1995), 59–60.
26 W.K. Hancock, *Professing History* (Sydney: Sydney University Press, 1976), 39; D.A. Low, ed., *Keith Hancock: The Legacies of an Historian* (Melbourne: Melbourne University Press, 2001), 249–68.

complex. It seemed important that the story should emerge. My chapter on the foundations of the *Dictionary* in my memoir remained the main historical source on this great pioneering enterprise until the publication based on the full archives was told in *The* ADB*'s Story*, edited by Melanie Nolan and Christine Fernon in 2013.[27] For me, my years at the *Dictionary* returned me to Australian history and led, through Hancock's mentorship, to my study of the history of Australian science.

Against this backdrop, the female autobiographical gaze was further enriched during the late 1990s by a trio of participant women writers, set in a specific historical period, with their gender specific titles: Susan Ryan, *Catching the Waves* (1999); Wendy McCarthy, *Don't Fence Me In* (2000); and historian Anne Summers, *Ducks on the Pond* (1999). All three, writing in mid-career, published vivid accounts of their contributions to Australia's political, feminist and organisational life.[28] Summers, a history graduate of the University of Sydney, with her PhD study and book, *Damned Whores and God's Police*, behind her, overviewed her creative role as an activist in the Women's Liberation Movement of the 1970s and her key participation as an advisor on Women's Affairs to two Australian prime ministers, Bob Hawke and Paul Keating.[29] Her title, 'Ducks on the Pond', relayed the words shearers cried out when a women was seen approaching their male domain. A new gendered autobiographical form was on the shelves, and more was to come with Cassandra Pybus's light-hearted and partly fictionalised memoir, *Till Apples Grow on an Orange Tree*.[30]

This genre continued to evolve, and the letters of daughters to mothers as sources for autobiography figure in the works of two historians composing their memoirs in the twenty-first century. Alice Garner, daughter of the writer Helen Garner, cut her teeth in history at the University of Melbourne in the late 1980s where she became attracted to French history through her lecturer, Peter McPhee. Garner spent time in France working on both her MA thesis and her PhD thesis, the latter being a study of changing

---

27   Melanie Nolan and Christine Fernon, eds, *The* ADB*'s Story* (Canberra: ANU E Press, 2013).
28   Susan Ryan, *Catching the Waves: Life In and Out of Politics* (Sydney: HarperCollins, 1999); Wendy McCarthy, *Don't Fence Me In* (Sydney: Random House, 2000); Ann Summers, *Ducks on the Pond: An Autobiography, 1945–1976* (Ringwood: Viking, 1999).
29   Ann Summers, *Damned Whores and God's Police: The Colonization of Women in Australia* (Ringwood: Penguin Books, 1974).
30   Cassandra Pybus, *Till Apples Grow on an Orange Tree* (Brisbane: University of Queensland Press, 1998).

place across two centuries in a fishing village at the Bassin de Arachon.[31] Garner's autobiographical *the student chronicles* is a slight, evocative record of student days at the University of Melbourne drawn from her diaries and letters, which recall those pre-computer days of the late 1980–90s when students hand-drafted their essays, typed them up with effort, used card catalogues and microfiche, kept their lips firmly closed through tutorials, and struggled at the onset of the Dawkins era when managerialism was 'sliding its cold fingers down the wrinkly collars of Arts faculty staff'.[32] Keeping all her essays for the record and her scattered recollections, she reconstructs some of the confusions, rawness and habits of student life.

The second historian is Sheila Fitzpatrick, whose memoir *My Father's Daughter* offers a frank, probing and, at times, poignant account of her relationship with her father, the notorious Melbourne radical historian, Brian Fitzpatrick, and her high dependence as a child on his attention and regard: 'Daddy, are you watching? I'm going to jump.'[33] In a sense, her father was her childhood. After education in the Department of History at the University of Melbourne, she had escaped his influence by taking up a scholarship to study Soviet history and politics at Oxford University when his unexpected death at the end of her first year sent her spiralling into extended grief and a determination to distance herself physically from Australia. Fitzpatrick's essay in this volume brings the reflective skill of the historian to an examination of her own mode of writing family memoir. It provides further demonstration that, in Australia, the canvas for women historian autobiographers presents itself as Janus-faced. We have moved into the pertinent examination of the varied nature and processes of history in the telling of a personal life, while we have also remained closely tied to the remembrance of childhood and youth.

In *A Spy in the Archives*, Fitzpatrick uses her diaries and letters to her mother to provide a detailed memoir of her experience as a doctoral student in Moscow working in the Soviet Archives in the mid to late 1960s in the period of the Cold War.[34] At a time when the study of Soviet history was in its infancy, she and her fellow exchange students

---

31 Alice Garner, *A Shifting Shore: Locals, Outsiders, and the Transformation of a French Fishing Town, 1823–2000* (Cornell: Cornell University Press, 2005).
32 Alice Garner, *the student chronicles* (Melbourne: Miegunyah Press, 2006), 107. The lower-casing is original to the title of the book.
33 Sheila Fitzpatrick, *My Father's Daughter: Memories of an Australian Childhood* (Melbourne: Melbourne University Press, 2010), 2, 230.
34 Sheila Fitzpatrick, *A Spy in the Archives* (Melbourne: Melbourne University Press, 2013).

from Britain 'felt like cosmonauts who had landed on the moon', and she writes vividly of the drabness of the Brezhnev age – the people poorly dressed, the challenge of inconvenient stores, learning Russian, a people-less life, and the gossip and obsession with spying. But the core of the book is her historian's account of working in the archives on A.V. Lunacharsky, the first Soviet Commissar of Enlightenment after the 1917 Bolshevik Revolution, alongside one of his former assistants, Igor Sats, who became a key mentor: 'untapped archives', Fitzpatrick recalls, 'plus a primary informant willing to give you a running commentary on what you read in the archives the day before is something that only happens once in a lifetime'.[35] In time she would be 'outed' as a spy, a so-called 'ideological saboteur', and face scrutiny and diverse modes of bureaucrat overview and control. But, leaving Russia for marriage in England, her research task complete, she allowed, 'I am very much at home in this funny atmosphere'.[36] It laid the foundation for her rise as a leading Soviet historian.

For my own part, writing autobiography as a woman in what is called the 'seventh age' or later, as I have done with my *A Woman of Influence* in 2014, is as yet a rare phenomenon in Australia and elsewhere.[37] What was my impulse towards it? I had written *Breakfast with Beaverbrook* in my late 60s, yet my life had remained richly active. I was also given a mental push by an American literary academic, Carolyn Heilbrun, who deplored that whenever she read an autobiography written by a woman in her 50s or beyond, it was always confined to her youth or romance: 'She abandons age, experience, wisdom to search the past, usually for romance, always for the beginnings of childhood.' But, as Heilbrun argued, 'the story of age, of maturity before infirmity, before meaningless old age, has never been told except perhaps by Shakespeare who told everything, provided he could tell it of men'.[38]

And so I engaged to write with some passion of my long career as a historian of Australian science, as a biographer and of those men and women who had influenced and enriched me in my personal and professional development. It is a story of interconnections. Importantly, late in life candour becomes important; one has nothing to lose, and there

---

35 Ibid., 170.
36 Ibid., 1, 329.
37 Ann Moyal, *A Woman of Influence: Science, Men & History* (Perth: UWA Publishing, 2014).
38 Carolyn G. Heilbrun, *Writing a Woman's Life* (London: The Women's Press, 1989), quoted in Moyal, *A Woman of Influence*, ix.

is an eagerness on the part of readers to share in the intimacy of one's story. So my text turned into a stretching, allusive conversation with my readers where identity became entwined with other lives and where my work as a historian played an integral part. For, as Alan Moorehead, whose biography I wrote working among his papers for several years at the National Library of Australia, declared: 'And so a writer's books are the chapters of his life.'[39]

I wave to Beaverbrook returning to England in recent years as a senior historian to look at the Beaverbrook papers in the Parliamentary Archives at the House of Lords and to reassess this remarkable participant historian, archival proprietor and writer, and how we worked together when I was young. As a reviewer of my book summed up aptly: 'The act of remembrance begins as a personal, private and often spontaneous activity but once shared with others, memories become collective remembering.'[40] Or, perhaps, as Jill Ker Conway writes in her excellent *When Memory Speaks*: 'We're heard when we speak confidently out of our understanding of our own experience. … We should play close attention to our stories. … We are all autobiographers.'[41]

---

39 Ann Moyal, *Alan Moorehead: A Rediscovery* (Canberra: National Library of Australia, 2005), frontispiece. See also Alan Moorehead, *A Late Education: Episodes in a Life* (London: Hamish Hamilton, 1970).
40 Susan Steggall, 'Cultivating Minerva', review of *A Woman of Influence* by Ann Moyal, *ISAA Review*, 13.2 (2014), 101–4.
41 Jill Ker Conway, *When Memory Speaks: Reflections on Autobiography* (New York: Knopf, 1998), 177–80.

Nation-Defining Authors

5

'A gigantic confession of life': Autobiography, 'National Awakening' and the Invention of Manning Clark[1]

Mark McKenna

> Perhaps this is the worst deceiver of all – we make up our pasts.
> — Doris Lessing

By any measure, Manning Clark (1915–91) is Australia's most well-known and controversial historian. Born only seven weeks before Australian soldiers landed at Anzac Cove on 25 April 1915, Clark's intellectual life was framed by the great ideological struggle of the twentieth century, which began with the Russian Revolution in 1917 and ended with the fall of the Berlin Wall in 1989. By the time of his death on 23 May 1991, he had also witnessed the slow yet inexorable decline of the British connection in Australia.

As professor of Australian history at The Australian National University (ANU) in Canberra, Clark produced an exceptional volume of work over a period of 40 years; three volumes of historical documents (the bedrock

---

1   An earlier version of the present chapter appeared in the journal *Life Writing*: '"National Awakening," Autobiography, and the Invention of Manning Clark', *Life Writing*, 13:2 (2016), 207–20. The author and editors are grateful for permission to republish.

of university courses in Australian history for more than two decades), *A Short History of Australia* (which was translated into several European and Asian languages and sold widely overseas), an extremely controversial short book on his visit to the Soviet Union in the late 1950s – *Meeting Soviet Man* – another on the writer Henry Lawson, the ABC Boyer Lectures in 1976, a collection of essays, two volumes of short stories, hundreds of articles, reviews, newspaper op-eds and two volumes of autobiography. Five further volumes of speeches, letters, history and autobiographical writings were published posthumously. From 1938, the time of his scholarship to Oxford at age 23 until his death in 1991, Clark also kept personal diaries, documenting his inner life often with fierce and uncompromising honesty, as well as tracking the personal lives of many of his friends and colleagues in sometimes brutal fashion, all of it in his barely legible ink scrawl, a script once compared to 'micro barbed-wire'.[2] In addition, he kept copious notebooks over the same period mapping his reading and the conceptual development of his work. Taken together, this output, most of it completed while he was still teaching, easily exceeded that of many of his contemporaries. And yet, remarkably, the above list of publications excludes the work for which he is best known, his six-volume *A History of Australia*, published between 1962 and 1987. Clark's six volumes comprised well over one million words and their extraordinary popularity played a large part in keeping Melbourne University Press afloat for over two decades (selling an average of 40,000 copies per volume).[3]

In media interviews, Clark's personal story of the creation of the six volumes became part of his success, as if the nation were waiting for the next instalment in the story of its own creation. In the 1970s and 1980s, he was interviewed both after each volume was published and when he had completed successive drafts. Clark's ability to dramatise the writing process usually involved a disarming cocktail of self-deprecation and special pleading, particularly in the 1980s ('I haven't done everyone justice and I regret that I did not have more ability … I know I've made a lot of mistakes … I don't want to sound too pompous. I've got a reputation for being a bit of a bullshit artist').[4] Clark created the illusion that his readers were buying both *A History of Australia* and a latter-day version of Rousseau's *The Confessions*, a deeply personal impression of the past and

---

2 Mark McKenna, *An Eye for Eternity: The Life of Manning Clark* (Melbourne: Miegunyah Press, 2011), 29.
3 See Appendix to this chapter for bibliographic details of Clark's *oeuvre*.
4 Clark interviewed by Ken Brass, *Weekend Australian Magazine*, 2 March 1985.

life itself. He frequently referred to his historical writing as the 'child of his heart'. For Clark, there was no distance between the historian and the past he inhabited.

In the public eye, from his retirement in the early 1970s until his death in 1991, Clark wore his trademark dress – the slightly tattered, black three-piece suit, the watch chain dangling from the fob pocket, the long, thin legs anchored in paddock-bashing boots and the grave, goatee-bearded face of the old man crowned by a crumpled, weather-beaten Akubra. Across Australia, he was renowned as a historical oracle. At the height of his fame in the 1970s and 1980s, he was awarded a Companion of the Order of Australia (1975), named Australian of the Year (1981) and won almost every major Australian literary award. In 1988, the year of Australia's Bicentenary, Clark (and his hat) seemed to be everywhere. He was the frequent subject of cartoonists' caricatures; he penned major critical essays interpreting the historical significance of the Bicentenary for magazines such as *The Bulletin* and *Time Australia*, and was easily the nation's most prominent public intellectual. In his last years, after his retirement from teaching, Clark addressed Australia Day events and citizenship ceremonies; launched books; opened art exhibitions, fetes, music festivals, opera and theatre productions; endorsed rock bands; spoke at school speech nights, Australian Labor Party campaign rallies and church services.

To understand the many causes he fought for from the 1960s to the 1990s is to understand how instrumental his public life was in changing the face of Australia in the twentieth century. Almost two decades before the White Australia policy was dismantled, Clark called for an end to the prejudice and inhumanity inherent in racial discrimination. He opposed the Vietnam War; condemned the proliferation of nuclear weapons; supported the land rights and treaty demands of Indigenous Australians; championed the arts and the importance of teaching Australian history in schools and universities; campaigned to save the Great Barrier Reef, Fraser Island and the Franklin River; spoke against the logging of old-growth forests; lent his name to numerous petitions to save significant historical sites; backed heritage legislation; protested against the Soviet Union's incarceration of Alexander Solzhenitsyn and the repression of the Solidarity movement in Poland; enthusiastically embraced multicultural Australia; personally encouraged generations of writers and artists; and worked to challenge longstanding stereotypes of Australia abroad, especially in the United Kingdom. In the last two decades of his life, Clark appeared in every possible media site, including midday television, house and garden programs, and even managed a cameo role as the preacher in the 1985 film production of the Peter Carey novel, *Bliss*. In all of these appearances and writings, Clark deftly cast his public interventions through the lens of his personal experience. The public telling of autobiographical stories – the modus operandi of the public intellectual – became the means through which Clark established a popular audience and created himself as a national prophet.

In the seven years I spent working on Clark's biography between 2004 and 2011, I never doubted the importance of what I was doing.[5] To be sure, I experienced many moments of exasperation and exhaustion. To come close to Clark, to know him intimately and, at the same time to keep my distance was always a struggle. This is the biographer's dilemma: to resolve the tension between closeness and distance, to know and reveal the subject without becoming the subject's ventriloquist. Gradually, I realised that there was something that transcended even the weight of Clark's scholarship and the substantial impact of his public life. On a human level alone – as child, adolescent, lover, friend and father – his life was lived and remembered with such an acute theatrical sensibility that it spoke to readers regardless of their gender, cultural background or nationality. Clark's life contained contradictions numerous and large enough for all of us to recognise shards of our own experience. It was both Australian and universal. But it was also a life given over to public examination in a way that few of us would dare contemplate, one burdened by extreme self-consciousness and a pathological desire to be remembered as a great man. Much of Clark's archival legacy – his anguished diaries, his voluminous correspondence with others (including more than 50 years of letters to his wife Dymphna), his eulogies for departed friends and his irrepressible ministering of others at times of personal crisis – was, as Ken Inglis shrewdly remarked in 1991, more about 'self than subject'.[6] Nearly everything Clark wrote and said was self-referential. Narrating the lives of others became a way of seeding the autobiography of C.M.H. Clark in the Australian imagination.

---

5   McKenna, *An Eye for Eternity*.
6   The remark by Ken Inglis is drawn from a set of hastily written notes by Inglis shortly after Clark's death and given to me. The notes are still in my possession. Clark's papers are held at the National Library of Australia (NLA, MS 7550), as are those of Dymphna Clark (NLA, MS 9873).

One of the greatest challenges I encountered in writing Clark's biography was not only the question of how to deal with the work of previous biographers such as Brian Matthews and Stephen Holt, but also the far more pressing problem of how to deal with Clark's *autobiographical* writings.[7] My intention was to write Clark's life as it was *lived*, not as he remembered it. Yet this proved tremendously difficult because he had stamped so much of his own memory on the public image of his life. To write Clark's biography, I had to somehow wrest control of the life from the extremely controlling voice of my subject. Perhaps the most graphic example of this was Clark's tendency to leave directional notes to his biographers throughout his papers. But the sheer volume of his autobiographical writings exacerbated the struggle for biographical distance. To avoid paraphrasing Clark's various accounts of his life and merely accepting his version of events, I had to disarm his autobiographical voice and test his interpretations and recollections against the perspectives of others.

Clark's best-known volumes of autobiography were published in quick succession in 1989 and 1990. First, *The Puzzles of Childhood*, which tells the story of his parents' lives and the 'nightmares and terrors' of his childhood, and then *Quest for Grace*, which picks up the story from his days as a student at the University of Melbourne and Oxford in the 1930s and ends just before the first volume of *A History of Australia* is published in 1962. In addition to these two volumes, Clark's autobiographical writings extended to reflections on historical writing (*An Historian's Apprenticeship*), essays, speeches and interviews. In fact, it is perfectly reasonable to include Clark's histories in the same category. For, as Clark remarked, 'everything one writes is a fragment in a gigantic confession of life'.[8] He saw all of his writing as inherently autobiographical.

Both as historian and public intellectual, Clark helped to destroy the belief that Australian history was merely a dull, insignificant appendage to British imperial history. Leading much of the post-1960s public debate around 'new nationalism', he transformed popular understandings of Australian history, an achievement that will undoubtedly prove to be his most lasting contribution. The origins of Clark's *A History of Australia*

---

7   Stephen Holt, *Manning Clark and Australian History, 1915–1963* (Brisbane: University of Queensland Press, 1982); Holt, *A Short History of Manning Clark* (Sydney: Allen & Unwin, 1999); Brian Matthews, *Manning Clark: A Life* (Sydney: Allen & Unwin, 2008).
8   Manning Clark, 'A Long Time Ago', in his *Speaking Out of Turn: Lectures and Speeches, 1940–1991* (Melbourne: Melbourne University Press, 1997), 79.

can be found in the profound schism between the established pastoral background of his pious, Protestant mother (a direct descendant of Samuel Marsden) and the working-class larrikinism of his Anglo-Catholic father of part-Irish descent, a division that Clark dramatised at every opportunity, portraying the religious divisions of his family as Australia's writ large. More than any other writer of his generation, Clark succeeded in aligning the trajectory of his own life with a larger narrative of national awakening.

His histories were *autobiographical* not only because he infused the past with his own experience but also because he often invented the thoughts and emotions of historical characters. As they rise from their graves and perform their soliloquies, they appear as thinly veiled shadows of their author's alter ego: they are 'tormented' by doubt and guilt, led on by some 'madness of the heart', and inevitably brought down by their 'fatal flaw'. Women appear in *A History of Australia* in much the same vein as Dymphna Clark appears in the pages of his diary. They are either the temptress or the punisher, more often the latter; women with a sharp, vindictive streak who undermine men's idealism and fail to understand the enormity of their husband's creative genius. In the pages of Clark's history, potted autobiographies rain down one after another, almost as if Clark were conducting an oratorio. In this light, it seems entirely appropriate that *A History of Australia* was made into a musical in 1988 (*Manning Clark's History of Australia: The Musical*). Clark's grand narrative – with its now familiar but at the time quite revolutionary schema of seeing Australia's past through the prism of three great belief systems: Protestantism, Catholicism and the Enlightenment – lurches from the inspired to the droll, finding tragedy, pathos and existential crisis on every stump and street corner. Part Gibbon, part Macaulay, part Carlyle, and steeped in the language of the Old Testament, it is entirely character driven, mostly a succession of flawed, tormented males, who walk on stage at the allotted time to play out the drama of their biographical roles. At regular intervals, the ghosts of Dostoevsky, Tolstoy, Chekhov and Henry James emerge from behind the arras to provide a guiding aphorism or two. Both in everyday speech, and in the persona of the writer, Clark spoke through the voices of the canon, peppering his language with literary and biblical quotations; Dostoyevsky, Tolstoy and the Book of Ecclesiastes were among his favourite sources of inspiration.

5. 'A GIGANTIC CONFESSION OF LIFE'

Clark was probably the first historian in Australia to write at length about the inner life of his characters (sketches that frequently mirrored his emotional state at the time of writing). Much of the emotion in his work is grounded in an acute religiosity, the parson's son ministering the souls of Australia's flawed men – Wentworth, Lawson, Burke and Wills, John Curtin and Manning Clark. His feeling was not only for his characters, it was also for place. Until Clark's six volumes, historical melancholy was something Australians imagined resided only in the layered, built environment of Europe. Like Sidney Nolan, Patrick White and Arthur Boyd, Clark found this melancholy in the land itself, a melancholy not only of exile but one born of an awareness of the continent's antiquity and the horror of the violent dispossession of Indigenous people; a dispossession that is not so much documented in his work but rather recurs as an underlying tragic refrain. *A History of Australia* succeeded in attracting a large popular readership because of its narrative flair and Clark's mercurial ability to convince his audience that the story of his own life was a unique window onto Australian history.

A handful of critics and reviewers noted the autobiographical dimension of Clark's history. John Rickard was particularly astute on the way in which Clark increasingly relied on personal experience as the volumes progressed: 'the project which began as history', Rickard observed, 'has become autobiography'.[9] Inglis thought fellow historians Bede Nairn and Allan Martin were both concerned that Clark had moved from history to fiction and autobiography, with each volume hanging on an encounter between an Anglophile villain (Alfred Deakin, Robert Menzies) and an Australian tragic hero (Henry Lawson, John Curtin).[10] Richard White was another who observed that, in the last volumes, 'history and memory had come too close'.[11] Reviewing Volume Five in 1981, Edmund Campion noted that the woman seen crying out at the railway station at the end of the book was actually Clark's mother. He drew attention to the way in which Clark introduced his personal memories of Anzac Day in the 1920s and 1930s into the history, just as he did with his memories of songs, radio advertisements and the Bodyline cricket series. 'This personal note is something new in our historians', reflected Campion. 'Indeed, it is so

---
9   John Rickard, review of *A History of Australia*, vol. 6 by Manning Clark, *Times on Sunday*, 23 August 1987.
10 This characterisation of Nairn and Martin comes from the file of notes given to me by Ken Inglis.
11 Richard White, review of *The Quest for Grace* by Manning Clark, *Australian Society*, November 1990, 39–40.

noticeable in Manning Clark that when I first read Volume Six I thought of suggesting to Melbourne University Press that they reject it as his autobiography.'[12]

Perhaps the first question regarding Manning Clark's volumes of autobiography (and all autobiography for that matter) is why he decided to write them? To defend oneself *against* biographers (as Doris Lessing described her motive for writing autobiography); to claim one's life *before* the 'ferrets' (as Kate Grenville described biographers when donating her papers to the National Library of Australia) usurp and misrepresent it; to 'set the record straight', as so many politicians claim is the starting point for their memoirs; or, as former Labor minister Barry Jones reflected when writing his autobiography *A Thinking Reed*, 'to explain my life to myself', to subject oneself to gruelling self-examination and at the same time give an existing audience a more personal insight into the object of their admiration.[13] The very term autobiography suggests that the decision to write is self-generated. I am a significant someone, therefore I am an autobiographer. Few autobiographers find themselves at their writing desk because they want to test or reconstitute the boundaries of the genre itself. Historical context, celebrity marketing and the vagaries of the publishing industry are usually far more important determinants in the shaping and publishing of autobiography.

Clark's autobiographies, written towards the end of his life when he was already a well-known figure, were prompted initially not by the urgent need for self-examination about which he spoke so frequently in public, but much more practically by the suggestion of former Labor senator Susan Ryan, who in the late 1980s worked as an editor for Penguin after leaving politics. Ryan wrote to Clark and asked him if he would consider writing his autobiography.[14] Both volumes of Clark's autobiography were therefore the direct result of his publisher's initiative. Clark received a $5,000 advance from Penguin to write *The Puzzles of Childhood*. Ryan, who had witnessed Clark's enormous public impact firsthand during her time in parliament, recognised a commercial opportunity when she

---

12   Edmund Campion, 'Manning Clark', *Scripsi*, 5:2 (1989), 183–7.
13   Doris Lessing, *Under my Skin: Volume One of my Autobiography* (London: HarperCollins, 1994), 14; Susan Wyndham, 'Kate Grenville's New Life as a Single Woman', *Sydney Morning Herald*, 21 March 2015, www.smh.com.au/good-weekend/kate-grenvilles-new-life-as-a-single-woman-20150304-13vbim.html; Barry Jones, *A Thinking Reed* (Sydney: Allen & Unwin, 2006), 1.
14   Clark on Susan Ryan's invitation in his interview with Andrew Rutherford, *Sunday Age*, 14 October 1990, 11.

saw one. Within months of publication, her decision was vindicated. *The Puzzles of Childhood* won national literary awards, climbed to number one in the list of bestselling non-fiction, while Qantas Airways purchased 500 copies to distribute to their passengers on long-haul flights. Although Clark claimed to Humphrey McQueen that he was 'upset' by Penguin's marketing campaign for the book – 'books should make their own mark without aids from P.R. promoters who probably have not read the book. Penguin makes me feel what I have to say is a commodity' – he appeared to revel in the opportunity to 'confess' his life story to the media.[15]

The particular cultural and political context in which Clark's autobiographies were written did much to shape their voice and narrative. They were completed in the shadow of his failing health and the death of many of his closest friends ('my contemporaries, or more accurately, my near contemporaries all seem to be dying').[16] These were the years that followed the constitutional crisis that had divided Australian society so deeply in 1975, when Governor-General Sir John Kerr dismissed Labor Prime Minister Gough Whitlam from office. As one of the leading intellectuals of the Labor Left, Clark was at the forefront of the campaign that condemned Kerr and the conservative parties and demanded a republican constitution. These were also the years of growing consumerism, increasing affluence and economic growth and rampant mining development. The tide of often vague, ill-directed nationalism that accompanied the demise of British Australia, which Clark had ridden so successfully, had helped to push Australian authors, artists and celebrities to the fore remarkably quickly. In Whitlam's Australia, intellectuals were accorded a public platform and authority they had never claimed before. Publishers were keen to capitalise on this cultural awakening and the booming genre of autobiography was no exception. The emotive style of Clark's autobiographies proved an exception to James Walter's identification of 'the dominance in Australian biography of an empiricist, positivist tradition – strictly chronological, favouring the public life over the private, description over analysis and the preservation of emotional distance – at least up until [the early 1980s]'. But, in other respects, his work was typical of broader literary and cultural trends. As Bruce Bennett noted as early as 1998, so many Australian autobiographies published in the late twentieth century, particularly those by authors such as Patrick

---

15   Clark to Humphrey McQueen, 7 July 1989, Papers of Humphrey McQueen, NLA, MS 4809, Folder Addition 31.5.1990, 'Correspondence with Manning Clark, 1988–1990'.
16   Clark to McQueen, 15 August 1988, in ibid.

White, Donald Horne and Geoffrey Dutton, sought to trace a life as 'part of a national allegory'.[17] Clark's autobiographies were probably the prime example.

In *The Puzzles of Childhood*, Clark casts his first years in the harsh light of his latter-day celebrity status. Thus, from the moment of his birth, he is destined to become a national prophet. Early in the book we read his mother's words to the infant Manning: 'one day [you] will be a famous man'.[18] Clark's mother's observation seems remarkably perceptive given that at this stage her son had not even begun to walk or talk. Other examples of remembering past experience through the imperatives of Clark's latter-day status as a national prophet abound. In *The Quest for Grace*, Clark continuously complains of the English condescension towards Australians that he experienced in Oxford. 'It made me very conscious of myself as an Australian.' Playing cricket for Oxford, he claimed that the English 'treated [him] as an outsider … they didn't accept me as an ordinary human being and I've never forgotten it'.[19] Yet in his diary during these years there is very little if any evidence of these sentiments. He certainly remarks on his experience of English superiority, but the young Clark is painfully aware of what he perceives to be the far more cultured existence in England. He yearns to be accepted. In fact, his depiction of his experience in England in the late 1930s in *The Quest for Grace* demonstrates how he has retrospectively coloured his memories through the prism of post-Dismissal Australia. A similar rewriting of the past can be observed in Clark's history.

The last three volumes of *A History of Australia*, all written in the wake of the Dismissal, give greater stress to Australian nationalism. The earlier schema of the grand contest between Catholicism, Protestantism and the Enlightenment falls away. In its place is the simplistic polarity of the Old Dead Tree (Britain) and the Young Tree Green (Australia). Clark's depiction of the Anglo-Australian relationship becomes increasingly crude. 'Colonials don't make their own history,' he proclaims, 'decisions are made for them in London.'[20] The Dismissal sharpened Clark's anti-

---

17 Bruce Bennett, 'Literary Culture since Vietnam: A New Dynamic', in Bruce Bennett and Jennifer Strauss, eds, *Oxford Literary History of Australia* (Melbourne: Oxford University Press, 1988), 255; and James Walter, quoted by Bennett, ibid., 287.
18 Manning Clark, *The Puzzles of Childhood* (Ringwood: Penguin, 1989), 48.
19 Clark interviewed in *Australian Playboy*, July 1981, 31–4.
20 Glen Mitchell, 'Interview with Professor Manning Clark', *University of Wollongong Historical Journal*, 1:1 (1975), 65–75.

5. 'A GIGANTIC CONFESSION OF LIFE'

British sentiments. As public intellectual, historian and autobiographer, he wrote both his life story and the nation's history in the image of late twentieth-century nationalism. The purpose of Clark's life, as he told it, was to hammer the last nail in the coffin of British Australia. He appears to be born to oversee the end of Empire.

The opening page of *The Puzzles of Childhood* contains a story he first told in 1979. It is December 1919 and Clark is four years old. He is sitting on the backyard lawn of his home in Burwood. Looking up in the sky, he sees a mechanical bird soaring above. Curious, he asks his mother what it might be. She explains that the bird is the plane piloted by Keith and Ross Smith; they are on the last leg of their flight from London to Sydney. It is one of Clark's first memories, but like so many of his memories, the facts do not quite match the power of the story. In December 1919, Sir Keith and Ross Smith landed not in Sydney but in Darwin. Due to mechanical problems, their plane did not arrive in Sydney until three months later, on 14 February 1920. As the *Sydney Morning Herald* reported, it was not the first plane that Sydneysiders had set eyes on but 'the thrill came when one thought, as he gazed, this plane had come from England!' Thousands of people stood on rooftops to catch a glimpse of the plane, which was escorted by three others as it approached the city from the south. The flight path *did not* take the planes over Clark's home in Burwood, but over the city's northern suburbs. First sighted over Mascot, the Smith Brothers flew over the heads, down to the city, then north towards Mosman, before circling back over the harbour, down over Hyde Park and on to Mascot to land. Even if Clark had the date wrong, he would have needed to be on his roof at Burwood, a four-year-old boy with sure feet and a telescope, in order to see the Smiths' plane. Fundraising flights also took place in the weeks after the historic occasion – perhaps Clark had mistakenly remembered one of these flights? It is certainly possible that he did see a plane in the sky from his backyard in Burwood in February 1920, but the story as Clark tells it, this powerful opening image of his autobiography, is not about the young Clark, it is about the old Clark.

His apocryphal tale of an innocent child gazing up to the sky to see the arrival of the first flight from England to Australia is a memory tailor-made for the grand man of history. His first memory is of a historically significant event. The giant bird in the sky – the portent of war waged from the air, of the coming age of technology and globalisation – brings with it the historical forces of modernity that will shape twentieth-century Australia. Memory obediently serves the titanic public figure, lining up family stories and national history until they seem to be one and the same journey. Like so many of Clark's stories, their telling allowed him to be present in the past. He became the witness, already the historian at only four years of age. The final effect was to make the path he chose to follow appear as his inevitable destiny.

More than twenty-five years after Clark's death, it is also possible to see that Clark's autobiographies rest on a pillar of falsehoods and half-truths. Perhaps it is commonplace to observe that 'autobiographies tell more lies than all but the most self-indulgent fiction'.[21] The late Gunter Grass, no stranger to autobiographical fiction himself, reflected that in autobiography, 'the conventions of literary reminiscence and historical recollection are flawed'. Autobiographical truth, Grass insisted, 'all too easily gives way to the old literary lies. The past is elusive, memory plays tricks, the self of narrative is a stranger to the self who writes'.[22] The fictive quality of autobiography has long been established. But Clark's autobiographical writings point not only to the notorious unreliability of autobiography, resting as it does on the paper-thin house of memory, but to much larger questions, such as the relationship between autobiographical truth and celebrity status and the autobiographer's right to 'own' their life story. There is a wonderfully revealing moment in an Australian Broadcasting Corporation (ABC) radio interview conducted after the publication of *The Puzzles of Childhood* in 1989. Interviewing Clark, ABC journalist Terry Lane was perplexed by his uncanny ability in the book to know precisely what his father and mother were thinking and feeling at any given point in time, not to mention his astonishing recall of the thoughts and emotions of his childhood self. 'But how can you possibly know these things?', Lane asked Clark incredulously. Slightly unnerved, Manning replied: 'Well Terry, it's my view of my life and my view can't be wrong'. Clark's deadpan response put a swift end to Lane's line of questioning.[23]

Yet it also raised a crucial question for biographers and readers: to what extent can the autobiographer's interpretation and recollection of his life be challenged? Can the biographer know his subject's life better than the subject knows himself? 'There is your life as you know it and also as others

---

21 A.S. Byatt, quoted in Allan Massie, 'Writing of, or from, Yourself', *Spectator*, 27 January 2010, www.spectator.co.uk/2010/01/writing-of-or-from-yourself/.
22 Ian Brunskill, 'An Added Ingredient', review of *Beim Hauten der Zwiebel* by Gunter Grass, *Times Literary Supplement*, 27 September 2006, 3–4.
23 'Terry Lane Talks with Manning Clark', ABC Spoken Word Cassette, 1990 (copy in Manning Clark House, Canberra).

know it,' wrote James Salter in his memoir *Burning the Days*, 'it is difficult to realise that you are observed from a number of points and that the sum of them has validity.'[24] It was precisely this perspective that Clark rejected. He claimed sole authority to interpret his life. But the autobiographer's recollection of his life can indeed be shown to be wrong. Because so much of Clark's life was lived on the public record, and because he archived his diaries and correspondence so meticulously, it is possible to test many of the claims that he makes in his autobiographies. In fact, the issue of autobiographical truth is crucial in understanding Clark's role in late twentieth-century Australia. As Salter further reflected when explaining his methods of recollection in his memoir:

> What I have done is to write about people and events that were important to me, and to be truthful though relying, in one place or another, on mere memory. *Your language is your country* Leautaud said, but memory is also, as well as being a measure, in its imprint, of the value of things. I suppose it could be just as convincingly argued that the opposite is true, that what one chooses to forget is equally revealing.[25]

Clark concurred with Salter in so far as he relied on what Virginia Woolf described as 'moments of being' – recollections that were deeply inscribed in his memory precisely because of their self-revelatory nature.[26] He did not want to write an autobiography that resembled his impression of Kaplan's biography of Dickens, 'one of those American academic biographies which tells you what he had for breakfast but not what you want to know'.[27] If memory was to be employed then it was not an instrument of reference so much as an instrument of self-discovery.[28] Yet Clark also conspicuously failed to take account of the possibility that what he had misremembered, invented, exaggerated or repressed was potentially more revealing than all of the words set down in his autobiographies. 'What I was trying to do', Clark explained, 'was to draw a picture of memory … a portrait of the inside of my head.'[29] However, his claim to have relied mostly on memory in writing his autobiography is only partially true. Indeed, the evidence

---

24   James Salter, *Burning the Days* (New York: Vintage, 1997), 4.
25   Ibid., xi.
26   Hermione Woolf, *Moments of Being: Autobiographical Writings*, introduced by Hermione Lee (London: Pimlico, 2002).
27   Clark to McQueen, 30 April 1989, McQueen Papers, NLA, MS 4809, Folder Addition 31.5.1990.
28   On this distinction, see Samuel Beckett, *Proust and Three Dialogues* (London: John Calder, 1999; first published in 1965), 29.
29   Clark interviewed by Peter Craven, *Sunday Herald*, 8 October 1989, 42.

in Clark's papers shows that he wrote his autobiographies in the same way that he wrote his history, as a series of character sketches interspersed with personal recollections, a performer improvising from primary sources and a mystic led through life by a series of epiphanies. Far from relying on memory alone, Clark carried out extensive research, especially for *The Puzzles of Childhood*. He wrote to various churches and historical societies seeking information on his parents' lives. He copied documents relating to his ancestors such as Samuel Marsden. He sourced newspaper articles and local histories to provide historical context. And he made an attempt to read reflections on autobiography by writers such as Michael Holroyd.

Nor was he the only researcher. Dymphna carried out most of his research. The archives are full of copious notes in her handwriting. She corrected grammar and punctuation, she suggested rephrasing and she corrected dates, places and memories. As Clark's editor, some of her marginal comments are telling:

> did you or did you not know where you stood? …

> Was it at Port Jackson (not Botany Bay) that the Aborigines told the British to go away? …

> She needs to be identified – wife or flame? … she has been doing it off and on for 140 pages! …

> Do you think it tactful to talk about [your brother's] generosity to 'those more gifted' [like yourself]? What about 'to those with gifts different from his own'

> Poor you, trapped in this terrible heart-dimming straitening institution, for all these years, pitiful, come on now!

After 50 years of marriage, Dymphna was clearly exasperated by the self-serving nature of Clark's recollections. For her, the lack of truthfulness in Clark's autobiographies undermined their claims to authenticity and their pretensions to literary greatness. For Clark, although he seemed to remain blissfully unaware of his tendency to self-aggrandise, he was nonetheless painfully conscious of his tendency to omit certain details and events in telling the story of his life.[30]

---

30 Dymphna's comments can be found in the Manning Clark Papers, MS 7550, Series 25, Box 173, 'Correspondence and drafts relating to Quest for Grace'. The first folder includes her handwritten editing notes.

As he wrote both volumes of autobiography throughout the late 1980s, Clark frequently exhorted himself to tell the truth about his life. 'How to be truthful without exposing one's own swinishness', he wrote searchingly, and 'how to be honest without offending someone?'[31] Despite his many promises to friends such as Humphrey McQueen that he would not recoil from writing an unvarnished account of his life ('Is the non-truth worth the paper on which it is written? I believe passionately we should all face the truth about ourselves'), the pages of his diary reveal his guilt and self-loathing because of his failure to do so.[32] On 11 March 1988, as he was beginning to write *The Puzzles of Childhood*, he wallowed in self-pity and disillusionment:

> Last night in bed had an attack of angina. I know my travelling and lecturing are killing me, but, maybe, that is what I want, the pain of living is now so intense. My wife is still taking revenge on me for my past iniquities. My closest friend, the one in whom I placed complete trust, has deserted me in my hour of need, the attacks on my work and character continue and will probably go on for a while after I am dead. I have lost faith in the autobiography.[33]

By the time both volumes of autobiography were published in 1990, Clark was firmly convinced that he had failed the task of self-examination that he had set for himself:

> The two volumes of the autobiography suffer from my failure to address myself to three subjects which have caused me much pain and made me the instrument of pain to other people. They are – First – my infidelities to Dymphna, infidelities of the heart more than the body, and my failure to examine when and why they began. I remember in the beginning my fear of whether I could keep her individual love, or whether she ever loved me. Second, my corruption of other people ... my [name deleted] who became a drunk just as I was wiping the filth of the gutter off my body. I made a drunkard seem attractive to him ... Third, those volumes do not confess to another fatal flaw ... inwardly I go to pieces when criticised, can never speak again to the character sketchers or critics who list the errors in my work. I never forget and never forgive. I do not retaliate, I punish them with silence and do not speak to them again ... a curt nod, a blank face, a horrible face ... cutting them, avoiding them. I have not

---

31 Ibid.: Clark's notes to self on first draft of *The Quest for Grace*.
32 Clark to McQueen, 28 July 1988, McQueen Papers, NLA, MS 4809, Folder Addition 31.5.1990.
33 Manning Clark, Diary, 11 March 1988, NLA, MS 7550, Series 2.

really tried to change, but I doubt whether I could change, that rush of blood to the head floods the rational me. I shake inwardly ... there has been no improvement except in surface courtesy.[34]

These reflections scribbled hastily in Clark's diary appear far closer to the truth. They demonstrate a capacity for self-criticism that his autobiographies conspicuously lack. As did one particularly frank note that Clark left for his biographer in his papers. In a folder marked 'Illustrations' for *The Quest for Grace*, there is a handwritten list in ink of the photographs and the order they appeared in the book. They are numbered with the captions from 1 to 10. Then, a line is drawn at the bottom of the list, in what appears to be fresher ink than the list above, almost certainly added at a later time, most probably as Clark pored over his papers in the last months of his life leaving comments for those he knew would come to his papers after his death. Underneath the line drawn earlier he wrote in fresh ink: 'The photographs, like the book, say nothing – the book is a lie, as it says nothing of what I lived through'.[35] Clark sets up a conversation with the biographer whom he knows will come sniffing like a bloodhound to the archive he has constructed. He plays with his own truth, giving prominence to earnest descriptions of his virtues on the one hand, while at the same time suggesting that the whole edifice of his self-invention is nothing but a charade, as if he does not know the truth himself.

Combing through Clark's autobiographies and finding examples of factual errors or misremembered encounters is a pastime one could indulge in for many years. In the pages of *The Puzzles of Childhood* and, *The Quest for Grace* things happen that never took place. People are born before their time. They die six years too early or four years too late. They stand for Labor Party preselection when they never did and they are remembered for doing all manner of things that never occurred. Consistent with Inglis's observation that Clark's recollections of others were often more about 'self than subject', his portrayal of many characters serves merely as a vehicle for dispensing praise to himself. And, of course, Clark's memories of his parents differ from those of his siblings, both of whom stated after the publication of *The Puzzles of Childhood* that they could not recognise their parents' marriage in his agonised portrayal, just as his accounts of events

---

34   Ibid., 13 March 1990.
35   Manning Clark Papers, NLA, MS 7550, Series 25, Box 175, Folder, 'Illustrations for Quest for Grace'.

5. 'A GIGANTIC CONFESSION OF LIFE'

and friendships differ from the memories of others, some of whom wrote forcefully to tell him how disappointed they were in his recollections. These differences of memory and perspectives are not unusual. And catching Clark out is not my purpose. But a handful of Clark's untruths and fabrications go to the heart of his credibility as a historian.

The most notorious example that I discovered of Clark's misremembering – his claim to have been present in Bonn the morning after *Kristallnacht* in November 1938, one repeated frequently in public during the last years of his life – still unsettles me because so much of the circumstantial evidence suggests that he knowingly lied. It was Dymphna who was in Bonn the morning after *Kristallnacht*. She wrote to Clark, who was then in Oxford and would not arrive in Bonn until three weeks later. It was her memories of *Kristallnacht* that Clark largely appropriated in order to claim a greater role for himself in one of European history's darkest moments. Clark had actually omitted the story of his presence that November morning in Bonn from all the drafts of *The Quest for Grace* that Dymphna edited before the book's publication. Not until the final typescript draft, when he finally decided on the title and Dymphna's editing was complete, did he decide to insert the claim that he was present in Bonn and that he had indeed seen the smashed glass from the Jewish shop windows on the streets and watched as the smoke from the burning synagogues filled the sky. It was not until the book was published that Dymphna read Clark's last-minute insertion, although she had certainly heard him make the claim previously on radio and television. It is possible that Clark chose to wait until the final draft to insert the claim of his presence the morning after *Kristallnacht* so as to avoid her marking up his claim as false. As she acknowledged after Clark's death in a private interview, '[Manning] says he arrived the morning after *Kristallnacht*. That's not true'.[36]

Writing about their peers, mentors and influences, let alone their achievements, historians are adept at making the activities of their own kind appear momentous. Nonetheless, Clark's autobiographies do so to a far greater extent than those of most of his peers. He saw himself as the leader of an intellectual vanguard whose self-appointed responsibility was to lead Australia out of its Anglo-centric torpor towards an independent, republican, multicultural and more Indigenous-centred future, a completely new vision of the nation. However, this is not to suggest

---

36   Quoted in McKenna, *An Eye for Eternity*, 638.

that many of his pronouncements were not prescient. In 1981, when he was asked to name Australia's national day, Clark argued that the country had yet to agree on one. He pointed out that Indigenous Australians were absent from the national anthem and invisible in the national flag and constitution. 'Our national day in the future,' he said, 'will be that day in which we made the great step forward on the Aborigines and on the non-British descendants and on [the] question of what sort of society are we going to have in Australia.'[37]

Janet Malcolm has written that '[i]f an autobiography is to be even minimally readable, the autobiographer must step in and subdue what you could call memory's autism, its passion for the tedious. He must not be afraid to invent. Above all he must invent himself'.[38] Manning Clark heeded Malcolm's advice. His autobiographies were an attempt to adapt his life story to the needs of Australia at Empire's end. His recollections are always pointing to the future, his authorial voice always pleading for entrance to Valhalla. Clark's autobiographies provided the great man's origin story and they further invented him as a national prophet, the man who would lead Australia out of the wilderness of what he called 'British philistinism' towards a largely unknown and ill-defined but somehow more enlightened Australian future. Towards the end of his life, he sensed that the way in which he had framed this quest – the old dead tree versus the young tree green – was quickly becoming irrelevant. 'The problems of my generation, or the way I formulated them have passed away – maybe are [already] rotting in history's ample rubbish bin.'[39] Like so many of his intellectual contemporaries, Clark was also alienated from the nation he sought to advance. He told McQueen that he had grown tired of living in 'a country inhabited by a people who display a vast indifference to what matters in life – and an unwillingness to listen to what you have to say'.[40] This seems a strange comment coming from someone who was listened to more than any other intellectual in late twentieth-century Australia. No matter how much of a national figure Clark became, he still craved to be showered in even greater public acclaim. As he wrote to Humphrey McQueen in 1984, 'On Tuesday 22 January at 4pm

---

37   Clark interviewed by Alan Tate, *The Virgin Press*, October–November 1981, 20.
38   Janet Malcolm, 'Thoughts on Autobiography from an Abandoned Autobiography', in her *Forty-one False Starts: Essays on Artists and Writers* (Melbourne: Text Publishing, 2013), 297–8.
39   Clark to McQueen, 24 April 1989, McQueen Papers, NLA, MS 4809, Folder Addition 31.5.1990.
40   Clark to McQueen, 12 March 1990, in ibid.

a BRONZE BUST of me will be unveiled in the Chifley Library. My LITERARY SLANDERERS will not be there. My friends will be. Please come if you can'.[41]

In the last weeks of Clark's life it was rumoured that he was writing a third volume of autobiography. A rough draft clearly existed, as his diaries appear to indicate. Ian Hancock, Clark's former colleague at ANU, recalled that the departmental secretary was 'shocked' as she typed up the first pages of the manuscript. 'She was shaking when she told me about it. It was full of scandalous revelations. But I think Dymphna put her foot down and refused to allow its publication.'[42] Perhaps Clark had finally decided to abide by his many exhortations to bare all. But no such manuscript has survived in his papers.

In early 1990, convinced that his death was now 'only a year or so away', Clark looked again to posterity when he penned the final line of his last letter to Humphrey McQueen before McQueen left Japan for Australia:

> [I] have tried, but alas failed to recreate the experience in [*The Quest for Grace*] of the confessions of a great sinner, & a failed human being … This ends the Clark part of the Clark-McQueen correspondence. I enjoyed it. You have always been very good to me. My love to you, Ever, Manning.[43]

In the months ahead, Clark read the reviews of *Quest* in the literary pages of the broadsheet press, which, as with most of his later work, shifted dramatically from almost foolish adulation to snarling condemnation. Friend and fellow historian Noel McLachlan claimed that Clark had produced 'the first Australian intellectual biography', one 'as revelatory as Rousseau's but better', in which 'astonishingly little seems to be held back', while Andrew Riemer politely referred to Clark's 'parochialism' in which Clark presents 'the world seen from Melbourne', riding forth 'like a latter-day Quixote, tilting at windmills perhaps, but keeping alive the noble flame of his idealism'.[44] Richard White, however, had come closest to revealing Clark's literary conceit: 'Manning Clark's Australia is Manning Clark himself.'[45]

---

41   Clark to McQueen, 19 January 1984, in ibid.
42   Ian Hancock to author, May 2007.
43   Clark to McQueen, 12 March 1990, McQueen Papers, NLA, MS 4809, Folder Addition 31.5.1990.
44   McLachlan's review in *The Australian Magazine*, 20–21 October 1990; Riemer in *Sydney Morning Herald*, 13 October 1990.
45   White, review of *The Quest for Grace*.

Clark's autobiographies – clearly unreliable, undeniably self-indulgent and yet somehow strangely compelling despite their countless literary flaws – stand not only as allegories of national awakening but also as the final expression of Clark's fictive historical style. For Manning Clark, it was not the facts of history that shaped us but the impression – emotional, intellectual and spiritual – that the telling of history and one's life story left behind. As he told *Playboy* magazine in 1989: 'I remember very vividly that one of my boyhood roles at school, both the state school and at Melbourne Grammar, was the telling of stories. I don't mean fibs of course, but I was a storyteller.'[46]

Appendix: Clark's books

There were many reprintings and subsequent editions of Clark's works.

Only the first editions have been itemised.

A History of Australia

Vol. 1. *From the Earliest Times to the Age of Macquarie.* Melbourne: Melbourne University Press, 1962.

Vol. 2. *New South Wales and Van Diemen's Land, 1822–1838.* Melbourne: Melbourne University Press, 1968.

Vol. 3. *The Beginning of an Australian Civilisation, 1824–1851.* Melbourne: Melbourne University Press, 1973.

Vol. 4. *The Earth Abideth for Ever, 1851–1888.* Melbourne: Melbourne University Press, 1978.

Vol. 5. *The People Make Laws, 1980–1915.* Melbourne: Melbourne University Press, 1981.

Vol. 6. *The Old Dead Tree and the Young Tree Green, 1916–1935.* Melbourne: Melbourne University Press, 1987.

---

46 Clark interviewed by *Australian Playboy*, July 1981, 31–4.

Short history

A Short History of Australia. New York: New American Library, 1963.

Other monographs (during his lifetime)

Meeting Soviet Man. Sydney: Angus & Robertson, 1960.

The Discovery of Australia: 1976 Boyer Lectures. Sydney: Australian Broadcasting Commission, 1976.

In Search of Henry Lawson. Melbourne: Macmillan, 1978.

Books of documents

Select Documents in Australian History, 1788–1850. Sydney: Angus & Robertson, 1950.

Select Documents in Australian History, 1851–1900. Sydney: Angus & Robertson, 1955.

Sources of Australian History. London: Oxford University Press, 1957.

Edited volume

Making History, with an 'Introduction' by Stuart Macintyre and other chapters by R.M. Crawford and Geoffrey Blainey. Melbourne/Ringwood: McPhee Gribble/Penguin Books, 1984.

Collection of essays

Occasional Writings and Speeches. Melbourne: Fontana/Collins, 1980.

Scholarly pamphlets

Abel Tasman. Melbourne: Oxford University Press [in the 'Australian Explorers' series], 1959.

The Quest for an Australian Identity. Brisbane: University of Queensland Press, 1980 [James Dulig Memorial Lecture].

Children's history

The Ashton Scholastic History of Australia, by Manning Clark, Meredith Hooper and Susanne Ferrier. Sydney: Ashton Scholastic, 1988.

Autobiographies (during his lifetime)

The Puzzles of Childhood. Ringwood: Viking, 1989.

The Quest for Grace. Ringwood: Viking, 1990.

Short stories

Disquiet and Other Stories. Sydney: Angus & Robertson, 1969.

Manning Clark: Collected Short Stories. Ringwood: Penguin Books, 1986.

Posthumous

A Historian's Apprenticeship. Melbourne: Melbourne University Press, 1992.

Manning Clark's History of Australia, abridged by Michael Cathcart. Melbourne: Melbourne University Press, 1993.

Dear Kathleen, Dear Manning: The Correspondence of Manning Clark and Kathleen Fitzpatrick, 1949–1990. Melbourne: Melbourne University Press, 1996.

Speaking out of Turn: Lectures and Speeches, 1940–1991. Melbourne: Melbourne University Press, 1997.

The Ideal of Alexis de Tocqueville, ed. Dymphna Clark, David Headon and John Williams. Melbourne: Melbourne University Press, 2000.

Manning Clark on Gallipoli. Melbourne: Melbourne University Publishing, 2005.

Ever, Manning: Selected Letters of Manning Clark, 1938–1991, ed. Roslyn Russell. Sydney: Allen & Unwin, 2008.

6
Ceci n'est pas Ramsay Cook: A Biographical Reconnaissance

Donald Wright

I

> ... before they go about collecting evidence, historians must have a reason for looking, a question in mind, and that question will determine what evidence is found, and how it is interpreted.
>
> — Peter Lamont

Wanting to interview someone about the use and abuse of history by governments, the Canadian Broadcasting Corporation turned to Ramsay Cook, professor emeritus at York University.[1] The conversation centred on the problems that arise when a government advances *a version* of the past as *the* past. At one point, Cook cited René Magritte's famous 1929 painting, *The Treachery of Images (Ceci n'est pas une pipe)*, to comment on just what a complicated business writing history is. In the same way that Magritte's painting of a pipe is not a pipe, he said, 'History as it is written is not the past; it is a representation of the past'.[2] Listening to Cook's defence of historical complexity, I realised that his biography would make the perfect third volume to my study of the historical profession in English

---

1 For a brief summary of Cook's career, see Michael Behiels and Marcel Martel, 'Introduction', in Behiels and Martel, eds, *Nation, Ideas, Identities: Essays in Honour of Ramsay Cook* (Toronto: Oxford University Press, 2000).
2 Ramsay Cook, CBC Radio, *The Sunday Edition,* 16 June 2013.

Canada. Genuinely surprised, Cook wondered if I would not be wiser and saner after completing a biography of Donald Creighton – a notoriously difficult man and, curiously enough, his doctoral supervisor – to turn my attention to something more distant and less controversial, 'like early Inuit settlements in Greenland'.[3] Still, he would think about it. Eight days later he agreed, on two conditions. First, I was to treat this project as I would any project, as an independent piece of research and writing. Second, I was to read *The Rise of the Indian Rope Trick: The Biography of a Legend* by Peter Lamont.

Of course, I was pleased, but what did a history of a magic trick have to do with anything? *The Rise of the Indian Rope Trick* is about many things – the rope trick itself, the West's fascination with the 'mysterious' East and, as its subtitle suggests, the problem of biography.[4] Obscured by imperfect memories, competing accounts, contested facts, archival silences, stretches, compressions, elisions and omissions, to say nothing of the biographer's own reasons for undertaking the project in the first place, biography is not the person in the same way that history is not the past. Like Magritte's pipe, it is a representation of the person. Hermione Lee called it 'an artificial construct' while Mark Twain likened the challenge of writing a biography to that of reconstructing a dinosaur from 'nine bones and 600 barrels of plaster'.[5] In telling me to read *The Rise of the Indian Rope Trick*, Cook was sending me a message: Wright, the best you will ever do is a representation of me so read widely, be thorough in your research, ask tough questions, check your own reasons at the door and take nothing for granted. In other words, do your homework. This essay, therefore, constitutes my first real homework assignment: a biographical reconnaissance of Ramsay Cook's childhood, adolescence and early 20s.

A reconnaissance, according to the *Oxford English Dictionary*, is 'a survey, inspection, etc., carried out in order to gain information of some kind'.[6] To this end, I intend to map the main features, key influences and recurring themes in Cook's life as a child and adolescent growing up in Canada's prairie west and later as a graduate student at Queen's. If I am

---

3 Ramsay Cook, email to author, 19 June 2013.
4 Peter Lamont, *The Rise of the Indian Rope Trick: The Biography of a Legend* (London: Little, Brown, 2004).
5 Hermione Lee, *Biography: A Very Short Introduction* (Oxford: Oxford University Press, 2009), 122, doi.org/10.1093/actrade/9780199533541.001.0001; Mark Twain, 'Is Shakespeare Dead?' in Charles Neider, ed., *The Complete Essays of Mark Twain* (New York: Doubleday, 1963), 422.
6 'reconnaissance, *n.*', *The Oxford English Dictionary* (Oxford: Oxford University Press, 1989).

right, the key to understanding the most important historian and public intellectual of his generation, a man who consistently articulated an open, decent and tolerant Canada, is to be found there.[7] But my use of the word reconnaissance is also historiographical. According to Ian McKay, a strategy of reconnaissance obviates the need for synthesis and comprehensiveness at the same time as it accepts 'the contingency, difficulty, and political riskiness of any and all attempts to generalize beyond the particular – and the inescapable necessity of doing so'. Explicitly political, McKay's strategy of reconnaissance is also linked to what he calls 'a multi-generational and protracted struggle for equality and justice'.[8] By locating paths both taken and not taken in the past, and by identifying men and women who reasoned and lived otherwise, who found ways to oppose prevailing capitalist certainties and bourgeois orthodoxies, or liberal rule, McKay aims to contribute to the historical struggle to imagine and achieve a more equitable and democratic present. McKay's own reconnaissance has focused on those rebels, reds and radicals who challenged Canada as a project of liberal rule. My reconnaissance has a different focus because Cook was neither a rebel nor a radical. He was a liberal who did not have much to say about property and its unequal distribution.

But he had a lot to say about minority rights and equality. And as Elsbeth Heaman reminds us, the struggle for minority rights and equality is historical and ongoing, not over and done with.[9] A biographical reconnaissance of Ramsay Cook, therefore, is the necessary first step in understanding where his ethical voice came from. It was that voice that enabled him as a historian to put social, ethnic and linguistic complexity at the heart of his interpretive understanding of Canada's past and present. Cook's intellectual journey, like that of every historian, began early in life.

---

7   What do I mean by public intellectual? As Doug Munro writes, 'the term evades ready definition because the range of individuals to whom it is applied is so amorphous, the issues they confront so varied, the methods they employ so contrasting, and the circumstances and contexts within which they function can be so different'. Ramsay Cook was not a 'cultural critic' and he did not occupy the 'corridors of power', except briefly in 1968. But from a place of 'civic obligation' and 'moral imperative', he engaged, in print and in person, with what the Royal Commission on Bilingualism and Biculturalism called the 'greatest crisis' in Canadian history – the threat of Quebec independence. Doug Munro, *J.C. Beaglehole: Public Intellectual, Critical Conscience* (Wellington: Steele Roberts, 2012), 64.
8   Ian McKay, *Reasoning Otherwise: Leftists and the People's Enlightenment in Canada, 1890–1920* (Toronto: Between the Lines, 2008), 3, 2.
9   See E.A. Heaman, 'Rights Talk and the Liberal Order Framework', in Jean-François Constant and Michel Ducharme, eds, *Liberalism and Hegemony: Debating the Canadian Liberal Revolution* (Toronto: University of Toronto Press, 2009).

II

> This is the story of a boy and the wind.
> — W.O. Mitchell

'Canadians born on the prairies are especially fortunate in at least one respect', Ramsay Cook once said, because 'their childhood has been immortalized' in *Who Has Seen the Wind,* a novel about one boy's coming of age in a small prairie town in the 1930s.[10] The town itself has a couple of churches, a school and a newspaper; the main street features shops and businesses with names like Nelson's Bakery, Harris's Hardware and Blaine's Store; there is a hotel, a pool hall and a small restaurant, the Bluebird Café, owned by a man from China named Wong. Laying 'wide around the town' is the Saskatchewan prairie, 'the least common denominator of nature', and it, more than anything else, gives the novel its evocative power.[11] Cook's fondness for W.O. Mitchell – he even named his sailboat *The W.O. Mitchell* – comes from his memories of growing up in small towns in Saskatchewan and Manitoba. But it is more than simple nostalgia, because the wind in *Who Has Seen The Wind* is God and God – or at least organised religion – played a central role in Cook's childhood and adolescence: his father, George Russell Cook, was a United Church minister and his mother, Lillie Ellen Cook, was a United Church minister's wife.

When Russell Cook was 14 years old his father died, leaving him with no inheritance and a difficult decision: he could work on the fishing docks of Grimsby – a busy port city on the east coast of England where the Humber estuary meets the North Sea – or he could emigrate. Having already spent a year or two collecting and selling cod livers, he chose to emigrate. To countless late Victorian and Edwardian British boys, the 'very word "Canada" seemed to epitomize adventure'. In those days, Canada meant the North West, 'an ill-defined and variously defined' place of cowboys, Indians, horse thieves and whisky traders, of forts, outposts and shacks belonging to old trappers, of prairies, rivers, coulees (ravines) and footpaths walked by both 'the war-whooping scalp hunter' and the noble

---

10   Ramsay Cook, 'William Kurelek: A Prairie Boy's Visions', in Cook, *Canada, Quebec, and the Uses of Nationalism* (Toronto: McClelland and Stewart, 1986), 147.
11   W.O. Mitchell, *Who Has Seen the Wind* (Toronto: Macmillan, 1947), 3. On using literature to write history see Ramsay Cook, 'The Uses of Literature in Cultural History', *The English Quarterly* 4:3 (Fall 1971), 25–30.

red child of the great plains.[12] Seeking adventure and perhaps hoping to escape 'the rigidities of the English class structure', Cook boarded the *Lake Manitoba* in Liverpool in April 1913 with $25 in his pocket. He was one of about 150,000 Britons emigrating to Canada that year 'in search of a better standard of living'.[13]

Too young to homestead, Cook worked as a farm labourer in Saskatchewan, not far from Carlyle, a town settled primarily by British settlers and named after Thomas Carlyle, the great nineteenth-century historian. When the war broke out a year later, he did not enlist. He would have been just 16 years old. But as the war dragged on, the pressure to enlist increased. The local newspaper even suggested that candidates in the 1917 general election who opposed conscription 'should be put in the front line trenches without a gun'.[14] Still, Cook continued to work as a labourer until he was conscripted under the terms of the Military Service Act and taken on strength by the 1st Depot Battalion, Saskatchewan Regiment, on 28 May 1918. He never made it overseas: only 24,000 men of the nearly 400,000 men who registered for conscription ever reached the front. Although his service record provides few clues, he may have been exempted under the rules of what the Act called 'Domestic Position': if a family member had enlisted, and 'especially' if that family member had been 'wounded or killed', one could apply for an exemption.[15] Cook's brother had enlisted as a private in the British Expeditionary Force, in the 10th Service Battalion Lincolnshire Regiment, or the Grimsby Chums, and been killed at Vimy Ridge on 11 April 1917. His silver cigarette case had stopped the first bullet, but not the second.

After being struck off strength on 13 January 1919, Cook returned to Carlyle and to the woman he had married just six months earlier, Lillian Ellen Young, the daughter of a local farming family. With help from his mother in England, Russell and Lillie Cook purchased three quarters, or 480 acres, near Alameda, a town just south of Carlyle that had been settled in the 1880s by a handful of families from England and Scotland and by German Americans from Michigan. They also started a family: a son, Vincent; a daughter, Luella; and, in 1931, another son, George Ramsay. Born in the farm house of a local midwife – and, according to family

---

12   R.G. Moyles and Doug Owram, *Imperial Dreams and Colonial Realities: British Views of Canada, 1880–1914* (Toronto: University of Toronto Press, 1988), 40, 49.
13   Robert Craig Brown and Ramsay Cook, *Canada, 1896–1921: A Nation Transformed* (Toronto: McClelland and Stewart, 1974), 57.
14   'Additional Locals', *Alameda Dispatch,* 7 December 1917.
15   Parliament of Canada, *Military Service Act 1917*, Section 11.

history, during an early winter blizzard – he was named George after his father and both of his grandfathers.[16] At least initially, Russell Cook made a go of it as a mixed farmer – principally grain and Holstein cattle – but as the Great Depression entered its second year, as prices dropped and markets disappeared, he fell further and further behind. Although only a child at the time, Ramsay Cook can still picture the family farm 'more or less blowing away' in 1936.[17] Twenty-three years earlier, Russell Cook had faced a similar fork in the road when his father died: he could stick it out on a recalcitrant farm or he could take a chance.

Entering St Andrew's College, the theological college of the United Church of Canada on the campus of the University of Saskatchewan, he took a chance. He was 39 years old, hardly the typical 18- or 19-year-old first-year theology student, but a few years earlier he had become a lay supply minister in the United Church, conducting services in churches that were either too small or too poor to have a regular minister. He liked the work, and when a United Church minister and administrator told him that he would make a good minister, he thought, well, why not? Studying theology was not easy, but St Andrew's was a lot of fun: he curled on a college rink, served as vice-president of the St Andrew's Undergraduate Association, and on at least one occasion found himself decorating the dining hall in purple and gold, the college colours.[18]

In addition to his studies, Cook had a mission field in Raymore and Punnichy, which required him to lead two services every Sunday in addition to fulfilling his pastoral care duties, visiting shut-ins, holding the hands of the dying and comforting the bereaved. Ramsay Cook remembers his father returning from Saskatoon on Friday night or sometimes Saturday morning and leaving again on Monday morning, sometimes as early as four o'clock, to catch the train back to Saskatoon. It was exhausting, especially in the winter months when he had to walk from Raymore to Punnichy if the roads were not ploughed.[19]

---

16 Ramsay Cook's birth announcement states that he was born in the 'Nursing Home of Mrs R.W. Wood on Saturday, 28 November 1931'. Nursing homes were not licensed and midwives did not have formal training. Still, they got the job done. See 'Births', *Alameda Dispatch*, 11 December 1931.
17 Author's interview with Ramsay Cook, 14 July 2014.
18 'Theologs Hold Banquet', *The Sheaf*, 21 February 1939, University of Saskatchewan Archives (USA).
19 Author's interview with Ramsay Cook, 14 July 2014.

Initially, the Raymore congregation complained about having to pay 'a married student preacher' because it meant more mouths to feed. But Cook quickly earned their trust and admiration for his efforts to turn Raymore United into a vital social institution by improving the Sunday school, keeping the church clean, ensuring that the bells were rung according to a schedule, and assisting in a vegetable drive for the 'dried-out areas of the province'.[20]

A 'deeply religious' woman with a 'caring, gentle soul', Lillie Cook also won over the congregation, readily assuming her responsibilities as a minister's wife.[21] Her experience was not the experience of the minister's wife on the Depression-era prairies depicted by Sinclair Ross in his novel *As for Me and my House*. Mrs Bentley is unhappy, unfulfilled and, above all else, tired – tired of being 'close to the financial breaking point', tired of being 'frumpy' because she cannot afford a new dress, and tired of being the object of the congregation's gaze, especially the gaze of the Ladies' Aid in the form of its president and 'first lady of the congregation'.[22] For her part, Lillie served as secretary of the Ladies' Aid and treasurer of the Women's Missionary Society. It was the women who kept these small churches going, organising church suppers, raising money for repairs to the manse, teaching Sunday school, and hosting endless teas.[23] In 1937, the church leadership thanked the Ladies' Aid 'for their exceptionally good showing in raising over $400 for church purposes in a hard year'; a few years later, it acknowledged that were it not for the Ladies' Aid 'it would be very difficult for us to carry on'.[24]

In 1940, Russell Cook graduated from St Andrew's and, a few months later, announced his intention to seek a new pastorate. Having come to appreciate what it called his 'conscientious and uncomplaining service', the church leadership urged him to stay and was even prepared to 'guarantee' a salary of $1,200, although it is unlikely that it could have.[25] After all, it had paid him occasionally in farm products – including bunches of

---

20 Minutes of the Raymore Union Congregation, 16 May 1936 and 8 September 1936, Saskatchewan Archives Board (SAB), Minutes of the Raymore Union Congregation, A381.XV.A.5777.
21 Author's interview with Ramsay Cook, 14 July 2014.
22 Sinclair Ross, *As for Me and my House* (Toronto: McClelland and Stewart, 1957; first published in 1941), 9, 10, 6. Readers never learn Mrs Bentley's first name.
23 See Marilyn Färdig Whitely, '"Doing all the Rest": Church Women of the Ladies' Aid Society', in Sharon Anne Cook, Lorna McLean and Kathryn O'Rourque, eds, *Framing Our Past: Constructing Canadian Women's History in the Twentieth Century* (Montreal and Kingston: McGill-Queen's University Press, 2006).
24 Minutes of the Raymore Union Congregation, 24 January 1937 and 25 February 1940, SAB, Minutes of the Raymore Union Congregation, A381.XV.A.5777.
25 Ibid., 24 January 1938.

rhubarb that he called Saskatchewan strawberries – and, as a result, he had accumulated too many debts to too many local merchants. 'We were very poor', Ramsay Cook now says. 'But I didn't know we were poor. The whole town was poor.'[26] Not far from Raymore was Wynyard, a larger centre with a larger congregation. Located south of an enormous drainage basin – named the Quill Lakes because of their location on the migratory routes of waterfowl and shorebirds – and first settled by Icelanders in 1904, Wynyard had grown quickly, attracting immigrants from Norway, Sweden, Great Britain, Poland, Germany and Ukraine. In 1941, it had a population of 1,080, making it the largest town in the district. But it too had trouble paying its minister, and Cook's debts kept growing. It was time to make another change.

Canada and Great Britain – his two great loves – were at war with Germany, and this time Cook was determined to serve. Canada was a British country and he was a British subject, making his loyalties complementary, not contradictory. When the 1939 Royal Tour of King George VI and Queen Elizabeth made its way through Saskatchewan, he took his family to catch a glimpse of the first reigning monarch to visit North America. Ramsay Cook recalls being shuttled to five or six different whistle-stops and walkabouts on the royal route, including Melville, a small town northeast of Saskatoon, its grain elevator proudly decorated to form, according to the *Regina Leader-Post,* a 'mighty welcome'.[27] Somewhere in the crowd of 60,000 people was a little boy on his dad's shoulders. George VI was not only the King of Great Britain, he was the King of Canada,[28] and each Christmas Russell and Lillie Cook gathered Vincent, Luella and Ramsay around the radio to listen to *their* king's annual broadcast.

To serve his two countries, Cook tried to join the air force but was told that he was too old. He said that he could train young pilots on the Link Trainer, even though he had never used a Link Trainer, much less flown a plane. The air force wisely declined his kind offer. He then tried to join the army as a chaplain, although it involved negotiating with a reluctant United Church and the threat that if he was not permitted to join the Canadian army then he would move to the United States and join the American army. In the

---

26 Author's interview with Ramsay Cook, 14 July 2014.
27 'Bold Welcome to King and Queen at Melville', *Regina Leader-Post,* 5 June 1939. See also Mary Vipond, 'The Royal Tour of 1939 as a Media Event', *Canadian Journal of Communication,* 35:1 (2010), 149–72.
28 Although sometimes called the King of Canada, George VI was not technically the King of Canada. Elizabeth II became the first monarch to be proclaimed Queen of Canada pursuant the *Royal Style and Titles Act* 1953.

end, the United Church relented. Stationed at Camp Shilo in Manitoba, Cook moved his family to Brandon. Now that he was earning a modest but reliable salary, he paid his debts and bought a small house.

Brandon was not Alameda, Raymore or Wynyard; it was a city and, for the first time in his life, Ramsay Cook did not have to cut across the yard to an outhouse. He remembers listening to the speeches of Winston Churchill, singing patriotic songs at school and watching *Canada Carries On*, a series of short propaganda films on the war effort.[29] More importantly, he understood that 'there was a larger world outside and that something quite terrible was taking place'.[30] Because both his father and his brother – who had left college to join the Royal Canadian Army Service Corps in 1940 – were doing their bit, Ramsay would do his. In Wynyard, he had collected old bones from the surrounding fields to be used in the production of industrial glues.[31] Now he followed the news coming out of Ottawa and London on a couple of old maps and an atlas; he cheered the exploits of Buzz Beurling, the 'Falcon of Malta', Canada's most successful fighter pilot; he wore a sweatshirt bearing the Union Jack and the title of Vera Lynn's popular song, 'There'll Always Be An England', and once punched a kid who begged to differ; he knitted woollen squares that were sewn together to make blankets for the Red Cross; he counted his nickels and dimes to buy War Savings Certificates; and he collected scrap metal, tin cans and glass bottles.

But Cook also experienced that moment in every child's life when he learned that the 'larger world outside' was not what it said it was. Reading anti-Japanese propaganda in the form of comic books took him back to the summer of 1940 when he and his parents visited his brother, then stationed in Victoria, British Columbia, and spent a month in a rented cottage.[32] One day a boy about Ramsay's age showed up and, although he was Japanese Canadian, Russell and Lillie Cook were delighted that their son had a summer playmate. For the next couple of weeks, the boys were inseparable, for the most part spending their days fishing off a small dock.

---

29 On the National Film Board and *Canada Carries On*, see Pierre Véronneau, 'La Propagande du Geurre de l'État Canadien: Le Cas de l'Office National du Film de 1940 à 1945', *Bulletin d'Histoire Politique*, 16:2 (2008), 151–62.
30 'American Society During World War II: An Interview with Prof. George Ramsay Cook', Center for American Studies, University of Tokyo, *Oral History Series*, 7 (1982), 1.
31 On the collection of bones and fat for military uses, see Ian Mosby, *Food Will Win the War: The Politics, Culture, and Science of Food on Canada's Home Front* (Vancouver: UBC Press, 2014).
32 On anti-Japanese propaganda in American comic books see Paul Hirsch, 'This Is Our Enemy: The Writer's War Board and Representations of Race in Comic Books, 1942–1945', *Pacific Historical Review*, 83:3 (2014), 448–86, doi.org/10.1525/phr.2014.83.3.448.

A young Ramsay Cook, left, fishing with his Japanese Canadian friend near Victoria, British Columbia, 1940

Source: York University Libraries, Clara Thomas Archives & Special Collections, Ramsay Cook fonds, ASC25757. With permission of Eleanor Cook.

The comic books depicting Emperor Hirohito as 'a fire breathing dragon' and Japanese soldiers as subhuman and 'essentially more cruel' than German soldiers did not make any sense. His friend, who had taught him how to bait a hook, cast a line and wait for the tug, was not cruel and he certainly did not breathe fire. He was 'human', Cook said, and he 'made me think differently'. Although 'I still probably thought that Emperor Hirohito breathed fire, I knew that there was at least one Japanese who didn't'.[33]

III

> Because that settlement and that land were my first and for many years my only real knowledge of the planet, in some profound way they remain my world, my way of viewing. My eyes were formed there.
>
> — Margaret Laurence

Demobilised in 1946, Russell Cook received a pastorate in Morden, about 200 kilometres south-east of Brandon in the Pembina Valley. Like Raymore and Wynyard, Morden was a small town servicing a large farming district, principally wheat but also corn and apples. A run of stores and businesses with names like Turner's Bakery, Dack's Pharmacy, Goode's Confectionary and Atkins' Hardware lined Stephen Street. There was a restaurant or two, a hotel, a bowling alley, a pool hall and a grocery store run by a man named Mark Ki who had emigrated from China in 1902. There were several churches, at least 12 according to one count, each denomination having enough adherents in what was an ethnically, linguistically and religiously diverse region, a microcosm really of the prairies that emerged at the turn of the century when Clifford Sifton, as Canada's minister of the interior, opened the west to immigrants from Scandinavia and eastern and central Europe. The large Mennonite farming population alone supported three separate churches. Meanwhile, the *Morden Times* covered Morden as well as Winkler, Darlingford, Rosebank and Plum Coulee.

---

33 'American Society During World War II: An Interview with Prof. George Ramsay Cook', 6. See also Ramsay Cook, 'JACS and my Discovery of Japan', *Japanese Association of Canadian Studies Newsletter*, 100:4 (2015), 3–4.

Because Cook understood that for any church to achieve what a St Andrew's classmate had called 'vitality',[34] he turned St Paul's United Church into a centre for both worship and fellowship by making its presence felt every day of the week, not just one day. In its 1940 Statement of Faith, the United Church of Canada had declared that 'God has appointed a Ministry in His Church for the preaching of the Word, the administration of the Sacraments, and the pastoral care of the people'.[35] As a minister, Cook preached God's word and administered His two sacraments, but 'he most enjoyed spending time with everyday people in common places like the coffee shop, the curling rink, [and] kids' hockey games'.[36] Within days of arriving in Morden in December 1946, he organised a special children's service and a Christmas cantata; in January, he planned a service to celebrate Canada's new Citizenship Act; and in February, March and April, he held events and led services to mark Valentine's Day, Shrove Tuesday, St Patrick's Day, Easter and the Battle of Vimy Ridge. On any given Sunday, he could lead services at three and sometimes four different churches that did not have their own ministers. He was also the chaplain to the Morden Branch of the Canadian Legion, eventually serving as its president. 'They are my boys,' he always said.[37]

Meanwhile, Lillie Cook threw herself into her obligations as a minister's wife, joining the Women's Association and the Women's Missionary Society, opening the manse to the congregation and the community, assisting in the Food for Britain drive, and helping with the Valentine's Tea, the St Patrick's Day dinner and the annual Lilac Tea held each June. The Women's Association did not get much rest because the church hall had to be either 'gaily decorated' with red hearts, 'handsomely decorated' with green shamrocks or filled with bouquets of violet lilacs.[38] Within seven months of their arrival, Russell and Lillie had increased the membership of the congregation by welcoming the old, the young and the in-between. To keep teenagers interested in the life of the church – a problem now four decades old in Protestant churches across the country – they created youth groups, although that initiative did not take root, especially among

---

34 'Theologs Hold Banquet', *The Sheaf*, 21 February 1939, USA.
35 United Church of Canada, 'Statement of Faith', (1940), www.united-church.ca/beliefs/statements/1940 (accessed 25 May 2015).
36 'Spiritual Leadership: Rev. George Cook', mordenmb.com/wp-content/uploads/2012/08/11-Spiritual-WebLg.pdf (accessed 25 May 2015).
37 Author's interview with Ramsay Cook, 14 July 2014.
38 'Around the Town', *Morden Times*, 19 February 1947; 'Around the Town', *Morden Times*, 19 March 1947.

teenage boys. However, Lillie Cook revitalised the Canadian Girls in Training, even leading the senior group.[39] In fact, she included the girls – dressed in what W.O. Mitchell described as their smart uniforms of 'white middies, blue skirts, and blue ties' – in meetings of the Women's Missionary Society.[40]

Religiously driven and civic-minded, Russell and Lillie Cook lived their values on a daily basis, emanating hard work, delayed gratification, service to others and education, an example not lost on their children. Vincent had gone to St Andrew's College, but joined the army and, after the war, made it his career. After high school, Luella studied nursing in Brandon, winning the Bronze Medal and the General Proficiency Prize in 1947. Two years later, she received a scholarship to do postgraduate work in nursing at the University of Western Ontario.[41] Ramsay was still in high school, of course, but it was expected that he would go to university. Reflecting on his childhood and adolescence, Cook remembers something else about his parents: their tolerance and their commitment to equality. His mother's family was a bit Orange – his grandmother once refused to take a particular medicine because it had alcohol in it, making it, she said, 'Catholic' – but his mother was not, not in the slightest. His father, meanwhile, was 'a man with no prejudices': yes, he sometimes grumbled about Germans during the war, and he was not pleased when the barber in Raymore, a German man named Mr Schindelka, cut Ramsay's hair 'the way Hitler wore his hair', but on balance he lived his faith, believing that everyone was equal in the eyes of God. One of the few times Ramsay Cook ever saw his father angry was also in Raymore when the Native people would haul wood into town. Their price was already low, they were asking 'almost nothing', but still people 'pushed the price down', and 'I remember how *angry* he was that people would cheat the Indians, as we called them in those days'. 'I admired my father greatly'; 'he was a wonderful man.'[42]

---

39 On the CGIT, see Margaret Prang, '"The Girl God Would Have Me Be": The Canadian Girls in Training', *Canadian Historical Review,* 66:2 (1985), 154–84, doi.org/10.3138/CHR-066-02-02; and Patricia Dirks, 'Shaping Canada's Women: Canadian Girls in Training versus Girl Guides', in Cook, McLean and O'Rourque, *Framing Our Past.*
40 'Around the Town', *Morden Times,* 30 March 1949; Mitchell, *Who,* 47.
41 'Around the Town', *Morden Times,* 28 May 1947; 'Around the Town', *Morden Times,* 31 August 1949.
42 Author's interview with Ramsay Cook, 14 July 2014.

Russell and Lillie Cook's tolerance and commitment to equality came naturally to them – it was who they were – and it came from the second great commandment – 'Thou shalt love thy neighbour as thy self' (Matthew 22:39). But it was also born on the prairies: 'if there is a word' that captures prairie political culture 'it is equality'.[43] Of course, racism, nativism and anti-immigrant sentiment found plenty of expression on the prairies in the first decades of the twentieth century. In his 1909 book, *Strangers Within Our Gates*, J.S. Woodsworth worried about the 'mixed multitude' of people from eastern and central Europe 'being dumped into Canada by a kind of endless chain': 'how shall we weld this heterogeneous mass into one people?'[44] The Protestant Church was one answer. A public school system was another. And attracting as many as 20,000 members worried about strangers, foreigners and Catholics, the Ku Klux Klan was yet another in 1920s Saskatchewan.[45] But, in the main, political, religious and civic leaders looked to the churches, the schools and, after the Second World War, the Canadian Citizenship Act.

'For years,' the *Morden Times* observed, 'Canadian-born citizens have suffered the humiliation of being classified according to their hereditary nationality', as Ukrainian Canadian, German Canadian and Chinese Canadian. But soon 'Canadian citizens will be able to travel the world and say with pride, "I am a Canadian."'[46] In subsequent editorials, Ray Evans – the *Times*'s editor whom Cook remembers as a 'tolerant' newspaperman but 'shaky' businessman – lamented Canada's residual 'Anglo-Saxon superiority complex', adding that the best answer to persistent prejudice was to banish the hyphen altogether: no longer should we 'tag ourselves as French-Canadians, Scotch-Canadians, Polish-Canadians, or other hyphenated Canadians'.[47] John Diefenbaker – then the member of parliament for Lake Centre, Saskatchewan, later the prime minister of Canada – agreed when, speaking in favour of the Act, he imagined an 'unhyphenated nation' premised on 'unity out of diversity'.[48]

---

43   Roger Gibbins and Sonia Arrison, *Western Visions: Perspectives on the West in Canada* (Peterborough: Broadview, 1995), 46.
44   J.S. Woodsworth, *Strangers Within Our Gates* (Toronto: F.C. Stephenson, 1909), 203.
45   See James Pitsula, *Keeping Canada British: The Ku Klux Klan in 1920s Saskatchewan* (Vancouver: UBC Press, 2014). See also Jonathan Fine, 'Anti-Semitism in Manitoba and the 1930s and 40s', *Manitoba History,* 32 (1996), 26–33.
46   'Editorial', *Morden Times,* 11 December 1946; 'I Am a Canadian', *Morden Times,* 15 January 1947.
47   Ramsay Cook, email to author, 11 May 2015; 'Pride and Prejudice', *Morden Times,* 30 April 1947.
48   Quotation in Richard Sigurdson, 'John Diefenbaker's One Canada and the Legacy of Unhyphenated Canadianism', in D.C. Story and R. Bruce Shepard, eds, *The Diefenbaker Legacy* (Regina: Canadian Plains Research Centre, 1998), 75.

Russell Cook agreed as well, holding a special service at his church to mark the Act's coming into effect and, a few weeks later, becoming a Canadian citizen. He still subscribed to the *Methodist Recorder*, a British weekly; he listened to Churchill's speeches on the radio; and J.R. Green's *Short History of the English People* – a history not of Carlyle's great men but of the English people, of men like himself, 'figures little heeded' in conventional 'drum and trumpet history' – had a permanent place on the family bookshelf.[49] But after 34 years on the prairies, he had exchanged his broad accent for a flat accent and become a Canadian, adding that 'more should be made of the citizenship ceremony by the public'.[50] And because he saw himself as one more immigrant in a country full of immigrants, he never brandished his English birth, appeals to race being a political dead end.

In Raymore and Wynyard, Rev. Cook had opened his churches to any and all, from the Scottish farmer to the Chinese merchant.[51] Where the Anglican Church – until 1955 the Church of England in Canada – tended to be ethnically English, the United Church was not, making it 'as Canadian as the maple leaf and the beaver'.[52] And because welcoming 'newcomers to Canada' mattered to him, he would do the same thing in Morden, a town with many first-generation Canadians, or 'not-yet Canadians', to borrow W.O. Mitchell's phrase.[53] In 1948, Morden United hosted a special Kinsmen banquet honouring that year's recipient of its award for 'meritorious community service'. Mark Ki had come to Canada 46 years earlier, working first in British Columbia, at one point as a cook at the Sullivan Mine in Kimberley, before opening a small business in Morden in 1919, a common enough economic strategy for Chinese men on the prairies. He quickly integrated, joining the Morden Gun Club, taking up curling, giving his time and money to the Freemason's Hospital and in 1939 winning a contest for the best-decorated store window to celebrate the Royal Tour. When he received his citizenship award, the

---

49 J.R. Green, *A Short History of the English People* (London: Macmillan, 1888), xvii–xviii.
50 'Citizenship Court', *Morden Times*, 15 October 1947.
51 Ramsay Cook recalls that the Chinese restaurant owner in Wynyard joined his father's church. Ramsay Cook, email to author, 20 May 2015.
52 John Porter, *The Vertical Mosaic: An Analysis of Social Class and Power in Canada* (Toronto: University of Toronto Press, 1965), 519, doi.org/10.3138/9781442683044.
53 'About the Town', *Morden Times*, 1 June 1949; Mitchell, *Who*, 131.

Times praised his 'quiet, unostentatious doing of good deeds' and when, a few months later, he received his actual citizenship, it described the event as 'historic'.[54]

Morden was not perfect. The 1947 ice carnival included 'squaws', 'braves', a 'chief', and a beautiful 'Indian maiden'; two years later, the carnival included a couple of boys in blackface on skates providing yet 'more laughs' to the 1,200 spectators; and the *Times* referred to the Japanese as Japs.[55] But Canada was not perfect either. The imagined Indian as a romantic figure doomed to disappear was everywhere; 'elements of blackface continued to appear until the early 1950s' in Canadian amateur music and theatre; and the *Globe and Mail* also referred to the Japanese as Japs.[56] Moreover, and to its credit, the *Times* described Canada's two languages as 'enriching', adding that the problem is not the French language, it is the 'holier-than-thou attitude adopted by many otherwise intelligent Canadians'.[57] A couple of years later, it ran a guest editorial marking the anniversary of Booker T. Washington's death that called Jim Crow a contradiction and an embarrassment to American leadership in the Cold War.[58] On balance, Morden was a decent town and as good a place as any to attend high school.

Ramsay Cook was now 15 years old, almost 16, and coming into his own physically, flexing his muscles, and discovering a passion for competition and testing himself through sports. School was easy. But sports demanded more from him. In Brandon he had joined the YMCA, learned to dive, and in 1946 won the provincial diving championship and the western Manitoba swimming championship. In Morden, he played hockey in the winter and baseball in the summer. But he also curled, ran the 100-yard dash and, when he was older, hung out at the local pool hall playing snooker and smoking what he and his friends called two-centers, a single cigarette sold for two cents by a Chinese shopkeeper.

---

54   'Mark Ki Receives Citizenship Award', *Morden Times*, 12 May 1948; 'Mark Ki Becomes Canadian Citizen at Local Court Sitting', *Morden Times*, 15 September 1948. See also Allison Marshall, *Cultivating Connections: The Making of Chinese Prairie Canada* (Vancouver: UBC Press, 2014), 81–93. Mark Ki sold his business in 1948 and moved to Winnipeg, where he died in 1957. He lived a happier life than the Chinese restaurant owner in *Who Has Seen the Wind*, who commits suicide.

55   'Local Skaters', *Morden Times*, 12 March 1947; 'Ice Show of '49', *Morden Times*, 16 March 1949. Ramsay Cook participated in the 1949 ice carnival as one of the male skaters, but not in blackface.

56   Elaine Keillor, *Music in Canada: Capturing Landscape and Diversity* (Montreal and Kingston: McGill-Queen's University Press, 2008), 163.

57   'Canadian Unity', *Morden Times*, 12 November 1947.

58   'Booker T. Washington', *Morden Times*, 30 November 1949.

Because the *Times* covered local sports almost religiously – a strike was not thrown and a goal was not scored without the *Times* reporting it – Cook became something of a local celebrity. After one baseball game, the *Times* described how 'Speedy Ramsay' had crossed the plate; after a hockey game, it reported that he had picked up an assist when 'he carried the puck to the blue line' and 'dropped a pass' to neatly set up an insurance goal; after another hockey game, it singled out his hat-trick in a 'shellacking' of Winkler, Morden's great rival; and after a 16-rink high school bonspiel in Carman, readers learned that he and his teammates had brought home the 'curling laurels'.[59] It is not clear when, because the articles were not signed, but Cook started working at the *Times* as a cub reporter on the sports beat as early as December 1948. Actually, one story was signed 'GRC', or George Ramsay Cook, almost certainly making it his first publication: do not worry, he told his readers, 'the boys will be curling their best to keep the Sifton Trophy in Morden'.[60] For the next couple of years, the sports page was sprinkled with words like 'razzle dazzle', 'thrills and spills', 'pucksters', and 'batsters'.

The *Times*'s coverage missed one element, though: intensely competitive, Cook often got into fights, a fact that did not go into his reporting. As one of the smallest boys, he used his size and speed to his advantage. If that did not work, he would drop the gloves, letting everyone know that he could not be pushed around. Of course, his parents were not amused, objecting 'strenuously'.[61] It was the same in baseball, although his best friend, Paul Sigurdson, managed to restrain him. Cook's hero was Ted Williams, a player known for his bat *and* his temper. But he most resembled his other Boston hero, Dom DiMaggio, aka 'The Little Professor', because, like Cook, he was short and wore glasses.

By his own admission, Cook was a 'desultory' student.[62] Because the curriculum was easy and grades came effortlessly, he 'never worked' because he did not have to.[63] Still, he won awards and prizes, receiving two Kinsmen scholarships in grade 10, one for the highest overall average

---

59 'Junior Ball Clubs Split Games on Labour Day', *Morden Times*, 8 September 1948; 'Morden Scholars Capture High School League Title', *Morden Times*, 30 March 1949; 'Hockey', *Morden Times*, 12 January 1949; 'Local High School Curlers Add More Conquests', *Morden Times*, 25 February 1948.
60 GRC, 'School Rinks Will Defend Sifton Cup', *Morden Times*, 22 December 1948.
61 Ramsay Cook, email to author, 11 May 2015.
62 Ramsay Cook, 'Who Broadened Canadian History?' H. Sanford Riley Lecture, University of Winnipeg, 19 October 2009. Copy in possession of author.
63 Author's interview with Ramsay Cook, 14 July 2014.

and the other for English and history.[64] Grades 11 and 12 were more of the same. He did little to no work, got good grades, but had no idea what he wanted to do, except maybe to work in Winnipeg at Baldy Northcott Sporting Goods. The ministry was never on the table and his parents never expected that of him. His brother, yes – in fact, the Raymore congregation had recommended him for the ministry. But with graduation approaching in the spring of 1950, and with his father pushing him to make a plan, Cook agreed to meet one of the lawyers in town, a friend of his father's, thinking maybe that would not be such a bad thing to be.

History did not interest him, especially after he had been condemned to read George Brown's mind-numbing but widely used textbook, *Building the Canadian Nation* – a title, Cook says, that pretty much 'described its contents'.[65] Relentlessly teleological, it was a standard account of discovery, exploration, settlement, colonial growth and nationhood. Canada from sea to sea was not 'forecast', Brown wrote, it was 'prophesied', making the prairies – once the 'Indians gave up their old way of life' – first colonies and later provinces, but never a focus, Manitoba appearing twice in the index, Saskatchewan and Alberta once.[66] To a kid at Maple Leaf Collegiate in Morden, Manitoba, especially a bright kid, history written from downtown Toronto could not 'but deceive and deceive cruelly'.[67]

The spring of 1950 brought more than the end of high school when the Red River flooded, forcing the evacuation of some 70,000 people up and down the Red River valley, including 550 people from the small Franco-Manitoban village of St Jean who were taken to Morden where service organisations, churches and women's auxiliaries set up emergency shelters, arranged billets, gathered used clothing, collected old toys and made hundreds of sandwiches. As a member of a quickly convened Red Cross committee, Rev. Cook opened Morden United as a clearing station and dining room for the 'long cavalcade of trucks and cars' and people leaving St Jean.[68] Later he would be singled out by one of the many evacuees who, although 'foreign of language and faith', believed

---

64 'Graduation', *Morden Times*, 12 May 1948.
65 Cook, 'Who Broadened Canadian History?'
66 George W. Brown, *Building the Canadian Nation* (Toronto: Dent, 1942), 177, 336.
67 W.L. Morton, 'Clio in Canada: The Interpretation of Canadian History' (1946), reprinted in Carl Berger, ed., *Approaches to Canadian History* (Toronto: University of Toronto Press, 1967), 47. 'Teaching inspired by the historical experience of metropolitan Canada', Morton argued, 'cannot but deceive, and deceive cruelly, children of the outlying sections.'
68 'Shelter 550 Evacuees Here', *Morden Times*, 17 May 1950.

that she had found 'unity and true socialism' in Morden.[69] The arrival of so many francophones – 'especially those of the opposite sex' – filled a young Ramsay Cook 'with both curiosity and a sense of adventure': 'there was something exotic about them'. Looking back, Cook now sees the flood as part of his discovery of French Canada. He had played hockey and baseball against teams from Letellier and St Norbert, which were 'positive, if sometimes bruising, meetings'. But the 1950 flood was 'more dramatic and personal'. Of course, there was no mention of bilingualism, biculturalism, founding nations or asymmetric federalism – unless, he jokes, those 'heated discussions' took place 'at the local beer parlour' – but there was enough innocent flirting to satisfy an 18-year-old boy.[70]

On 27 May 1950, Cook graduated from high school in front of nearly 800 people packed into the Legion auditorium. In a 'well-delivered' valedictory address that 'held the attention of the audience', he told his peers to 'aim high', reminding them that 'a successful person is one who had done his best'. Despite his lousy study habits, he won the Governor General's Medal for his 'exceptional' marks, athletic accomplishments and popularity.[71] He also won the languages prize, even if French was 'poorly taught' at Maple Leaf Collegiate.[72]

That fall Cook left Morden to attend university and, although he did not know it then, he would never live in a small prairie town again. But he never resented where he had come from, or felt that he had been deprived because Raymore did not have an art gallery, or because Wynyard did not have a museum, or because Morden did not have a library. The prairies had something else: they had, he says looking back on his childhood, 'a lot of freedom'.[73] As long as he was home in time for supper, he was allowed to go to the edge of town, explore the fields, walk the stream beds and run beyond the next rise. In this, his childhood was like something out of *Who Has Seen the Wind* and its promise of wide open spaces to young boys whose hair was 'as bleached as the dead prairie grass itself'.[74] And it was like something out of Wallace Stegner's *Wolf Willow*, a memoir of growing

---

69 'St. Jean Evacuees Return to Flood Ruined Homes', *Morden Times*, 14 June 1950.
70 Ramsay Cook, 'Introduction', in Ramsay Cook, *Watching Quebec: Selected Essays* (Montreal and Kingston: McGill-Queen's University Press, 2005), viii–ix. The sentence, 'there was something exotic about them', comes from author's interview with Ramsay Cook, 14 July 2014.
71 'G.A. Fitton, Brandon, Speaks to Grads Friday', *Morden Times*, 31 May 1950.
72 Cook, 'Introduction', *Watching Quebec*, ix.
73 Author's interview with Ramsay Cook, 14 July 2014.
74 Mitchell, *Who*, 11.

up in miniscule Eastend, Saskatchewan, a place he called a 'kid's paradise'. Using the metaphor of imprinting – that phase 'in the development of birds, when an impression lasting only a few seconds may be imprinted on the young bird for life' – Stegner believed to his last days that he too had been imprinted, or 'marked by the space and geography of the plains'.[75]

The prairies marked Cook in the same way, imprinting an abiding love and need for nature, the outdoors, wildlife and especially birds. As a 10-year-old boy in Wynyard, he learned to identify the prairies' many birds – the meadow lark, the northern goshawk and the western tanager – using a simple guide book; he spent the money he earned as a paper boy on bird pictures from the Audubon society; and he 'collected birds' eggs, blew the yolks out and, with his hands scratched and dirty from a day spent free, 'carefully stored the shells in a sawdust-filled box', his own cabinet of curiosities. 'I always claimed that I collected only one egg per species, but I often found what I decided was a better example in some gopher-skin-strewn hawk's nest high in a tree.'[76]

For these reasons and more, Cook reacted quickly and viscerally to a 1974 book that he felt looked down on small prairie towns like the ones that had made him, and he let the author have it in a review written with what he called, quoting Stegner, the 'angry defensiveness of the native son'. At this point a full professor at York University, Cook turned *Grass Roots* upside down. The Winklers, Biggars and Miamis were not stuck in the past; they were stuck in the present. It was the car, television and chain stores that were turning their main streets dusty and tired. And while he acknowledged that these towns and villages could be 'pinched and prejudiced', they could be 'attractive' and 'humane' too. 'The devoted school teacher can still be found,' he said, 'and the doctor who'll make a house call when asked' and 'lawyers and merchants who know when a bill shouldn't be collected'. As well, there are clergymen like his father 'who have never heard of [Marshall] McLuhan but who help people who are lonely or alcoholic or just mixed up'.[77] Forty years later, it is still one of his favourite reviews, precisely because it was defensive and

---

75 Wallace Stegner, *Wolf Willow* (New York: Viking, 1962), 21. For Stegner's reference to Eastend as a 'kid's paradise', see Page Stegner, ed., *The Selected Letters of Wallace Stegner* (Emeryville, CA: Shoemaker Hoard, 2007), 118. For Stegner's reference to having been 'marked by the space and geography of the plains', see Jackson J. Benson, *Wallace Stegner: His Life and Works* (New York: Penguin, 1996), 31.
76 Ramsay Cook, email to author, 23 May 2015.
77 Ramsay Cook, review of *Grass Roots* by Heather Robertson, in *Canadian Forum* (March 1974), 43.

therefore honest. In the end, Cook's experience was Margaret Laurence's experience. When thinking about her hometown of Neepawa, Manitoba, she admitted that it could be an 'isolated hell'. But it could be 'a place of incredible happenings, splendours, and revelations', and for the longest time that 'settlement and that land' were 'my only real knowledge of the planet'; it was, she said, 'where my world began'.[78]

The prairies were not a hinterland to the commercial empire of the St Lawrence River. They were Ramsay Cook's only real knowledge of the planet and the place where his world began. But that was about to change.

IV

> It never crossed my mind, when young, that I might become a professional historian.
> — A.J.P. Taylor

Winnipeg was still the largest city on the prairies when Cook began his studies at United College in 1950. It was also the most tolerant as the 'old barriers between ethnic groups' fell and 'the once impregnable fortress of British-Canadian culture was undermined' by 'an evolving, plural approach to questions of identity'. Of course, Winnipeg had been a diverse city since its beginnings, but in the postwar period its civic leaders displayed an 'increasing openness to newcomers'. Forty years earlier, Woodsworth had asked how a 'heterogeneous mass' might be welded 'into one people'. The answer, most of Winnipeg's citizens now believed, lay in pluralism and 'a determined effort' to build bridges across ethnicity, religion and language.[79] Cook remembers United College, then a couple of buildings on Portage Avenue at Good Street, as a place where kids with Jewish, Ukrainian, Polish, German, Scandinavian and West Indian backgrounds went to classes and shared a dormitory with kids from English, Scottish and Irish backgrounds. Although Winnipeg was New York City compared to Raymore, Wynyard and Morden, and although United College, with 1,500 students, was enormous compared to Maple

---

78 Margaret Laurence, 'Where the World Began', in Laurence, *Heart of a Stranger* (Toronto: McClelland & Stewart, 1976), 213, 219.
79 Royden Loewen and Gerald Friesen, *Immigrants in Prairie Cities: Ethnic Diversity in Twentieth-Century Canada* (Toronto: University of Toronto Press, 2009), 92, 78. 'Winnipeg', Allison Marshall writes, 'was a more tolerant place to live than many other cities in Western Canada'. Marshall, *Cultivating Connections*, 11.

Leaf Collegiate, a four-room, four-grade high school, they all shared one defining characteristic: cultural diversity. Thinking about his childhood and adolescence, Cook is not sure that he ever lived in a town that had a majority British population. Actually, every town did, but that is not the point. Rather, his memory is. Ethnic, religious and linguistic difference, or multiculturalism, although that word had not been invented yet, was 'the normal state of things' on the prairies.[80]

Initially, Cook did not want to study history, thinking instead that first-year chemistry would be more interesting. After the 'insufferably boring' history that he had been compelled to sit through at Maple Leaf Collegiate, he would have watched paint dry if he could get credit for it. But when the assistant registrar explained that taking chemistry necessitated 'thrice weekly bus trips to the Fort Garry campus of the University of Manitoba', he said thanks but no thanks. She then suggested the American history survey, adding that the department had 'an excellent reputation'. Maybe it did, but Cook did not care about things like that. He cared about the classroom – a five-minute walk across campus. 'On such weighty considerations my career choice was made, though I did not suspect it at the time.'[81]

United College's Department of History was small, just three full-time professors, but it was the centre of the Arts Faculty and, in a way, of the university because its members were tough-minded men with strong opinions who were not afraid to stick their necks out.[82] And they were wonderful teachers who pushed their students to think for themselves and make connections between the past and the present. Where George Brown had killed the past, Harry Crowe, Ken McNaught and Stewart Reid brought it back to life. Cook loved it and although he 'had no conception of what historians did for a living', he quickly shelved his plans for law school.[83] The next four years saw him grow intellectually, push his mind and discover its reaches, broaden his horizons and debate the world.

---

80   The 1931 and 1941 censuses confirm that Alameda, Raymore, Wynyard and Morden had more 'British Races' than other 'Races', although the 1941 census identified 427 Britons and 408 Scandinavians in Wynyard. Cook, 'Introduction', *Watching Quebec*, viii.
81   Cook, 'Introduction', *Watching Quebec*, ix.
82   Kenneth McNaught, *Conscience and History: A Memoir* (Toronto: University of Toronto Press, 1992), 89. For example, in 1953, Kenneth McNaught, Harry Crowe and Stewart Reid formed the United College Association, a faculty association, with the goal of securing faculty representation on the Board of Regents and improving salaries. See also Michiel Horn, *Academic Freedom in Canada: A History* (Toronto: University of Toronto Press, 1999), doi.org/10.3138/9781442670570.
83   Cook, 'Who Broadened Canadian History?'

The *Morden Times* had made a handful of references to famine in China and polio in India, but it was more interested in Princess Elizabeth's engagement to Lieutenant Philip Mountbatten, the royal wedding and the birth of Prince Charles. At United College, Cook discovered that the world was bigger than the royal family and that history was the key to unlocking it. The Cold War and the Korean War; Israel and the Arab states; McCarthy and the Rosenbergs: it was an exciting time to be a student of history.

Crowe, McNaught and Reid took an interest in young people, hosting meetings of the History Club in their homes and inviting students to Tony's, the campus cafeteria and coffee shop in the basement of Wesley Hall next to the ancient boiler room. With 'a semi-permanent cigarette drooping from his mouth', Crowe would hold forth on politics, especially American politics, while students sat transfixed.[84] The senior senator from Wisconsin, Joseph McCarthy, was a favourite target. Often McNaught would join Crowe, and together they would solve the world's problems. When the conversation turned to history, they would refer to the Winnipeg General Strike as class warfare and not, as George Brown had, simply the result of postwar unemployment. Every now and then, Reid would show up, turning the conversation to British politics, decolonisation, the National Health Service and especially the Labour Party, the subject of his doctoral thesis. A crusty Scot, Reid was 'argumentative' and 'disagreed' with everyone but, like Crowe and McNaught, 'he was a *really good* teacher'.[85]

Captivated, Cook began to see himself in his professors, thinking that they led interesting lives. The coffee, cigarettes and conversations also confirmed and strengthened his growing interest in civil liberties. So when a law student wrote a column in the college newspaper criticising those 'propagandists' and 'fellow travellers' who would rail at witch hunts and threats to academic freedom but disdain America's leadership in the 'crucial struggle of our time', he responded. If only one professor is intimidated – or worse, hounded – it is one too many, Cook said. McCarthyism, he added, is a 'manifestation of a certain type of thought' in American politics – which Richard Hofstadter would identify later as the paranoid style – but there is another type of thought in American politics, Cook noted,

---

84 Ramsay Cook, *The Teeth of Time: Remembering Pierre Elliott Trudeau* (Montreal and Kingston: McGill-Queen's University Press, 2006), 98.
85 Emphasis not mine. Author's interview with Ramsay Cook, 14 July 2014. Fifteen or so years later, Cook dedicated a collection of essays 'To the Memory of J.H.S. Reid'. See Ramsay Cook, *Canada and the French-Canadian Question* (Toronto: Macmillan, 1966).

stretching from Jefferson to Franklin Delano Roosevelt, and it is in this tradition 'that the hope of western democracy lies'. Not to be outdone, the law student responded in kind, thanking Cook for confirming his thesis that every 'self-righteous pseudo-intellectual' believes that he is heir to Jefferson yet this same 'left-wing thinker' has nothing to say about the 'millions' of victims and 'proposed victims' of communism. Still the competitive kid who never backed down from a fight against some hayseed from Winkler, Cook hit back: congressional committees are one thing, but 'kangaroo courts' are another, and academic freedom is too important to be left in the hands of 'cowards' and 'character assassins'.[86] The exchange ended in a draw, but Cook had discovered the letter-to-the-editor, which became a favourite medium for usually quick, occasionally sustained, often ironic, but always forthright commentary.

In addition to its informal sessions at Tony's, the Department of History organised an annual exchange on some aspect of international relations with Macalester College in St Paul, Minnesota: United College faculty and students would go down one year, Macalester faculty and students would come up the next. To Cook, it was heady stuff and in the spring of 1953 he was selected to give a presentation, which meant that summer he had to prepare a paper on 'the problem of peace in the Middle East', as well as fertilise sunflowers and corn at the Morden Experimental Farm. In his self-deprecating way, he now likes to remind people that, in case they are wondering, he failed to find a solution, but the paper contains the first expression of what became two of the animating themes of his career: a distrust of nationalism and a commitment to liberalism. Drawing on articles in *The Nation* and *The New Statesman,* two left journals, he asserted that the record of the West in the Middle East is the record of generals, oil executives and Coca-Cola salesmen, making it 'a record of conquest, broken promises, expediency, and exploitation'. Meanwhile, local elites draw on the language of nationalism and national self-determination to advance their own narrow class interests, transforming 'the foreigner' into 'the whipping boy' and deflecting attention from persistent social and economic inequality. But it is the intractable 'misery of the people',

---

86   The 1953 exchange took place in the *Manitoban*, the student newspaper of the University of Manitoba, but was reprinted in *The Brown and Gold*, the Manitoba yearbook. See *The Brown and Gold*, 1954, University of Manitoba Archives and Special Collections.

Cook concluded, that must be addressed by policies rooted in the 'liberal principles' of 'liberty, equality, and fraternity' if the place that 'gave birth to Western civilization' is not also to become its 'graveyard'.[87]

In his fourth year, Cook had the opportunity to study with a visiting professor, William Rose, whose courses in Eastern European history and Eastern European nationalism were unlike anything he had taken before. Rose himself was a fascinating man whose life read like something out of a novel: a poor farm boy from Minnedosa, Manitoba, he went to Oxford on a Rhodes Scholarship and then Leipzig to do a PhD, but the First World War interrupted his studies and he found himself interned in Poland as an enemy alien of the Austro-Hungarian Empire. He quickly learned the language, fell in love with the culture and, when the war ended, did a PhD in Poland on Polish history, becoming a key interpreter of Eastern and Central Europe to Great Britain when he was named director of the School of Slavonic Studies at the University of London.[88] Now retired and nearly 70 years old, Rose returned to his alma mater and took his Winnipeg students beyond Britain and France to that part of Europe where Clifford Sifton's 'stalwart peasant in a sheepskin coat' and his 'stout wife' had come from – where, for some of them, their parents and grandparents had come from.[89]

As he did in all of his courses, Cook jumped in with both feet, 'struggling to pronounce Eastern European names and to distinguish between Pan Slavs and Slavophils'.[90] But Rose was a patient teacher – 'very fatherly' and 'very kind' – and when he delivered a public lecture – in a subfusc in the tradition of Oxford and Cambridge – Cook sold copies of his books at the back of the hall.[91] As both a historian and commentator on current events, Rose saw nationalism as a positive force, leading to national independence and the end of empire. Polish nationalism, he believed, could be a force even for moral regeneration. Cook was not convinced. After all, he had studied with Crowe, McNaught and Reid, all socialists who distrusted the nation as a bourgeois deceit and instead pinned their hopes on

---

87 Ramsay Cook, 'Nationalism in the Middle East', *Vox Wesleyana*, 1954, University of Winnipeg Archives, AC-9-27.
88 See Daniel Stone, 'William Rose, Manitoba Historian', *Manitoba Historical Society Transactions*, Series 3, 31 (1974–75) and Daniel Stone, ed., *The Polish Memoirs of William John Rose* (Toronto: University of Toronto Press, 1975).
89 Quotation in Brown and Cook, *A Nation Transformed*, 63.
90 Cook, 'Introduction', *Watching Quebec*, x.
91 Author's interview with Ramsay Cook, 14 July 2014.

internationalism. Besides, he was a kid from the prairies with, in his words, 'an instinctive suspicion that what passed as nation-building in Ontario' was really 'industrial tariff protection' to be paid for by the western farmer in the form of more expensive farm machinery.[92] As part of his courses with Rose, Cook read Johann Gottfried Herder, the eighteenth-century German philosopher and intellectual father of nationalism, who insisted that the nation consisted of a people, or *volk*, with a shared ethnicity and language, and, in turn, that the nation was the natural basis of the state. Reading Herder against the backdrop of 'the Second World War and the destruction of most of Europe's Jews', and reading him on the prairies that did not have, and never would have, a shared ethnicity, Cook, frankly, 'disliked him'.[93] Still, Rose taught him that nationalism was a force in history that could be its own field of study.

Encouraged by his professors, especially by Ken McNaught who recognised something pretty special in him, Cook decided to pursue graduate work, either at Toronto or Queen's.[94] Toronto had a bigger program, but Queen's offered a bigger scholarship. And he now thought that he might like to work in Ottawa, in the Department of External Affairs, where the action was and where the bright and ambitious set their sights. Cook was both, but his ambition was not crass and he was not a young man on the make. Money, status and rank did not matter to him. Ideas did, and he was increasingly drawn to a life of the mind. He had found in history a new language that could be a moral language because it included questions of right and wrong, making it, he said many years later, 'an essential component of a developing moral imagination'.[95] History compels the writer to enter the lives of real people and to see them as men and women struggling, striving, succeeding, failing, doing good things and sometimes doing very bad things. In short, it compels the writer to walk a mile in someone else's shoes, which is the essence of a moral imagination.

---

92 Cook, 'Who Broadened Canadian History?'
93 Cook, 'Introduction', *Watching Quebec*, x. Guy Laforest believes that Cook misread Herder and was too quick to dismiss nationalism, believing that 'une autre lecture, plus nuancée, de la pensée herdérienne et de la nature du nationalisme dans le monde contemporain' is possible. Of course, Laforest has never agreed with Cook. See Guy Laforest, 'Herder, Kedourie et les errements de l'antinationalisme du Canada', in Raymond Hudon and Réjean Pelletier, eds, *L'engagement intellectuel: Mélanges en honneur de Léon Dion* (Québec: Les Presses de l'Université Laval, 1991).
94 In his memoirs, Ken McNaught fondly remembered Ramsay Cook as a bright student who 'let me get away with nothing'. McNaught, *Conscience and History*, 85.
95 Ramsay Cook, 'Identities Are Not Like Hats', *Canadian Historical Review*, 81:2 (2000), 260.

Understood as a moral discipline, history was replacing religion in Cook's life. Attending Sunday school, singing in the church choir, listening to his father's sermons and watching his mother leave the house to attend yet another meeting of the Women's Association, the Women's Missionary Society or Canadian Girls in Training gave him an ethical and moral compass, a sense of obligation and service. As the son of a United Church minister and a United Church minister's wife, he had learnt right from wrong in his childhood and adolescence, but now in his early 20s, he felt his faith recede to the point where he became an agnostic. Neither epiphanic nor sudden, it was a process with no clear beginning and no clear ending. He did not, like Michael Bliss, one day take a shower, decide that God was a 'superstitious invention', and watch his faith go down the drain.[96] At some point, though, he decided that the answers to questions of equality and inequality, tolerance and intolerance, nationalism, patriotism, self-determination, identity and minority rights, would be found in the archives, not in the Sermon on the Mount, while answers to questions of life and death would be found not in the Psalms of David but in the poetry of T.S. Eliot and W.B. Yeats, and in *Who Has Seen the Wind*, ultimately a novel about the unalterable mystery of death.[97]

V

> Canada is a supreme act of faith.
>
> — Arthur Lower

Every generation had to work out Canada's reason for being, according to Arthur Lower. For him, that reason was a nation independent of Great Britain, separate from the United States, neither English nor French, but united by history and geography, by the shared historical experience of living on the northern half of North America. 'You can call it nonsense', he wrote, 'you can call it what you will', but nationalism gives 'form and substance to the vague and formless': 'I have faith that we will win through,

---

96 Ramsay Cook, email to author, 15 May 2015. Michael Bliss had been studying for the ministry and even had a mission field in the Northwest Territories, but during a long shower in the fall of 1961, he became a lifelong sceptic. See Michael Bliss, *Writing History: A Professor's Life* (Toronto: Dundurn, 2011), 94.
97 See Ramsay Cook, 'Donald Creighton: Tribute to a Scholar', *University of Toronto Bulletin*, 25 February 1980; and Cook, *The Teeth of Time*.

that Canada is not a mere name' on some world map.[98] Lower could have never guessed that the 'brilliant young man' with the mop of red hair who had come from Manitoba to work with him in the fall of 1954 would call it nonsense and, within five or six years, emerge as one of the key figures in the articulation and defence of a new reason for being.[99] And Ramsay Cook could not have known that the formidable figure who had agreed to supervise his MA thesis would introduce him to a subject that, 60 years later, still fascinates him.

Lower co-taught a seminar on French Canada. From behind stacks of paper, he emphasised French-Canadian culture while Fred Gibson, who never knew when to stop, covered French-Canadian politics. Cook loved it. Ken McNaught had made Canada interesting, but here was a part of the country that Cook barely knew existed and that was on the cusp of something revolutionary. Quebec's traditional, defensive and Catholic nationalists were being challenged by a new generation of neo-nationalists who talked about a modern, bureaucratic, secular Quebec that was master in its own house. It was a lively seminar: Lower, who had the 'hide of an elephant', lived for the fight and expected his students to challenge the generalisations that he lobbed into a seminar for effect; and Gibson, who knew everything there was to know about national politics from having worked in Ottawa at what was then the Public Archives and as an assistant to Mackenzie King in the sorting of his papers, was a 'very demanding teacher'.[100] He was also a fun teacher because he knew where the bodies were buried and how to tell a good story. Later, Gibson hired Cook as a research assistant for a project on the 1909 to 1911 naval debate, which had broken along linguistic lines, pitting English-speaking Canadians who believed Canada had a duty to the mother country against French-speaking Canadians who foresaw Canada being dragged into Britain's wars. In short, the naval debate was the clash of two nationalisms.[101] The seed had been sown and Cook was nearing one of the key insights of his career: Canada's problem was not too little nationalism, it was too much.

---

98 Arthur Lower, Diary, 23 February 1964, Queen's University Archives, Arthur Lower fonds, 5072, box 57, E75.
99 Arthur Lower, *My First Seventy-Five Years* (Toronto: Macmillan, 1967), 324. On Cook as a public intellectual, see Patrice A. Dutil, 'Ramsay Cook's Quest for an Intellectual "Phoenix", 1960–1968', in Behiels and Martel, *Nation, Ideas, Identities*.
100 Author's interview with Ramsay Cook, 14 July 2014.
101 See Brown and Cook, *Canada, 1896–1921*, ch. 13 'The Clash of Nationalisms'.

That seminar and that research taught him something else: French Canadians were not 'one minority among many' and they could claim rights that, for example, Ukrainian Canadians could not. The Ukrainians had become Canadians by choice; the French had become Canadians by conquest.[102] Equality, he realised, was not sameness and equal treatment was not the same treatment. And if groups could be treated equally *and* differently, then French language and education rights were compatible with equality, not contradictory. John Diefenbaker's unhyphenated Canadian could never include French Canadians, especially French Canadians outside of Quebec, because the hyphen was all that stood between them and assimilation. At Lower's urging, Cook became a faithful reader of *Le Devoir*, Quebec's newspaper of record edited by the neo-nationalist André Laurendeau. Then a classmate introduced him to *Cité Libre*, a small, left-liberal, anti-clerical, pro-labour journal edited by an up-and-coming intellectual named Pierre Trudeau. Laurendeau and *Le Devoir*; Trudeau and *Cité Libre*; neo-nationalists on the one hand, Citélibristes on the other: although he did not fully appreciate it, Cook had a front row seat at the prelude to the Quiet Revolution. 'My interest in Quebec was born at Queen's', he now says.[103]

Cook shared something else with his thesis supervisor: a commitment to liberalism and a concern for what had happened during the Second World War when 21,000 Japanese Canadians were interned and basic civil liberties were mocked by a security state. Because Lower had been a founding member and first chair of the Civil Liberties Association of Winnipeg in the 1940s, he was able to give Cook access to his personal papers and put him in touch with F.R. Scott, the McGill law professor and longtime champion of civil liberties in a province plagued by a reactionary and corrupt government, and with Andrew Brewin, the Toronto lawyer who had led the legal fight against the planned deportation of Japanese Canadians after the war.[104] A 'taskmaster', Lower also instructed Cook to look for the forest and not just the trees, to look beyond the minutes of meetings, press reports and parliamentary debates by reading widely in

---

102 Cook, 'Introduction', *Watching Quebec,* x–xi.
103 Author's interview with Ramsay Cook, 14 July 2014. See Michael Behiels, *Prelude to the Quiet Revolution: Liberalism vs Neo-Nationalism, 1945–1960* (Montreal and Kingston: McGill-Queen's University Press, 1985).
104 For the history of civil liberties in Canada, see Christopher MacLennan, *Toward the Charter: Canadians and the Demand for a National Bill of Rights, 1929–1960* (Montreal/Kingston: McGill-Queen's University Press, 2003) and Dominique Clément, *Canada's Rights Revolution: Social Movements and Social Change, 1937–1982* (Vancouver: UBC Press, 2008).

the history of liberal thought. Using the Douglas Library's card catalogue, Cook went into the stacks where he read the Magna Carta's promise 'that there exists a rule of law and that everyone, including the King, must be governed by it'; he studied the seventeenth-century's vindication of liberty in the Habeas Corpus Act and the Bill of Rights; and he read A.V. Dicey's insistence that freedom was dependent on parliamentary sovereignty, an independent judiciary and the rule of law.[105]

However, one book shone above the others, as if it cast a great light. Lord Acton's *History of Freedom and Other Essays* confirmed Cook's experience growing up on Clifford Sifton's prairies and now his experience studying French Canada. The schools in Raymore, Wynyard, Brandon and Morden, the lectures, seminars and bull sessions at United College, the coffee and cigarettes at Tony's, and the debates over Canada and the French-Canadian question at Queen's came together in a moment of clarity. A nation founded on 'race', Acton said, is a nation founded on 'a fictitious unity'; the idea that the 'State and nation must be co-extensive' is a lie; and the 'divided patriotism' stemming from 'the presence of different nations under the same sovereignty' is not a bad thing, it is a good thing because it resists 'centralisation', 'corruption' and 'absolutism': 'The co-existence of several nations under the same State is a test, as well as the best security, of its freedom.'[106] 'On first reading Acton, I thought of Canada', Cook said many years later.[107]

Opening with a nod to Lord Acton, 'Canadian Liberalism in Wartime' argues that Canadian liberalism had been encouraged by the presence of two main cultures, although it still remains vulnerable to governments in both wartime and peacetime: the War Measures Act in the First World War was an obvious example, as were the amendments to the Immigration Act and the Criminal Code to deal with the Winnipeg General Strike. The Second World War again saw the federal government use the War Measures Act and the Defence of Canada Regulations to intimidate,

---

105 Ramsay Cook, 'Canadian Liberalism in Wartime: A Study of the Defence of Canada Regulations and Some Canadian Attitudes to Civil Liberties in Wartime, 1939–1945' (MA thesis, Queen's University, 1955), iii, 11. Nineteen years later, he published a version of his thesis in a *festschrift* to his supervisor and friend. See Ramsay Cook, 'Canadian Freedom in Wartime, 1939–1945', in W.H. Heick and Roger Graham, eds, *His Own Man: Essays in Honour of Arthur Reginald Marsden Lower* (Montreal and Kingston: McGill-Queen's University Press, 1974).
106 Lord Acton, 'On Nationality', in John E.E. Dalberg Acton, *The History of Freedom and Other Essays* (New York: Cosimo, 2007), 288, 285, 289, 290.
107 Cook, *The Teeth of Time*, 12. Another Manitoba historian, W.L. Morton, also found Lord Acton's insights helpful to understanding Canada. See Morton, 'Clio in Canada'.

silence, jail and, in the case of the Japanese, intern. The removal of the Japanese Canadians from their homes and the disposal of their property at fire sale prices was, Cook wrote, a 'flagrant abuse' made possible by years of 'strong prejudice', wartime hysteria and the government's assumption of 'arbitrary powers'. The internment confirmed the dictum, he wrote, that 'once a government is allowed to assume extraordinary powers it will use them'. While there were important voices of dissent in the press, parliament, organised labour and civil liberties associations, why were they so few in number? Why were such 'illiberal security regulations' met with such 'silence'? Because, he concluded, Canada did not have an eighteenth century, meaning Canadian liberalism had been inherited, not won. Later, in the last third of the nineteenth century and opening decade of the twentieth century, railways and tariffs were the great national questions. 'With tangible economic questions rather than abstract constitutional points the main concern of Canadians, our Burkes and Foxes have been Galts and Siftons.'[108]

An impressive piece of research and writing for a 23-year-old graduate student, 'Canadian Liberalism in Wartime' is also moving: Cook's childhood friend, the little boy who had taught him how to fish, would have been interned along with his family, their property seized and effectively given away. Of the 'several blots' left on Canadian liberalism by 'wartime security regulations', the 'case of Japanese Canadians' is 'the blackest'. Perhaps this explains his anger, restrained and academic, but present between the lines. Once conceived as a moral discipline, historians must be prepared 'to pass judgment', Cook argued, sounding not unlike his parents. The apple had not fallen all that far from the tree after all. Cook's judgement of a government that allowed internal security to trump civil liberties *and* of Canadians that failed to stop that government and its technocrats, that had allowed liberalism to become 'chamber of commerce oratory', was quick and unambiguous.[109] And on that note, he closed his thesis in the same way that he had opened it, with a nod to Lord Acton: 'Liberty is not a means to a political end. It is itself the highest political end.'[110]

---

108 Cook, 'Canadian Liberalism in Wartime', 233, 237, 278, 279.
109 Ibid., 238, 268, 270. His point about the apathy of Canadians was confirmed at his thesis defence in the fall of 1955 when the chair, a distinguished Queen's mathematician, admitted that 'he had lived through the war without ever knowing that the War Measures Act or the Defence of Canada Regulations existed'. Ramsay Cook, email to author, 29 May 2015.
110 Acton, *The History of Freedom and Other Essays*, 22.

Cook began his PhD at the University of Toronto in the fall of 1955 and in time became the leading historian and public intellectual of his generation by developing the themes in his MA thesis – equality, minority rights, anti-nationalism and the benefits of what Lord Acton called 'divided patriotism'. But have I committed the biographer's sin, the one Cook cautioned me against when he told me to read *The Rise of the Indian Rope Trick* by Peter Lamont? Has my reconnaissance – carried out at moment in history when security concerns mean that even the Supreme Court of Canada can hold a secret hearing – determined what evidence I found and how I interpreted it? Maybe. But that is the question all biographers confront. And is my biographical reconnaissance of Ramsay Cook not Ramsay Cook in the same way that Magritte's pipe is not a pipe? Yes, of course: the problem of biography is the problem of Magritte's pipe. Then why write biography? Because like the rise of the Indian rope trick, it is 'a victory of imagination over reality'.[111]

---

111 Lamont, *The Rise of the Indian Rope Trick*, 232.

Discipline-Defining
Authors

7

Intersecting and Contrasting Lives: G.M. Trevelyan and Lytton Strachey

Alastair MacLachlan

This essay is about history and biography in two senses. First, it examines two parallel and intersecting, but contrasting lives: that of George Macaulay Trevelyan (b. 1876), probably the most popular historian and political biographer of early twentieth-century England – a Fellow and in old age the Master of Trinity College, Cambridge, an independent scholar for 25 years and, for 12 years, Regius Professor of Modern History – and that of his slightly younger Trinity protégé, Giles Lytton Strachey (b. 1880), a would-be academic rejected by the academy, who set himself up as a critical essayist and a historical gadfly – the writer credited with the transformation of a moribund genre of pious memorialisation into a 'new' style of biography. Second, the essay explores their approaches to writing nineteenth-century history and biography, and it assesses their works as products of similar but changing times and places: Cambridge and London from about 1900 to the 1930s.[1]

---

1 I shall therefore ignore Trevelyan's later writings (he died in 1962), and concentrate on the biographies written by Strachey (S) and Trevelyan (T), with a focus on their nineteenth-century studies.

'Read no history', advised Disraeli, 'nothing but biography, for that is life without theory'. But 'life without theory' can be intellectually emaciated, and a comparative biography may have the advantage of kneading into the subject theoretical muscle sometimes absent in single lives, highlighting the points where the two lives intersected and what was common and what distinctive about them. As such, it may limit what Terry Eagleton called 'the remorseless linearity and covert anti-intellectualism of the biographical form', and may provide some of the broader contexts Trevelyan found through an engagement with geography and history, and some of the clarity and coherence Strachey sought through 'the new biography'.[2]

The two men had much in common. Born within four years of each other, they belonged to the late Victorian intellectual aristocracy. They shared common Whig ancestries, home lives steeped in literature and history, and curiously coincident but contrasting Anglo-Indian backgrounds. Both were residual, godless products of the early nineteenth-century evangelical movement. At Cambridge, they were scholars of Trinity College, graduates of the tiny as yet unnamed History Faculty, and defenders of the belletristic tradition of historical writing against the new gospel of scientific history proclaimed by Professor J.B. Bury in a famous inaugural of 1903. Above all, they both were members of the elite 'Cambridge Apostles': a society with a distinctive collective identity at the turn of the twentieth century, marked by intense devotion to the ethical and philosophical values formulated by G.E. Moore, shared by their friends, 'Goldie' Dickinson, Bertrand Russell, Leonard Woolf and Maynard Keynes, and subsequently embraced by 'Bloomsbury'.

A comparative study, however, needs to address difference as well as similarity, and I shall also suggest divergences of nature and nurture, which helped to shape their distinctive styles of living, thinking and writing. Some were perhaps biologically or at least sexually determined; some went back to the distinctive features of their homes, families and early educational experiences. Others were developed in Cambridge, where despite close elective affinities, there were acute tensions between the two men, articulated in radically dissimilar ideals of 'reality' and

---

2   Benjamin Disraeli, *Contarini Fleming* (New York: Harper, 1832), Part 1, ch. 23; Ray Monk, 'Life without Theory: Biography as an Exemplar of Philosophical Understanding', *Poetics Today*, 28:3 (2007), 527–70, doi.org/10.1215/03335372-2007-007; Terry Eagleton, 'First Class Fellow Traveller', review of *Patrick Hamilton: A Life* by Sean French, *London Review of Books* (*LRB*), 15:23, 2 December 1993.

'phenomena', goodness and the proper ends of life. Some of these tensions focused on their 'Apostolic' characters and their relationship with Moore, while others were the products of constructed identities: the increasingly different personae they forged for themselves in the decades before, during and after the First World War.

These temperamental differences resulted in two very different 'archives'. Shortly before he died, Trevelyan burned virtually all his personal papers. He could not, of course, destroy what he had written to other people. Genuinely self-effacing and incurious about himself, he never in his opinion 'wrote a private letter worth printing'. He did not keep a diary; his sex life was unrecorded and unremarkable. On the other hand, in the period up to the First World War, he aspired to the role of a public man of letters, and he viewed his writings not as disinterested research, but as 'Tracts for the times'. Before, during and after the war, he was a committed internationalist, an active conservationist and a recreational champion. So his life is imbedded in the history of English politics and society to a degree unusual in a conventional academic historian.[3]

Strachey kept virtually all his papers. Unlike Trevelyan, he was immensely curious about himself: 'I am an egoist', he told his sister, and everything he wrote – biographies, literary essays, plays, dialogues, poems – bore the imprint of his idiosyncratic personality. He was an inveterate gossip and a prolific, candid letter writer; his personal archive consisted ultimately of over 30,000 items stored in boxes, trunks and suitcases. Unlike Trevelyan, Strachey was an aesthete and intellectual mandarin: public life repelled him. He shrank from contact with what he called 'the phenomenal world' – a world, as he saw it, marked by 'stupidity, vulgarity and falseness'. Like many chronically sick people, he found it hard to cope with healthy, boisterous, interfering people like Trevelyan. If, as Leonard Woolf claimed, he was 'keenly interested' in politics, he was also acutely aware of the costs of social activism. Though public affairs impinged on his life more than he recognised, notably during the First World War, what he really valued

---

3   G.M. Trevelyan, *An Autobiography and Other Essays* (London: Longmans, Green, 1949), 1–2; GMT to Robert Calverley Trevelyan, 20 May 1949, in Peter Raina, *George Macaulay Trevelyan: A Portrait in Letters* (Edinburgh: Pentland, 2001), 154; David Cannadine, *G. M. Trevelyan: A Life in History* (London: HarperCollins, 1992), xiv, 1–55.

was literature, music, art and talk. His ethic was one of beauty, truth and friendship, focused on 'good states of mind' rather than on public duty and good conduct.[4]

Thus, increasingly, Strachey scorned the civic sermons and literary pretentions of would-be mentors like Trevelyan and, since he could be witheringly dismissive, there is much comedy in their *mésalliance*.[5] To some degree, this then is a study in contrasts. Trevelyan had a career; Strachey a life. 'Trevy', as he was known to friends, found fulfilment outside writing in a wide range of political, social, international and institutional activities; Strachey found his in conversation, correspondence and personal relationships.

In August 1918, the 42-year-old Trevelyan – author of three reverential biographies of nineteenth-century liberal heroes: Garibaldi, John Bright and Grey of the Reform Bill – was sitting in a railway carriage in northern Italy, on his way home from front-line duties. On his lap was an exceedingly unreverential study of four nineteenth-century lives, *Eminent Victorians*, by Lytton Strachey. The train was slow, and he was able to finish it at 'one long sitting,' he told Lytton, 'with the most intense pleasure, approval and admiration'. He congratulated Strachey on his 'judgement' and 'historical sense', and concluded in his most avuncular manner: 'you have found a method of writing about history which suits you admirably, and I hope you will pursue it'. In Brixton Prison, another 'Angel' or ex-'Apostle', the philosopher Bertie Russell, was chortling over Lytton's pages, only to be told by a warder that incarceration for wartime sedition was no laughing matter. Second thoughts convinced Trevy that *Eminent Victorians* was no laughing matter either.[6]

Why Trevelyan came to deplore Strachey's biographical style can partly be explained by homes and families. In an essay read to the Bloomsbury 'Memoir Club' in 1922, Strachey remarked that 'the influence of houses

---

4 S to D. Bussy, 8 January 1908, Robert Taylor Mss, Princeton, Box 18/12; Leonard Woolf, review of *Lytton Strachey, Vol 1: The Unknown Years, 1880–1910* by Michael Holroyd, *New Statesman* (*NS*), 26 November 1965.

5 S to L. Woolf, 24 February 1905, Harry Ransome Humanities Research Center, University of Texas at Austin (HRHC), Strachey Mss, Box 4, folder 4; 'Shall We Go the Whole Hog?', Paper to the Cambridge Apostles, 25 February 1905, British Library (BL) Strachey Mss, Additional Mss (Add. Ms.), 81,890; Todd Avery, ed., *The Works of Lytton Strachey: Early Papers* (London: Pickering Masters, 2011), 99–104.

6 T to S, 12 August 1918, BL, Add.Ms., 60,732, ff. 195–6; Bertrand Russell, *The Autobiography of Bertrand Russell* (3 vols; London: Allen & Unwin, 1951–69), vol. 1, 34; Michael Holroyd, *Lytton Strachey: The New Biography* (*LSNB*) (London: Chatto & Windus, 1994), 427.

on their inhabitants might well be the subject of a scientific investigation'. And he explored the atmospherics of place and the formation of personality in his own case at 69 Lancaster Gate, the huge Victorian terrace, where he grew up. 'To reconstruct that grim machine', he suggested, 'would be to realize with … real distinctness the essence of my biography.' It was a building where 'size (had) gone wrong' and had become 'pathological'. At once too large with seven floors and half-landings it was also pokey, dowdy and rundown. There were times when he and his sisters wondered if it was 'one vast "filth packet," and we the mere *disjecta membra* of vanished generations'. Yet alongside Dickensian decomposition, went a Victorian assurance and stability that came from the house as 'an imperturbable mass – the framework, almost the very essence – so it seemed – of our being'.[7]

Trevelyan's formative experiences, in some respects curiously similar, in their setting and ambience were very different. He grew up largely at Wallington, the family home on the edge of the Northumbrian moors. Built 'on the model of great French chateau', Wallington is stately, commodious, compact. Begun in 1688, the red-letter year of aristocratic liberation, by the mid-eighteenth century it had become a quintessentially Whig home, improved in fashionable Palladian style. It was crowned in the nineteenth century, by the creation of a great central saloon – 'one of the most remarkable rooms in any English country house', its balustrades decorated by the family's Pre-Raphaelite friends with 'portrait medallions of famous Northumbrians, culminating in the mid-nineteenth-century Trevelyans'. Like the drawing-room at Lancaster Gate, it was 'a temple erected to the spirit of Victorianism'. But the Trevelyans loved it. Trevy's father, George Otto, thought it the finest room in England. In the writing room stood the desk where Trevy's great-uncle, Thomas Macaulay, wrote his *History of England*; in the study, the table on which his father completed his *Life and Letters of Lord Macaulay* two weeks before Trevy's birth. Little wonder Trevy was convinced at the age of 18 that history would be his 'task in life', and that he wrote as if before 'a bust of Lord Macaulay'.[8]

---

7   Lytton Strachey, 'Lancaster Gate', in Michael Holroyd, ed., *Lytton Strachey by Himself: A Self-Portrait* (London: Heinemann, 1971), 16–28; S.P. Rosenbaum, *The Bloomsbury Group Memoir Club* (Basingstoke: Palgrave Macmillan, 2014), 110–12.

8   George Otto Trevelyan, 'Wallington', *Country Life*, 53 (1918), 22, 29 June 1918; R. Trevelyan, *Wallington, The National Trust* (London: The National Trust, 1994), 56–63; Stefan Collini, 'Like Family, like Nation', review of *G.M. Trevelyan: A Life in History* by David Cannadine, *Times Literary Supplement* (*TLS*), 16 October 1992, 3–4; Collini, *English Pasts* (Oxford: Oxford University Press, 1999), 10; John Batchelor, *Lady Trevelyan and the Pre-Raphaelite Brotherhood* (London: Chatto & Windus, 2006); Cannadine, *Trevelyan*, 11, 28.

Like many elite British families, the Trevelyans cared as much for the rural surrounds as for bricks and mortar. Although he lived much of his life in urban settings, Trevelyan thought of himself as a countryman. He was one of those late Victorian 'pilgrims of scenery', for whom 'landscape theology' served as a substitute religion. So, when he thought of Wallington, he thought immediately of the gardens, park and the estate, as it eased out to the 'moors and sheep runs that sweep up to the Scottish border', which he evoked in some of his best early essays. So home and nature coalesced: if Lancaster Gate for Strachey connoted rupture, disintegration, '*degringolade*', here was repose, fusion, seamless continuity.[9]

The Stracheys were an old, West Country gentry family and, according to their most recent biographer, were 'extremely conscious of their heritage and of their extensive familial connections'. To an outsider such as Leonard Woolf, 'the atmosphere of the dining room at Lancaster Gate was that of British history and of the comparatively small ruling middle class which for the last hundred years had been [its] principal makers'.[10] Lytton's oldest uncle, Sir Edward, lived in Sutton Court, the ancestral home at Stowey in Somerset – a largish fifteenth-century country house, greatly extended in Elizabethan times by the formidable Bess of Hardwick. Though modest by the standards of Bess's other homes, it reminded Lytton that his 'father and mother belonged by birth and breeding to the old English world of country-house gentlefolk'. But it also ironically highlighted the gap between their straightened material circumstances and the 'secure world of dynastic strength, piety and imperial power' whence they came.[11]

For the Stracheys were a large, long-lived dynasty – 10 or more children were common, and all five of Lytton's uncles lived into their 80s – so that his father, Richard, a third son, had to make his own way in the world. The same was true of his mother's immediate family, the Grants

---

9   Collini, 'Like Family, like Nation'; T to G.O. Trevelyan, 2 June 1918, Philip Robinson Library, University of Newcastle (PRL), Trevelyan Mss, GOT 94; G.M. Trevelyan, 'The Middle Marches', *Independent Review* (*IR*), 5 (1905), 231–40; Trevelyan, *Clio, a Muse, and Other Essays Literary and Pedestrian* (London: Longmans, Green, 1913), 56–81.
10 Barbara Caine, *Bombay to Bloomsbury: A Biography of the Strachey Family* (Oxford: Oxford University Press, 2005), 3; Leonard Woolf, *Sowing: An Autobiography of the Years 1880–1904* (London: Hogarth Press, 1960), 190.
11 John St Loe Strachey, *The Adventure of Living: A Subjective Autobiography* (London: Hodder and Stoughton, 1922), ch. 3; 'Sutton Court', *Country Life*, 45 (1910), 22 January 1910; Sir Edward Strachey, *Materials to Serve for a History of the Strachey Family*, ed. John St Loe Strachey (London: Office of The Spectator, 1899); Charles Richard Sanders, *The Strachey Family, 1588–1932: Their Writings and Literary Associations* (Durham, NC: Duke University Press, 1953), 28–40; W.C. Lubenow, 'Authority, Honour and the Strachey Family', *Historical Research*, 76:194 (2003), 511–34.

7. INTERSECTING AND CONTRASTING LIVES

of Rothiemurchus. Here, too, there was the whiff of vanished ancestral real estate, and Jane Grant's debt-encumbered forebears had to seek fame and fortune in the Empire, above all, in India. The Stracheys, too, had become primarily an Anglo-Indian family: servants of the East India Company and the Raj, 'continuously from the days of Clive and Hastings' – its colonial officials, army officers, engineers, railway builders, explorers, cartographers, meteorologists, historians and scientific collectors. Among them were Lytton's uncle, Sir John, acting Viceroy and finance minister during the 1870s, and Lieutenant General Sir Richard Strachey, Lytton's father, who, 'in length of service and variety of his claims to distinction', was described as 'the most remarkable of the Stracheys who for four generations … ha[d] given to India the best portion of their lives'.

In 1872, shortly after what he intended as a final return from India, the family acquired its first permanent home, Stowey House, a Georgian mansion, on Clapham Common, once the home of James Stephen, a leading member of the sect. Here, in 1880, Lytton was born. His birthplace, though clearly not of his choosing, was ironically emblematic – enough to prompt an absurdly tendentious essay on the decline of Victorian values by Gertrude Himmelfarb: 'From Clapham to Bloomsbury: A genealogy of Morals'.[12] But, in 1884, the family moved to Lancaster Gate – in Bayswater, known for its colonial connections as 'Little India'. And Sir Richard, though greatly admired by Lytton, by now 67, was cut off from his younger children by age, deafness and outside interests: a kindly but remote, olympian figure.[13]

Thus, the household Lytton inhabited for quarter of a century was dominated by his mother, Jane, and his unwed sisters, Dorothy, Pippa, Pernel and Marjorie. Intelligent, cultured, independent women, they did much to nurture Lytton's knowledge and love of literature. But they overindulged the sickly lad. Perhaps that was the trouble: to Lytton, the female, nursing-home atmosphere of Bemax and Dr Gregory's Rhubarb Oil was claustrophobic and inhibiting. But it was also wonderfully stimulating and reassuring. There were many Victorian worlds. And alongside his father's world of technological, scientific and scholarly advancement was the mince, quince and runcible spoon world of Edward Lear: what Leon Edel, in a deft evocation of Lytton's childhood, describes

---

12   Gertrude Himmelfarb, *Marriage and Morals among the Victorians* (New York: Knopf, 1986), 23–49.
13   Caine, *Bombay to Bloomsbury*, 68–9; Holroyd, *LSNB*, 5–6.

as 'a verbal world, an eternal nursery' where he danced, dressed up, wrote and acted plays with his sisters, or played 'Blue Fly' to his mother's 'Bumble Bee'.[14]

The Trevelyans too were, by origin, an ancient West Country gentry family. For centuries they had lived at Nettlecombe Court, a honeystoned Elizabethan country house with an estate of 20,000 acres in South Somerset. Here, they perennially served as knights of the Shire – Country Tories, obscure, independent, invariably out of office. Then a series of fortuitous marriages, inheritances that included Wallington and three generations of administrative, political and cultural distinction raised them above the common run of squires. Trevelyan's grandfather, Charles Edward, who inherited Wallington from a cousin, was an energetic, self-made civil service mandarin, so unbending as to be pilloried by Anthony Trollope in the character of 'Sir Gregory Hardlines'.[15] An ardent liberal reformer, he helped transform India's trade and education, presided over Irish Famine relief, initiated the rebuilding of Whitehall and authored the famous Northcote–Trevelyan report, British public administration's 'Bill of Rights'.[16] Life for him was a battlefield, where the forces of altruistic moral progress constantly had to be mobilised against tradition and vested interest. Even more important than his embattled reformist imprint was his marriage to Hannah, beloved sister to Thomas Macaulay, the essayist and historian. Over the years, Macaulay became virtually a member of the family, sharing their house in Calcutta and at Western Lodge on Clapham Common. Living next door to the hallowed 'Battersea Rise' – into the 1850s the shrine of progressive Evangelicalism – the Trevelyan household was closer in spirit to the original 'Saints' than were the later inhabitants of Stowey House.[17]

---

14 Holroyd, *LSNB*, 18ff; Leon Edel, *Bloomsbury: A House of Lions* (London: Hogarth Press, 1979), 35; Lytton Strachey, correspondence with Jane Strachey 1885–1897, with frequent insect greetings, HRHC, Strachey Mss, Box 3, folders 7–8; Box 4, folder 1; Box 5, folders 3–5.
15 G.M. Trevelyan, *An Autobiography and Other Essays*, 1–5; Laura Trevelyan, *A Very British Family: The Trevelyans and their World* (London: I.B. Taurus, 2006), 8, 12–15, 24–25; Anthony Trollope, *The Three Clerks: A Novel* (London: Richard Bentley, 1858).
16 The Northcote–Trevelyan Report of 1854 established the DNA of the modern civil service: recruitment by competitive examination, a graded hierarchy and promotion on merit.
17 John Clive, *Macaulay: The Shaping of the Historian* (New York: Knopf, 1973), 316–18, 344, 351–3; Humphrey Trevelyan, *Public and Private* (London: Hamish Hamilton, 1980); Christopher Tolley, *Domestic Biography: The Legacy of Evangelicalism in Four Nineteenth-Century Families* (Oxford: Clarendon Press, 1997), 196–219, doi.org/10.1093/acprof:oso/9780198206514.001.0001; L. Trevelyan, *A Very British Family*, 32–7.

Yet Charles's son, George Otto, proved an oblique specimen of evangelical descent: 'a hearty Protestant', he inherited his father's reforming zeal and his uncle's bookishness. But he 'did not understand Christianity'. Described as 'a busy pushing man … for ever writing, speaking, questioning … ready with remedies for all things', George Otto was a leading Liberal who enjoyed high office in all four Gladstone governments. Yet he never quite decided whether to be a 'stormy' reformer after the manner of his father, or an orthodox Whig like Uncle Tom. He loved the House of Commons, but shied away from the drudgery of political office. Life was too easy; he loved Wallington; he was wealthy and he spread himself thin. A gifted polymath, part politician, part historian, part biographer, a clever versifier, accomplished essayist and classicist, he had, he said, 'a craving for literature, like … some people for drink'. He had inherited his uncle's narrative skill, to which he added a classical refinement and aristocratic sensibility: qualities evident in all he wrote, from *The Competition Wallah*, his critical sociology of Anglo-Indian manners after the Mutiny, and *Cawnpore*, his horror narrative of 1857, to his fond recreation of the world of eighteenth-century Whig politics in *The Early History of Charles James Fox*, and his multi-volumed *The American Revolution*. Best of all was his 900-page *Life and Letters of Lord Macaulay*, perhaps the finest Victorian biography.[18]

As the setting of George Otto's first writings indicated, in the nineteenth century the Trevelyans also had become an Anglo-Indian family. In three tours of duty spanning the period from 1826 to 1865, Charles Edward served as First Assistant to the Resident in Delhi, private secretary to the Governor-General in Calcutta, Governor of Madras and eventually Finance Minister for the whole Raj. During his last years on the subcontinent from 1862 to 1865, he and Hannah lived next door to Colonel Richard Strachey, then Secretary for Public Works. Charles thought him 'sanguine, ambitious and strongly disposed to partisanship'.[19] Their politics were very different. As political advisor to the evangelistic Governor-General, Lord William Bentinck, in the 1830s, Trevelyan became a crusader for the replacement of traditional Hindu and Muslim beliefs by Christianity,

---

18 G.M. Trevelyan, *George Otto Trevelyan: A Memoir* (London: Longmans, Green, 1932), 20–2; G.O. Trevelyan, *The Competition Wallah* (London: Macmillan, 1864); G.O. Trevelyan, *Cawnpore* (London: Macmillan, 1865); G.O. Trevelyan, *The Early History of Charles James Fox* (London: Longmans, Green, 1881); G.O. Trevelyan, *The American Revolution* (London: Longmans, Green, 1899); G.O. Trevelyan, *Life and Letters of Lord Macaulay* (London: Longmans, Green, 1876).
19 Raleigh Trevelyan, *The Golden Oriole: A 200-Year History of an English Family in India* (London: Secker & Warburg, 1987), 411–12, 436.

of indigenous learning by western scholarship and of native vernaculars by English. Cured of superstition and error, 'trained by us to happiness and independence, and endowed with our learning and institutions', Indians, he believed, would learn to govern themselves, and 'we shall exchange profitable subjects for still more profitable allies'.[20]

Richard Strachey, by contrast, was typical of the new breed of technocrats who dominated the Raj after the Mutiny. If institutional and educational reform had been the galvanising principle of British rule in the 1830s, modernisation and territorial consolidation were those of the following decades. The system after 1857 was stiffer, more remote: its watchwords control, efficiency, hierarchy and difference rather than reform, progress and assimilation. The downward filtration expectations of the Bentinck era were now seen as a delusion. Far more useful to the imperial project than evangelical teachers, seeking to inculcate 'the diffusive benevolence' of British education, were the builders and modernisers of India's economic infrastructure that would underpin its prosperity under the rule of Viceroys such as the Tory Lord Lytton, after whom Lytton Strachey was named.[21] So, in the 1870s, as the Trevelyans reaffirmed the Whig vision of Indian self-development and self-government, the Stracheys and their friends restated their belief in enlightened colonial despotism. 'The only hope for India', Sir John Strachey wrote in 1903, was 'the long continuance of the benevolent but strong government of Englishmen': an 'illusion of permanence' accepted by the family till 1914.[22]

---

20   R. Trevelyan, *The Golden Oriole*, 139–58, 214–15, 285–7, 326; Charles E. Trevelyan, *On the Education of the People of India* (London: Longman, 1838); Eric Stokes, *The English Utilitarians and India* (Oxford: Oxford University Press, 1959).
21   Thomas R. Metcalf, *Ideologies of the Raj: The New Cambridge History of India*, Vol. 3, Part 4 (Cambridge: Cambridge University Press, 1988), 66–159.
22   C. Trevelyan, House of Commons, Select Committee on East Indian Finances, *The Times*, 31 July 1873; Letters on The Famine in Bengal, *The Times*, 27 November 1873; G.O. Trevelyan, *The Competition Wallah*; James Fitzjames Stephen, *Liberty, Equality, Fraternity* (dedicated to Sir John Strachey; London: Smith Elder, 1873), xix–xx; Sir John Strachey, *India: Its Administration and Progress* (3rd ed., with new preface; London: Macmillan, 1903) x–xi; Metcalf, *Ideologies of the Raj*, 206–11; Ranbir Vohra, *The Making of India: A Political History* (New York: Armonk, 2014), 87; Francis G. Hutchins, *The Illusion of Permanence: The British in India* (Princeton: Princeton University Press, 1967), doi.org/10.1515/9781400879649. The family repeatedly stated this belief up to 1914: Lytton Strachey, 'The First Earl of Lytton', *IR*, 12 (March 1907), 332–8; Strachey, 'The Guides', *Spectator*, 15 August 1908; Lady Jane Strachey, 'That India Should Not Be Allowed Self-Government', Speech to Lyceum Club, 15 March 1910, quoted in Caine, *Bombay to Bloomsbury*, 49–50; Joan Pernel to S, 1 March 1914, BL, Add.Ms., 60,726, f. 4.

7. INTERSECTING AND CONTRASTING LIVES

The Trevelyan household, like the Stracheys', was a happy one. But it was also masculine and highly politicised. If Lytton was, to some degree, 'made feminine by the femininity of his environment', Trevelyan was made 'manly' by his. Instead of sisters, he had brothers; instead of amateur theatricals, they played Napoleonic war games; they spent hours of outdoor activities on the estate and they walked on a heroic scale. For George especially, mountain walking was a regular tonic and a spiritual experience: 'the best means whereby a man might regain possession of his own soul, by rejoining him in sacred union with nature'. Every Easter from 1899, the 'Trevies' and their friends went on 'The Man Hunt', a five-day game of fellside running, scrambling and sleeping rough in the Lake District, devised by George in an attempt to recreate the excitements of the great chase in Robert Louis Stevenson's *Kidnapped*.[23] Yet the brothers – Charles the radical politician, Robert the classicist, and George the historian – were no philistines. Admittedly, they had no small talk. They lectured one another; they were abrupt, plain-speaking, often rude. But they also recited and wrote poetry. George started serious writing at eight with a biographical collage of British leaders in the Napoleonic wars, and at school he composed enormous sub-Tennysonian verse epics on 'Columbus', 'Sir John Franklin', and 'The Prophet' or 'A Song of the People'.[24]

By upbringing and education, as well as lineage, George Trevelyan belonged far more decisively than Lytton Strachey to the political elite. Following his brothers, he was sent to Wixenford, an exclusive preparatory school where the headmaster was a distant cousin of the great Dr Arnold. He went then to Harrow, where his history teacher and housemaster Edward Bowen – author of Harrow's school songs – was a close family friend. The school, remodelled after the pattern of Arnold's Rugby, was at the peak of its prestige, having already produced five nineteenth-century prime ministers. But, by the 1880s, Harrow had also become a High Tory preserve, and Trevelyan's politics were radical Liberal. When he was not in the library immersed in Ruskin, Shelley and Tennyson, or in his study, 'keeping the

---

[23] Cannadine, *Trevelyan*, 144, 146; Mary Moorman, *George Macaulay Trevelyan: A Memoir by his Daughter* (London: Hamish Hamilton, 1980), 68–70; G.M. Trevelyan, 'Walking', in *Clio, A Muse and Other Essays*, 1–19, esp. 3–4; R.C. Trevelyan, *Windfalls: Notes and Essays* (London: Allen & Unwin, 1944); Alan Hankinson, *Geoffrey Winthrop Young: Poet, Mountaineer, Educator* (London: Hodder & Stoughton, 1995), 45–6.

[24] Trevelyan's school poetry can be found in *Prolusiones ... Scholae Harroviensis* (Harrow: Privately Printed, 1892), 51–5; ibid. (1893), 31–44, 54–59; precis of poems in *The Harrovian*, 18 February, 5 July 1893; Christopher Tyerman, *A History of Harrow School, 1324–1991* (Oxford: Oxford University Press, 2000), 355–70, doi.org/10.1093/acprof:oso/9780198227960.001.0001.

flame of [his] liberalism bright in this dark corner', he was firing off daily screeds to brother Charles, about 'true democracy', 'the gospel of the poor', and 'the progress of the human race', signing his letters 'God Save Ireland', 'God Save the People', or GSI and GSP, for short. But saving Ireland or the People was not Harrow's line, and Trevelyan found himself 'the democratic exception in this high-class establishment'. As a militant agnostic he also refused to take Confirmation – a refusal the headmaster responded to, he said, 'with a religious bigotry worthy of Ignatius Loyola'.[25]

Lytton's schooling, apart from a brief stint at Marie Souvestre's academy, where his French and English literary skills were nurtured, was less select and fortunate. There was Abbotsholme, a spartan, religiose establishment, which advertised itself as 'an advanced Educational Laboratory', devoted to producing the cultural missionaries who would rescue the Empire from degeneracy through 'the natural method' of physical and mental toughening later associated with 'Outward Bound'. After two terms, Lytton's health gave way completely. So he was sent instead to Leamington College, a demi-semi public school that practised the more traditional arts of philistinism, buggery and bullying. Here he learnt to deflect peer hostility by playing clever court jester, a role that soon became second nature. Here, too, he experienced 'that extraordinary sense of melt[ing] into a body literally twice as big as one's own' – boys blessed with the looks, physiques and popularity he so lacked.[26] The discovery of Plato's *Symposium* in 1896 came to him 'with a rush of … surprise [and] relief to know what I feel now, was felt 2000 years ago in glorious Greece'. But living in the shadow of Reading Gaol, he had to fight a sense of uncleanness. By the time he left school, he was an unusual mix: timid, irresolute, insecure, 'naturally biddable', but also self-dramatising, droll, outrageous and secretly rebellious. With his supercilious talk, stick-insect physique, and give-away voice – described as the 'breathless squeak of an asthmatic rabbit' – he was also a provocation: a 'queer' who made even discreet homosexuality dangerous.[27]

---

25   Moorman, *George Macaulay Trevelyan*, 21–2; T to G.O. and C. Trevelyan, 23 February, 9 November, [n.d.] November 1892, 5 July 1893, PRL, Trevelyan Mss, GOT 87; T to C.P. Trevelyan, 23 January, 13 February, 19 March, 'Easter', 'April-May', 13, 14, 17, 21 May, 1, 18, 25, 29 June, 5, 19 July 1893 (all from Harrow), PRL, Trevelyan Mss, CPT, Ex 194; Trevelyan, *An Autobiography and Other Essays*, 3, 9, 15.
26   Holroyd, *LSNB*, 28–32; Caine, *Bombay to Bloomsbury*, 113–15.
27   S, Diary, 13 November 1996, in Holroyd, *Lytton Strachey by Himself*, 86; Julie Anne Taddeo, *Lytton Strachey and the Search for Modern Sexual Identity: The Last Eminent Victorian* (New York: Harrington Park Press, 2002), 22–3; Holroyd, *LSNB*, 42–3; W.G. Robertson, *Time Was: The Reminiscences of W. Graham Robertson* (London: Hamish Hamilton, 1931), 16–17.

Trevelyan was a 'serious gowk': irreligious, but terribly earnest. And he recognised it: 'I am forced to confess,' he wrote his brother, 'we inherit the moral stamina produced in Grandpa by religion and apply it straight to our infidel sense of duty.' Shortly before going up to Cambridge, he told Charles of his tasks in 'the battle for life'. His ideal was 'the wedding of the modern democratic spirit, the spirit of duty in its highest form, to modern literature'. But, he wrote, 'literary people are not most of them, democratic', and 'Cambridge people are intellectual but not serious'. So, 'unless I keep my fire ever kindled within me, I shall soon forget my "motif" and become a mere "littérateur"'![28] In addition to the hard work that earned him a First, a Prize essay and a Trinity fellowship at the age of 21, he was active in many progressive causes – Irish Home Rule, opposition to British policies in Egypt, India and, above all, 'the Devil's kitchen in South Africa'. He wrote passionately on the 'Condition of England' problem, and devoted much of his spare time to adult education, organising Trinity summer schools and teaching at the Working Men's College in London.[29]

Strachey arrived in Cambridge seven years later, in 1899. University for him was not 'a battle for life', still less a test of political engagement or good works. Rather it was a liberation, a place of unrestrained talk and enduring friendships – with the male core of 'Old Bloomsbury' – or, as Leon Edel puts it, 'a romp, a lark, a phallic universe'.[30] Early in his first year, he was 'taken up' by Trevelyan. As a junior fellow, Trevy was responsible for sponsoring Lytton's election to a College Scholarship, to the elite Sunday Essay Club and, above all, to the Cambridge Apostles. He was greatly impressed with Lytton's poetic and literary abilities, and he looked to him as a potential ally in the defence of the literary and humane traditions of English historical writing. 'He will write history well some day, and I am leading him out of cynicism into the dry land of Carlylean defiance and pity,' Trevelyan told his mother, 'he is worth leading and I am getting very fond of him.' 'He is most friendly and kind,' Strachey told his mother, 'and very much like I imagined his father to be.' But there was an undertow of passive aggression in his response: 'He is very eager', he wrote, but 'too

---

28   T to C.P. Trevelyan, 19 July, 4 August 1893, PRL, Trevelyan Mss, CPT, Ex 194; Moorman, *George Macaulay Trevelyan*, 35–6; L. Trevelyan, *A Very British Family*, 117.
29   T to G.O. Trevelyan, 12 May, 17, 20 October, 12 December 1900, PRL, Trevelyan Mss, GOT 91; G.M. Trevelyan, 'Past and Future', in C.F.G. Masterman, ed., *The Heart of Empire* (London: Unwin, 1901), 398–415; G.M. Trevelyan, 'The White Peril', *The Nineteenth Century*, 50 (1901), 1043–55.
30   Edel, *Bloomsbury*, 39, 44; Lytton Strachey, 'A Sermon Preached before the Midnight Society', 5 May 1900; Strachey, 'Conversation and Conversations', 3 November 1901, BL, Add.Ms., 81,813, folder 1, 8.

earnest, patristic and virulent' and 'somewhat piteous'.[31] Lytton found the 'overwhelming enthusiasm' and heavy-handed mentoring 'alarming', and he started poking fun, as in the parable of 'Cleanthes the Stoic':

> 'For the last six months,' said Cleanthes, 'I have been very busy. I have written four more chapters of my history of Cos … I have given several lectures … attended countless … committees, boards and syndicates … walked from Athens to Corinth … twenty five times … taken a great deal of exercise, and done a great deal of work, a great deal of talking and a great deal of good.'[32]

The tension reflected not only temperamental dissonance, but also generational change. Generational rupture was to become one of the leitmotifs of Strachey's thought. His father, born within months of the battle of Waterloo, was too old. So were the 'bilious' uncles he recalled at Lancaster Gate. Admittedly, his mother was younger, and Lytton was strongly tied to her aesthetically and emotionally; however, she was 'a consenting and approving Victorian', was 'not up to date in morals', and 'ha(d) never heard of buggery – at any rate in her own family'. There was much he could not tell her: 'Oh, how dreadful to be a mother,' he said to Maynard Keynes, 'how terrible to love so much and know so little.'[33] According to Russell's somewhat jaundiced verdict:

> J.M. Keynes and Lytton Strachey both belonged to the Cambridge generation about ten years junior to my own. We were still Victorian; they were Edwardian. We believed in ordered progress by means of politics and open discussion … The generation of Keynes and Strachey … aimed rather at a life of retirement among fine shades and nice feelings, and conceived of the good as consisting in the passionate mutual admirations of a clique of the elite.[34]

---

31   T to S, 2 March 1900, 22 March 1902, BL, Add.Ms, 60,732, ff. 180–5; T to Caroline Trevelyan, 1 December 1900, PRL, Trevelyan Mss, GOT 94; S to Joan Pernel Strachey, 10 March, 3 May 1900, BL, Add.Ms., 60,724, ff. 86–92; S to Jane Strachey, 11 March, 29 April 1900, 24 March 1902, HRHC, Strachey Mss, Box 4, folder 2; Holroyd, *LSNB*, 61–2; Cannadine, *Trevelyan*, 41–2.

32   Strachey, 'Aphorisms', BL, Add.Ms., 81,916, no. 40; partly printed in Gabriel Merle, *Lytton Strachey (1880–1932): Biographie et critique d'un critique et biographe* (Paris: Honoré Champion, 1980), 911.

33   Vanessa Bell to Virginia Woolf, 18 January 1918, New York Public Library, Berg Collection, Virginia Woolf Papers, Incoming Correspondence; Quentin Bell, *Virginia Woolf, A Biography* (2 vols; London: Hogarth Press, 1972), vol. 2, 60; Virginia Woolf to Vanessa Bell, 17 January 1918, in Nigel Nicolson and Joanne Trautmann, eds, *Letters of Virginia Woolf*, Volume II (London: Hogarth Press, 1976), 212–13; S to John Maynard Keynes, 27 February 1906, King's College, Cambridge, (KC), Keynes Mss, PP/45/316/2, f. 130.

34   Bertrand Russell, 'Portraits from Memory', *The Listener*, 17 July 1952, 97, reprinted in Russell, *Portraits from Memory and Other Essays* (London: Allen & Unwin, 1956), 73–5.

7. INTERSECTING AND CONTRASTING LIVES

In Trevelyan, this sense of generational rupture was wholly absent. Independent he might be; rebel he was not. George Otto, born in 1838, active in politics and history writing until the First World War, was his natural confidante on matters literary, historical and political, as was Lady Caroline, born in 1849 and into the 1920s an advanced reformer, on his social, educational and personal concerns. And if his parents' interests reached into the twentieth century, his own reached back to the nineteenth, through his father to Macaulay and Holland House, and through his mother to the Manchester mercantile dynasties and the world of the First Reform Bill. So completely did he project the values of his elders that by the time he reached his 30s, he was seen by his Cambridge juniors as an 'old dear' – an anachronism.[35]

By 1900, the Trevelyans had become very wealthy. Frugal habits, astute marriages, culminating in George Otto's to Caroline Philips, the inheritor of a cotton fortune, and a large copyright income from Macaulay's and George Otto's books saw to it that the brothers enjoyed large private incomes. But George was too angular a character, too complicit with the demise of privilege, too much a son of Clapham simply to enjoy his position. Somehow he had to earn it. So, he spoke of the need for self-discipline and drove himself all his life.[36] The Stracheys were relatively poor, and Lytton was painfully aware that his family had come down in the world. Long before Virginia Woolf patented the phrase, he wrote of his longing for 'a room of one's own', and he envied the 'uncontending ease' of the Trevelyans. But he had none of their guilts either. Cosseted from infancy, he believed he had a right to the good things of life. It could never be said of him as of Trevelyan, 'his was a character inadequately warmed by self-indulgence'. Like the Carpenter, he wanted another slice.[37]

It was in the Apostles that the differences between Trevelyan's late Victorian angst and Strachey's Edwardian levity came to a head. Discussions at the turn of the century, under the influence of G.E. Moore – the great Cambridge guru of the era – focused on the distinction between

---

35 S to Leonard Woolf, 23 March 1903, 1 June 1905 (on Russell as 'a medieval figure'), 6 February 1907 (Rupert Brooke on Trevy as 'an old dear'), HRHC, Strachey Mss, Box 4, folder 5.
36 Cannadine, *Trevelyan*, 47; John Burrow, review of *George Macaulay Trevelyan* by Mary Moorman, *The Times*, 1 July 1980; John Vincent, 'G.M. Trevelyan's Two Terrible Things', *LRB*, 2:12, 19 June 1980.
37 S to Duncan Grant, 23 August 1909, BL, Add.Ms., 57,932; 'Walruses and Carpenters', *Spectator*, 9 December 1911. This article was signed 'Z', as were a number of Strachey's other contributions to the *Spectator* between 1908 and 1912. In this article, S refers to Trevelyan and Dickinson as 'Walruses' and to himself and some of his fellow Apostles as 'Carpenters'.

'reality' and 'phenomena', and on the nature of 'the good'. Was 'reality' a timeless area of truth and contemplation or was it the material world? And was being good or doing good more important: was the active or the contemplative life the ideal? Trevelyan was fully convinced that 'the only way of getting at reality, was by <u>the phenomenal expression of it</u>'. As he put it to his mother, 'If life consisted of right thinking, it might be successfully lived; but, it consists also of right doing and right creating, <u>a very different matter</u>'. There was no point in feeling or even being good if one did not improve the world. 'Action', he told the Apostles, was 'the main thing in life': it was only by action, that one could make oneself a human agent capable of ethical thinking at all. Doing good also meant fighting evil: 'Liberalism,' he told Moore was 'the forcible social realization of the principle of Hatred of Evil, which I take … to be an essential part of love of good.'[38]

For Moore and Strachey, however, the ultimate realities were 'good states of mind'. These were intrinsic and were not associated with 'instrumental actions'. They consisted of timeless, passionate states of contemplation and communion. The appropriate subjects of contemplation and communion were a beloved person, beauty and truth, and the 'prime objects in life were love, the enjoyment of aesthetic experiences and the pursuit of knowledge' – to the exclusion of all else. Strachey deplored the belief that 'you are definitely improved if you do social work and go into Parliament or an engagement at the Working Men's College', and that 'the dynamic life is the proper one to lead'. This view was, for him, 'detestable. I want to throttle it', he said, 'put it out of the way. The phenomenal world oppresses me like an undigested nightmare'.[39] According to Russell, there was 'a long drawn out battle' between Trevelyan and Strachey for the soul of the Apostles, 'in which Lytton was on the whole victorious'.

---

38   T to Caroline Trevelyan, April–May 1896, PRL, Trevelyan Mss, GOT 89, ff. 84–5; T to G.E. Moore, July–September 1895, esp. 26 July 1896 (a 20-page letter); Moore Papers, Cambridge University Library (CUL), Additional Mss, 8330, 8T/12/4-8; Cambridge Apostles' Papers, Minute Books, 1893–1898, KC: KCAS/39/1/12: 6 June 1896, 13 February, 1 May 1897, and esp. 21 May 1898 in response to Moore's paper entitled, 'Shall we think without acting, or act without thinking?'.
39   John Maynard Keynes, 'My Early Beliefs', a paper read to the Bloomsbury Memoir Club in 1938, is the classic formulation. See S.P. Rosenbaum, *The Bloomsbury Group: A Collection of Memoirs, Commentary and Criticism* (revised ed.; Toronto: University of Toronto Press, 1995), 82–95; S to G.E. Moore, 11 October 1903, CUL, Moore Papers, Additional Mss, 8330, 8T/44/1; Leonard Woolf, 'George or George or Both' Paper to the Cambridge Apostles, 9 May 1903, summarises the conflict between George Trevelyan and George (or, as he preferred, G.E.) Moore: Leonard Woolf Archive, Part 2, O/2 University of Sussex Special Collections; Strachey, 'Shall We Go the Whole Hog?', Paper to the Cambridge Apostles, 25 February 1905, BL, Add.Ms., 81,890, in Avery, *The Works of Lytton Strachey: Early Papers*, 99–103.

7. INTERSECTING AND CONTRASTING LIVES

Russell thought it was all about sex – and homosexual relations, hitherto dormant, became rampant in the society under the influence of Strachey and Keynes – but it ranged more widely: it was also about art and politics, good states of mind and good deeds, the active and the passive life.[40]

At this stage in his career, Trevelyan, according to Leonard Woolf, was 'a fiercely political young man'. In 1903, in protest at Bury's inaugural on 'the science of history', he left the introverted world of academe to devote himself to public writing and good works, and in 1904, he married Janet, daughter of Mary Ward, the celebrated novelist, philanthropist and grandchild of Dr Arnold.[41] Living on the edge of Pimlico, they were both prominent in a range of progressive causes – children's play centres, conservation, land reform, open diplomacy. And George was a member of various organisations formed in support of national independence and reform movements in Europe and the Middle East. In 1903, he had established and funded a new progressive journal, *The Independent Review*, a twentieth-century '*Edinburgh*' review of 'advanced views on politics and ideas … above party', and he recruited congenial Apostles including Russell, Dickinson, Roger Fry and Strachey to write for it. Infused with the ethic of service to the people, and by the *philosophe* ideal of stamping out ignorance and prejudice through education – inspired, he said, by 'the career and example' of Voltaire to put his 'wealth' and 'talent' to more than 'the selfish … egotism which we know as "academic"' – he also lectured many times a week at adult educational institutions: the Working Men's and Morley Colleges, Toynbee Hall, and Mary Ward's charitable foundation, the Passmore Edwards Settlement in Bloomsbury.[42]

But it was primarily as a historian and biographer that he meant to galvanise 'the modern democratic spirit'. His books were all designed as public statements, books that would 'make a difference', Liberal 'tracts for

---

40 Russell, *Autobiography*, I, 74; Cannadine, *Trevelyan*, 42; Richard Deacon, *The Cambridge Apostles: A History of Cambridge University's Élite Intellectual Secret Society* (London: R. Royce, 1985), 55–68 overstates the case.

41 G.M. Trevelyan, 'The Latest View of History', *IR*, 1 (1903), 395–414. On the marriage with Janet Ward, see 56 letters between T and Janet Ward in 1903 and 1904; also Janet Ward to Mary Ward, 9 February, 3 April 1904, PRL, Trevelyan Mss, MM 2/2/1; T's letters to his parents, 1903–4, PRL, Trevelyan Mss, GOT 96. Strachey's take on the wedding is found in S to Leonard Woolf, 20 March 1904, in Paul Levy, ed., *The Letters of Lytton Strachey* (London: Penguin 2005), 23–4.

42 'A Plea for a Programme', *IR*, 1 (1903), 1–27; T to S, October 1903, BL, Add.Ms., 70,732, f. 187; Moorman, *George Macaulay Trevelyan*, 51; John Sutherland, *Mrs. Humphry Ward: Eminent Victorian, Pre-eminent Edwardian* (Oxford: Clarendon Press, 1990); Janet Penrose Trevelyan, *The Life of Mrs. Humphry Ward* (London: Constable, 1923).

the times'. He honestly believed that the lives of the heroes he laid before the public – freedom fighters such as Garibaldi or reformers such as John Bright, teaching by example – could transform brutalised artisans into good citizens and culturally fulfilled human beings. 'Service to mankind,' he wrote, 'though it may be the same thing as service of truth, must be put first, in so far as the two are separate. I do not mean I should falsify history to serve any end, but that I must act as an interpreter of history, in the truest sense, to all those who ... read books.' But to reach the reading public, history must be accessible. Hence, Trevelyan's opposition to the new 'scientific' orthodoxy promoted by Bury – to the methods of painstaking research and dry 'objectivity', which so easily turned into 'unenlightened pedantry'.[43]

He had inherited Macaulay's view of history as a branch of literature and an essential part of the national culture, and he was a great believer in the symbiosis of literary history and progressive politics. But he surpassed his great-uncle in his enthusiasms and sensibilities. Unlike Macaulay, he genuinely warmed to the freedom fighters and radicals of the past. Much of his enthusiasm came from Carlyle. The greatest of Victorian prophets, the Sage of Chelsea was at the height of his repute in Trevelyan's early years. And Trevy was a fervent disciple. Like Carlyle, he believed that history was 'the essence of innumerable biographies', that its function was to 'breed enthusiasm' and that its method was imaginative, empathetic, rhetorical and exemplary. History, he said, was 'a perpetual evangel': it was 'man's ... attainment that [was] the great lesson of the past and the great theme of history'. Here too, one can sense the presence of Lord Acton, the presiding genius of the Cambridge History, who first set him on the path of historical writing. For Acton insisted on the importance of individuality, morality and free choice: 'soul cannot be mixed with soul', he declared, 'each individual stands apart'.[44]

---

43   Moorman, *George Macaulay Trevelyan*, 51–2; T to G.O. Trevelyan, 1 August 1895, [undated] 1896, PRL, Trevelyan Mss, GOT 88, ff. 11–13, 89, ff. 30ff; Vincent, 'G.M. Trevelyan's Two Terrible Things'.
44   Victor Feske, *From Belloc to Churchill: Private Scholars, Public Culture and the Crisis of English Liberalism* (Chapel Hill: University of North Carolina Press, 1996), 4–5, 141–2, 150; Cannadine, *Trevelyan*, 26–31; Trevelyan's passion for Carlyle can best be followed in his correspondence with his parents and brothers between 1895 and 1901: see PRL, Trevelyan Mss, GOT 88–94; CPT, Ex 195–7; Raina, *George Macaulay Trevelyan*, 21, 82; G.M. Trevelyan, 'Carlyle as an Historian', *The Nineteenth Century*, 48 (September 1899), 493–503; Trevelyan, 'Carlyle, Cromwell and Professor Firth', *IR*, 4 (1904–5), 302–8; Trevelyan, *England in the Age of Wycliffe* (London: Longmans, Green, 1899), 3–5; Trevelyan, 'Lord Acton's Liberalism', *IR*, 2 (1904), 651–6.

The familiar nodal points of the Whig story naturally formed the substance of Trevy's early writing. But his treatment of these episodes broadened and radicalised ancestral themes in a way that reflected the social, economic and international preoccupations of his age. His histories focused on the heroic action of individuals – Wycliffe, Hampden, Bright, Grey, above all Garibaldi, whose career he celebrated in three vivid volumes from 1906 to 1911 – to bring about religious and political freedom, democracy, reform and national liberation against the odds. As such, they illustrated a fundamentally optimistic storyline: a progressive morality tale wrought by heroes against injustice.[45] But just as important to him as 'Clio the evangel' was 'Clio the muse'. Trevelyan was a poet manqué: to study the past was to experience 'the poetry of Time'. History for him was the repository of 'rest and beauty so alien to the spirit of our age', 'an ever-present antidote' to its 'social ills' and 'visions of ugliness'. So his progressivism was undercut by nostalgia. In recapturing the landscapes of the past – and his sense of place was far more acute than his understanding of persons – Trevelyan, the celebrant of unspoilt nature, critic of industrialisation, would-be rescuer of ordinary lives from the urban 'abyss', also mourned the collapse of traditional communities and the passage of time itself.[46]

Biographers are in the character business, and Trevy's heroes were impossibly noble. He was baffled by psychological complexity, divided loyalties, mixed motives, worldliness, cynicism. Sexual relations disturbed him. Private life lay outside his brief. His idealisation of, and self-identification with, Garibaldi was especially strong. But it was also, in Richard Holmes's telling epithet, 'pre-biographic': a form of self-projection never counterbalanced by the process of distancing or disillusion. By rewalking all Garibaldi's marches across Italy – reliving and internalising the story – Trevelyan acquired a second, adventitiously heroic, identity. By fusing his persona as a frustrated political activist with his protagonist's, and his protagonist's agency with Italy's, he joined the personal with the national. Conversely, Garibaldi's enemies were villains out of *grand guignol*, building futile barriers against the flow of history. Trevelyan's biographies were very successful, but in the long run their

---

45 G.M. Trevelyan, *Wycliffe*; Trevelyan, *England under the Stuarts* (London: Methuen, 1904); Trevelyan, *The Life of John Bright* (London: Constable, 1913); Trevelyan, *Lord Grey of the Reform Bill* (London: Longmans, Green, 1920; partly written before 1914). For Garibaldi, see below, fn. 47.
46 G.M. Trevelyan, 'The Latest View of History', 412–14; Trevelyan, *Clio, A Muse and Other Essays*, 140–76; Trevelyan, 'The Present Position of History', Inaugural Lecture, Cambridge 1927, 15–16, also published in *Clio, A Muse and Other Essays* (2nd ed.; London: Longmans, 1930), 177–96; Cannadine, *Trevelyan*, ch. 4; Trevelyan, 'The White Peril', 1043–55.

success was intellectually disabling. He went on telling familiar reverential stories into the 1920s – adding further slabs to the public tombstones Strachey ridiculed in *Eminent Victorians*.[47]

Strachey was one of those whom Trevy had lined up to write against the new scientific orthodoxy in *The Independent Review*. But Strachey's view of the journal was ambivalent – he called it 'The Phenomenal Review' – and his response to Bury was never published. For his essay on 'The Historian of the Future' found *both* Bury and Trevelyan guilty of confusing identity and purpose, the nature of history with the good it was supposed to do. Unfortunately, he continued – drawing on Moore's distinction between intrinsic and instrumental value – people were never satisfied with things of value, but had to question their uses or the ends they served. Literature, music and art, however, were simply good in themselves; it was otiose to show they produced good results. So, too, history: it was not a vocational discipline like law or medicine, nor was it a moral parade ground or a social service industry. Its role was to amuse and delight. Its value was purely aesthetic. 'The past is irrevocable,' Strachey wrote, 'its good and evil are fixed and done with; and we can look at it dispassionately as if it were a work of art.'[48]

Yet Lytton's first formal attempt at writing history was far from dispassionate. Rather, it was a piece of family piety. Both Lytton's uncle and family friend Fitzjames Stephen had written in defence of Hastings's policies in India and against his detractors. So Lytton's fellowship essay on 'Warren Hastings, Cheyt Sing and the Begums of Oude' was a chip off the family block. Written at a time when enlightened colonial despotism was being celebrated as never before, it was engaged and partisan.[49]

---

47   G.M. Trevelyan, *Garibaldi's Defence of the Roman Republic* (London: Longmans, Green, 1907), 2–4, 7, 23–4; Trevelyan, *Garibaldi and the Thousand* (London: Longmans, Green, 1909), 3, 7–9; Trevelyan, *Garibaldi and the Making of Italy* (London: Longmans, Green, 1911), 289–91, 296; Lucy Riall, *Garibaldi: The Invention of a Hero* (New Haven, CT: Yale University Press, 2007), 13–14; Richard Holmes, *Footsteps, Adventures of a Romantic Biographer* (London: Penguin, 1985), 66–8; Alastair MacLachlan, 'Becoming National: G.M. Trevelyan, The Dilemmas of a Liberal (Inter) nationalist', in 'Nationalism and Biography: European Perspectives', Jonathan Hearn and Christian Wicke, eds, *Humanities Research*, XIX:1 (2013), 28.
48   S to Leonard Woolf, 28 August 1903, HRHC, Strachey Mss, Box 4, folder 5; Lytton Strachey, 'The Historian of the Future', BL, Add.Ms., 81,893, no. 2; Avery, *Lytton Strachey: Early Papers*, 51–64; S to J.T. ('Frank') Sheppard, 17 March 1906, KC, Sheppard Papers, JTS 2/194.
49   Sir James Fitzjames Stephen, *The Story of Nuncomar and the Impeachment of Sir Elijah Impey* (2 vols; London: Macmillan, 1885); Sir John Strachey, *Hastings and the Rohilla War* (Oxford: Clarendon Press, 1892). Strachey acknowledged the advice of his uncle in the writing of his thesis. For the 'imperial moment' in biography, see Sir William Hunter's *Rulers of India* series (28 vols; Oxford: Clarendon Press, 1889–1902), including L.J. Trotter, *Warren Hastings* (1890); John Knox Laughton's *English Men*

Hastings had fallen foul of the prevailing parliamentary and commercial mode of governance advocated by Burke and the Whig managers at the time of his impeachment in 1786, and subsequently endorsed by James Mill and Macaulay in their utilitarian evaluations of Hastings's rule.[50] Picking through the controversies of Hastings's eight-year trial required painstaking research and close forensic analysis, but superseding Macaulay required more than scientific weighing of evidence. To Lytton:

> In general, books are read solely for the pleasure they give; and … Macaulay will triumph, until there arises a greater master of the art of writing, who will … invest the facts of Indian history with the glamour of literature, and make truth more attractive than fiction.

So his account transformed his hero from the autocrat of orthodox Whig accounts into benevolent imperial icon, and substituted a morality tale on malignant political partisanship for one on Oriental despotism. Like Macaulay and Trevelyan, he could not bear history to be dull; like them he was inclined to substitute ornate description, rhetoric and melodrama for cool analysis. Torn between documentary fact-finding and dramatic storytelling, between history as science and history as art, his essay was characterised by a confusion of styles and targets – a narrative puffed out by heated refutations of Burke or Mill, and critical evaluation of evidence subverted by elaborate literary tableaux. The examiners were unimpressed, and twice he was denied a fellowship.[51]

---

of Action series (16 vols; London: Macmillan, 1889–1905), including Sir Alfred Lyall, *Warren Hastings* (1891); and the *Builders of Greater Britain* series (12 vols; London: Chapman & Hall, 1890–1904), including G.B. Malleson, *Life of Warren Hastings: First Governor-General of India* (1894).

50   For the Strachey and Stephen families' hostility to 'the great criminals' (Lytton's term) Burke, Mill and Macaulay, see K.J.M. Smith, *James Fitzjames Stephen: Portrait of a Victorian Rationalist* (Cambridge: Cambridge University Press, 1988), ch. 6, doi.org/10.1017/CBO9780511558597; Lytton Strachey, 'The Political Wisdom of Burke', *Spectator*, 31 October 1908; Strachey, Letter (in reply to Professor J.B. Bury), 7, 14 November 1908 (both signed Z); Sophia Weizman, *Warren Hastings and Philip Francis* (Manchester: Manchester University Press, 1929); F.G. Whelan, *Edmund Burke and India: Political Morality and Empire* (Pittsburgh: Pittsburgh University Press, 1996); Edward Strachey, 'James Mill', *Spectator*, 15 April, 1 July 1882.

51   Lytton Strachey, 'Warren Hastings, Cheyt Sing and the Begums of Oude' (1905, 1906), unpublished, two versions in Firestone Memorial Library, Princeton University, Robert Taylor Collection, Mss, 121, 122; 'Introduction' of the later version in Michael Holroyd and Paul Levy, eds, *The Shorter Strachey* (Oxford: Oxford University Press, 1980), 225–32 at 225; earlier version in BL, Add.Ms., 81,890 (Greaves Essay Prize, September 1901); later version, *Spectator*, 12 March 1910; S.P. Rosenbaum, 'Lytton Strachey and the Prose of Empire', in Susan Dick, Declan Kiberd, Dougald McMillan and Joseph Ronsley, eds, *Omnium Gatherum: Essays for Richard Ellmann* (Montreal: McGill-Queen's University Press, 1989), 122–33; Bruce B. Redford, 'The Shaping of the Biographer: Lytton Strachey's Warren Hastings, Cheyt Sing and the Begums of Oude', *Princeton University Library Chronicle*, 43 (1981), 38–52.

Cast back into 'a limbo of unintimacy' at Lancaster Gate, Lytton had to earn a living with periodic short essays and book reviews. At Cambridge, in his scatalogical verses, smutty dialogues, short stories and especially his papers to the Apostles – on bodily functions and propriety, art and indecency, aesthetics and morality, progress and savagery, self-control and self-expression, marriage and the death of love – he had learnt that the best way to startle, amuse and delight his peers was to deploy humour, irony, mockery, a sense of paradox and of disproportion; qualities he was to perfect in *Eminent Victorians*.[52] And from 1904 on, in essays and book reviews – 10 for Trevelyan's journal – he began to apply his iconoclasm to historical and literary subjects, and to complement his subversive stance with a style that Barry Spurr has aptly termed 'camp mandarin'.[53] Over the next decade, he cultivated a cosmopolitan, Francophone persona, and he fine-tuned his exotically 'queer' sensibility in recoil from what he depicted as Victorianism.

'To someone born in 1880,' he wrote, 'the Victorian age has the odd attractiveness of something at once very near and very far off; like … those queer fishes one sees behind glass at an aquarium.' Simultaneously modern and ancient, an age of science and faith, it was somehow 'unaesthetic to its marrow bones'. The Victorian age, he wrote, 'great in so many directions' – he was thinking of its scientists and empire builders – 'was not great in criticism, in humour, in the realistic apprehension of life'. The Victorians were ineradicably 'phenomenal'. From this deficiency flowed multiple defects: the crushing conventionality, the Puritan morality, the work ethic, the infinite deferment of pleasure, the intellectual dishonesty, the lack of self-awareness, intuition or psychological insight, the 'ineradicable instinct for action and utility' that destroyed all sense of art. Victorianism, he suggested, was shaped by a tug of war between Puritanism and Romanticism, propriety and conviction, excessive moralism and rampant

---

52   Apostles' Essays 1902–1912, Dialogues, Short Stories, all in Avery, *Lytton Strachey: Early Papers*, 1–199; Cambridge Apostles' Papers, Minute Books 1902–9, 1909–1914: 10 May, 25 October 1902; 31 January, 14 March, 16 May, 14 November 1903; 20 February, 21 May, 19 November 1904; 25 February, 27 May, 2 December 1905; 27 October 1906; 27 May 1907; 24 October 1908; 28 May 1910; 20 May 1911; 27 January, 11 May 1912, KC: KCAS/39/1/14-15.
53   Barry Spurr, 'Camp Mandarin: The Prose Style of Lytton Strachey', *English Literature in Transition 1880–1920*, 33:1 (1990), 31–45; G.L. Strachey, *Landmarks in French Literature* (London: Williams and Norgate, 1912).

materialism, self-denial and self-expression, which, like the meeting of two weather systems, generated what he called an 'atrocious fog … of sentiment'.[54]

These were the characteristics he explored in a number of different guises in some of the writers Trevelyan particularly admired: Scott, Carlyle, Tennyson, Sidgwick, Morley, Maitland.[55] But Strachey singled out three for particular disparagement. One was George Meredith. In 1906, Trevelyan had written a study of *The Poetry and Philosophy of Meredith*. Strachey's response was scathing, for typically, instead of focusing on the poetry, Trevy filled his book with its 'social messages' and 'moral teaching', crushing 'all sense of art between the millstones of [his] earnest moral endeavour and deep political conviction'. Six years later, when he contributed to the Memorial Edition of Meredith's works, Strachey's criticism extended from the expositor to the subject: the Victorians, he remarked to Virginia Woolf, 'seem to me a set of mouthing, bungling hypocrites'. Another target was Macaulay, with whom he warred all his life: a Puritan turned Philistine, who invariably confused culture with better street lighting and morality with middle-class respectability.[56] But the most scathing of his essays was reserved for Trevelyan's other great-uncle, Matthew Arnold, the high priest of Victorian cultural criticism who had popularised the idea of great literature as a form of moral uplift. Entitled 'A Victorian Critic', and opening with the suggestion that 'an Old Victorian Club' should be started in 'some quiet corner of Pimlico', the essay asked sarcastically, 'how could anyone … take literature seriously', when there was life to be

---

54   Holroyd, *LSNB*, 139–40; S to Leonard Woolf, 9 September 1904, in Levy, *The Letters of Lytton Strachey*, 32–3; Lytton Strachey, 'A Statesman: Lord Morley', *War and Peace*, 5 (February 1918), in Strachey, *Biographical Essays* (*BE*) (London: Chatto & Windus, 1948), 281–4; Strachey, 'A Victorian Critic', *NS*, 1 August 1914, in Strachey, *Literary Essays* (*LE*) (London: Chatto & Windus, 1948), 209–13.
55   Lytton Strachey, 'Not by Lockhart', *The Speaker*, 15 October 1906; Strachey, 'Some New Carlyle Letters', *Spectator*, 10 April 1909; Strachey, 'Catullus and Lord Tennyson', in Avery, *Lytton Strachey: Early Papers*, 159–64; for Sidgwick, see Holroyd, *LSNB*, 139–40; S to John Maynard Keynes, 11 March 1906, and Keynes to S, 8 March 1906, KC, Keynes Mss, PP/45/316/2, ff. 152–3, 158–9; S to G.E. Moore, 28 March 1906, CUL, Moore Mss, T8/44/7; for Maitland, see Apostles' Paper, 20 May 1911, in Paul Levy, ed., *The Really Interesting Question and Other Papers* (London: Weidenfeld & Nicolson, 1974), 121–6.
56   S to Leonard Woolf, 2 December 1905, HRHC, Strachey Mss, Box 4, folder 5; G.M. Trevelyan, *The Poetry and Philosophy of George Meredith* (London: Constable, 1906); Clive Bell, Review, in *Cambridge Review*, April 1906; S to Clive Bell, 17 March 1906, BL, Add.Ms. 71,104, ff. 13–14; S to Woolf, 8 November 1912, in Leonard Woolf and Lytton Strachey, eds, *Virginia Woolf and Lytton Strachey: Letters* (London: Hogarth Press, 1956), 42–3; Strachey, 'Macaulay's Marginalia', *Spectator*, 16 November 1908; S to G.L. Dickinson (on 'the damned weed of Macaulayism'), 26 May 1918, KC, Dickinson Papers, GLD/5/23; Strachey, 'Congreve, Collier and Macaulay', *Nation & Athenaeum* (*Nation*), (34), 13 October 1923, 'Macaulay', *Nation*, (42), 21 January 1928, both in *LE*, 53–7, 195–201.

lived, action to be taken, duty to be done? Hence 'that ingenious godsend, the theory of the Criticism of Life', which enabled one to write poetry and be 'an inspector of schools', admire Shakespeare and Samuel Smiles, serve the Muses and Mammon.[57]

'A Victorian Critic' was published on 1 August 1914, and the differences between Strachey and Trevelyan were sealed by the outbreak of the First World War. Six months earlier, the two of them had discussed Bury's *A History of Freedom of Thought*, which described the growth of religious toleration in early modern Europe. Bury explained how 'religious warfare and persecution had been abolished by the quiet thinking of rationalists and sceptics' who showed that intolerance simply did not work. Trevelyan was convinced that the same transformation could take place in military thought, and he declared himself a convert to Norman Angell's 'practical' pacifism, which argued that war was counterproductive, unsustainable and hence impossible. Strachey's response to the congratulatory story of 'Toleration Victorious, all *coleur de rose*' was quite different. Was it really possible, he asked, that 'such [a] deeply rooted instinct as the love of persecution … should have disappeared?' Intolerance had merely 'shifted its concern' from metaphysics and science to life and literature; instead of burning heretics and imprisoning astronomers, the authorities now persecuted writers and suppressed indecency: if not Galileo, then Oscar Wilde.[58]

In August 1914, after a brief opposition to British intervention in the name of practical pacifism and international rationality, Trevelyan became an ardent liberal warrior. Granted his commitment to public duty and progressive causes, his activism and his need to improve the world, he was programmed to subscribe to most wartime 'myths'. He was soon convinced that this was a war of duty and national honour, of little peoples against ancient dynastic empires, of self-determination, liberty and democracy against militarism and autocracy. It was, for him, a war that would complete the progressive nineteenth-century story and eventually through the foundation of a new international order lead to the ending of war itself. Too blind for active service, he spent his war in

---

57 Lytton Strachey, 'A Victorian Critic', *LE*, 209–14.
58 T to S, 16 December 1913, BL, Add.Ms., 60,732, ff. 193–4 (arranging a meeting at Strachey's country retreat); J.B. Bury, *A History of Freedom of Thought* (London: Home University Library, 1913); G.M. Trevelyan, 'Norman Angell's New Book', *War & Peace*, 2 (March 1914), 164–5; [Strachey], '*Avons-nous changé tout cela*', *NS*, 22 November 1913, 204–6; Strachey, 'Bonga-Bonga in Whitehall', *NS*, 17 January 1914, 459–60.

7. INTERSECTING AND CONTRASTING LIVES

non-stop public service: diplomatic and military missions to Serbia and Romania; propaganda activities in Rome and the United States; and for three years Commandant of the British Red Cross Unit on the Italian Front. He also wrote morale-boosting articles on behalf of Britain's allies, and a series of upbeat essays that combined metahistory and propaganda on the meaning and significance of the war.[59]

Strachey, on the other hand, after a frisson of patriotism in August 1914, was almost as overdetermined by his scepticism to become a pacific bystander and a conscientious objector on non-religious grounds. Convinced that the war was a cock-up not a conspiracy, that it constituted a relapse from cosmopolitan civility into superstition and barbarism and that the real enemies of freedom were conformity, censorship and conscription – that Puritanism was more pernicious than Prussianism – he wrote anti-war essays, dialogues and poems, retired to oases like Garsington where he could enjoy the comforts of prewar civilisation, and turned his appearance before a military tribunal in 1916 into a pacifist farce. In his writings, he argued that self-righteous activism was more likely to bring misery than was self-indulgent harmlessness, that the private pleasures of friendship, love and beauty were preferable to the duties of patriotism, comradeship, honour and self-sacrifice, that the wartime abuse of language and manipulation of literary greats for nationalist purposes was ridiculous, but that militarism like religious intolerance could vanish – that the pen could prove mightier than the sword. And, in *Eminent Victorians*, he toppled wartime idols.[60]

Eminent Victorians is not simply revisionist biography. It is primarily a polemic, intimately linked to militant pacifism. Under pressure of war, Strachey had reduced the 12 Victorian 'silhouettes', with which he had started in 1913, into a study of just four 'disagreeable' ones. The aim, said Strachey, shortly after the book's publication in May 1918, was 'to make

---

[59] I have examined Trevelyan's wartime experiences and writings at length in MacLachlan, 'Becoming National', 23–44.
[60] Lytton Strachey, 'Voltaire and Frederick the Great', *Edinburgh Review*, 222 (October 1915), 351–73; Strachey, 'King Herod and The Rev. Mr. Malthus', undated but probably late 1914, BL, Add.Ms., 81,892, no. 6 (shorter version in Levy, *The Really Interesting Question*, 107–10); Strachey, 'Boccaccio and General Lee', 'Sennacherib and Rupert Brooke' (both mid-to-late 1915), BL, Add. Ms., 81,892, nos. 5, 2; Levy, *The Really Interesting Question*, 40–44; Strachey, 'Militarism and Theology', May 1918, 'Peace and Peace Traps', June 1918, 'The Claims of Patriotism', July 1918: all in *War & Peace*, 5 (1918), 249–50, 269–70, 292–3. His most extreme pacifist views can be found in his unpublished 300-line poem, 'Last Night I Dreamt I went to Hell', BL, Add.Ms. 91,908 (unfoliated), written between 1915 and 1922.

a protest' against 'a whole set of weaknesses which ha[d] been hitherto either ignored or treated as virtues'. Starting with the worldly ecclesiastic (Cardinal Manning) and moving on to the pitiless humanitarian (Florence Nightingale), the obtuse educationalist (Thomas Arnold) and the maverick crusader (General Gordon), Strachey's portrait gallery anatomised four power-hungry public figures and four instrumental philosophies – religious ambition, self-promoting philanthropy, public school morality and missionary imperialism – that had led Britain into war and deluged it in blood.[61]

Mary Ward accused Strachey of 'literary Prussianism', and her son-in-law – despite his approbation on a first reading – came to agree.[62] For Strachey placed under the microscope much that Trevy held most dear. While both men might deplore prelatical religiosity and missionary imperialism, for Trevy liberal reformism had not only inspired his prewar writing but also, in the shape of public school chivalry and conscience-salving humanitarian service, had informed his activities during the war. Alongside Manning, the ambitious ecclesiastic, and Gordon, the bible-bashing adventurer, were the great vocational do-gooders of the age: Florence Nightingale and Thomas Arnold. Lytton's Dr Arnold had no obvious redeeming features. All hustle and bustle, bursting with sexual fears, obsessed by 'moral evil', he was an obtuse, sanctimonious humbug, who 'strove to make his pupils Christian gentlemen', but proved only 'the founder of the worship of athletics and … good form'. *Eminent Victorians* is an anti-heroic text. Like Trevelyan, the Victorians loved heroes, and with Arnold the pedestal was set particularly high. He, most clearly of all the eminences, was commemorated in one of those pious 'obituary notice[s]' Strachey lambasted in his Preface, Dean Stanley's *Life and Correspondence of Dr. Arnold* – the work used almost exclusively for his study, and one that he manifestly despised. Chronologically barely a Victorian – born in 1795 he died four years into Victoria's reign – Arnold was the most Victorian of them all: the most

---

61 Lytton Strachey, *Eminent Victorians* (*EV*), ed. John Sutherland (Oxford: Oxford University Press, 2003), xi–xii; Noel Annan provides what is still the best brief introduction to *EV*, in Strachey, *EV* (London: Collins, 1959), see esp. 9–12; Blanche Athena Clough to S, 1 October 1918, S to Clough, 20 October 1918, BL, Add.Ms., 60,662, ff. 108–10.

62 Mary Ward in *TLS*, 11 July 1918, in Sutherland, *Mrs Humphry Ward*, 201; 'Is there a Menace of Literary Prussianism?', *Current Opinion*, 65 (October 1918), 253–4; 'Literary Shock Tactics', *Current Opinion*, 65 (July 1918), 182–3; Trevelyan's initial approval probably derived from his avuncular attitude to Strachey, his misjudgment of Strachey's underlying motives, and the fact that he was just returning from front-line carnage.

earnest, morally embattled, 'disagreeable' – and influential. He disciplined and indoctrinated the Victorians and made them dutiful, pharisaical, conformist, emotionally stunted – and immensely energetic.[63]

Strachey had started his book with Cardinal Manning. It seemed a curious choice, for on the face of it, here was a totally unrepresentative figure: a Catholic Cardinal in an overwhelmingly Protestant country, a revival of 'that long line of … clerics which … had come to an end … with Cardinal Wolsey … coming to maturity with the first onrush of Liberalism and living long enough to witness the victories of Science and Democracy'. But the choice was deliberate. Begun shortly after a visit to Rome in 1913 – the Rome of St Pius X, the anti-modernist Catholic warrior – Strachey's Manning was a representative not an aberrant figure: at once a modern figure fighting alongside London dock-workers for social justice and an ambitious, superstitious medieval relic. For all its seeming progressivism and modernity, Victorian England in Strachey's view was fundamentally a credal society, a society of believers, and it had more in common with the thirteenth than with the eighteenth century.[64]

How Manning, the champion of Papal infallibility and defender of the *Syllabus Errorum* – Rome's denunciation of 'the favourite beliefs of the modern world' – came to be buried as a hero in the world's first modern metropolis, Strachey explored initially through an account of the Oxford Movement. Again, it was no accident that he began his study with the spiritual and theological agonies of the Tractarians. For, as Sir Edmund Gosse explained, the Victorian age proper opened not, as liberal historians had it, in an atmosphere of parliamentary, economic and administrative reform but 'in a tempest of theology'. And the Oxford Movement, 'as might be expected from the place and time of its birth', was 'very remote from modern and secular influences'; indeed, it was the work of superstitious freaks at war with the values of modern, civilised behaviour. Thus described, Strachey's Victorian age was a rupture or a relapse in English history: a religious throw-back or a counter-enlightenment, sandwiched

---

63 Edmund Gosse, 'The Agony of the Victorian Age', *Edinburgh Review*, 228 (October 1918), 276–95; John Gardiner, *The Victorians, An Age in Retrospect* (London: Hambledon Continuum, 2003), 4–5, 131–2; Arthur Penrhyn Stanley, *The Life and Correspondence of Thomas Arnold, D.D.* (London: B. Fellows, 1845); A.O.J. Cockshut, *Truth to Life: The Art of Biography in the Nineteenth Century* (London: Collins, 1974), 87–105.

64 Strachey, *EV*, 9–10; Holroyd, *LSNB*, 285–6; on Pius X and the 'grim Cardinals', see Leonard Woolf to S, 4 January 1915, in Frederic Spotts, ed., *Letters of Leonard Woolf* (New York: Harcourt, 1989), 210; on 'Old Catholic' versus 'New National Rome', R.J.B. Bosworth, *The Whispering City: Rome and its Histories* (New Haven, CT: Yale University Press, 2011), 141–4.

between one age of secular cosmopolitan enlightenment and what he had hoped, writing early in 1914, would be another. But as 1914–18 showed, 'militarism and theology' were recurring vices: progress in morals and civilisation was an illusion, and history moved in a cycle of flux and reflux, ages of agnosticism and disbelief interspersed with ages of faith, and peaceful progress with war.[65]

'Every war', writes Paul Fussell, 'is ironic because … its means are so dramatically disproportionate to its ends. But the Great War was more ironic than any before or since. It was a hideous embarrassment to the prevailing meliorist myth … It reversed the idea of Progress.' Strachey was well attuned to this irony. History for him was continually ironic and disproportionate in its effects – for it was invariably the outcome of chance, circumstance and personality. If there was any meaningful movement to the relationship of past and present, it was not an evolutionary continuum, a benign Whig narrative of progress or of liberalism and reform, but one of generational rupture, a seesaw or a cyclical affair, as David Hume had proposed. Victorian England was a credal society; so was the England of 1917 – the England of Horatio Bottomley, Churchill and Lloyd George. As the war showed, credal societies kill, and *Eminent Victorians*, which started with the credulous clerics of Oxford, ended amidst the catacombs of Omdurman. Submerged for most of the book, the killing gradually worked its way into its fabric, finally coming out into the open in the last paragraph when the 'future lay with … Kitchener and his Maxim-Nordenfeldt guns', and in a last bathetic shrug of the shoulders, 'it all ended very happily – in a glorious slaughter of 20,000 Arabs, a vast addition to the British Empire, and a step in the peerage for Sir Evelyn Baring'.[66]

If *Eminent Victorians* was a wartime polemic, pervaded by the vehemence of conscientious objection, *Queen Victoria* (1921) was clearly a book of peace. It was 'a five act comedy,' Lytton told Leonard Woolf, not a satire. Anatomical dissection made way for 'a more subjective spirit of romance',

---

65 Strachey, *EV*, 15–35; Gosse, 'The Agony of the Victorian Age', 278–9; Strachey, 'Militarism and Theology', 249–50. On history as flux and reflux, Lytton Strachey, 'The Eighteenth Century', *Nation*, (45), 29 May 1929, in *BE*, 199–202; Strachey, 'Congreve, Collier and Macaulay', 55–7.
66 Paul Fussell, *The Great War and Modern Memory* (New York/London: Oxford University Press, 1975), 7–8; Strachey, *EV*, 243. Churchill, Bottomley and Lloyd George feature as Moloch, Beelzebub and Belial in Strachey's 'hellish' anti-war poem. He also wrote a fragment on Churchill in 1921, which formed the basis of E.M. Forster's 1922 Dialogue, 'Our Graves in Gallipoli', All in BL, Add.Ms., 91,908; see also S to John Maynard Keynes, 10 December 1919 (on Keynes's *Economic Consequences of the Peace*), 5 May 1923 (on Churchill's war memoirs), KC, Keynes Mss, PP 45/316/5, ff. 64, 158.

and melodramatic exposure for a cadenced narrative, initially whimsical and playful, mildly subversive and malicious at its core, but at the end and in memory, roseate and nostalgic.[67] Yet if the play of accident is more nuanced, and the breaks between acts less violent, the themes of *Eminent Victorians* are still visible. For Strachey, it was 'the interplay of circumstance and character that makes up the sum of every human life'. And, as with the story of his eminences, *Queen Victoria* opened with a series of chance events, starting with the sudden death of the Prince Regent's only child, Princess Charlotte, and followed by the unlikely chance of Victoria's birth.[68] Ruptures became 'turning points', and the great turning points of the reign were connected with the Prince Consort.

Albert, not Victoria – a responsive but not a creative character – was the true begetter of the Victorian age. Victoria, for Strachey, was not very Victorian – but Albert was. With his arrival in 1840, Lord Melbourne – an eighteenth-century survivor: cynical, civilised, slightly sentimental, 'an autumn rose' – was swept aside. Victoria was transformed from feisty, young Hanoverian queen into staid Victorian 'Hausfrau … walking … her children [and] inspecting … lifestock'. Soon:

> The last vestige of the eighteenth century had disappeared; cynicism and subtlety were shrivelled into powder; and duty, industry, morality and domesticity triumphed over them. Even the chairs and tables had assumed in singular responsiveness, the forms of prim solidity. The Victorian age was in full swing.[69]

Albert appears as a kinder version of Dr Arnold, and his attempts to educate and indoctrinate court and government are frustrated by some very un-Victorian characters – by Palmerston, a jaunty Regency throwback, and by Edward VII, a post-Victorian who proved 'strangely resistant' to his father's moral engineering, and grew into something very different,

---

67 S to Leonard Woolf, 16 December 1919, Berg Collection, Strachey Mss, Strachey–Woolf Letters; *TLS*, 7 April 1921, 215; *Times*, 7 April 1921; *Nation*, (31), 16 April 1921; Clive Bell to S, 'Saturday', April 1921, BL, Add.Ms., 50,559, ff. 126; Dorothy Bussy to S, 17 April 1921, BL, Add. Ms., 60,661, f. 237.
68 Strachey, Queen Victoria, Manuscript Preface (unpublished), HRHC, Strachey Mss, Box 2, folder 7; Lytton Strachey, *Queen Victoria* (*QV*) (Harmondsworth: Penguin, 1971; first published 1921), 10–12, 21, 24. See A.N. Wilson, *The Victorians* (London: Hutchinson, 2002), 24–6 for the much-repeated speculation that Victoria was not the Duke of Kent's daughter; for speculation about Albert's birth, Strachey, *QV*, 82.
69 Strachey, *QV*, 54–7, 118.

at once another George IV and the exemplar of a more modern kingship.⁷⁰ Unlike Arnold, Albert is a tragic as well as a comic figure. The pressure of unrelenting duty, endless activity and constant dissatisfaction destroys his health and brings about his early death, the other great turning point of the reign. Had he lived, Strachey asked in an unusual counterfactual, 'perpetually at the centre of affairs … virtuous, intelligent … with the unexampled experience of a whole lifetime of government', would not 'such a ruler', armed with 'the prescriptive authority' of wisdom and age, have 'convert[ed] England into a State as … organized, as elaborately trained and as autocratically controlled as Prussia herself'? But, as it was, 'what chance gave, chance took away. The Consort perished in his prime; and the English Constitution, dropping the dead limb with hardly a tremor, continued its mysterious life as if it had never been'.⁷¹

The death of Albert put Victorianism in aspic or black crepe for nearly a generation, as the widowed queen's mawkish grief reached its hideous apotheosis in the Albert Memorial.⁷² But, politically, Victoria lacked the directing intelligence, skill and perseverance to manipulate 'the complex and delicate principles of the Constitution' to the Crown's advantage. Rather, 'the threads of power which Albert had so laboriously collected, fell from her hands into the vigorous grasp of … Mr. Gladstone, Lord Beaconsfield and Lord Salisbury'. Then, gradually Albert's dead hand loosened and a third Victoria emerged, as the product not of an abrupt transformation but a gradual metamorphosis: a reflection of Albert

---

70   Strachey, *QV*, 123–50, 151, 154; on Edward VII, Lytton Strachey, 'A Frock-Coat Portrait of a Great King', *Daily Mail*, 15 October 1927; Leonard Woolf, 'To See the Kings Go Riding By', *Nation*, (42), 22 October 1927, 118; David Cannadine, 'The Last Hanoverian Sovereign?: The Victorian Monarchy in Historical Perspective', in A.L. Beier, David Cannadine and James M. Rosenheim, eds, *The First Modern Society: Essays in Honour of Lawrence Stone* (Cambridge: Cambridge University Press, 1989), 138–9, 158–9.
71   Strachey, *QV*, 147–8, 176–8. Strachey's counterfactual was based largely on Baron Stockmar, *Denkwürdigkeiten aus den Papieren des Freiherrn Christian Friedrich von Stockmar* (Braunschweig: F. Vieweg und Sohn, 1872) which he read with some difficulty, 'about 1 page an hour'. See S to Dora Carrington, 26 February 1919, BL, Add.Ms., 62,890; Frank Hardie, *The Political Influence of Queen Victoria, 1861–1901* (London: Oxford University Press, 1935); Cannadine, 'The Last Hanoverian Sovereign?', 139–46. Cannadine modified his position in 'From Biography to History: Writing the Modern British Monarchy', *Historical Research*, 77:197 (August 2004), 289–312, doi.org/10.1111/j.1468-2281.2004.00211.x.
72   Strachey, *QV*, 190–1; S to Dora Carrington, 21 September 1919, BL, Add.Ms. 62,891; S to Vanessa Bell asking her opinion of the Albert Memorial, 1 March 1919, Robert Taylor Collection, Princeton, Strachey Mss, Letters to Vanessa Bell; Strachey started to lampoon the Albert Memorial very early: in his first Apostle's Paper, he imagined the Prince Consort rising from his seat and standing naked in front of shocked Victorians.

still, but also of Disraeli, that most un-Victorian of characters.[73] So, to the last years of her reign, which in their 'solid splendour' seemed, in Strachey's opinion, 'hardly paralleled' in England's history; so also to the iconic figure of the Golden and Diamond Jubilees. Amid the 'established grandeur' of Lord Salisbury's imperial Britain, Victoria had become a fixture, 'a magnificent immovable sideboard in the huge saloon of state'. In many ways, it was an affectionate portrait – half ironic, half-admiring. Trevelyan, who typically missed the subversive undertow and believed that Strachey had come to scoff but stayed to admire, told a friend that the most important event in the history of twentieth-century English biography was 'the conquest of Strachey by Queen Victoria'. To the more committedly anti-Victorian among his Bloomsbury friends, Lytton had lost his passion. 'Carrington and the young men', they thought, had taken the edge off his writing, and changed the claws of *Eminent Victorians* into the soft-pawed pussy touch of *Queen Victoria*.[74]

After the war, Trevelyan had expected to go on writing in the same manner as before, returning to the 'world of reform [he] so loved'. But fashion had changed, and the public had no time for his prewar heroes. Commented Harold Laski in 1919, for example, 'I re-read Trevelyan on Italy, and to my astonishment, found a large part of it merely brilliant rhetoric, where ten years ago I remember being swept off my feet by it'.[75] When *Grey of the Reform Bill* was eventually published early in 1920, it sold poorly. The writing – literary, rhetorical, respectful, a frock-coat biography with all the proprieties intact – seemed irredeemably Victorian. And Trevelyan's 'dignified aristocrat', whose career 'ennoble[d] the annals of English statecraft', was more of an effigy than a man. In Grey's case, this was especially unfortunate. As a young man, he was overbearing, vain and moody. He had fallen passionately in love with the fashion icon of the age, Georgiana Duchess of Devonshire. Thereafter, even in Fox's louche

---

73 Strachey, *QV*, 238–9; Lytton Strachey, 'Dizzy', *The Woman's Leader*, 12, 16 July 1920, in *BE*, 264–7.
74 Strachey, *QV*, 224–5, 240–1; T to S, 6 May 1921, BL, Add.Ms., 60,732, f. 198; Trevelyan, quoted in Charles Richard Sanders, *Lytton Strachey: His Mind and Art* (London: Oxford University Press, 1957), 227; Leonard Woolf, 'The Biography of Kings', *Nation*, (36), 21 March 1925, 859; Anne Bell and Andrew McNeillie, eds, *The Diary of Virginia Woolf*, Volume III (London: Hogarth Press 1980), 28 November 1928, 208–9.
75 Cannadine *Trevelyan*, 15, 101–4; Moorman, *George Macaulay Trevelyan*, 129; T to G.O. Trevelyan, 1 April 1919, PRL, Trevelyan Mss, GOT 107; Harold Laski to Oliver Wendell Holmes, 14 December 1920, quoted in Feske, *From Belloc to Churchill*, 167.

circle, he had a reputation, and his affairs continued well into his 70s. None of this made its way into Trevelyan's biography, which was written well within the 'Great Wall of Victorian respectability'.[76]

Absent from Trevelyan's work were precisely the features that concerned Strachey: the play of personality, the texture of a life, psychic interiority in all its contradictions, rather than the spurious coherence retrospectively given to a public career. Also missing were the qualities Lytton had made fashionable, enabling him to strip away the Victorian varnish from political biography: irreverence, a probing imagination, a sense of irony, ambiguity and paradox. With all their talk of liberty, democracy, reform and free trade, Trevelyan's ancestral Whig heroes had become derided *Eminent Victorians* – or, as Leonard Woolf put it when *John Bright* was reissued in 1927, 'antediluvians and patriarchs'. So Trevelyan backed off. His need for heroes never entirely dissipated, but they were now heroes in eclipse: not Garibaldi the heroic national unifier, but Manin, the noble republican failure; not Lord Grey of reform, but Edward Grey, the man of good intentions who was powerless as the lamps went out. The heroes of the Risorgimento or English Liberalism were always shaping or imposing themselves on events; now they could only respond to or flee from them. In the dialectic between predestination and free will, Trevelyan, once the champion of moral choice and free action, moved towards determinism.[77]

Perhaps then, it was better to avoid biography. So the focus of Trevy's writing altered, as did its tone and texture. *British History in the Nineteenth Century* (1922) coincided chronologically with his work on Bright and Lord Grey, but it could hardly have been more different. This was a book shorn of rhetoric and imaginative colour, lacking obvious artistic form. It was impersonal, undramatic, dry – almost 'dry-as-dust' – without heroes or villains, or with plaudits so widely and evenly spread as to be virtually neutral. Pitt and Fox, Grey and Canning, Melbourne and Peel, Aberdeen and Palmerston, Gladstone and Disraeli were all well-meaning men of principle and courage who 'in the main wrought greatly and beneficently'.

---

76 G.M. Trevelyan, *Lord Grey of the Reform Bill*, passim; one reviewer complained that Grey was 'morally … about ten foot tall', *Nation*, (27), 26 March 1920, 159; *TLS*, 25 March 1920. For the skeletons in Lord Grey's cupboard: Amanda Foreman, *Georgiana: Duchess of Devonshire* (London: HarperCollins, 1998). *The Duchess*, the movie of 2008, presents a very different Charles Grey; see www.imdb.com/title/tt0864761/ (accessed 8 October 2016).
77 Leonard Woolf, 'John Bright and Liberalism', in Woolf, *Essays in History, Literature, Politics, Etc.* (London: Hogarth Press, 1927), 218–22; G.M. Trevelyan, *Manin and the Venetian Revolution of 1848* (London: Longmans, Green, 1924); Trevelyan, *Grey of Fallodon* (London: Longmans, Green, 1937).

Thus described, modern British political history embodied the philosophy both of Burke and Bentham: the 'conservative principles which constitute one half of our social happiness', and 'the spirit of liberalism … never neglected without disaster'. Historical change was brought about not by the triumph of progressive heroes, but through the interplay of reformers and stabilisers – 'the two party system'. Trevelyan had once written that genuine wisdom 'does not always consist in sympathy and tolerance. The world is moved in the first instance by those who see one side of a question only'. Now, he believed it was the consensualists who were the wisest: 'no one party could cover all the ground'.[78]

He still saw the nineteenth century – which he opened in 1782 on the eve of reform – in evolutionary, liberal terms. Whereas Strachey's Victorian age was saturated in theology, his was a secular, improving society. Indeed, coming after Strachey's corrosive anatomy, Trevelyan's, for all its spiritual anaemia and industrial ugliness, was upbeat and reassuring. But it was an academic rather than a literary portrait. Strachey and his literary imitators viewed Trevelyan's history as a 'tiresome' Victorian relic. Trevy, for his part, was convinced that 'Lytton had poisoned history, traduced the Victorians and created a fashion for cheap … nasty … one volume biographies, designed to meet the demand for sensational literature'.[79] Just how far the rot had gone – how far standards were set by the 'suave practitioners of denigration' – was illustrated in 1923 by the fate of a book dedicated to Trevelyan, F.A. Simpson's *Louis Napoleon*. Simpson was a scrupulous literary historian in the Trevelyan mould – a Trinity don who, thanks to Trevy, had landed the life Fellowship that passed Lytton by. But his publishing career was abruptly terminated by a destructive anonymous review in the *Times Literary Supplement*:

> History (there is no use denying it) is mainly about dead people. But it is the duty of historians to convince us that they were once alive … Mr Simpson's … grave narrative disdain[s] the bright colours, the quick, undignified movement of reality, without [which] one may write sound history but never get [the past] to live.

---

78   G.M. Trevelyan, *British History in the Nineteenth Century (1782–1901)* (London: Longmans, Green, 1922); Cannadine, *Trevelyan*, 107–9, 120–1; Trevelyan, *England in the Age of Wycliffe*, 181; Trevelyan, 'The Latest View of History', 412; G.M. Trevelyan, *The Two-Party System in English Political History* (Oxford: Clarendon Press, 1926); Feske, *Belloc to Churchill*, 175–8.
79   Cannadine, *Trevelyan*, 44.

Trevelyan was outraged: the Strachey-esque comments were a call for a history that was all sail but no ballast, all 'personality and pageant' but no politics, 'unimaginable in a serious study'.[80] Convinced that the popularity of the new biography had led to a decline in the art of writing history and that the old alliance between freelance literary history and progressive politics had broken down, he returned to the academy. Keen to avail himself of 'the aura of authority' that a senior academic position might confer, he succeeded Bury as Regius Professor of History at Cambridge in 1928 – the culmination of a fence-building exercise going back many years.[81]

Yet he had not abandoned the pursuit of popular literary history. His tactics may have changed; the goal remained the same. Despite his formal academic position, he still believed 'the appeal of history … [wa]s in the last analysis poetic', and he saw himself as the heir of Walter Scott, Macaulay and Carlyle, rather than as Bury's spiritual successor.[82] He was delighted when Strachey abandoned critical Victorian biography to devote himself to a romantic evocation of Elizabethan court society, in what he believed was his 'greatest work', his *Elizabeth and Essex*: 'not a piece of satire but a piece of life'. So much the more was he appalled when Strachey returned to his most satirical manner in his last published set of essays, *Portraits in Miniature*, especially as the most deflating pieces were on the Trevelyan family icons, Macaulay and Carlyle.[83] By the time Strachey died in 1932, it was clear that generational and temperamental differences, exacerbated by the war and by their increasingly divergent postwar lifestyles, friendships, tastes and judgements as to the role of biography and history had turned to mutual antipathy. To Strachey's Bloomsbury friends, 'Old Trevy' was now 'the complete insider … the

---

80 Philip Guedalla, review of *Louis Napoleon and the Recovery of France, 1848–1856* by F.A. Simpson, *TLS*, 25 January 1923, 55; G.M. Trevelyan, 'The Writing of History', *TLS*, letters, 1 February 1923, 76; Guedalla, 'The Writing of History', *TLS*, letters, 8 February 1923, 92; Strachey in fact hated Guedalla's writing, which he saw as a crude parody of his own: Carrington, file of correspondence to Noel Carrington, Tate Gallery Mss, TGA 797/2/22, 7 August 1922.
81 Feske, *Belloc to Churchill*, 151–5, offers the best analysis of Trevelyan's retreat to academe; G.M. Trevelyan, 'History and Literature', *History*, 9 (1924), 81–91, doi.org/10.1111/j.1468-229X.1924.tb00409.x; Leonard Woolf, 'The New Art of Biography', *Nation*, (38), 12 December 1925, 404; A.F. Pollard, 'The Progress of History', *TLS*, 26 June 1930, 521–2.
82 Trevelyan, 'The Present Position of History', 106; Cannadine, *Trevelyan*, 196, 159–60; G.M. Trevelyan, 'Walter Scott: The Novelist as Historian', *The Times*, 21 September 1932.
83 T to S, 28 November 1928, BL, Add.Ms., 60,732, ff. 200–1; Lytton Strachey, *Portraits in Miniature* (London: Chatto & Windus, 1931), which included 'Six Historians': Hume, Gibbon, Macaulay, Carlyle, Froude and Creighton; for Virginia Woolf on Trevelyan's reaction, see S to Roger Senhouse, 30 December 1930, Berg, Strachey Mss, Strachey-Senhouse Letters; Holroyd, *LSNB*, 653.

perfect product of the university machine'. To Trevelyan and his fellow dons, Strachey was an irritating gadfly – and a supercilious intellectual. 'As to intellectuals,' Trevy told his daughter in 1942, 'one of the greatest disappointments of my life has been the decadence of that class (if you can call it a class), of which I first became aware when Lytton Strachey came up to Cambridge.'[84]

Historical texts, like other literary artefacts, carry their own internal imperatives. And it is possible that comparative biography – especially when it tries to highlight temperamental and generational differences – may explain too much, thereby rendering writings textually undernourished and biographically 'overdetermined'. As Strachey once put it, quoting Mallarmé, 'poetry is not written with ideas, it is written with words': 'these things that we have made are as much alive as we are, and we have become their slaves'.[85] Yet it is difficult to believe that Strachey and Trevelyan were so enslaved; for history is written with ideas and philosophies as well as with words. And their families, backgrounds, lifestyles, assumptions, moments and milieus were not irrelevant to their choice of subjects and to their treatment of them. As such, biography may help to elucidate the sources of their early friendship and the growing antipathy between them. Clio, like all the muses, speaks in tongues, and examining Clio's historians surely helps us to decipher them.[86]

---

84   For Trevelyan on Virginia Woolf, see Cannadine, *Trevelyan*, 39, 255; T to Mary Moorman, 10 April 1941, PRL, Trevelyan Mss, MM 1/4/29; Anne Bell and Andrew McNeillie, eds, *The Diary of Virginia Woolf*, Volume IV (London: Hogarth Press, 1982), 24 August 1933, 174; Bell and McNeillie, eds, *The Diary of Virginia Woolf*, Volume V (London: Hogarth Press, 1984), 26 October, 5 November 1940, 333, 337; Feske, *Belloc to Churchill*, 152–3; T to Mary Moorman, 30 June 1942, PRL, Trevelyan Mss, MM 1/4/30.
85   Lytton Strachey, Introduction to George H.W. Rylands, *Words and Poetry* (London: Hogarth Press, 1928), in *LE*, 16–19; Strachey, 'Peace and Peace Traps', 269–70.
86   Trevelyan, *Clio, A Muse and Other Essays*.

8

An Ingrained Activist: The Early Years of Raphael Samuel

Sophie Scott-Brown

When Richard Lloyd Jones looked back on his wartime school days at Long Dene, a progressive boarding school in Buckinghamshire, one particular incident stuck in his mind.[1] He remembered being kept awake during the hot summer of 1944. It was not the heat alone that was responsible for this, nor was there any particular physical reason why he should have been so wakeful. Part of the school's ethos was a strenuous emphasis on the pupil's participating in forms of outdoor and rural work such as harvesting. All that fresh air and exercise should have been quite sufficient to exhaust even the most active of small boys. What kept Richard Lloyd Jones awake was the incessant talking of a young, hyperactive 'Raf-Sam'. Lloyd Jones did not recall exactly what it was that so animated his young classmate, late into that sticky summer's night, but a reasonable assumption would be that it was politics, specifically communist politics, as the nine-year-old Raphael Samuel was already practising his skills as an aspiring communist propagandist and organiser.[2]

---

1   Lloyd Jones later became permanent secretary for Wales (1985–93) and chairman for the Arts Council of Wales (1994–99).
2   Quoted in Sue Smithson, *Community Adventure: The Story of Long Dene School* (London: New European Publications, 1999), 21. See also: Raphael Samuel, 'Family Communism', in Samuel, *The Lost World of British Communism* (London: Verso, 2006), 60; Raphael Samuel, 'Country Visiting: A Memoir', in Samuel, *Island Stories: Unravelling Britain* (London: Verso, 1998), 135–6.

Raphael Samuel (1934–96) was an unconventional historian. A member of the Communist Party of Great Britain (CPGB), and later the youngest member of the Historians' Group of the Communist Party (HGCP), in his youth, he left the party in 1956. He was a founding figure in the first British New Left movement and later an adult education history tutor at the trade union – affiliated Ruskin College, Oxford. As a historian, he was best known as the moving force behind the early History Workshop movement (1967–79) and the *History Workshop Journal* (1976–). He was also renowned for his approach to oral and local history, and for his pioneering work in the history of popular culture and public history. Compared to some of his close contemporaries, such as Perry Anderson (b. 1938) or E.P. Thompson (1924–93), Samuel is a relatively neglected figure.[3] Where accounts do exist, interpretations are divided. Given his early membership of the CPGB and association with the HGCP, he has naturally been viewed in relation to a trajectory of postwar British cultural Marxist historiography, and here he has often been found wanting. He is described by some as populist and romantic, as a man of a different and dying era ('the last comrade of the first New Left') or, more emotively but still as disingenuously, a confused Marxist, whose work, whilst creative, lacked structure and critical force.[4]

Others, however, present a different perspective, challenging the use of Marxism as a framework for understanding Samuel's politics and history. Ken Jones, for example, has argued that Samuel occupied a 'non-

---

3   On E.P. Thompson, see: Perry Anderson, *Arguments in English Marxism* (London: Verso Editions, 1980); Scott Hamilton, *The Crisis of Theory: E.P. Thompson, the New Left and Postwar British Politics* (Manchester: Manchester University Press, 2012); Bryan Palmer, *E.P. Thompson: Objections and Oppositions* (London: Verso, 1994); Harvey J. Kaye and Keith McCelland, eds, *E. P. Thompson: Critical Perspectives* (Philadelphia: Temple University Press, 1990). On Perry Anderson, see: Gregory Elliot, *Perry Anderson: The Merciless Laboratory of History* (Minneapolis: University of Minnesota Press, 1998); Paul Blackledge, *Perry Anderson, Marxism and the New Left* (London: Merlin, 2004).
4   Harvey J. Kaye, *The Education of Desire: Marxists and the Writing of History* (London/New York: Routledge, 1992), 99; Dennis Dworkin, *Cultural Marxism in Postwar Britain: History, the New Left, and the Origins of Cultural Studies* (Durham/London: Duke University Press, 1997); Kynan Gentry, 'Ruskin, Radicalism and Raphael Samuel: Politics, Pedagogy and the Origins of the History Workshop', *History Workshop Journal*, 76 (2013), 187–211, doi.org/10.1093/hwj/dbs042; David Selbourne, 'On the Methods of the History Workshop', *History Workshop Journal*, 9 (1980), 150–61, doi.org/10.1093/hwj/9.1.150; Selbourne, 'The Last Comrade: Raphael Samuel, the Ruskin Historian Who Died Last Week Was the Conscience Keeper of the Old Left', *The Observer*, 15 December 1996, 24; Richard Hoggart, 'Review of Theatres of Memory', *Political Quarterly*, 66:3 (1995), 215–16; Patrick Wright, 'Review of Theatres of Memory', *The Guardian*, 5 February 1995; Stefan Collini, 'Speaking with Authority: The Historian as Social Critic', in *English Pasts: Essays in History and Culture* (Oxford: Oxford University Press, 1999), 95–102; Eric Hobsbawm, *Interesting Times: A Twentieth-Century Life* (London: Abacas, 2002), 212.

conformist' position in relation to the wider intellectual left. Jones recast his apparent populism into part of a creative and democratic pedagogical politics.[5] In Samuel's own conception, the Workshop took its stance on the democratisation of history, rather than the reformulation of Marxism, part of an attempt to democratise history and make 'working-class men and women producers of their own history'.[6] Building on this, Hilda Kean has pointed to the Workshop as a means of expanding both the range of the historical subject matter and those considered to be engaged in historical work. She further contended that it did this by fostering an inclusive and democratic learning environment and demystifying the research process.[7]

These accounts suggest that the Workshop, as a political intervention and educational initiative, relates more to a species of left-libertarian politics, characterised, across its various guises, by an anti-authoritarian and decentralised conception of direct democracy and a view of the individual as an agent for social change. In education, this corresponds with what Susan Askew described as a 'liberatory model'. Whilst primarily concerned with education for social change and social justice, this model considers knowledge as intrinsic (rather than extrinsic), stressing individual change as the prerequisite for larger change and emphasising the need for an empathetic understanding of social relationships. As a mode of teaching practice, it adopts a person-centred approach in which learning is a personalised, reciprocal process and participatory activity. Askew acknowledged that, within this framework, the exact role of the educator can be unclear or unexamined, but generally it involves a shift from an authoritative position to one of facilitation and critique.[8]

---

5   Ken Jones, 'Raphael Samuel: Against Conformity', *Changing English: Studies in Culture and Education*, 5:1 (1998), 17–26, doi.org/10.1080/1358684980050103.
6   Raphael Samuel, 'Afterword: History Workshop 1966–1980', in Samuel, ed., *People's History and Socialist Theory* (London: Routledge Paul, 1981), 410–17; 'General Editor's Introduction', in Samuel, ed., *The History Workshop: A Collectanea 1967–1991* (Oxford: History Workshop 25, 1991).
7   Hilda Kean, 'Public History and Raphael Samuel: A Forgotten Radical Pedagogy?', *Public History Review*, 11 (2004), 51–62; Kean, 'People, Historians and Public History: Demystifying the Process of History Making', *Public Historian*, 32:3 (2010), 25–38, doi.org/10.1525/tph.2010.32.3.25.
8   Susan Askew, 'Educational Metamorphosis', in Susan Askew and Eileen Carnell, *Transforming Learning: Individual and Global Change* (London: Continuum International Publishing, 1998), 84, 89–91. For this in particular application to history see Jorma Kalela, *Making History: The Historian and the Uses of the Past* (London: Palgrave Macmillan, 2012), 159–64.

Sheila Rowbotham, an early Workshop participant, endorses the idea of Samuel as a liberatory educator, saying:

> Raphael was not simply a writer but a renowned organiser, the kind who was an initiator of great projects with the capacity to yoke his fellow to the concept and carry them on regardless of grizzles and groans … He was the world's most adept hooker, and ruthless behind the charm.[9]

She added that:

> Writers leave visible traces, they contrive their own record. Organisers, in contrast, have a powerful impact upon those within whom they have direct contact but tend to live on in oral memory alone.[10]

What made Samuel distinctive as a historian, then, was not a particular argument that he advanced about the past, nor a specific theory of history that he proposed, but his entire *way of being* a historian. As much as reclaiming a radical view of the past, Samuel exemplified a radical approach to the role of the historian. Samuel's politics were enacted through his practices of history as much as in his historical writing. This makes him as an individual as important to 'read' as any of his texts. But, as Rowbotham's comment suggested, personalised and performative practices leave little trace on the documentary record. They are deeply embedded in context, perceived emotionally as much as grasped conceptually. This is where the intimate perspective of the biographical approach can provide valuable insight, situating the individual within a web of their social, cultural and historical relationships and permitting an all-important sense of dynamism, adaption and response, to thinking and acting.

This essay explores Samuel as an intellectual personality distinguished by a remarkable capacity to recognise and galvanise history-making as an everyday social activity and potential tool of social critique. It focuses on Samuel's formative years, from his early communist childhood through to his student years, arguing that it was during this period that he absorbed the values of communism as a moral framework and developed the distinctive intellectual and practical skills of the grassroots activist and aspiring party organiser, highly distinctive from those of the traditional historical scholar or political theorist. These were the values and skills that shaped his later practices as a historian.

---

9   Sheila Rowbotham, 'Some Memories of Raphael', *New Left Review*, I/221 (January/February 1997), 128–32.
10 Ibid.

Communism as a way of life

Samuel was born on 26 December 1934, in North London, to Minna and Barnett Samuel, part of an extended Jewish family. Minna Samuel was the daughter of Jacob and Fanny Nerenstein, who had migrated to England from Grodno, Polish Russia, at the turn of century. Once in England, they had settled in the East End of London, where Minna was born in 1906 followed by two younger sisters, Miriam and Sarah. Here the family ran a bookshop and publishing house specialising in Jewish literature, Shapiro Valentine & Co. on Wentworth Street, East London. Minna married Barnett Samuel (1906–71), a London solicitor from an orthodox Jewish family, in 1931 and moved to Hampstead Garden Suburb in North London. The marriage was short-lived, Minna and Barnett separated in 1941 when Samuel was not quite seven years old, later divorcing in 1946. Minna raised Samuel, their only child. On returning to London following evacuation during the war, Minna and Samuel lived in Kentish Town, North London.[11]

The most-defining feature of Samuel's early upbringing was communist politics, which dominated every aspect of his young life. This communist childhood was the subject of some of his most powerful pieces of historical writing, in particular his series of essays on 'The Lost World of British Communism' published in the *New Left Review* during the mid-1980s. Historian and ex-communist John Saville criticised the essays, arguing that Samuel's communism was of a highly particular, even peculiar, kind, far from representative of a broader experience:

> I do not deny the validity of Raphael Samuel's own personal history, especially in his younger days … The historian in him, however, might have acknowledged that it was a very unusual story, typical of some, perhaps many, Jewish comrades but not in any way relevant to the working-class militants who were joining the Communist Party at the time that Raphael was growing up in the 1940s.[12]

Saville may have intended this remark as a criticism but, in fact, this was the point that Samuel was making in the 'Lost World' essays, rejecting the idea that any sort of uniform experience of communist politics actually existed, that it always entailed a close and complex relationship with other

---

11 Gareth Stedman Jones, 'Samuel, Raphael Elkan (1934–1996)', *Oxford Dictionary of National Biography* (Oxford: Oxford University Press, 2004).
12 John Saville, *Memoirs from the Left* (London: Merlin, 2003), 9.

factors. His own experience was not only that of a Jewish comrade, but also that of a child brought up by a single mother during the war years on the home front. Above all, it must be understood as a communism shaped and mediated by the values implied by Popular Front politics.

In 1935, at the seventh international congress (a meeting of all the national communist parties), Georgi Dimitrov, the General Secretary of Comintern, announced the official transition towards a policy of Popular Front to be effective immediately amongst all the national branches of the party. The Popular Front replaced the previous policy of 'Class Against Class' (1928–35) in which the respective parties followed a narrowly prescribed class politics at the exclusion of those who did not pursue this line.[13] In adopting this policy in 1928, the CPGB had differentiated itself from the British Labour Party (BLP), the political arm of the British left, by rejecting all gradualist approaches to socialism and aggressively asserting a view of class interests as clear, unified and utterly incompatible with one another.[14] The switch to the Popular Front had been prompted in part by the catastrophic fate that had befallen the Communist Party of Germany. As a result of the 'Class Against Class' line, the German party had become so isolated that they had been incapable of opposing Adolf Hitler's attacks against them. They had subsequently been wiped off the German political spectrum and rendered powerless.[15] Now Dimitrov urged the respective national branches of the Communist Party to collaborate, not just joining forces with other left-wing or centrist political groups such as the British Labour or Liberal parties, but also showing a willingness to cooperate with any social or cultural group who were opposed to fascism. He also stressed the importance of reclaiming national histories for the political

---

13 Matthew Worley, *Class Against Class: The Communist Party in Britain Between the Wars* (London: I.B. Taurus, 2002).
14 See: David Cannadine, 'The Twentieth Century: Social Identities and Political Identities', in Cannadine, *Class in Britain* (London: Penguin, 2000), 126–44; Stuart Macintyre, *A Proletarian Science: Marxism in Britain 1917–1933* (London: Lawrence & Wishart, 1986). See also Ross McKibbin, *Classes and Culture: England 1918–1951* (Oxford: Oxford University Press, 1998), doi.org/10.1093/acprof:oso/9780198206729.001.0001. McKibbin argues that the perceived tranquillity of England's interwar (1918–39) social order gravely underestimates the degree of social antagonism that lay below the surface.
15 Jim Fyrth, 'Introduction: In the Thirties', in Fyrth, ed., *Britain, Fascism and the Popular Front* (London: Lawrence & Wishart, 1985), 9–29; Kevin Morgan, 'The Communist Party and the Popular Front, 1935–1938', in Morgan, *Against Fascism and War: Ruptures and Continuities in British Communist Politics, 1935–1941* (Manchester: Manchester University Press, 1989), 33–55.

left. Invocations of a lost 'national' past were a key feature cutting across fascist rhetoric, a tactic that had proved gallingly effective as a form of psychological propaganda.

Amongst the CPGB, there had always been some uneasiness with the deeply isolationist implications of the 'Class Against Class' policy, so the notion of a united or Popular Front was greeted with relative consensus amongst the party's membership.[16] Despite the shift in stance, however, the Labour Party remained mistrustful of the CPGB and rejected all overtures towards a united front.[17] The CPGB was, however, more successful in its engagement with the public sphere. One implication of the change was that the party became more attractive to radically inclined intellectuals, writers and artists. Once viewed with hostility as inherently bourgeois, the party now softened its stance, seeing them as important potential weapons in the battle of ideas.

Another fruitful area for the party was its association with the numerous grassroots initiatives that emerged during this period, initiatives from which it would previously have remained aloof. One example of this was the Left Book Club (LBC), run by the charismatic editor Victor Gollancz, which, whilst never explicitly affiliated to the CPGB, harboured strong communist sympathies. Intent upon revitalising an ailing popular left-wing movement, the LBC became one of the most effective methods of circulating left-orientated literature to a wide audience.[18] Similarly, communists were also able to collaborate in campaigns such as Aid in Spain (Samuel later recalled that it was her frustration with the Labour Party's position on the Spanish Civil War that first turned his mother further towards the radical end of the political spectrum).[19] For a Jewish family such as Samuel's, another important dimension of this increased appeal was the party's strong opposition to all forms of fascism and active campaign against former MP Oswald Mosley and the British Union of Fascists (BUF). Whilst Britain was never in the grip of state fascism as Spain, Germany and Italy were, the BUF's hostility towards migrant

---

16   Matthew Worley, 'Comrade Against Comrade: The CPGB in Crisis', in Worley, *Class Against Class*, 116–54. James Eaden and David Renton argue that as early as 1931 the Communist Party line had been in transition. James Eaden and David Renton, *The Communist Party of Great Britain since 1920* (London: Palgrave Macmillan, 2002), 50, doi.org/10.1057/9781403907226.
17   Morgan, 'The Communist Party and the Popular Front', 35–6.
18   Paul Laity, 'Introduction', in Laity, ed., *Left Book Club Anthology* (London: Victor Gollancz, 2001), ix–xxxi.
19   Samuel, *The Lost World*, 66.

communities, including Jewish ones, in the name of a selective vision of the national past was enough to provide a chilling glimpse into the implications of fascist politics.

In September 1936, the BUF attempted to march through Cable Street in East London where a significant proportion of the population were Jewish. Angry protestors confronted the BUF, resulting in a pitched street battle and the abandonment of their planned march.[20] The CPGB took a considerable role in organising the protest, offering those frustrated with what was perceived by some as indecisiveness on the part of Anglo-Jewish community leaders (often divided amongst themselves on matters of both politics and religion) an assertive alternative form of leadership.[21] As Samuel's uncle, the scholar and historian Chimen Abramsky, said later, 'if you were for democracy Communism was the place to go'.[22] Strategically, the CPGB's switch proved successful, resulting in a substantial increase in its membership, peaking during the war at 56,000.[23] It was not, however, without tension, creating, amongst the membership, a dualistic, even conflicting, set of demands on both their thought and loyalties. For some, such as Palme Dutt, the party's arch theoretician, this policy of inclusivity and alliance risked obscuring or undermining *class* as the key political category of analysis or critique.[24] This concern was further emphasised following the outbreak of the Second World War when class divisions were increasingly overridden by invocations of a British nation unified in defiance of a common enemy.

There was also the question of the relationship to the Soviet Union. On the one hand, the party sought to identify with indigenous political traditions, united by a common commitment to democracy, but at crucial moments it showed an enduring allegiance to Moscow. It refused to condemn communist suppression of anarchist factions in

---

20 Nigel Crosby, 'Opposition to British Fascism 1936–45', in Crosby, *Anti Fascism in Britain* (London: Macmillan Press Ltd, 2000), 42–80.
21 David Cesarani, 'Who Speaks for British Jews?', *New Statesman*, 28 May 2012, 23–7. See also James Eaden and David Renton, 'The Zig Zag Left 1928–39', *The Communist Party of Great Britain since 1920*, 58; Raphael Samuel, 'Jews and Socialism: The End of a Beautiful Friendship?', *The Jewish Quarterly*, 35:2 (1988), 8–10.
22 Ada Rapaport-Albert, 'Chimen Abramsky Obituary', *The Guardian*, 19 March 2010. Samuel's mother Minna was also an 'implacable opponent of Oswald Mosley's Blackshirts'. Paul Conway, 'Minna Keal 1909–1999', www.musicweb-international.com/keal/ (accessed 19 June 2014).
23 Noreen Branson, 'Appendix I Communist Party Membership', *History of the Communist Party of Great Britain 1931–1951* (London: Lawrence & Wishart, 1997), 252.
24 See, for example, Rajani Palme Dutt, 'Intellectuals and Communism', *Communist Review* (September 1932), 421–30.

the Spanish Civil War, its newspaper, *The Daily Worker*, defended the Moscow trials and the party as a whole complied with the implications of the Nazi Soviet Pact (1939), switching to a policy stance of imperial war in August 1939, only returning to a position of 'social patriotism' following the Soviet Union's entry into the war in June 1941. It must be stressed that Samuel would have understood this only indirectly at the time of its actual happening. He was four-and-a-half when the party line changed following the Nazi–Soviet pact in August 1939, six-and-a-half when it changed back in June 1941. Unlike the older members of his family, and several of his contemporaries, Samuel was 'born into' communism. Later, as a historian and left-wing intellectual, he would become aware of the broader political and conceptual contexts in which this was situated. It was first received, however, as a child. Saville's critique of the 'Lost World' essays as an 'incoherent personal sociology', might, in another light, be more rewardingly seen as communism from a 'child's eye view', encountered not as a theory of political economy that carried consequences for the daily lives of adherents but in terms of a series of direct, firsthand experiences and perceptions.[25]

In the first place, Samuel's communism was a real family affair. Not only his mother but, in total, 13 members of his extended family, including aunts, uncles and cousins, were actively involved in the CPGB, or in the respective national equivalent in the country in which they lived. If not actual members, many were supportive of radical political positions.[26] As a result, continuous political activity was 'normal', infused within his day-to-day life and domestic spaces. Political meetings were conducted in the living room, fellow comrades looked after him after school, political leaflets adorned the kitchen table, and his mother knitted white-ribbed socks intended for use by the Red Army.[27] It shaped his child's play through learning the names of Russian towns, marking out the military positions of the Red Army on a map and singing Russian songs, and had all the qualities of an intriguing imaginary world with its own secret language, a pantheon of heroic figures and legends, and even its own promised land (the Soviet Union).[28] In all these ways, Samuel became attuned to politics as part of normal everyday life.[29]

---

25 Saville, *Memoirs from the Left*, 9.
26 Samuel, *The Lost World*, 63. Some members of Samuel's family lived in France, others in America.
27 Ibid.
28 Ibid., 59–62.
29 Ibid., 61, 66.

This youthful communism also furnished him with an early ethical framework for judging his behaviour and that of others. This hinged around an absolute antithesis to anything resembling individualism (the defining trait of bourgeois culture), the centrality of collectivism and the paramount importance of sustained political education and activity.[30] All of this carried firm implications for how to behave both amongst comrades and non-comrades, and provided a structure for how to behave in both public and private.[31] To this extent, Samuel would later say that communism provided him with a 'complete social identity' that had even greater significance for a child in the dark and confusing times of the war on the home front. Like many other city children, he was evacuated to the countryside (Buckinghamshire) and sent to a boarding school (Long Dene). Here, separated from his family and social network for the first time, his burgeoning sense of communist identity carried reassuring connotations of the home he had left behind.[32] As he grew older, advancing towards more complex forms of abstract thinking, Marxism certainly provided him with a conceptual framework and explanation of the world. In his own words:

> Marxism, or what we called Marxism, reinforced this cosmic sense. It dealt in absolutes and totalities, ultimates and finalities, universals and organic wholes … As a political economy, it showed us that capitalism was a unified essence … As a science of society, if offered itself as an all-embracing determinism, in which accidents were revealed as necessities, and causes inexorably followed by effects. As a mode of reasoning, it provided us with a priori understandings and universal rules – laws of thought which were both a guide to action and a source of prophetical authority.[33]

However, the important point here is that initially his communism had been non-theoretical. It had been primarily social and behavioural.[34]

An important early influence on him was Minna, his mother. Born Minnie Nerenstein on 22 March 1909 in East London, she was raised in a deeply religious household with Yiddish as her first language. She was

---

30   Ibid.
31   The second of Samuel's essays 'Staying Power' focuses on the ways in which this ethical framework was constructed, transmitted and reproduced amongst the wider membership. Samuel, *The Lost World*, 77–156.
32   Samuel, *The Lost World*, 67–8.
33   Ibid., 49.
34   On communism as providing a 'total identity', see Thomas Linehan, *Communism in Britain: From Cradle to Grave 1920–1939* (Manchester: Manchester University Press, 2007).

a bright child, winning a scholarship to Clapton Country Secondary School run by Mrs Harris, a progressive Fabian Socialist. She proved herself to be a talented musician and her talent took her to study at the Royal Academy of Music. Minna was forced to quit her music studies in order to help run the family business following the death of her father Jacob in 1926. Following her marriage to Barnett and their move to Hampstead Garden, she soon found the genteel environs of 'The Suburb' claustrophobic after the bustle of the East End.[35] Politics offered Minna activity and intellectual stimulation. She joined the Hampstead Garden Suburb Labour Party, becoming secretary of the women's group. Together with Barnett, she formed a committee for refugee children from Germany, throwing herself wholeheartedly into the venture, seized and driven by the urgency of the situation. Barnett, a far less effusive personality, drew back at this whirlwind of activity, causing a rift to open up between the couple. Minna's radicalism increased through her work on Spanish Aid. Disappointed in the Labour Party's policy on Spain, she drifted further towards the radical left. In 1939, Minna followed her younger sisters in joining the CPGB, a move that precipitated the eventual breakdown of her marriage to Barnett in 1941.

Communism, with its levelling concept of 'comrade', allowed Minna to escape the confines of 'the ghetto', the 'suburb' and married life. She threw herself into party life with gusto, becoming a progress chaser in an aircraft factory and later the key organiser of the large Slough branch of the CPGB. At different times, she assumed the roles of literature secretary, class tutor and engagements secretary for the Worker's Music Association. For a significant portion of Samuel's childhood, Minna was a one-woman dynamo of public activity, organising, teaching and public speaking.[36] Importantly, this was not communism as political theory but as a form of personal and social liberation.

If Minna's influence on Samuel was characterised by activism then that of his uncle, Chimen Abramsky, was defined by its deep intellectualism. Abramsky was born in Minsk, Russia, in 1916, the son of Yehezkel Abramsky, a rabbi and gifted Talmudic scholar. The young Abramsky

---

35 Hampstead Garden Suburb was the brainchild of the social reformer Henrietta Barnett, who had envisaged a community of mixed social classes living together in pleasant green surroundings.
36 Samuel, *The Lost World*, 63–8; Raphael Samuel, 'Country Visiting: A Memoir', *Island Stories*, 132–52; Alex May, 'Keal, Minna (1909–1999)', *Oxford Dictionary of National Biography* (Oxford: Oxford University Press, 2004), www.oxforddnb.com.ezproxy.library.uq.edu.au/view/article/73220 (accessed 10 October 2016); Paul Conway, 'Minna Keal: 1909–1999'.

received little formal schooling but had a procession of private tutors, later becoming a student at the Hebrew University of Jerusalem. During a visit to family in London, he became stranded by the outbreak of the Second World War. Taking a job in Shapiro Valentine & Co., Abramsky met and married Miriam Nerenstein, Minna's younger sister and Samuel's aunt. He joined the party in 1941, becoming the 'patriarch' of the family's communism. Abramsky was a renowned bibliophile, extraordinarily widely read and learned. He was meticulous in his scholarship, an expert in socialist and Jewish history, a lively conversationalist and a compelling teacher. Samuel's aunt, Miriam Abramsky, was equally strong in her political convictions, but preferred to express them through her warm and welcoming hospitality. The Abramskys' modest London household provided a second home for Samuel as he was growing up. It also provided an intellectual haven for a steady stream of scholars, intellectuals and leading political and religious figures, all of whom came to engage in intense political and philosophical debate that would often carry on late into the night. For all the gravity and passionate nature of the discussion, this was also a house of laughter, friendship and fun.[37]

In Samuel's later autobiographical writing, a distinction in tone suggests something of his relationship to these two figures. In writing of his mother, whilst not uncritical, he was consistently affectionate and enthusiastic in his depiction of her as a constant whirlwind of energy and activity. The warmth of these portrayals would imply, at the very least, his strong identification with her activities. His writing on his uncle, by contrast, is respectful but much cooler in tone.[38] Equally, Abramsky's tribute to him following his death in 1996 was similarly reserved in some of its judgements, describing his nephew as a 'Narodnik' – referencing a nineteenth-century Russian populist movement – in his political views and personal manners.[39] These subtleties in tone suggest his attraction to

---

37 Rapaport-Albert, 'Chimen Abramsky Obituary'; 'Professor Chimen Abramsky: Historian', *The Times*, 19 March 2010; Samuel, *The Lost World*, 63; Peter Dreier, '*The House of Twenty Thousand Books* by Sasha Abramsky', *Huffington Post*, 8 June 2014, www.huffingtonpost.com/peter-dreier/the-house-of-twenty-thousand-books_b_5467086.html (accessed June 2014); Sasha Abramsky, *The House of Twenty Thousand Books* (London: Halden Publishers, 2014); Sasha Abramsky, 'The House of Twenty Thousand Books', YouTube, www.youtube.com/watch?v=h37Gf-awf0E&feature=youtu.be, June 2014 (accessed June 2014).
38 Samuel, *The Lost World*, 63.
39 A Narodnik was a term used to describe a member of the nineteenth-century Russian populist movement. Chimen Abramsky, 'Raphael Samuel', *Jewish Chronicle*, 17 January 1997.

and admiration for his mother's activism, whilst his more reserved respect for Abramsky's deep intellectualism could, it seems, be a point of division between the two men.

Further proof of Minna's influence can be seen in his early ambition to the role of the party organiser.[40] In this ambition he followed his mother (the key organiser for the Slough branch of the party), indicating once again the significance of her influence upon him. In terms of the overall CPGB organisational structure, the 'organiser' was drawn from amongst the rank-and-file membership. They were distinguished from their comrades by their self-taught intellectual prowess forming a sort of 'proletarian clerisy'. The role of the organiser forged a bridge between the wider body of party members and the party's hierarchy.[41] His aspiration to this role provides an intriguing insight into his youthful character. As a precocious and intelligent child from a family who had become well established within the party structure (Abramsky also held key party positions serving as the secretary of the party's Jewish committee, the editor of *The Jewish Clarion* and chairman of the party's Middle East Committee), Samuel might well have aspired to a more 'authoritative' position.[42] And yet, he remained attracted to this particular role that placed him in much closer relation to the rank-and-file membership.

In the 'Lost World' essays, he supplied his readers with some descriptions of the nature and the implications of these sorts of more practical 'activist-leadership' roles in the party drawing on both his personal experiences and official party documentation to do so. They make revealing reading:

> In the localities, too, authority was expected to be self-effacing. Branch secretaries were expected to *comport themselves as co-workers*, taking on a good deal of the dogsbody work, as the price of the trust which reposed in them. At branch meetings he/she was to *exercise a pastoral care, drawing the members in by allocating tasks to them, 'involving' them in the processes of decision making* … [and] *encouraging new comers to 'express' themselves*.[43]

---

40 Brian Harrison, 'Interview with Raphael Samuel', 18 September 1987, transcripts in author's possession, copies deposited at Raphael Samuel Archive (hereafter RSA), Bishopsgate Institute, London; Samuel, *The Lost World*, 88.
41 Ibid., 201.
42 Rapaport-Albert, 'Chimen Abramsky Obituary'.
43 Samuel, *The Lost World*, 125 (emphasis added).

And:

> One started at the *'level' of the sympathiser, emphasising common ground, 'building' on particular issues*, while at the same time *investing them with Party-mindedness*. Plied with Party literature, invited to Party meetings, above all *'involved' in some species of Party work* … the sympathiser was drawn into the comradeship of the Party by a hundred subtle threats.[44]

The role, as he recalled and described it, has some notable features. First, it was an acutely social role dealing directly with people. Second, it required the individuals in question to have a clear consciousness of their own performance in relation to the people they were dealing with, coming across as a co-worker, being welcoming and inclusive and so on. Third, much depended upon the individual's ability to synthesise different areas of expertise into a collective endeavour and identify areas of common ground between their interests and the person(s) they were engaging with. Finally, it called upon skills in using that common ground as the basis to infuse the subject with 'party mindedness', to provoke an internal transformation, all the more plausible and effective because the subject was complicit in the process. To summarise, this role utilised forms of intelligence and skill both pragmatic and profoundly psychological in character.

There are two key points to take from Samuel's early childhood communism. First, his earliest encounters with communism were profoundly social, rather than theoretical, in nature, experienced as a way of life rather than a political idea. Second, this Popular Front, wartime communism was heavily characterised by a complex dualism that bore significant consequences for the development of his thinking and behaviour. The party of his youth trod a precarious line between cooperation and critique, between unifying invocations of the nation and the divisive implications of class politics, between loyalty to Britain and to the Soviet Union. The organiser, the role he came to aspire to, further rehearsed this duality, being simultaneously part of but also at a distance from the wider movement. All these factors prompted in him an early but acute self-consciousness in terms of his positioning in relation to others and their positioning in relation to him. Intellectually, it accustomed him to moving deftly between descriptive modes and equipped him with the capacity to continually connect the particular instance with the wider picture that, at this time, was provided by communism as a political cause.

---

44 Ibid., 125–6 (emphasis added).

The Historians' Group of the Communist Party

The HGCP (1946–56) exemplified something of this dualism in its attempt to integrate Marxist political analysis with a reclaiming of the national past. The group formed in 1948 and contained a mixture of old and young, academic and non-academic historians.[45] Samuel was the group's youngest member, joining in 1951 as a schoolboy. As Bill Schwarz has argued, the group's work constituted a more substantial theorisation of popular frontism and its call for a battle of ideas.[46] This was, in part, conveyed through the historical work produced by its members who, it has been argued, laid the grounds for the development of critical cultural history.[47] A less acknowledged but important dimension of its activities lay in its educational-activist agenda, which aimed to encourage and support history-making as a common social activity and political tool in the battle of ideas. Despite drawing its initial impetus and objectives from the Popular Front, the group worked in very different times, which, inevitably, impacted upon the nature of its work.[48] The group's working life was conducted against the backdrop of the Cold War, and the increased hostility that this fostered towards British communists, the original enemies within, put even greater pressure on the need to forge direct links between Marxism as a critical political-economic theory and the domestic past.[49] At the same time, the stark dividing line imposed by the Cold War meant that there was also increased pressure for conformity to the party line. This produced tensions within the party, in particular towards the intellectuals and artists amongst the membership whose work,

---

45   Eric Hobsbawm, 'The Historians' Group of the Communist Party', in Maurice Cornforth, ed., *Rebels and Their Causes: Essays in Honour of A.L. Morton* (London: Lawrence & Wishart, 1978), 21–47.
46   Bill Schwarz, '"The People" in History: The Communist Party Historians Group 1946–1956', in Richard Johnson, Gregor McLennan, Bill Schwarz and David Sutton, eds, *Making Histories: Studies in History-writing and Politics* (Minneapolis: University of Minnesota, 1982).
47   Jim Obelkevich, 'New Developments in History in the 1950s and 1960s', *Contemporary British History*, 14:4 (2000), 125–6, doi.org/10.1080/13619460008581606; Harvey J. Kaye, *The British Marxist Historians* (Cambridge: Polity Press, 1984).
48   For further discussion of this, see Alastair MacLachlan, *The Rise and Fall of Revolutionary England: An Essay on the Fabrication of Seventeenth Century History* (London: Macmillan 1996), doi.org/10.1007/978-1-349-24572-7; Dennis Dworkin, *Cultural Marxism in Postwar Britain: History, the New Left, and the Origins of Cultural Studies* (Durham, NC/London: Duke University Press, 1997).
49   See Harriet Jones, 'The Impact of the Cold War', in Paul Addison and Harriet Jones, eds, *A Companion to Contemporary Britain* (Oxford: Blackwell, 2005), 24–6.

naturally, demanded conceptual and creative freedom. Always suspicious of this bourgeois figure, at the peak of Cold War hostilities, the party would make little room for anything suggesting ideological deviation.[50]

Psychologically, the experience of the Cold War, particularly in western countries such as Britain, exacerbated the already profoundly complex situation for party members, caught between their political convictions and their own ethnic identities. Something of this dilemma was illustrated by the CPGB's 1951 shift to 'The Road to British Socialism', an apparently ground-breaking shift away from Moscow, part of an attempt to revive flagging membership.[51] In reality, however, this break was limited, as demonstrated by the party's refusal to allow the HGCP to undertake a historical study of the party and its subsequent failure to publicly critique the decisions and actions of Moscow following the Yugoslav split in 1948 or after the disastrous events of 1956.

As Schwarz suggested, Christopher Hill's essay 'The Norman Yoke' is often seen as emblematic of the group's activities. This essay saw Hill break from his usual terrain of seventeenth-century high politics and turn his attention towards popular ideology.[52] Tracing the trajectory of popular accounts and invocations of 'The Norman Yoke', he demonstrated how the story had been continually made and remade in line with shifting political agendas and values. He concluded with the argument that only in Marxism were the key political principles of the story, 'the recognition of class struggle as the basis of politics, the deep sense of *Englishness* of the common people', distilled and clarified.[53] But, he warned, these principles *needed* the imaginative framework of historical storytelling to garner widespread appeal.[54] The work of Hill and others with the group offered a bold and compelling attempt at uniting national history with Marxist theory. In pursuit of this more rigorous analysis of the English

---

50 On the Communist Party and intellectuals, see Andy Croft, 'Authors Take Sides: Writers in the Communist Party 1920–1956', in Kevin Morgan, Nina Fishman and Geoff Andrews, eds, *Opening the Books: New Perspectives in the History of British Communism* (London: Pluto, 1995), 83–101; Andy Croft, 'The Boys Around the Corner: The Story of Fore Publications', in Andy Croft, ed., *A Weapon in the Struggle: A Cultural History of the British Communist Party* (London: Pluto Press, 1998), 142–62. For a source more contemporaneous to the times, see Neal Wood, *Communism and British Intellectuals* (London: Gollancz, 1959).
51 Harry Pollitt, 'The Road to British Socialism', *Looking Ahead* (London: Communist Party of Great Britain, 1947).
52 Christopher Hill, 'The Norman Yoke', in John Saville, ed., *Democracy and the Labour Movement: Essays in Honour of Dona Torr* (London: Lawrence & Wishart, 1954), 11–67.
53 Ibid., 66 (emphasis added).
54 Ibid. (emphasis added).

past, a number of the group, along with other non-Marxist historians, set up the journal *Past and Present* (1952–), which, whilst never a party mouthpiece, proclaimed itself dedicated to the championing of a new, scientific approach to history, an approach that distilled and clarified the colourful events and personnel of history, revealing their connection to deeper shifts in political-economic structures.

To return to this experience from Samuel's perspective, it must be remembered that on joining the group he was still a schoolboy, not a trained historian. Moreover he was, at this time, a committed activist and his interest in history was entirely ideological. His excitement was then piqued by the prospect of political battle rather than the musk of ancient documents. He was, at this time, far less invested, intellectually or emotionally, in the literal substance of the more specific historical debates that took place amongst the group (which is not to say that he was ignorant of or oblivious to them). It was, therefore, natural that he would be just as inspired by the group's other main *raison d'être*, its educational activities. This manifested not only in the dissemination of its historical work but in the organisation of large events and conferences and the facilitating of publications, such as *Our History* or the *Local History Bulletin* to encourage a wide cross-section of popular participation in history-making.

Later, in the wake of protracted and heated debates surrounding the trajectory of British Marxism, Samuel, in his private notes, wrote critically on the subjugation of the HGCP's educational work to the historiographical debates taking place amongst the academic membership:

> Another great weakness which was also the site of division with the group was local history. Betty Grant almost alone when she joined the group and produced a remarkable document [on this] Lip service was paid to this and she soldiered on with Our History.
>
> But if one compares the local history bulletin and Our History … this looks a very poor relation compared to the ambitious Past and Present.[55]

A handwritten aside to this:

> P&P [Past and Present] epoch making [another sentence not legible] Belligerently professional.[56]

---

55   Raphael Samuel, 'Notes on Communist Party Historians Group', Samuel 134/ British Marxist Historians, RSA.
56   Ibid.

For Samuel, the HGCP had several important influences. Not only did it demonstrate the importance of history as a crucial tool in the battle of ideas, the work of members such as Hill also showed creativity in traversing between nation, theory and in bringing to the fore focus on popular ideologies as a means of exploring political consciousness. On the other hand, his experiences with the group also left him with a sense of frustration at the degree to which the more prestigious academic battles so often took precedence over the educational-activist agenda.

Oxford student politics

Samuel had long been practising the skills of the aspiring organiser, but it was during his student days that he really began to develop independently his political ideas, practices and values, in particular his skills in recruitment and political organisation. In 1952, he went up to Oxford to read modern history at Balliol College under the supervision of Christopher Hill. Whilst under pressure from the party to be a good student, the majority of his time and efforts were spent on political activity. In this area, his output during this time was tremendous. He was actively involved in both the Oxford town party branch and the university's student group throughout his undergraduate years, becoming its secretary in the second year of his degree. He engaged with a range of other left-wing groups and initiatives, including the Socialist Club. He was the key moving force behind numerous political petitions and campaigns, always remaining alert to potential recruitment opportunities for the party. Towards the end of his Oxford years, he set his sights increasingly towards working with the Oxford Labour Club.

Samuel, committed to a minority political party that, in the Cold War years, was viewed by many with hostility and suspicion, had to work extremely hard in order to gain a voice in Oxford student political debate. Reinforcing this was the fact that he was now encountering a greater number of people who were not only acutely aware of the pragmatic implications of political power but came from families accustomed to exercising it and who, quite reasonably, expected to do so themselves in the future. One strategy he adopted for dealing with these issues was simply to cultivate a considerable flexibility in his political vocabulary. So intently did Samuel attempt to seek out common ground in discussions that he was even willing to adopt the less 'esoteric' political language of liberalism, resplendent with references to that comforting cover-all

8. AN INGRAINED ACTIVIST

concept of tolerance. In the course of this process, he recalled, he could not help becoming 'a bit liberal' himself, emphasising the extent to which he truly immersed himself into other people's political languages.[57]

Another tactic he adopted was organising campaigns on issues that cut across party-political lines. One revealing instance of this was his efforts to forge an alliance with existentialist philosophers against the prevailing dominance of Oxford analytical philosophy. The motivation behind this was that whilst both the analytical and the Marxist approach to philosophy gave a privileged position to materialist explanation, analytical philosophy was characterised by the stress that it placed on the pursuit of 'objectivity' in knowledge and in its emphasis on 'words' rather than 'things'. Marxism rejected both the notions that language could be detached from the material conditions and productive relationships in which it was embedded or that knowledge could ever be entirely 'objective' or value free. Samuel, as a communist, found common ground in his critique with those attracted to existentialist philosophy with its austere insistence on existence over essence. It was during this venture that he encountered Charles Taylor, a Canadian philosophy student (and future co-founder of the first New Left).[58]

There were further examples of his attempts to find issues or campaigns that brought together a number of disparate strands of the left-wing student body. He worked intently on a campaign against the hydrogen bomb in response to the H-bomb tests that were carried out on Christmas Island in 1953.[59] His work on this campaign actually took him into a realm outside of the official party policy of this time. He also dedicated a considerable amount of energy on issues relating to anti-colonialism, becoming active in the campaign against the British Government's deposition of the Guyanese Government in 1954. During his various campaigning activities, he encountered other figures who would go on to play key roles in the first New Left, including Stuart Hall, a Jamaican Rhodes Scholar graduate student, and Peter Sedgwick, a grammar school boy from a Christian family in Liverpool.[60]

---

57 Ibid.
58 Ibid.
59 Harrison, 'Interview with Raphael Samuel', 18 September 1987.
60 Harrison, 'Interview with Raphael Samuel', 20 October 1987.

Apart from these specific campaigns, a more structured example of Samuel's attempts to liaise across political lines can be seen in his involvement, at the behest of the party, with the Oxford Socialist Club. The club, a 1930s breakaway group that had formed out of what had been the Oxford Labour Club, had been dormant for some years. The CPGB, committed to 'The British Road to Socialism', viewed the club as an opportunity to create a 'broad front organisation', and so Samuel, along with several of his friends, set about reviving it. In part, it acted as space that allowed for those outside of the official party to interact with communist ideas and politics. Hall later described debate in the club as wide ranging, pre-empting many of the issues that would later come to preoccupy the first New Left.[61] Hall also recalled Samuel's remarkable ability to bring even the most expansive and apparently abstract of questions in socialist political philosophy back into some kind of direct connection with worker unrest at the local Cowley car plant, an early glimpse of his prowess for connective thinking![62] He became closely involved with the club's journal, *The Oxford Left*, initially taking charge of publicity (Trinity 1953), advancing to the editorial board (Hillary 1954) and eventually becoming the sole named editor (Michaelmas 1954).[63] The journal gives some sense of Samuel's interests and political approach during this time. Articles such as 'The Mind of British Imperialism' demonstrated his concern and astute sensitivity towards the internal dynamics of political mentalities and the ways in which these were reformulated over time.[64]

After 1954, however, Samuel began to harbour some scepticism about the party's strategic use of the club, feeling that it 'stopped people being faced with the hard question of whether or not they would become Communists'.[65] This discomfort could be construed as an example of his unease with the 'The British Road to Socialism' stance of the CPGB and his absorption of the Cold War Cominform concern to demarcate

---

61 Stuart Hall, 'The Life and Times of the First New Left', *New Left Review*, 61 (January–February 2010), 182.
62 Stuart Hall, oral communication with author, May 2012, Hampstead, London.
63 Both the Socialist Club and the club's journal, *The Oxford Left*, anticipated many of the themes and issues that preoccupied the first New Left and dominated the contents of *Universities and Left Review*, addressing issues such as the role of intellectuals, colonial issues, questions of contemporary socialism and the politics of popular culture.
64 Raphael Samuel, 'Socialism and the Middle Classes', *The Oxford Left*, Hillary Term (1954); Raphael Samuel, 'The Mind of British Imperialism', *The Oxford Left*, Michaelmas Term (1954).
65 Harrison, 'Interview with Raphael Samuel', 18 September 1987. Whilst the CPGB had committed to 'The British Road to Socialism' in 1951, it was only after the death of Stalin in 1953 that a greater sense of the party 'opening up' was experienced.

and clarify political positions. Equally, for a 20-year-old man, still making the journey from youth to adulthood, such sectarianism might also be connected to the psychological and emotional processes of late adolescence and the desire for sharply defined lines between those who were 'one of us' and those who were 'fellow travellers', to be approached with caution. From another perspective, this can also be seen as evidence of his belief in alliance between openly *different* factions amongst the left.

Samuel's growing interest in the Oxford Labour Club was in keeping with his doubts concerning the use of the Socialist Club in party strategy. It was also compatible with his desire to forge connections beyond the confines of student life and his efforts to expand the grounds for intellectual debate. Following the CPGB's 1951 policy transition and later the death of Stalin in 1953, there was a slight thaw in the intensity of the Cold War hostility, which mellowed, marginally, the general feeling towards communists. On becoming the branch secretary of the communist student group, he became even more concerned to take the Labour Party seriously as a political force. This drew him into a closer relationship with the Labour club, which brought him perilously close to being in direct violation of his instructions from the CPGB, whose relationship with Labour remained profoundly uneasy throughout this time.[66] The intellectual and emotional constitution of the Labour club students was distinct from those who identified with the harder line of communism. Communists, Samuel would later suggest, formed a sort of 'literati', typically harbouring interests in literature, poetry or philosophy and often knowing very little about the practicalities of political life.[67] Despite articulating a formal (theoretical) appreciation for the natural sciences, the student communists that he engaged with were more likely to approach politics on the basis of larger metaphysical or moral terms. The Labour club, by contrast, had a more pragmatic character in its understanding of political power,

---

66   Harrison, 'Interview with Raphael Samuel', 18 September 1987. Whilst the CPGB initially sought a close working relationship with the Attlee-led Labour Government, by 1947, after repeated rejections, the party began to criticise Labour Party policy. Following the defeat of Labour in 1951, the relationship remained hostile. See also Keith Laybourn, *Marxism in Britain: Dissent, Decline and Re-emergence, 1945–c.2000* (London/New York: Routledge, 2006), 21–2, doi.org/10.4324/ 9780203300626.

67   A sample of Samuel's immediate friendship group reflects this: Pearson and Hall were English literature students; Taylor a philosophy student; Sedgwick initially read classics, later changing to psychology.

largely because they could more confidently expect to exercise it. More importantly, it had a greater appreciation for the mechanics and apparatus of political power.

And so Samuel immersed himself in a complex world of alliance and negotiation, requiring a clever use of language and a strategic engagement with issues and other political groups. The technique that he most favoured, and utilised above all others, was, however, an even more personal one: the adoption of a self-consciously charming and agreeable public persona.[68] He later described this situation:

> I mean there wouldn't be a minute that I wouldn't be aware that I was a Communist until I left the Communist Party at 22. Anything I did, there would always be a kind of sense that it was in some way forwarding the cause – even if it was something like playing football or tennis or shove ha'penny or just sitting around, because even making oneself agreeable was in some sense making one's unpalatable politics more palatable … There was a sense of wanting to make the unpalatable palatable by showing a human face. Given that you actually had a politics that was zealous, the one thing you didn't do … in the Communist Party was be zealous about it because you wouldn't get a hearing for it in a hostile climate.[69]

As this comment suggests, there was no dividing line between political activism and socialising, between politics and personal relationships. Debates would take place over coffee in the common room or rage late into the night in student bedrooms. Quite often they were played as a form of sport involving posturing, jostling, teasing and sparring, all of which had entertaining, even comedic elements about them. He later recalled that he had:

> actually liked arguing with Tories, and we used to get quite a lot of fun – in a way, almost as court jesters. It was such an improbable thing for anybody to _be_ a Communist – and they were very tolerant of us, and we were delighted to be tolerated.[70]

Protests, attended by only a handful of people and promptly dispersed by the college rugby club, provided a sense of camaraderie and solidarity amongst the motley few who had turned out. In this sense, politics was the

---

68 One might view his earlier decision to anglicise his name to Ralph as part of this desire.
69 Harrison, 'Interview with Raphael Samuel', 20 October 1987.
70 Harrison, 'Interview with Raphael Samuel', 18 September 1987.

source of deep-rooted, long-lasting friendships, amplified and intensified in their intimacy by the single-sex college environments in which so much of this discussion and organising took place.[71]

His extraordinary pursuit of Dennis Butt, a fellow student, gives a striking illustration of this. Butt was a mature student and former wool sorter who had come to Oxford University from the independent, trade union – affiliated Ruskin College. A longstanding Labour man, he went on to become a 'prize recruit' for the CPGB and one of Samuel's closest friends.[72] In the process of attempting to recruit Butt, he immersed himself in the cultural, psychological and emotional values involved in Labour politics saying later that: '[M]y effort, which lasted about a year, to recruit him, as it were, on Labour ground. And I actually, without knowing it, made myself into a kind of labour person.'[73] This anecdote, analysed more closely, suggests a rough prototype for Samuel's later methodology as a historian-educator. First, he worked hard to understand not only the language of labour but also, through forming a close friendship with Butt, to understand the specific ways that Butt as an individual interpreted it. He then translated his own politics into a form tailored specifically to Butt, enabling him to communicate on a deeply personal and meaningful level with the man. This, in turn, allowed Butt to then 'metabolise' this politics more readily. Such a process reflects the organiser's insight into the need to 'involve' prospective members and make them complicit in the challenging and changing of their own ideas. It also echoes the sort of pedagogical strategy an effective teacher might use. Another notable dimension to Samuel's thinking revealed by this anecdote is that this process had an impact on him, too. He became 'a little bit labour', as he had become 'a little bit liberal' through his other activities. In the intensity of this learning process he was, therefore, not fully in control but also subject to having his own mindset challenged and changed.

Up until the age of 22, Samuel was a committed communist activist devoted to the party and convinced that his future lay in service to the cause. In 1956, the year of his graduation from Oxford with a first-class degree, this all-encompassing world was shattered. It received its first major blow following Nikita Khrushchev's revelations about the

---

71 Samuel later commented that these were 'extremely intense male friendships' sharing similarities with 'heterosexual relationships and jealousies'. Harrison, 'Interview with Raphael Samuel', 20 October 1987.
72 Harrison, 'Interview with Raphael Samuel', 18 September 1987.
73 Harrison, 'Interview with Raphael Samuel', 20 October 1987.

brutalities of Stalinism in the spring of that year. It was brought under further pressure by the refusal of the CPGB to permit open discussion amongst the membership or countenance internal reform amongst its own managerial infrastructure. The final straw came in the wake of the Soviet suppression of the Hungarian uprising in November and the CPGB's continued lack of decisive response. Shortly after this, Samuel, along with many other prominent members, left the party. Yet, although detached from the party, and increasingly disillusioned with the idea of political leadership, he did not abandon the sort of political work or values that had characterised his youth, rather he now turned to them all the more fulsomely. Looking back at that time, he explained: 'I really was an organizer and believed in organization and believed really in discipline, I suppose, and it was a belief in unity and above all … I … believed in being positive.'[74] Within a fortnight of leaving the party, he became the prime moving force behind the journal *Universities and Left Review*, part of a fledgling New Left movement, and subsequently an organising force for the Campaign for Nuclear Disarmament, the New Left club network and the inspired but ill-fated Partisan cafe. In this sense, as Hobsbawm, his former party comrade, would fondly recall, Samuel truly was an 'ingrained activist'.[75]

Samuel's youth provided an important crucible for both his intellectual interests and practices. As a young communist activist, growing up against the backdrop provided by the switch to popular front communism, his political work was practical and people-centred rather than primarily theoretical in nature. It aimed at engaging with and involving a range of people from both inside but also from outside of the party membership in political activity. For this, it was necessary to draw on a capacity to empathise and to consciously make use of his persona as a political tool. Outside of the formal CPGB policy position, this was further reinforced by the complexities provided by his wider social-cultural positioning, a Jewish family in English society, an only child surrounded by adults. He had always to work hard in order to gain a hearing; aware and sensitive to cultural differences, he could take nothing for granted. His aspiration to the specific party role of the organiser further reinforced this, developing in him ever more sophisticated analytical and communicative abilities. Whilst the roles of activist and organiser were, in the first place, embedded

---

74 Ibid.
75 Hobsbawm, *Interesting Times*, 212.

within the explicit context of the party and attached to a specific political agenda, they nevertheless imprinted upon him an important set of deep-rooted intellectual values and skills based around a capacity to both understand people outside of his own immediate sociocultural group and, as a result of this deeply personalised approach, to effectively engage with, even challenge, their existing ideas and, in the process, his own.

Recognising this distinctive form of applied intelligence not only restores to Samuel a greater sense of his complexity as an individual thinker, it also provides a valuable insight into the kind of person-centred, direct-action politics that he, through the Workshop, came to most exemplify. This suggests the need to reconsider the significance of the Workshop's political, pedagogical and historiographical agenda. The deeply contextualised and personalised nature of this form of intelligence also demonstrates the importance of applying a biographical approach to this sort of thinker. The great power of the organiser, particularly a communist one at the height of the Cold War, was the ability to work subtle transformations 'unseen and unheard'. It is only through close examination of the individual, situated within their network of relationships and acting in response to specific contexts, that its effects and implications can, even partially, be discerned.

The significance of engaging with different forms of intellectual skill and work lies not only in gaining a better understanding of individual figures such as Samuel but has significant implications for intellectual history more generally. Thinking is a fundamentally social activity that goes beyond the reading of particular text and occurs across a whole cross-section of communicative practices, many of which occur through direct person-to-person interactions. The potent transformative power of the personal relationship may leave little trace on the documentary record but, as Rowbotham suggested (quoted above), it can also linger longer in oral memory having, in the end, a deeper and more enduring effect on the individual or individuals who encounter it.

9

Pursuing the Antipodean: Bernard Smith, Identity and History

Sheridan Palmer

Identity mattered to Bernard Smith, probably more than for most people. As an illegitimate child and a fostered ward of the state, anonymity had haunted him, but it also drove his ambitions. By using these two opposing structures as tension rods, identity and anonymity, he sought validation through his work and recognition as an art and cultural historian. His revision of Australia's modern cultural evolution, written from a fiercely independent position, was based around colonial inheritance, cultural traffic and transformation, but it was also intended to shake up an 'uncritical culture' and situate it in a more conspicuous international position. From the mid-1940s, his historiography became the benchmark for scholars and artists in their pursuit of, or argument with, Antipodean identity and cultural autonomy, and this chapter seeks to explain why Bernard Smith's rethinking of antipodeanism – a term he coined – and his aim to legitimate Australian culture within a globalised postwar world was a pioneering and brilliant study of cultural origins and evolution; at a personal level it reflected his own genesis.

'To understand Australia one must look elsewhere'[1]

Writing to his friend Lindsay Gordon in 1948, Bernard Smith stated:

> I am becoming convinced that the conceptions of … Utopia, and 'working man's paradise' in the Southern Land is one of the central historical ideas running through Australian literature, art and politics. It is perhaps the myth-making of the voyager and the emigrant … another aspect of *Illusion and Reality*.[2]

Bernard Smith, 1948 passport photo
Source: Bernard Smith Papers, National Library of Australia.

---

1   Noel McLachlan, 'Godzone: The Australian Intellectual', *Meanjin* (Melbourne), 26:1 (1967), 6.
2   Bernard Smith to Lindsay Gordon, 23 November 1948, Bernard Smith Papers, National Library of Australia (hereafter NLA), Acc. 10.088, Box 19.

At the time, Smith was one of Australia's up-and-coming young intellectuals and had arrived in London on a British Council scholarship to study at the Courtauld Institute of Art.

His research project was a comparative survey of the origins of Australian art with that of British painting and architecture between 1788 and 1835, and to consider in greater detail the impact of the British on the South Pacific. He had already commenced this with his acclaimed analysis of Australia's sociocultural evolution from colonial settlement to 1945 in his first book, *Place, Taste and Tradition: A Study of Australian Art since 1788*. His area of research, however, was a relatively new field of enquiry, especially the impact of British imperialism in the Pacific and colonial settlement in the Antipodes, but his academic approach to the subject would prove significant on several counts. First, his meticulously incisive, polemical nature would evaluate British material from an Australian perspective, and second, he possessed an acute sense of identity as an outsider.

On his first meeting with Anthony Blunt, the director of the Courtauld Institute, Smith was taken aback by the Englishman's cultural superiority, conspicuous class-consciousness and the inference that Australia was subcultural; a hangover, he assumed, of a postcolonial mentality. Later, he discovered a letter that Blunt had written to John Summerson, the director of the Sir John Soane Museum at Lincoln Inn Fields, which proved his reaction had not been unfounded: 'This is to introduce Mr Bernard Smith from Australia, who has been hitherto working on the early phase of painting in and of Australia with remarkable results (contrary to the expectations aroused by the subject).'[3] What Smith did not know was that Blunt's private life was in complete turmoil and his 'chilling elegance' a mask for his personal and political alienation.[4] Nevertheless, Blunt's condescending and patronising manner made him feel like a 'mere colonial, a modern Antipodean' and it reinforced his perception that England was a self-absorbed nation. Historian Perry Anderson has defined this as a country that possesses a cultural tradition with an 'absent centre'. England, he wrote, 'may be defined as the European country which – uniquely – never produced either classical sociology or

---

3   Anthony Blunt to John Summerson, 19 October 1949 (copy), Bernard Smith Papers, NLA, MS 8680, Acc. 10.088, Box 33.
4   Smith later claimed that Blunt may have known about his communist affiliation and that MI5 were monitoring his movements and, given Blunt's undercover activity as a spy, it is understandable he would have been nervous about Smith's presence.

national Marxism ... [It] was never challenged as a whole from within'.[5] In this context, Bernard Smith would use his encounter with Blunt and other elitist Englishmen as a tuning fork to understand British hegemony both in its historical and modern form. Moreover, Smith's encounter with Blunt made him look at himself and what it meant to be Antipodean in the world, and to resituate it politically, culturally and globally.

Fortunately for Bernard Smith, Anthony Blunt moved him from the Courtauld Institute to that 'republic of learning' the Warburg Institute, where he studied under some of Europe's most brilliant scholars, most of whom were exiled from Hitler's Germany.[6] Under their guidance, he delved deep into British archives and libraries looking at some of the earliest material on the southern hemisphere and how *Terra Australis Incognita* had first been perceived – what he described as the upside-down long view of historical reconstruction. Smith also realised how profoundly the mythological memory had permeated history, and was reminded of his friend Lindsay Gordon's parting words: 'Somewhere in the primitive deep of the mind and the ritual of fare-welling ships there is something of [the] birth image mixed up with the hint of Styx.'[7] Myths, symbols and utopian or renewal concepts had imaginatively interlaced history since ancient time, and the publication of *mappa mundi*, especially from the early sixteenth and seventeenth centuries, was integral to the perception of *Terra incognita*.[8] Francis Bacon's *New Atlantis*, published in 1627, was an imaginative construction and a travel fantasy concerning a new utopia in the Pacific Ocean, which influenced thinkers such as the French Encyclopaedists, Immanuel Kant and Karl Marx as a model for renovating scientific, moral and social laws.[9] Indeed, Bacon's fictional 'Salomon House' became an institutional model for the Royal Society founded in 1660, which in turn influenced numerous other academies.[10]

---

5   Perry Anderson, quoted in Lesley Johnson, *The Cultural Critics: From Matthew Arnold to Raymond Williams* (London: Routledge & Kegan Paul, 1972), 12.
6   Blunt told Bernard that he could not read an Honours course at the Courtauld Institute as he had not completed an undergraduate degree nor was his subject compatible to the Courtauld Institute's research program.
7   Lindsay Gordon to Bernard Smith, 7 September 1948, Bernard Smith Papers, NLA, Acc. 10.088, Box 19.
8   See Bronwen Douglas, '*Terra Australis* to Oceania: Racial Geography in the "Fifth Part of the World"', *Journal of Pacific History*, 45:2 (2010), 179–210, doi.org/10.1080/00223344.2010.501696.
9   Bronwen Price, ed., *Francis Bacon's New Atlantis: New Interdisciplinary Essays* (Manchester/New York: Manchester University Press, 2002), 14–16.
10 Ibid., 15.

Other sources included Robert Burton's 'ideal kingdom': 'it may be in *Terra Australis Incognita* … perhaps under the Equator, that paradise of the world … the longitude for some reason I will conceal'.[11]

But it was perhaps Linnaeus's system of identification and classification that had significant implications for the New World. In a recent study of race and nationalism David Bindman noted that:

> Linnaeus offered a classification of humanity, based upon the Four Continents or Four Quarters of the Earth and the Four Temperaments associated with each … add[ing] a number of other categories, including the Wild Man and various forms of monster. The fourfold division was compatible with the idea of a lost primeval unity, the Judaeo-Christian Garden of Eden.[12]

Such diversification of *geographica* led men of science, theology and exploration during the Enlightenment to expect in the unknown fifth part of the world, 'human variety as on a scale of savagery to civilization, contingent on climate and environment'.[13] This literature was fundamental for Bernard Smith's understanding of how European artists, explorers and settlers imagined and visualised the landscape and inhabitants of the South Pacific during the eighteenth and nineteenth centuries, and which as he discovered, still persisted in postwar England. Australia, it seemed, had retained its mythical status amongst educated Englishmen such as Anthony Blunt and Sir Kenneth Clark, even if it was for the sake of rarefied amusement. But as Edward Said later argued, 'Men have always divided the world up into regions having either real or imagined distinction from each other'.[14]

As Bernard Smith uncovered a plethora of drawings, paintings, objects and specimens of flora and fauna, much of which lay hidden in museums and collectors' cabinets since it had been deposited during the eighteenth and early nineteenth centuries, he realised how much the sheer variation of species would have stupefied both learned and lay people and led them

---

11   O.H.K. Spate, 'The Pacific: Home of Utopias', in Eugene Kamenka, ed., *Utopias* (Melbourne: Oxford University Press, 1987), 23.
12   David Bindman, *Ape to Apollo: Aesthetics and the Idea of Race in the 18th Century* (London: Reaktion Books and the Paul Mellon Centre for Studies in British Art, 2002), 17.
13   Ibid.
14   Edward Said, *Orientalism* (London: Penguin Books, 1978), 39.

to believe they had 'gradually complete[d] the picture of the universe as a vast ordered chain of being'. The Antipodes had 'open[ed] a new road to the science of man', or, as Ernst Cassirer put it:

> the motto, 'Back to Nature' [could] be heard everywhere, in inexhaustible variations. Descriptions of the customs of primitive peoples were eagerly snatched up; there was a mounting urge to acquire a wider view of primitive forms of life … Diderot made a report of Bougainville on his trip to the South Seas his starting point for celebrating with lyrical exaggeration the simplicity, the innocence, and the happiness of primitive peoples.[15]

Shortly after commencing his research, Smith received an invitation to join a large project on the art of Cook's voyages. The New Zealand scholar Dr J.C. Beaglehole, who was working on an edition of Cook's Journals for the Hakluyt Society, wrote to him:

> Very interesting to me as we have been paddling around in NZ with the idea of the European trained eye impacted upon by Polynesian appearance and I should welcome extremely a treatment of the subject by one who has really made a study of it as you have. Also I am looking forward to your impressions of all the Cook stuff.[16]

The 'Cook stuff' consisted of some 3,000 material objects, journals and descriptive works of art, much of which had rarely been seen. Bernard Smith later admitted that 'none of us had the faintest idea of the scale of the task involved … [and it] determined much of my subsequent scholarly life … [and] also directed my Warburg research'.[17]

This material, which Smith had to catalogue, was considered 'low art' – apart from finished oil paintings by the professionally trained artist William Hodges – and belonged to ethnographic studies and natural history. For Bernard Smith, however, the attraction to early colonial or exploration art was twofold: it bridged the trained scientific eye with visual descriptions often made *in situ* by trained naturalists or untrained artists, and, importantly, it showed the origins of contact, exchange and cultural convergence. While his research demanded a comprehensive analysis of history, from scientific and botanical discoveries to philosophies of identity, politics, social and power relations, it was the art of topography,

---

15   Ernst Cassirer, *The Question of Jean Jacques Rousseau* (Bloomington/London: Indiana University Press, 1963), 49.
16   J.C. Beaglehole to Bernard Smith, 6 April 1950, Bernard Smith Papers, NLA, Acc 10.088, Box 4.
17   Bernard Smith to Doug Munro, 6 April 2000 (copy provided to author by Doug Munro).

botany and ethnography, or that which depicted the noble or ignoble natives that excited him. The intricate and superbly drawn flora and the crude realism or unsophisticated drawings and portraits of indigenous peoples provided a more accurate and comprehensive procession of discovery, and revealed the local agencies of encounter between nativism and imperialism, between 'the colonised and the colonisers'.

Moreover, Smith found this type of art far more valuable than 'high art' or the romantic landscapes and grand history paintings finished in the artist's studio for an elite audience such as the Royal Academy, where fashionable style was preferable to truth. 'Low art' provided information, and for Smith 'there was no embarrassment to look at [it]'.[18] This statement discloses his working-class background and Marxist beliefs, in that art should possess a social consciousness or combine a utopian aesthetic within its cultural production. As he put it, Marxism gave him a 'dislike for any kind of elitist attitude to a subject'.[19]

An excellent example of 'low art' is the sketch titled 'First Contact', originally thought to be by Sir Joseph Banks but more recently identified as being drawn by a young Ra'iatean native called Tupaia, who sailed on Cook's first voyage in 1768.[20] It is an extraordinary work of innocent vision and depicts the face of British imperialism as it engages with the exotic – a naval officer bartering a crayfish with a Māori. Indeed, it was this type of naive drawing that best encapsulates one of Bernard Smith's most important historical tropes, that of the 'revision of territorialism, possession and ownership as seen through the dramatic acquisition of the exotic as a potential commodity'.[21]

---

18   Bernard Smith, interviewed by Neville Meaney, 6 November 1986, NLA, Oral History Programme, TRC 2053/17.
19   Ibid.
20   Harold B. Carter identified Tupaia as the artist in April 1997 from a letter written by Banks in 1812 to Dawson Turner, a Fellow of the Royal Society. See Keith Vincent Smith, 'Tupaia's sketchbook', Electronic British Library Journal, 2005, www.bl.uk/eblj/2005articles/articles.html, in which he quotes Banks's letter: 'Tupaia the Indian who came with me from Otaheite Learnd to draw in a way not Quite unintelligible[.] The genius for Caricature which all wild people Possess Led him to Caricature me & he drew me with a nail in my hand delivering it to an Indian who sold me a Lobster but with my other hand I had a firm fist on the Lobster determined not to Quit the nail till I had Livery and Seizin of the article purchased.'
21   Sheridan Palmer, *Hegel's Owl: The Life of Bernard Smith* (Sydney: Power Publications, 2016), 122. This chapter draws extensively upon this biography.

But Bernard Smith did not intend to analyse Australia 'as a geographer might … in terms of physical structure and climate, nor yet purely in terms of literature and art, but something between the two'.[22] Synthesising complex ideas and finding interdisciplinary connections and overarching narratives reflected his pluralist methodology, but it also revealed his skill in locating interstices. The focus on art as a recording tool of the binary manifestations of science and nature, the empirical and the romantic, also repositioned the role of the artist as primary witness and descriptor of historical events and things that had never before been seen. This lifted the art of exploration out of its narrow confines towards a new visual plateau in which 'witness' art illuminated the root of contact with the exotic and unknown. It was an extraordinary lens through which the geopolitics of imperialism, identity and cultural convergence could be more thoroughly contextualised. Even James Cook and Joseph Banks had insisted that 'the drawings made on the voyages would provide a better idea of the matter under discussion than their own words'.[23] The philosopher Emmanuel Levinas also believed that '[t]he judgement of history is set forth in the visible. Historical events are the visible par excellence; their truth is produced in evidence'.[24] Between this descriptive 'low art' and literature on imperial exploration, Bernard Smith was able to conceptualise how the idea of a 'working man's paradise', or a new society in the great southern continent was envisaged.

One of Britain's most influential patrons and wealthy young 'experimental gentlemen', who helped determine the future of New Holland, was Joseph Banks. He accompanied Cook on his first voyage in 1768 and his advice that *Terra Australis* could become 'a food basket for both Great Britain's and Europe's immigrants, convicts and her "redundant poor"' was heeded by the House of Commons in the late 1770s.[25] It was pivotal to the colonising of New South Wales as well as relieving pressure on England's penitentiary problems and burgeoning population. As Smith noted, Australia:

---

22   Bernard Smith, 'The Artist's Vision of Australia', given as a talk on the BBC in 1950 and published in *The Listener*, 30 November 1950, 631–3, and later in *The Antipodean Manifesto: Essays in Art and History* (Melbourne: Oxford University Press, 1976), 159.
23   Bernard Smith, proposal to Yale University Press, 1978, Bernard Smith Papers, Mitchell Library, MSS 5202, add on 2039.
24   Emanuel Levinas, quoted in Peter Osborne, *The Politics of Time: Modernity and Avant-Garde* (London/New York: Verso, 1995), 123.
25   Alan Frost, 'The Planting of New South Wales: Sir Joseph Banks and the Creation of an Antipodean Europe', in R.E.R. Banks, B. Elliott, J.G. Hawkes, D. King-Hele and G.L. Lucas, eds, *Sir Joseph Banks: A Global Perspective* (Richmond: Royal Botanic Gardens Kew, 1994), 137.

inherited neither craft traditions nor the Grand Style of Sir Joshua Reynolds. The convicts and the 'redundant poor,' who constituted the early Australian community had been dispossessed of their cultural traditions almost as completely as they had been dispossessed of their land and their citizenship by the legal code of eighteenth century England. No country in the history of the world has begun the history of its art under more unpromising circumstances than Australia.[26]

But the priorities of imperial possession and mercantile expansionism also simultaneously presented a paradox of freedom and imprisonment, material wealth and reformism, scientific progress and economic materialism. As the influential Joseph Banks oscillated 'between the world of science and the world of taste', he and his circle of dilettante gentlemen created a concept of *Terra Australis* as a potential destination for the grand tourist. This quest to satisfy an elite appetite for curiosities enhanced the Antipodes not only as an appendage of Empire but as a utopia inhabited by the noble savage, weird animals and strange vegetation, which, in the public's imagination, confirmed those ancient perceptions of the Antipodes as a large, primitive counterbalance to the civilised northern hemisphere.

As the Europeans and British sailed into the South Pacific, they were confronted by their own limitations and constructed the spectacular 'unknown … in terms of the known'.[27] This, as far as Bernard Smith was concerned, illustrated 'the insular British mind' and how it reacted 'to the vast ocean spaces' and 'free-love' arcadias of the South Sea islands, in particular the Society Islands and Tahiti.[28] What it did achieve, however, was a new system of perception from which a transformative arts program developed in Britain and Europe. W.T.J. Mitchell has pointed out that '[j]ust as the landscape movement was at its height the islands of the South Pacific and the larger continental prize of Australia loomed to dislodge the Romantic pastoral'.[29] The exotic lands of the New World and the sensual nature of its Oceanic people introduced a new language,

---

26 Bernard Smith, 'Australian Art and War', Bernard Smith Papers, NLA, MS 8680, Box 2/65.
27 Greg Dening, 'Ethnography on my Mind', in Bain Attwood, ed., *Boundaries of the Past* (Melbourne: History Institute, 1990), 15.
28 Bernard Smith, *Imagining the Pacific: In the Wake of Cook's Voyages* (Melbourne: Miegunyah Press, 1992), xi.
29 Bernard Smith, *European Vision and the South Pacific: A Study in the History of Art and Ideas* (Oxford: Clarendon Press, 1960), 4; W.J.T. Mitchell, 'Imperial Landscape', in Mitchell, ed., *Landscape and Power* (Chicago/London: University of Chicago Press, 1994), 18.

both literary and pictorial, that helped change the nature of English art during the late eighteenth century away from classicism towards a poetic or mysterious sublime.

While exploration of the South Pacific may have initially romanticised the origins of European settlement in Australia, the anticipated utopia fell well short of being a working man's paradise. Instead, it became a colonial experiment in dispossession for the transported and the Indigenous inhabitants and a fatal attrition of native populations through murder and disease. What enabled Bernard Smith to analyse this period and its imperialist material so brilliantly was his acute sense of the 'unequal exchange' – typified by his meeting with Anthony Blunt – and his hostility to anything that subordinated ideas or relations of exchange. This yielded an understanding of power relations that gave his ideas and grasp of history real resonance, especially when he reached one of his most significant intellectual peaks during the height of the Cold War. Later in 1980, when he gave the Boyer lectures, *The Spectre of Truganini*, Smith drew upon the crime of dispossession that had occurred during the British invasion and colonisation of Australia, and the subsequent immolation of the Indigenous population. These brilliant essays on 'the locked cupboard of our history' revealed his sensitivity towards the injustice of conquest, whether historical or contemporary, and anything or anyone subverted by moral and ethical arrogance.[30]

Bernard Smith's two-year sojourn in England marked a major turning point in his career; it crystallised his scholarship and launched him into a school of international scholars, many of whom critically tested his intellectual credentials while also praising his ideas and achievements. For Bernard Smith, it confirmed the importance of measuring Australia against Europe, locating the intervals between reality and myth and synthesising the cultural and political strands that linked or locked these two countries together. As he said, 'I was looking for sources and the sources were northern European and still are'.[31]

---

30 Bernard Smith, *The Spectre of Truganini* (Sydney: Australian Broadcasting Commission, 1980), 10.
31 'Interview with Bernard Smith' by Rex Butler, in Butler, ed., *Radical Revisionism: An Anthology of Writings on Australian Art* (Brisbane: Institute of Modern Art, 2005), 76.

9. PURSUING THE ANTIPODEAN

The quest for identity

Later in his career, Bernard Smith gave a seminar paper titled 'On being Antipodean' in which he spoke of his 'identity paradox'. Identity was about the ontology of interactive relationships between people and place – to think of Europe was to think of the other.[32] His self-perception as the singular 'I', a *filius nullius* dispossessed of his natural parents, had taught him humiliation and social inferiority – 'Whose ya father Ben', the school boys would taunt or, as he later admitted, 'a state ward can't expect much'.[33] So embedded in Smith's identity was this notion of being different that he emotionally distanced himself from those who wielded authority.[34] In a letter to his friend Vincent Buckley in 1984, he expanded on this: 'many illegitimate children who do not succumb to self-pity experience a kind of distancing from society. One sees oneself almost as a kind of witness figure'.[35] This ability to stand apart and conscientiously monitor society would develop into a conceptual device with which to archive the Antipodes and map how the British constructed the Pacific as a place and shaped its possession and reception. He summed it up as 'I am thinking of distance, or more precisely distancing, as an intellectual tool both for aesthetic evaluation and for writing of history'.[36]

Bernard Smith also spoke of how his research in England in the late 1940s had made him 'look back at his own intellectual origins' and cultural inheritance. Born in 1916, he experienced the after effects of the Great War, the hardships of the Depression and witnessed, from a distance, the full panorama of the Second World War. Like many who matured during the angry decades of the 1930s and 1940s, when fascism and the European crisis dramatically altered concepts of identity, national boundaries and political power, he moved towards the left and joined

---

32 See Peter Beilharz, *Imagining the Antipodes: Culture, Theory and the Visual in the Work of Bernard Smith* (Cambridge: Cambridge University Press, 1997), doi.org/10.1017/CBO9780511470202.
33 Bernard Smith, *The Boy Adeodatus: The Portrait of a Lucky Young Bastard* (Ringwood: Penguin Books, 1985), 267; Smith, conversation with the author.
34 Bernard Smith claimed he was never abandoned as a child; he lived with his mother for the first six months of his life and once fostered saw her daily until the age of two, after which she wrote regularly, with Bernard corresponding with her once he had learnt to write. He also met his biological father on several occasions as a small boy but, from an early age, believed he did not belong to anyone. See Bernard Smith's first volume of autobiography, *The Boy Adeodatus*, for an account of his life to 1940.
35 Bernard Smith to Vincent Buckley, 8 December 1984 (copy), Bernard Smith Papers, NLA, Acc. 10.088, Box 66.
36 Smith, unpublished notes, Bernard Smith Papers, NLA, MS 8680, Box 7/55/155.

the Communist Party. This was the only party that he believed was politically and ideologically capable of renovating society and rectifying the hierarchical machine that Australia had inherited.

Also at this time in Sydney, Smith met a group of European refugee artists and scholars who had fled Nazism; outsiders defined by the dispossession of their cultural heritage and homeland. Though they had belonged to some of the great intellectual and artistic institutions of Europe, Europe was now their Antipodes. Not only did these exiled scholars dramatically expand Bernard Smith's knowledge, but they taught him to think on a global scale; it was through them that he began to develop his concept of 'antipodal inversion' and how cultural traffic affected provincial identity and its relation to metropolitan centres. Moreover, the refugees were firsthand witnesses of Europe's barbaric decline. Where once during the eighteenth and nineteenth centuries its imperial hand had dominated the South Pacific, in the 1940s Europe's and Britain's power lay dispersed and 'the disinherited' were the 'driving force for a revolutionary reconstruction of society'.[37] It made Smith look at what had been brought to Australia, what had been absorbed, transformed or rejected or, as he retrospectively put it:

> I was trying to define the business of what it is to be Australian, that is I was looking for what is typically Australian. But the only way you could logically define this, I thought, was to find out what is European, to distinguish what is European from what is Australian.[38]

For Bernard Smith, culture was a historical process and a man-made construction. The Pacific historian and ethnographer Greg Dening similarly believed that 'Culture' was an 'analytic concept … of all human behaviour considered as expression and communication. Culture is an observer's construct'.[39] Spatial and temporal distance was inherent in the observer's method, and Smith used it to identify intellectual and cultural patterns and to clarify and shape his discourse. It is why Dening wrote of Smith that he 'made us look at our own marginality in a positive way. Be Antipodeans, he told us'.[40]

---

37 H.G. Wells, *Experiment in Autobiography* (Harmondsworth: Penguin Books, 1934), 206–7.
38 Bernard Smith, interview with Hazel de Berg, NLA, Oral History Programme, TRC2053-17, Tape 1 (page 43 of typescript).
39 Greg Dening, 'Disembodied Artifacts: Edward Said's Culture and Imperialism', *Scripsi*, 9:1 (1993), 80.
40 Greg Dening, *Readings/Writings* (Melbourne: Melbourne University Press, 1998), 142.

If Smith's concern was how Australia emerged from its colonial cradle and arrived at its own distinctive modern position, this also coincided with his own personal quest for identity as he distanced himself from his past. For some, illegitimacy fosters a deep and lasting sense of invisibility and of never belonging, and certainly Smith had experienced this during his childhood: 'No, he is not one of us', he heard his foster sister Bertha tell a stranger. But he was also born with a ferocious determination to escape from the institutional constraints of his orphaned status and rise above his humble beginnings. In *Place, Taste and Tradition*, he wrote that '[a] national tradition arises from a people as they struggle with their social and geographical environment' – one could think that here he was reflecting on his own struggle to leave his social periphery.[41]

In his research leading up to his magnum opus, *European Vision and the South Pacific* (1960), Smith captured an important factor affecting new settlers as they came to terms with the country's unique qualities, qualities that he had himself experienced as a young primary school teacher when he worked in a remote part of rural New South Wales:

> For Australian nature was not merely something to be seen, but something to be revealed, something hidden from vulgar eyes and still unknown. The mystery of the bush could inspire not only fear but also hope … and the hopeful and melancholic conventions fused into a complex unity capable of reflecting the finest shades of experience and emotion. They are therefore landmarks in the emotional maturity … [of] Australian identity.[42]

Hope was the great mover of utopian ideas, and it kept Smith focused on his future. It was also central to Marxist thought.

By the late nineteenth century, after a new merchant capitalism emerged based upon the wealth of the gold rush, Australians began to assert themselves more confidently. This was evident in art, literature and architecture as well as the rapid growth of cities – the staging of the great International Exhibitions in Sydney, Melbourne and Adelaide, and the impressionistic paintings of a new national vision by Tom Roberts, Arthur Streeton and Charles Conder. By the early and mid-twentieth century,

---

41   Bernard Smith, *Place, Taste and Tradition: A Study of Australian Art since 1788* (Sydney: Ure Smith, 1945), 30.
42   Bernard Smith, 'The Interpretation of Nature during the Nineteenth Century', BA Honours thesis (Department of English, University of Sydney, 1952), copy in Bernard Smith Papers, NLA, MS 8680, Box 3/20/21, 23 and 78.

artists such as Margaret Preston, Russell Drysdale, Sidney Nolan, Arthur Boyd and Noel Counihan and the writers Miles Franklin, Vance and Nettie Palmer, Frank Dalby Davidson and Brian Penton, to name a few, were constructing an Australian idiom with even greater assurance. But this vigorous Antipodean character began to wane again after the Second World War as dominant metropolitan cultures altered Australian cultural values.

Others have noted that Bernard Smith's interpretations of Australian art and identity were consistently based around 'the circularity between Europe and Australia', and never on a distinctive entity in and by itself. Yet this was precisely because of the Eurocentric cultural inheritance that had been implanted with British possession in 1788, and that continued well into the twentieth century. It was what made Australians 'refer back' in order to 'mediate influences' or 'wilfully disrupt' received styles and reposition themselves within their own locality.[43] As he said, 'Even if the past is another country the historian has to find a way to get there'. For a cultural historian like himself, that route was through the dominant cultures of Europe and Britain.[44]

When Smith first arrived in England in 1948, he was concerned with this notion of identity and cultural revision. By the end of his two years there, and with extensive travels through Europe, he had developed a real sense of the cultural past and its global present, though he could never have stayed on in England nor felt comfortable in its class-based society – even though he had married a middle-class Englishwoman in Sydney in 1941. Bernard Smith was resolutely and defiantly Australian and, as he discovered, there simply was not enough interest in the Antipodes as a historical or modern cultural entity. Geographical distance and British principles of exclusion still hampered contemporary Australia almost as much as it had 150 years earlier. In a letter to his mother, he assured her he would not be staying on in England as he felt he could do much more important work back home.

Before leaving London in late 1950, Smith gave several broadcast talks at the British Broadcasting Corporation (BBC) on 'Australian Landscape Painting' and 'The Artist's Vision of Australia'. From the discovery by Cook

---

43   Geoffrey Batchen, in Ian Burn, *Dialogue: Writings in Art History* (Sydney: Allen & Unwin, 1991), xviii.
44   Bernard Smith, notes for review of T.J. Clark's *Farewell to an Idea*, July 1999, Bernard Smith Papers, NLA, MS 8680, Box 8/57/176.

and the importance of Sir Joseph Banks and Charles Darwin, Bernard led the listener through the unique qualities of the Australian landscape and how it created for artists a distinct way of seeing and a unique style of painting. From the colonial, picturesque, romantic and impressionist genres to the 'psychic centre' of the great outback, he finally arrived at Russell Drysdale who, he said, painted the landscape in its own terms of reference, as though he was 'half in love and half in fear of his subject … because the Australian landscape is … a wilful capricious thing, half-wild, half-tame, half-myth and half reality'.[45]

The pursuit of cultural autonomy

After returning to Sydney in 1951, Smith became frustrated by the impact that prevailing American and British cultural forces were having on Australian art, and he was determined that an Antipodean cultural identity should be more internationally acknowledged. Australians viewed the world through their entrenched nostalgic attachment to Great Britain and this had to be replaced by 'an Australian way of looking'. Moreover, the western world's new watchdog, America, was using its invasive cultural power to assert its metropolitan monopoly in Europe and Australia and, according to Smith, this was twentieth-century cultural imperialism.

The historian Robin Winks once observed that a scholar's subject matter or academic discipline usually holds 'an autobiographical meaning, in that one is often attracted to a discipline that appears to reflect the world as one understands it, rather than using the discipline to order the world'.[46] Bernard Smith used art and culture not only to understand 'the sociology of colonisation' and its relations of exchange but as a mirror for addressing his own personal 'position and position taking'.[47] One extraordinary construction for identity and cultural difference that he masterminded was the *Antipodeans* exhibition and its Manifesto in 1959.

As its originator and convener, Smith used the idea of myth-making to illuminate Australia's cultural autonomy and proclaim its distinctive originality; as he put it, 'We live in a young society still making its myths. The emergence of myth is a continuous social activity. In the growth and

---

45   Bernard Smith, 'Sir Russell Drysdale (1912–1981): A Memoir', *Art Monthly*, 110 (1998), 28.
46   Robin W. Winks, *The Imperial Revolution: Yesterday and Tomorrow* (New York: Oxford University Press, 1994), 8–9.
47   Bernard Smith, interview with author, 7 June 2001.

transformation of its myths a society achieves its own sense of identity'.[48] But with politics never far from his mind, it was also an agenda for his concerns about regionalism, contemporary cultural imperialism and the Cold War.

Ever since first proposing the idea to Sir Kenneth Clark in London in 1949, Bernard Smith had been keen to mount an exhibition showcasing the best of contemporary Australian figurative art, with the aim of touring it nationally and internationally. The plan was reactivated in 1957, when he heard the Melbourne architect Robin Boyd deliver a lecture on Australia's de-culturalisation and the 'featurist' and 'Austerica' banality of its urban design and architecture. He wrote excitedly to Boyd:

> I cannot tell you how much I admired and enjoyed your lecture … I am right behind you – but can anything really be done about it? … I should dearly love to think that one or two of our artists and architects were standing up squarely on their own feet and thinking out their own problems before an Australian and a world audience. Of course the waters of nationalism have always been treacherous ones to fish in – but at least they're deep.

As the letter shows, the genesis of the 'Antipodeans' had evolved:

> What is needed is a small compact group of artists (architects, painters, perhaps a sculptor), about 6 or 7 would be enough with a common purpose … one thinks of The Impressionists, de Stijl, The Pre-Raphaelite Brotherhood. … Better to make history than write about it. What is needed is a brotherhood of some kind … with a colourful title … The artists I can think of … who would qualify for what I have in mind are Sid Nolan, Arthur Boyd, John Brack. … If some sort of Antipodean Brotherhood did somehow crawl upsidedownedly into existence its birth would have to be veiled in mysteries … I can assure you I rarely write letters like this – but this is what you have brought me to … Meanwhile my congratulations on your magisterial stand against the … hands of Austerica.[49]

Art, Smith insisted, *had* to communicate as 'a recognisable shape, a meaningful symbol', and a reflection of society, and he used the *Antipodeans* exhibition as a platform to convert artists and audiences away

---

48   *The Antipodean Manifesto*, first published as a foreword to the *Antipodeans* exhibition held at the Victorian Artists' Society, East Melbourne, August 1959.
49   Bernard Smith to Robin Boyd, 22 September 1957 (copy), Bernard Smith Papers, NLA, MS 8680; these papers have recently been deposited in the NLA and are awaiting accessioning.

from the 'vacuous geometric patterning' of international abstraction, a style that emanated from the dominant New York School of abstract expressionism and the 'canonical dominance of Clement Greenberg's post-painterly abstraction'.[50] Bernard Smith had first witnessed this new art form at the 1950 Venice Biennale where Jackson Pollock's dribble technique or, as Bernard described it, the 'glamorous wallpaper of his own alienation' was on show.[51] He also had information that major American exhibitions, which had been touring Europe since the beginning of the Cold War, were funded by the CIA and New York's Museum of Modern Art (MoMA), which further intensified his hostility towards America's postwar cultural hegemony.

Bernard Smith qualified cultural imperialism as 'a study in inequality', and therefore 'what is vital and native to our tradition' needed to be protected. This was not xenophobic nationalism but, as Peter Beilharz has suggested, a more cryptic, hybrid form of nativism.[52] Australian artists, Smith wrote, had to 'battle for survival in the post-war years against powerful and at times overwhelming cosmopolitan tendencies, at times stimulating and vitalizing, at times devitalizing'.[53] With his sight fixed on Australia as it intersected with metropolitan cultural powers, Bernard chose seven artists who were 'distinctively Australian, without being self-consciously nationalistic'.[54] These were John Brack, Charles Blackman, Arthur and David Boyd, John Perceval, Clifton Pugh and the Sydney painter Robert Dickerson. To avoid being tagged nationalistic, the group, driven by Bernard's preferences, chose the word 'Antipodeans'. As he explained:

> Europeans have used [the term] in connection with this part of the world ever since the Greeks and there is no reason at all why we should sneer at it … no reason why painters … should not be able to find something worth saying both to their community and to the world at large.[55]

---

50   Gary Willis, conversation with the author, 2015.
51   Bernard Smith, *A Pavanne for Another Time* (Melbourne: Macmillan, 2002), 444.
52   'A day with Bernard Smith', La Trobe University Thesis Eleven symposium, 23 April 2003.
53   Smith, notes for a speech given at the annual dinner of the Fellowship of Australian Writers, 1 September 1959, Bernard Smith Papers, NLA, MS 8680, Box 20/24. Bernard later published a significantly revised version of events with 'The Truth about the Antipodeans' published in *The Death of the Artist as Hero: Essays in History and Culture* (Melbourne: Oxford University Press, 1988).
54   Bernard Smith to Sidney Nolan, 1 February 1960 (copy), Bernard Smith Papers, NLA, MS 8680.
55   Ibid.

He also suggested to Charles Blackman, the artist who designed the *Antipodean Exhibition* poster, that he should look at the primitive Antipode creatures illustrated in the 1493 medieval Nuremburg Chronicle, a copy of which was held in the Melbourne public library.

Antipodeans exhibition poster, 1959
Source: Private collection.

By refashioning the mythic past with the political present, Bernard Smith's promotion of antipodeanism declared a distinctive aesthetic while simultaneously asserting a national autonomy. As he said, '[i]t is natural that we should see and experience nature differently in some degree from artists of the northern hemisphere'.[56] Moeover, by establishing a regionalist, figurative style – Smith preferred calling it 'being oneself [or] standing on one's feet' – in opposition to international abstraction, Australian artists might have a chance of being noticed. Aesthetic individualism was important, but it was also about challenging the political giants and their cultural supremacy – though at the time he did not present it to the artists as such. In retrospect, he explained that the exhibition and Manifesto were 'not at bottom an attack on abstract art; it [wa]s an attack on the

---

56 'The Antipodean Manifesto', published in *The Antipodean Manifesto: Essays in Art and History* (Melbourne: Oxford University Press, 1976), 197.

policy of the State Department of the USA to use abstract art as a political instrument in opposition to the Soviet Union's use of socialist realism as a political instrument'.[57] Given the Cold War tensions in the late 1950s, Bernard Smith's obsession with power relations and dominant cultures was understandable, but it also reflected his hostility to anything that 'subordinated ideas or relations of exchange'. The price of survival had always interested him, whether that of the convict, the destitute, the state ward, Aborigines or the marginalised individual or artist – it resonated deeply with his outsider self.

The *Antipodeans* exhibition was an enormous success and consolidated the seven artists' professional reputations, yet it also became one of the most divisive events in the history of the Australian art world. Not only had it politicised art but it reignited antagonism between Melbourne and Sydney artists and provoked rivalry between the 'abs' and the 'figs' – Smith was accused of derailing abstraction and tying figurative art to the tracks and holding it ransom. Others like Helen Brack objected to the 'genius' factor that positioned one artist above another or, more specifically, one group above all others.[58] In this, Bernard Smith's Marxism and egalitarian beliefs had faltered and his selection of the artists was seen as elitist; his own defence was that he had chosen them for their political neutrality and distinctive Antipodean content. In Barbara Blackman's view, however, the exhibition was 'an irrefutable landmark in Australian art':

> Where tradition is wanting, certain prejudices and preconceptions may also be lacking. The Antipodeans made their gesture from necessity and out of direct experience and so have helped to shape the present particular contours of our art, a distinctive and virile growth alongside the modern art of other countries.[59]

The periphery versus the centre

While Bernard Smith did all he could to get the *Antipodeans* exhibition to London, he was stymied by the local antagonism of artists towards him, as well as by the British establishment and its cultural elites exemplified by Sir Kenneth Clark and Bryan Robertson, the director of the Whitechapel

---

57   Bernard Smith, cited in Beilharz, *Imagining the Antipodes*, 117.
58   I am grateful to Helen Brack, who was closely associated with the entire development of the *Antipodeans* exhibition, for discussing Bernard's authority in determining the exhibition and its controversial Manifesto.
59   Barbara Blackman, 'The Antipodean Affair', *Art and Australia*, 5:4 (1968), 607–16.

Gallery in London. Robertson had been developing a large exhibition of Australia's best contemporary artists, including the *Antipodeans*, and this was held in 1961 at the Whitechapel Gallery. To add insult to injury, Robertson bypassed Smith as a major critic of Australian art and invited the young Sydney architecture student and flamboyant art critic Robert Hughes to write the catalogue essay for the exhibition.

In the introductory essays, Clark and Robertson stressed that Australian culture had been moulded by isolation and the country was seen as a major food bowl producer in which the 'redundant poor' had been replaced by 'sun bronzed sheep farmers'.[60] The stigma of the 'working man's paradise' remained firmly rooted in the European psyche and the spinning of the myth was too irresistible for these cultured Englishmen, whose attitudes were diametrically opposed to Smith's. Robertson's colourful rhetoric emphasised the country's vast landscapes, immense distances and a heightened sense of isolation:

> A friction in the air itself finds expression in the edge and bite which underlies [its] art. A fierce, tough, often rather slangy imagery is invariably described in the most tender and loving manner … [but] the imagery itself, cut off from our European environment, is highly inventive and has one unifying factor: an unremitting sense of the drama of the isolated moment.[61]

He also claimed that '[a] nation based on an idea rather than on blood needs some transcendent image to reveal itself'. In a veiled reference to Smith, Robertson wrote:

> Power politics have made nationalism a dirty word … Australian artists … are at once passionately interested in *what is* Australian art and highly suspicious of the answer. At the same time, these problems do not concern the painters as much as critics and interpreters for who the painters feel mostly a proper and essential distrust.[62]

Hughes also parodied Smith, 'some things I am told, can only be seen clearly from a considerable distance' and that 'exoticism depends on where you stand'.[63] With his superb cast of phrase, Hughes continued, 'The first convict settlement was made here [Australia] in 1788. In the

---

60 Bryan Robertson, *Recent Australian Painting* (Whitechapel Art Gallery, exhibition catalogue, 1961).
61 Ibid.
62 Ibid.
63 Robert Hughes, in ibid., 13.

next few years, a cultural transplantation took place. But though you can ship works of art, you cannot put a climate of thought in a crate'. As he proceeded to decipher the past, uproot its traditions and uncover Bernard Smith's political mask, referring to him as a 'critic' who had 'evolved' an Australian mythology, Hughes took aim:

> Recently an 'opposition group' was formed in Melbourne under the leadership of the distinguished art historian Bernard Smith. His programmic intent was clear. Australia he argued lacks a tradition of art but possesses strong social traditions. It has acquired its own myths, heroes and white man's folklore. If the artist, then, is to function as an effective social unit his art must reflect this and draw its inspiration from it … The Antipodean notion of an image seems to concern a pressure point for a number of beliefs … which need have nothing to do with aesthetic sensation or the existence of the object itself. It is an art of association. Under this aspect, an image is the firing pin and not the grenade.[64]

Smith, however, was not to be marginalised and took his revenge.

In the John Murtagh Macrossan Memorial Lectures, which Bernard Smith titled 'The Myth of Isolation' and 'The Rebirth of Australian Painting' given at the University of Queensland in 1961,[65] he asserted that while there was 'some core truth at the heart of any myth', Australia had never suffered from cultural isolation, from neither Europe's Renaissance nor its modernist movement.[66] As a young pastoral society, its cultural identity had been formed upon a Eurocentric philosophical and cultural inheritance, and what had been brought to the colony was adapted, modified or changed by the geographic, climatic and developing social conditions, not formed under isolation. During the 1950s and 1960s, as in the late 1940s, the reception of Australians in London was usually simplistic, being seen more often as the poor, uncultured cousins from behind the black stump.[67] The London critic John Douglas Pringle, who had lived and worked in Sydney, understood how the British tended to misread Australia as a distant, inhospitable land of mythological proportions; he began his review of the Whitechapel exhibition tongue in cheek:

---

64   Ibid., 19–20.
65   The John Murtagh Macrossan lectures were published as *Australian Painting Today* (Brisbane: University of Queensland Press, 1962).
66   Smith, 'The Myth of Isolation', 16.
67   Sheridan Palmer, 'The Lone Antipodean – Bernard Smith's Post-War Modernism', *Eyeline Contemporary Visual Arts Magazine* (Brisbane), 78/79 (2013), 55.

> Many people in this country must imagine that contemporary Australian painting is a rather exotic art form discovered by Sidney Nolan in a cave near Alice Springs, round about the year 1940, and since handed on – under oath of secrecy sealed in wallaby blood – to Albert Tucker and Arthur Boyd.[68]

While Australia's cultural character had been carved out from its dominant European beginnings, Bernard Smith stressed that a culture on the periphery was able to develop in more vital ways precisely because it was less hampered by the ever prevalent 'graveyard of memory' or the heavy hand of European cultural traditions evident in major northern centres such as Paris, London and New York. Australian cultural identity was not inferior or forged through provincial isolation, but lay in its democratic difference.

The Macrossan lectures, though reaching only a small audience, were a brilliant riposte to those British who still clung to the notion of Australia as a colonial appendage. Bernard Smith also refuted their image of Australian art as some exotic, crude imitation of Europe's great painters, and accused them of having 'disastrously misrepresented modern Australian artists' as 'white noble savages'. These English values, Smith felt, were deeply entrenched and maintained by their imperial distance and cultural elitism.

Bernard Smith's willingness to 'stand alone' and question cultural hegemony gave him a reputation as a critical interventionist and a vitally important intellectual at a time when Australia's modern cultural identity was in a major developmental phase. His Antipodean discourse, though seen by some as inhibiting, was critical to artists as they aesthetically defined themselves during the Cold War and in an increasingly globalised world. Later he wrote, 'Distance is our *longue durée*, the near constant factor in our history, that does so much to transform our art – and if we are creative and intelligent we can put it to our advantage'.[69]

---

68 John Douglas Pringle, 'The Australian Painter', *Observer* (London), 4 June 1961. Pringle was a well-informed and brilliant editor who lived and worked in Australia during the 1950s and 1960s as editor of the *Sydney Morning Herald*.
69 Bernard Smith, opening address at the S.H. Ervin Gallery, 16 April 1984, for the exhibition 'Aspects of Australian Figurative Painting 1942–1962: Dreams, Fears and Desires', Bernard Smith Papers, NLA, MS 8680.

9. PURSUING THE ANTIPODEAN

Bernard Smith, 1978
Source: Bernard Smith Papers, National Library of Australia (photographer unknown).

For much of the remaining twentieth century, Smith's polemics on cultural identity and traditional inheritances set a benchmark for Australian critics and art historians, but his influence extended well beyond them to other disciplines such as anthropology, Pacific and cross-cultural studies, and artists working nationally and internationally. If *European Vision and the South Pacific* had established him as a major revisionist – one art critic considered it 'one of those mind-changing works which truly extend not just knowledge but the frame-work in which to place that knowledge'[70] – then his epic vision of Australia's cultural condition and his theories of contact, exchange and identity, together with his ability to steer a critical course through vast historical terrains, mark him as one of this country's most brilliant and pioneering intellectuals.

Indeed, *European Vision and the South Pacific* predated Edward Said's *Orientalism* (1978) by almost 20 years. For Smith, Australian artists mattered and he was emphatic that they deserved to be recognised internationally. On this he was prepared to stake his professional reputation and fight at the barricades of modernism and challenge the metropolitan systems of cultural elitism. Even when his peers and intellectual children considered him anachronistic, he remained a vital figure in Australia's cultural modernisation.

As a Marxist utopian, Bernard Smith believed in the future and found generational change exciting; it helped him absorb the zeitgeist of the day, which in turn helped him define his arguments and redefine his identity amongst the next generation of Australian art and cultural historians. In this, he was determined to maintain a visible and intellectual presence well into his old age, even if it meant being overtly provocative. In 2002, aged 86, Smith posed naked for the artist Carmel O'Connor's Archibald Prize portrait. The reclining, unclothed image of the father of Australian art history was deliberately designed to shake up bourgeois complacency, challenge the uncritical Australian culture and address the demise of figurative art. Smith insisted that his pose be constructed on the classical Roman sculpture known as the *Barbarini Faun*, or *The Sleeping Satyr*, which enabled him to incorporate complex connections and mythical metaphors. The faun or satyr was considered as representing the mythic messenger of man's origins, and Bernard Smith had always been interested in origins.[71] Moreover, the portrait was a final 'identity performance' with the aged and eminent art historian unashamedly parading as the emperor with no clothes and imparting his lesson aimed at the crisis of identity in the postmodern age.

---

70   Charles Nodrum, 'Bernard Smith and the Formalesque', unpublished article, courtesy of Charles Nodrum.
71   Friedrich Nietzsche, *The Birth of Tragedy; and, the Genealogy of Morals* (New York: Doubleday Anchor Books, 1956), 52.

What was important to Bernard Smith was to keep the dialogue open and arguments on traditional and contemporary art moving. He saw his role as reinvigorating the cultural debate, and in this his conscientious criticism was inescapable, even when attempts to dislodge him from his prominent position in Australian art history were made. So influential was his published work and extensive criticism that other art historians found it impossible not to use it as their matrix upon which to formulate their own theories of centre and periphery or metropolitan power and provincialism. Smith's critiques of cultural hegemony were adopted, interrogated and reconstructed by younger art historians and sociologists during the latter part of the twentieth century, which repositioned him at the core of a new plateau of revisionism and discourse on contemporary identity.[72] In particular, the neo-Marxists Ian Burn and Terry Smith appropriated the issue of provincialism in the 1970s and 1980s, and in the early 1980s the young art critic Paul Taylor and his colleague Paul Foss 'channelled' Bernard Smith's early theories of cultural imperialism and the importance, or unimportance, of locality. As the Australian art world's *eminence grise*, Bernard Smith was the benchmark and, as the art historian Rex Butler more recently claimed, we should continue to 'turn to the true precursor of revisionism' and the originator of 'the great Australian idea' of antipodal inversion or 'reversal to the rest of the world.'[73]

Bernard Smith questioned the Antipodean psyche and gave it significant cultural form as well as proclaiming its place in a globalised world. His intellectual and aesthetic landscape was vast, Antipodean, Eurocentric and universal, and he traversed these terrains confidently. It was cultural evolution that propelled his curiosity, for through culture it was possible to understand the socioeconomic and political mechanisms attached to power, and these were vital to his self-actualisation; it is what drove his desire to legitimate place and liberate the marginalised. Even when he used his own symbolic image of the outsider in order to understand hegemonic relations, class differences and inequality, it was ultimately situated within the larger disciplines of philosophical ideas on origins,

---

72   Some major texts indebted to Bernard Smith's historiography include Terry Smith, 'The Provincialism Problem', *Artforum*, 12:6 (1974), 49–52; Ian Burn, Nigel Lendon, Charles Mereweather and Ann Stephen, *The Necessity of Australian Art* (Sydney: Power Publications, University of Sydney, 1988); Heather Barker and Charles Green, 'No More Provincialism: Art & Text', *emaj*, 5 (2010), www.melbourneartjournal.unimelb.edu.au/E-MAJ.
73   Butler, *Radical Revisionism*, 12.

identity and identification; indeed, he believed we must classify in order to understand the historical agencies and shifting paradigms that have shaped us.

If Bernard Smith used myths to frame his discourse on antipodeanism and unravel the historical, scientific, cultural and political forces that moulded Australian art and its modern cultural identity, he was equally aware that utopias were an ideological construct of the emigrant and the intellectual voyager, and both were fundamental to historical processes and human progress. As he said, 'I am a communist, in so much as a utopian communist, I believe in the future—the hope is in the waiting'.[74] In other words, he had never shifted from his Marxist humanism and his belief that a better future was possible for the world.

---

74 Bernard Smith, conversation with the author, 2011.

Collective Biography

10
Australian Historians Networking, 1914–1973

Geoffrey Bolton[1]

The *Oxford English Dictionary* defines networking as 'the action or process of making use of a network of people for the exchange of information, etc., or for professional or other advantage'.[2] Although recently prominent in management theory, the art of networking has been practised over many centuries in many societies, but its role in the Australian academic community has been little explored. This essay represents a preliminary excursion into the field, raising questions that more systematic researchers may follow in time, and drawing unashamedly on the resources of the *Australian Dictionary of Biography*. Beginning on the eve of the First World War, the essay is bounded by the formation of the Australian Historical Association in 1973, at which date the profession provided itself with

---

1   This essay is a lightly edited version of the paper prepared by Geoffrey Bolton for the 'Workshop on Biographies and Autobiographies of Historians' held at The Australian National University in July 2015. Professor Bolton had intended to make further revisions, which included adding some analysis of the social origins of the Australian historians who participated in the networks he had defined. In all essential respects, however, we believe that the essay as presented here would have met with his approval, and we are very grateful to Carol Bolton for giving permission to make the modest editorial changes that we have incorporated.
  For biographical information and insights, see Stuart Macintyre, Lenore Layman and Jenny Gregory, eds, *A Historian for all Seasons: Essays for Geoffrey Bolton* (Melbourne: Monash University Publishing, 2017).
2   *Oxford English Dictionary*, www.oed.com/view/Entry/235272?redirectedFrom=networking#eid.

a formal structure for the creation and nurturing of networks that would benefit the scholarly advancement of individuals and the coherence of the discipline as a whole.

By 1914, each of the Australian states had established a university in its capital city, and all had made some provision for the teaching of modern history. Melbourne at its foundation in 1856 included modern history among the disciplinary responsibilities of one of its first foundation professors, the protean W.E. Hearn (1826–1922).[3] When Hearn became dean of law in 1879, he was followed by John Elkington (1841–88) as professor of history and political economy with tenure for life.[4] An entertaining lecturer but a cantankerous colleague, Elkington was no dynamo. When a royal commission in 1903 inquired about his research, he replied disarmingly: 'I have work in hand, but I have not committed myself to anything very extensive in book form so far.'[5] After Elkington was persuaded to retire in 1913, he was succeeded by Ernest Scott (1867–1939), who although lacking a university degree of any kind possessed a convincing record of publication, largely in the field of European maritime exploration in eastern Australia and the Pacific.[6] He would prove a much more energetic networker than Elkington.

At the University of Sydney, the standing of modern history was assured in 1889 when the discipline became one of the chairs created by the Challis bequest, although at first it was advertised at a lower salary than the others, and was only increased when no credible applicants came forward. The chair was awarded in 1891 to the 26-year-old G. Arnold Wood

---

3   Most of the individuals mentioned in this chapter have entries in the *Australian Dictionary of Biography*. Readers are also referred to Stuart Macintyre and Julian Thomas, eds, *The Discovery of Australian History, 1890–1939* (Melbourne: Melbourne University Press, 1995), which contains separate chapters on several of the *dramatis personae*.
4   Geoffrey Blainey, *A Centenary History of the University of Melbourne* (Melbourne: Melbourne University Press, 1957).
5   Quoted in Norman Harper, 'Elkington, John Simeon (1841–1922)', *Australian Dictionary of Biography* (*ADB*), National Centre of Biography, The Australian National University, adb.anu.edu.au/biography/elkington-john-simeon-6100/text10451, published first in hardcopy 1981 (accessed 19 December 2015). These years in the life of the Melbourne history department are recounted by Richard Sellick, 'Empires and Empiricism: The Teaching of History at the University of Melbourne, 1855–1936', in Fay Anderson and Stuart Macintyre, eds, *The Life of the Past: The Discipline of History at the University of Melbourne, 1855–2005* (Melbourne: Department of History, University of Melbourne, 2005), 3–38.
6   Stuart Macintyre, *A History for a Nation: Ernest Scott and the Making of Australian History* (Melbourne: Melbourne University Press, 1994). Scott's works included *Terre Napoleon: A History of French Explorations and Projects in Australia* (London: Methuen, 1910); *Laperouse* (Sydney: Angus & Robertson, 1912); and *The Life of Captain Matthew Flinders, R.N.* (Sydney: Angus & Robertson, 1914).

(1856–1928).⁷ He was to be a significant influence. Appointees at other Australian universities, most of them equally youthful, were expected to combine the teaching of history with other disciplines. Thus the University of Tasmania in 1893 appointed the 25-year-old William Jethro Brown (1868–1930) as one of its three foundation professors with responsibility for history and law, followed in 1906 by Robert Dunbabin (1869–1949) as lecturer in history and classics.⁸ George Henderson (1870–1944), at the age of 32, became professor of history and English language at the University of Adelaide in 1902.⁹ The two newest universities, Queensland (1911) and Western Australia (1913), made foundation appointments in the field. The University of Queensland appointed the 27-year-old Edward Shann (1872–1935) to a lectureship in 1911, but by 1913 he was poached as professor of economics and history by the University of Western Australia.¹⁰ Queensland then appointed two lecturers, Henry Alcock (1886–1947) and Alexander Melbourne (1888–1943). Both were still in their 20s, but Alcock was to be the senior; he had graduated from Oxford with first-class honours, whereas Melbourne was entirely Australian-educated.¹¹

By 1914, there were enough academic historians in Australian universities to call for some structured means of professional communication, but they were still too few to support a dedicated disciplinary association. A convenient umbrella existed in the Australasian Association for the Advancement of Science.¹² Established in 1888, largely on the initiative of the University of Sydney mineralogist and chemist Archibald Liversidge (1846–1927), the association conducted congresses at different cities in Australia and New Zealand every year or two, and soon established itself as a valued meeting place for the exchange of scholarly ideas as well

---

7   R.M. Crawford, *'A Bit of a Rebel': The Life and Work of George Arnold Wood* (Sydney: Sydney University Press, 1975), 108; see also John A. Moses, *Prussian-German Militarism 1914–18 in Australian Perspective: The Thought of George Arnold Wood* (Bern: P. Lang, 2001).
8   Alison Alexander, 'History', in Alison Alexander, ed., *The Companion to Tasmanian History* (Hobart: Centre for Tasmanian Historical Studies, University of Tasmania, 2005), www.utas.edu.au/library/companion_to_tasmanian_history/H/History.htm.
9   Tamson Pietsch, '*Imperium and Libertas*: G.C. Henderson and "Colonial Historical Research" at Adelaide', in Wilfrid Prest, ed., *Pasts Present: History at Australia's Third University* (Adelaide: Wakefield Press, 2014), 77–85.
10 C.B. Schedvin and J.E. Carr, 'Edward Shann: A Radical Liberal Before his Time', in Macintyre and Thomas, *The Discovery of Australian History*, 55.
11 Geoffrey Bolton, 'A.C.V. Melbourne: Prophet without Honour', in Macintyre and Thomas, *The Discovery of Australian History*, 111, 114.
12 The association changed its name to Australian and New Zealand Association for the Advancement of Science (ANZAAS) in 1930.

as outreach to a wider public.¹³ The association in its early decades was a broad church, accommodating many subjects from the social sciences and, even for a time, the humanities. Geography was a foundation participant, forming Section E, and in those years of fluid boundaries between disciplines it was easy for historians to take part in its proceedings. By the years preceding the First World War, the association was providing historians with a pulpit for expounding their ideas; at the 1911 Sydney congress, for example, Henderson was able to exhort his colleagues to use Australian materials as a means of training their students in research skills.¹⁴ Eventually, in 1928, History was to take over Section E, leaving Geography and Oceanography to re-establish themselves further down the alphabet as Section P.¹⁵

Even with the contacts provided by Australian and New Zealand Association for the Advancement of Science (ANZAAS), the number of historians at Australian universities was still limited, and their teaching responsibilities so demanding that the discipline could benefit from the stimulus of ideas imported from a wider world. At that time, the United Kingdom was the predominant source of such ideas, and the universities of Oxford and Cambridge were seen as the intellectual powerhouses. It was perhaps an unforeseen result of G. Arnold Wood's 37 years in the Sydney chair that Balliol College, Oxford, was to become for several decades a highly significant influence on many historians in Australia.

Balliol was one of the oldest colleges at Oxford, founded in 1263 by the widow of a nobleman with estates in Scotland and the north of England as penance for her husband's role in the highway robbery of the Bishop of Durham's treasury.¹⁶ After some centuries of mediocrity, enlivened at intervals by the production of alumni such as Adam Smith, Balliol came to the fore in the second half of the nineteenth century in the wake of reforms at Oxford University. These confirmed the arrangements by which the university served as the examining body that awarded degrees, but in its constituent colleges undergraduates lived communally and received most or all of their tuition. The BA in modern history took three years, a preliminary first year followed by six terms without written

---

13   Roy MacLeod, ed., *The Commonwealth of Science: ANZAAS and the Scientific Enterprise in Australia, 1888–1988* (Melbourne: Oxford University Press, 1988), ch. 1.
14   Elizabeth Kwan, 'G.C. Henderson: Advocate of "Systematic and Scientific" Research in Australian History', in Macintyre and Thomas, *The Discovery of Australian History*, 37.
15   MacLeod, *The Commonwealth of Science*, 365–6.
16   John Jones, *Balliol College: A History, 1263–1939* (Oxford: Oxford University Press, 1987), 2–3.

examinations until a week-long marathon at their conclusion. Graduates from other universities in the United Kingdom, the United States or the British Empire were excused the preliminary first year. A compulsory ingredient of the course for nearly a century was the study of a sequence of mediaeval charters, edited by Bishop William Stubbs (1872) and tracing the development of early English constitutional history; it became an influential model for the use of documents in undergraduate teaching.

Balliol had never lost its original connection with Scotland and the north of England, and under a notable Master, Benjamin Jowett (1870–93), and his successors, the college extended its outreach. If some Oxford colleges seemed like sheltered workshops for the privileged classes, Balliol placed its emphasis on intellectual excellence: the hallmark of a Balliol man, it was said, was his tranquil consciousness of effortless superiority. But it was not a socially snobbish college. Balliol, in Jim Davidson's words, 'had the reputation of requiring ability from its entrants rather than good connections. It led the way in taking Indians and later Africans'.[17] For Australians and other 'colonials', Balliol provided a more hospitable environment than most. It was not surprising that in the heyday of the British Empire, Balliol was well to the fore in producing Imperial statesmen such as Lord Milner and Lord Curzon, nor that when the South African millionaire Alfred Beit endowed a chair of imperial and Commonwealth history at Oxford it was located at Balliol.

But Balliol's sense of imperial mission was tempered by a strong sense of social conscience. This went beyond a belief in the civilising and humanitarian missions of Empire to an abiding concern with issues of inequality and poverty. The young G. Arnold Wood, who came up to Balliol in 1885, was remembered by his tutors as 'dyed in the wool in Puritan Nonconformity, Cobdenism, Gladstonian Liberalism, the humanitarian ideals of John Bright and the political philosophy of John Morley'.[18] Concern for Empire could tilt into anti-imperialism, and Wood famously took a lot of criticism in Sydney for his opposition to the South African war of 1899–1902. His values had been nurtured at Balliol and he integrated them into his teaching in Australia.

---

17   Jim Davidson, *A Three-Cornered Life: The Historian WK Hancock* (Sydney: University of New South Wales Press, 2010), 50.
18   Crawford, '*A Bit of a Rebel*', 1.

It was not surprising that when Wood's teaching produced a promising history graduate in James Fawthrop Bruce (1888–1978), who sought further study in Britain, he directed the young man to Oxford, and specifically to Balliol College, but the decision was not based merely on collegial loyalty. Balliol had built up one of the strongest and longest-lasting teams of history tutors of any college in Oxford. Foremost among them was Arthur Lionel Smith (1850–1924), tutor from 1882, dean from 1907 and master from 1916 until his death in 1924. A.L. Smith was a firm upholder of archival research as the foundation for sound historical writing, and he combined this approach with an insistence on the academic's responsibility for outreach into the wider community. He was a role model for many of his students. No doubt it helped that he was among the first generation of Oxford dons who were permitted to marry, and of his nine children, seven were daughters.[19] The Smiths were a hospitable couple who frequently invited undergraduates to their house, especially those from overseas. One daughter married the Australian medical researcher who later became Sir Hugh Cairns. The young Australians who went to Balliol remembered Smith with respect and affection.[20]

James Bruce returned from Balliol to Sydney in 1915 to take up an appointment as lecturer and deputy to Wood (associate professor from 1924).[21] One of his strengths was in the history of Renaissance Italy, where his teaching stimulated, among others, the young Max Crawford (1906–91), who, together with Wood's son F.L.W. (Fred) Wood (1903–89), was among the Sydney graduates to find their way to Balliol in the 1920s. An earlier example of the Sydney–Balliol axis was Hessel Duncan Hall (1891–1976). After taking a master's degree at Sydney, Hall studied under A.L. Smith between 1915 and 1918, and wrote a thesis that became his first publication on *The British Commonwealth of Nations* (1920). Oxford's only postgraduate degree at that time was the Bachelor of Letters, while the newfangled doctorate of philosophy arrived a few years later. But Duncan Hall, after working in adult education in England for a few years, failed to find secure academic employment in Australia and from 1926 he lived and worked overseas, producing in retirement a massive

---

19   Jones, *Balliol College*, 235.
20   See, for instance, his influence on Keith Hancock in Davidson, *A Three-Cornered Life*, 52–3.
21   B.H. Fletcher, 'Founding a Tradition: G.A. Wood and J.F. Bruce, 1891–1930', in B. Caine, B. Fletcher, M. Miller, R. Pesman and D. Schreuder, eds, *History at Sydney: Centenary Reflections* (Sydney: History Department, University of Sydney, 1992), 1–21.

history of imperial constitutional development entitled *Commonwealth* (1971). When the University of Queensland sent a history graduate to Oxford in 1916, Bevil Molesworth (1891–1971), he also gravitated to A.L. Smith and Balliol, and became a tutor in adult education, but in his case it became a lifetime career in Australia, leading to appointment as the Australian Broadcasting Commission's first director of talks.

Meanwhile, the Balliol tradition spread to Melbourne after Ernest Scott became professor of history in 1913. Aware of his lack of Oxford connections, Scott no doubt took advice from Wood in the matter of sending Melbourne graduates to the United Kingdom. In the years immediately after the First World War, Melbourne alumni admitted to Balliol included the philosophy graduates Clement Leslie (1898–1980) and Boyce Gibson (1900–72) and the history students Esmonde Higgins (1897–1960), Fred Alexander (1899–1996) and William Keith Hancock (1898–1988).[22] Leslie, after a short period lecturing in British universities, moved into industry and the public service. Higgins embraced radical politics, almost certainly to the detriment of his career prospects, but devoted himself to adult education, thus replicating one of A.L. Smith's abiding interests. Boyce Gibson was also involved in adult education for a few years before returning to a lifetime of teaching philosophy at the University of Melbourne, and Fred Alexander was to pursue what almost became a second career as director of adult education in Western Australia from 1941 to 1954. However, Alexander's main trajectory began as assistant lecturer to Shann at the University of Western Australia in 1924, where he remained until his retirement as professor in 1966. Hancock, after becoming the first Australian elected to a fellowship at All Souls, Oxford's ancient and prestigious graduate college, was offered the chair of history at Adelaide in 1924 in succession to Henderson – who was retiring after periodic bouts of depression – and took up the position in 1926. Hancock and Alexander maintained a lifelong contact in which old friendship was mingled with a competitive element.

Of course women who aspired to become historians did not participate in the Oxbridge networks, apart from Kathleen Fitzpatrick (1905–90),[23] and had to look elsewhere for stimulus and support. Jessie Stobo Webb

---

22 For particulars, see Elsie Lemon, ed., *The Balliol College Register, Fourth E, 1916–1967* (Oxford: Oxford University Press, 1969).
23 Elizabeth Kleinmetz, *A Brimming Cup: The Life of Kathleen Fitzpatrick* (Melbourne: Melbourne University Press, 2013), 66–72.

(1880–1944), who at the age of 28 was appointed lecturer in ancient history at the University of Melbourne in 1908, and who spent three decades as deputy to Scott and Crawford, did much to mobilise the resources in Melbourne for intellectual companionship.[24] An important source of such support was created in 1910 with the establishment of the Catalyst Club, a monthly discussion group bringing together professional women, writers, artists and academics.[25] This group found a home in the Lyceum Club, founded in 1912 on the model of a London initiative eight years earlier. Its membership was drawn from the same cohort as the Catalyst Club, with the addition of women notable in philanthropy and public service.[26] This soon became, and has remained for a century, an important meeting place for women of active intellectual and cultural interests. Jessie Webb's career illustrates the kind of enterprise that might be fostered by membership of such a group. With one friend from the Lyceum Club, she traversed Africa from Cape Town to Cairo; with another she went travelling in central Australia in an Austin Seven in 1928 – all this besides the intellectual companionship.

Curiously, the Lyceum Club did not strike such deep roots in Sydney. Wood's school of history produced several graduates with distinguished scholarly potential, whose careers followed varying trajectories. In 1920, Marjorie Barnard (1897–1987) was awarded an overseas scholarship, but her father did not allow her to take it up, and she worked as a librarian in Sydney before entering into the literary partnership with Flora Eldershaw (1897–1956) that produced several works of historical fiction and history based on colonial New South Wales. Barnard's older colleague Myra Willard (1887–1971) received a postgraduate scholarship in 1920 that enabled her, under Wood's supervision, to conduct research leading to the publication of her *History of the White Australia Policy* in 1923. It was the first book published by the Melbourne University Press and remained the standard authority on the subject for almost half a century.[27] Unfortunately, Willard wrote no more history, spending the rest of her working life as a teacher and educational administrator. The one that

---

24 Ronald T. Ridley, *Jessie Webb: A Memoir* (Melbourne: History Department, University of Melbourne, 1994).
25 Anne Longmire, *The Catalysts: Change and Continuity 1910–2010* (Melbourne: Anne Longmire and the Catalysts, 2011).
26 Joan M. Gillison, *A History of the Lyceum Club, Melbourne* (Melbourne: Lyceum Club, 1975).
27 See Sharon M. Harrison, 'Myra Willard, 1887–1971', in *The Encyclopedia of Women and Leadership in Twentieth-Century Australia*, www.womenaustralia.info/leaders/biogs/WLE0730b.htm (accessed 19 December 2015).

got away was Persia Campbell (1898–1974), whose scholarship to the London School of Economics enabled her to write and publish *Chinese Coolie Immigration* in 1923. She returned to Sydney for a few years but married an American in 1930 and spent the rest of her life as an academic in the United States, becoming an early and respected authority on consumer protection. In their choice of research topics, both Willard and Campbell foreshadowed an outreach towards East and Southeast Asia and the Pacific that would become one of the characteristics of the Sydney school of history, but initially they were lone pioneers.

The rising interest in Australia's place in international affairs following the end of the First World War led to the formation of a number of organisations in which university staff found themselves networking with likeminded individuals from the professional and business world. First in point of time was the Round Table movement, which had prewar origins. It followed a visit from a tireless publicist for the British Empire, Lionel Curtis, in 1910–11 and was intended to mobilise influential public opinion in the major centres of the Empire with a view to fostering closer ties between the member nations, perhaps ultimately leading to some form of imperial federation. Groups were formed in Melbourne, Sydney, Adelaide and Brisbane (though after a few years the Brisbane group faded out of existence). The Australians were not keen on the concept of imperial federation, but they saw value in monthly meetings among interested citizens who would then forward essays based on their proceedings to a central London publication, the *Round Table*. The movement flourished during the interwar period, and provided a model of intellectual cooperation between the universities and the wider community. Its historian, Leonie Foster, estimated that 26 per cent of the membership was drawn from an academic background, 42 per cent from other professions and 32 per cent from business or primary production.[28]

The Round Table provided a model for the League of Nations Union, which originated in the United Kingdom. Its aim was similar: the mobilisation of support among influential public opinion in the league's member nations. A Melbourne chapter was set up in 1921, its promoters including the lawyer John Latham (1877–1964), the constitutional lawyer Sir Harrison Moore (1867–1935), and the geologist and stockbroker E.C.

---

28   Leonie Foster, *High Hopes: The Men and Motives of the Australian Round Table* (Melbourne: Melbourne University Press, 1986); D.A. Low, 'Australians and the Round Table, 1910–2010' (paper read at seminar, 'Preparing for Perth: An Action Agenda for 2011', Canberra, 6 November 2010).

Dyason (1886–1949), whose constructive role in forging links between town and gown would repay further study. For three decades, Dyason was a successful businessman, a respected economic advisor to governments, a student of international relations with pacifist leanings, and, as Ernest Scott's brother-in-law, someone with good contacts at the University of Melbourne.

In 1924, Archibald Charteris (1874–1940), professor of international law and jurisprudence at the University of Sydney and formerly associated with the Royal Institute of International Affairs at Chatham House, London, founded the Australian Institute of International Affairs in Sydney.[29] Dyason was among those who within a few months started a Victorian branch, and in 1925 he helped to promote an Australian affiliate of the Institute of Pacific Relations, an American initiative designed 'to study the conditions of the Pacific people with a view to the improvement of their mutual relationships'.[30] The Victorian chapter of the institute merged with the local branch of the Australian Institute of International Affairs in 1932, but its Sydney counterpart in its early years was more robust. Duncan Hall led the Australian delegation to the first international conference of the Institute of Pacific Relations at Honolulu in 1925 (where he seems to have scored a chair at a reputable American university; another aspect of networking).[31] Persia Campbell, G.V. Portus (1883–1954) and the economist Richard Mills (1886–1952) published in 1928, on behalf of the Institute of Pacific Relations, *Studies in Australian Affairs*. Gradually from the 1930s, the Australian Institute of International Affairs and the Institute of Pacific Relations came to concentrate on foreign policy, while the study of current affairs in Australia was taken over by the Australian Institute of Political Science,[32] publishers since 1929 of the *Australian Quarterly*. This was another medium linking public intellectuals from within and outside the universities.

---

29   J.D. Legge, *Australian Outlook: A History of the Australian Institute of International Affairs* (Canberra: Department of International Relations, The Australian National University, 1999).
30   Quoted in Susan Hogan and Heather Radi, 'Campbell, Persia Gwendoline Crawford (1898–1974)', *ADB*, adb.anu.edu.au/biography/campbell-persia-gwendoline-crawford-9682/text17087, published first in hardcopy 1993 (accessed 19 December 2015).
31   Hall was professor of international relations at Syracuse University, in New York State, during the 1926–27 academic year.
32   Since 2006, the Australian Institute of Policy and Science.

By 1928, then, networking among Australian historians was facilitated by three different lines of access. Participation in the regular meetings of ANZAAS was consolidated by the recognition of history as a discipline deserving a section of its own. The institutes specialising in aspects of foreign and domestic policy brought together academics and members of the business and professional communities. And, less measurable but no less pervasive, the shared experience of overseas study, especially at Balliol College and, to a lesser extent, the London School of Economics, shaped the thinking of a significant number of historians and political scientists. But then the unexpected and tragic death of G. Arnold Wood in 1928 led to lasting change in the character of the Sydney and Melbourne departments of history.

In choosing Wood's successor in the Challis chair, the selectors made a bold decision, appointing the 28-year-old Melbourne graduate Stephen Henry Roberts (1901–71).[33] This meant passing over the two remaining members of Wood's staff, James Bruce and Fred Wood, both Balliol alumni. Bruce soon left to take an appointment as foundation professor of history at the University of the Punjab, which was to become one of the leading schools in the Indian subcontinent. Fred Wood left in 1935 to become professor of history at Victoria University College, New Zealand. From that time on, the Sydney connection with Balliol College weakened, although during the 1930s the economic historian R.B. Madgwick (1905–79) enrolled there as a postgraduate between 1933 and 1935. His doctoral thesis saw publication as *Immigration to Eastern Australia, 1788–1851* (1937). Maintaining a tradition, in his subsequent career 'he pioneered a massive scheme of adult education' as director of army education during the Second World War.[34]

The University of Sydney acquired in Stephen Roberts a young dynamo with a record of research productivity unequalled until Geoffrey Blainey in the 1950s. From a rural background, Roberts took a swag of prizes at the University of Melbourne, where he was then appointed assistant lecturer under Scott. His pioneering *History of Australian Land Settlement* (1924) was followed by *Population Problems in the Pacific* (1927), a work

---

33 For Roberts, I draw on D.M. Schreuder, 'An Unconventional Founder: Stephen Roberts and the Professionalisation of the Historical Discipline', in Macintyre and Thomas, *The Discovery of Australian History*, 125–45; Schreuder, 'A "Second Foundation": S.H. Roberts as Challis Professor, 1929–47', in Caine et al., *History at Sydney*, 27–45.
34 Andrew Spaull, 'Madgwick, Sir Robert Bowden (1905–1979)', *ADB*, adb.anu.edu.au/biography/madgwick-sir-robert-bowden-11032, published first in hardcopy 2000 (accessed 3 October 2016).

stimulated by attending the Institute of Pacific Relations conference at Honolulu in 1925. Awarded an overseas scholarship, he preferred instead of Oxford or Cambridge to enrol at the London School of Economics between 1927 and 1929, where his supervisors included Harold Laski (1893–1950). His doctoral thesis was published in 1929 as the two-volume *History of French Colonial Policy, 1870–1925*. The theme built on Scott's early interest in French exploration but also harmonised with the growing tendency of historians based at the University of Sydney to look to the Pacific and East Asia for their subject matter. This tendency was strengthened when G.C. Henderson, after his resignation from the University of Adelaide, devoted his energies to research on the history of Fiji using materials in the Mitchell Library; he was eventually appointed an honorary research professor in Roberts's department and participated in the creation of a fourth-year honours class in Australian and Pacific history.[35]

Roberts himself during the 1930s consolidated his reputation in international studies with *Australia and the Far East* (1935) and *The House that Hitler Built* (1937).[36] After the Australian Broadcasting Commission was formed in 1932, he was one of its first and most prominent news commentators. He involved himself with the Australian Institute for International Affairs, the Institute for Pacific Relations and the Round Table, but did not take the initiative in creating new networks. When the 150th anniversary of the founding of New South Wales was celebrated in 1938, he does not seem to have reached out to the Aboriginal counter-narrative of a day of invasion. Some of the most creative work was achieved by women writers working outside the academy, most of them identified with the fledgling Fellowship of Australian Writers. Flora Eldershaw, with Marjorie Barnard, Miles Franklin (1879–1954) and Dame Mary Gilmore (1865–1962) produced *The Peaceful Army* (1938), which recovered much useful material about pioneer women in New South Wales. Marjorie Barnard, with Flora Eldershaw, also wrote *Phillip of Australia* (1938), an account of the first four years of settlement, which was to find its counterpart three years later in Eleanor Dark's (1901–85) fictional reconstruction of the same period from an Aboriginal perspective, *The Timeless Land* (1941). It is evident that women writers moving across the borders of history and historical fiction experienced an

---

35 Kwan, 'G.C. Henderson', 44–6.
36 See Andrew Bonnell, 'Stephen Roberts as a Commentator on Fascism and the Road to War in Europe', *History Australia*, 11:3 (2014), 9–30.

enriching contact in Sydney in those years, though this was not always appreciated by the men who had hitherto dominated the writing of early colonial history such as C.H. Currey (1890–1970) and Malcolm Ellis (1890–1969). Ellis directed a particularly nasty accusation of plagiarism against Barnard when she published *Macquarie's World* in 1941, and the experience seems to have discouraged her for a time from major historical research.[37]

At the University of Melbourne, Crawford's arrival as professor in succession to Scott in 1937 was a more distinct harbinger of change, as he injected into his department's honours courses ingredients in the philosophy and theory of history that had not previously been prominent in university teaching. But Crawford's department also showed national leadership, since it was responsible in 1940 for the establishment of the journal *Historical Studies: Australia and New Zealand*, which under various changes of name has survived to this day as a forum for the publication of new research of a quality to meet international scholarly standards.[38] Previously, the most accessible outlets for academic and amateur alike had been the journals of the various state historical societies, of which probably the most substantial was Sydney's *Journal of the Royal Australian Historical Society*, but the pages of all of them combined somewhat uneasily the monographs of the scholar with the effusions of the enthusiastic amateur.

The onset of the Second World War thrust many historians into new and often unexpected company. Probably the most bizarre experience of all fell to Max Crawford when he found himself in a remote Russian provincial city as first secretary in the new Australian embassy to the Soviet Union. Robert Madgwick and Fred Alexander more predictably found service in army education, which led to an expansion of their interest in adult education nationally. The young political scientist and historian Fin Crisp (1917–84) worked in the Department of Post-War Reconstruction, often in cooperation with Paul Hasluck at the new Department of External Affairs. Alf Conlon's (1908–61) Directorate of Research and Civil Affairs, with its emphasis on postwar colonial policy, included a number of anthropologists such as Ian Hogbin (1904–89), Bill Stanner (1905–81)

---

37 Jill Roe, 'Barnard, Marjorie Faith (Marjory) (1897–1987)', *ADB*, adb.anu.edu.au/biography/barnard-marjorie-faith-marjory-12176/text21821, published first in hardcopy 2007 (accessed 19 December 2015).
38 Fay Anderson, *An Historian's Life: Max Crawford and the Politics of Academic Freedom* (Melbourne: Melbourne University Press, 2005), 68–72, 81–5; see also Stuart Macintyre and Peter McPhee, *Max Crawford's School of History* (Melbourne: History Department, University of Melbourne, 2000).

and Camilla Wedgwood (1901–55), but no historians, except for the youthful John Legge (1921–2016), subsequently a leading authority on the Pacific and Southeast Asia.[39]

It was only with the establishment of the Department of Post-War Reconstruction, and the establishment in 1945 of the Universities Commission and the Commonwealth Office of Education, that a renewed potential for networking among historians became feasible, though none could foresee the extent to which these instrumentalities might survive and wield influence in the postwar years.[40] Of greater consequence was the decision to establish The Australian National University (ANU) in Canberra as a research and postgraduate institution that might coordinate initiatives in scholarship on a nationwide basis. Even though unforeseen delays in the appointment of senior professors in the social sciences meant that it was to be well into the 1950s before this promise was fully implemented, nevertheless during that time at least two ANU postgraduates, Russel Ward (1914–95) and Allan Martin (1926–2002), produced work of national importance.[41]

With the arrival in 1957 of Sir Keith Hancock as professor of history and director of the Research School of Social Sciences, the pace accelerated. Hancock was conscious of ANU being The Australian *National* University, encouraging cooperation and major research endeavours throughout Australia. This sense of mission was evident not only in such ventures as the wool seminar, bringing together a wide cross-disciplinary group to consider Australia's major primary industry, but also in a project of continuing importance today: the *Australian Dictionary of Biography*.[42] Building on the biographical data collections that Laurie Fitzhardinge (1908–93) had put together, Hancock oversaw the development of Australia's largest scholarly network. Working parties were set up in each

---

39 There are essays on Conlon and his directorate colleagues in Geoffrey Gray, Doug Munro and Christine Winter, eds, *Scholars at War: Australasian Social Scientists, 1939–1945* (Canberra: ANU E Press, 2012).
40 Stuart Macintyre, *Australia's Boldest Experiment: War and Reconstruction in the 1940s* (Sydney: NewSouth Publishing, 2015), 304–8.
41 Russel Ward, *The Australian Legend* (Melbourne: Oxford University Press, 1958). Martin published a number of important journal articles during the 1950s, culminating in Peter Loveday and A.W. Martin, *Parliament Factions and Parties: The First Thirty Years of Responsible Government in New South Wales, 1856–1889* (Melbourne: Melbourne University Press, 1966).
42 D.A. Low, ed., *Keith Hancock: The Legacies of an Historian* (Melbourne: Melbourne University Press, 2001), including Geoffrey Bolton, 'Rediscovering Australia: Hancock and the Wool Seminar', 180–200, and Libby Robin, 'Woolly Identities', 201–12.

Australian state and territory, connected on a federal basis with Canberra and reinforced by regular meetings of a representative committee; academic historians cooperated with hundreds of contributors from many walks of life to produce articles that could be edited to a sterling standard; new research questions were identified and materials discovered that might not otherwise have received attention. It was a classic model of networking to add value to existing scholarly resources. If Hancock's intention of involving historians from outside the universities led to a long and stormy interaction with Malcolm Ellis, the diplomacy of the first general editor, Douglas Pike (1908–74), ensured that the *Australian Dictionary of Biography* would be quickly acknowledged as genuinely nationwide and participatory.[43]

More generally, during the 1950s, networking among the state universities tended to build on the lines laid down before the Second World War. Perhaps the most surprising phenomenon was the persistence of the Balliol College nexus at Melbourne, Adelaide and Western Australia, probably through the influence of academic staff who had gone through Balliol before the war. During the 1930s, the Australians who gravitated to Balliol College included John La Nauze (1911–90), Fin Crisp and Manning Clark (1915–93). I may digress here to comment on the later idea that the anti-British sentiment sometimes evident in the six volumes of Clark's *History* was due to the coldness and lack of appreciation that he met with at Oxford.[44] In 1956, when he was embarking on the first volume of this great project, he and his family spent their study leave attached to Balliol College. Some of the dons, including the mediaevalist Richard Southern (1912–2001), thought highly of him, and I experienced proof of this. In the term before the Finals examination in history, it was customary for the candidates to receive extra tuition and grooming from the senior fellow at Balliol. This man unfortunately fell ill, and it was to Manning Clark that the college entrusted the coaching of their undergraduates. Their confidence was well placed. Almost immediately he had them eating out of his hand. They long remembered the tutor who, when challenged by an American undergraduate as to what he knew

---

43 Melanie Nolan and Christine Fernon, eds, *The ADB's Story* (Canberra: ANU E Press, 2013), esp. Ann Moyal, 'Sir Keith Hancock: Laying the Foundations', 49–92; and John D. Calvert, '"Born to do this work": Douglas Pike and the *ADB*, 1962–1973', 101–19.
44 Manning Clark, *A History of Australia* (6 vols; Melbourne: Melbourne University Press, 1962–1987). Clark recounts his treatment at Oxford in those terms – *The Quest for Grace* (Ringwood: Viking, 1991), ch. 3 – but as Mark McKenna (in this volume) points out, his diaries during this time present 'very little if any evidence of these sentiments'.

about baseball, replied that it was a game occasionally played as a warm-up before minor Australian Rules games in Melbourne. Four of the 10 who sat the examination got first-class honours.

In the decade after 1945, the intake of Australian historians at Balliol reached a peak. They included Hugh Stretton (1924–2015), Max Hartwell (1921–2009), C.M. (Mick) Williams (1923–87), John Legge, Frank Crowley (1924–2013), Peter Phillips (1920–2010), Bede Nairn (1917–2006), and myself. My choice was no doubt affected by the fact that the four teaching staff at the University of Western Australia – Fred Alexander, 'Josh' Reynolds (1905–81), John Legge, and Frank Crowley – were all Balliol products, though too much should not be read into that; a senior don at Balliol once confessed to me sorrowfully that Crowley was the only Australian for whom Oxford and Balliol seemed to have done nothing. But the Balliol influence must have been pervasive. As late as January 1966, when I took the chair of modern history at the University of Western Australia, half of the 20 professors of history in Australia had either read the undergraduate course or completed a doctoral thesis at Balliol.

During the 1950s, the foremost school of history in Australia was probably Melbourne, where two Balliol alumni, Max Crawford and John La Nauze, each formal in suits, presided over dutiful departmental afternoon teas, but managed to coexist with a lively radical and Marxist subculture that included Alan McBriar (1918–2004) and Ian Turner (1922–78). Moreover, the loudest barracker for Melbourne's pre-eminence was the Balliol man Manning Clark, nostalgic in exile at the Canberra University College. When challenge came it was from two Balliol alumni, Stretton at Adelaide and Legge at Monash. Stretton's career at Balliol was remarkable. Arriving as a Rhodes Scholar in 1946, he was appointed as a fellow two years later, and this even before he graduated with first-class honours in 1948. At the age of 29, he became the college's dean, an office usually held by dons of much greater seniority. In 1954, at 30, he returned to Adelaide to take the chair of history, and there, despite the interventions of a reactionary vice-chancellor,[45] built up an array of talent including George Rudé (1910–93), the young Ken Inglis and Allan Martin. By the early 1960s, Adelaide was arguably the most dynamic department in

---

45 Evidence of Vice-Chancellor A.P. Rowe's antipathy towards Stretton can be found in Hugh Stretton, interviewed by Rob Linn, 14 November 2006, J.D. Somerville Oral History Collection, interview no. 760/4, State Library of South Australia, Adelaide (pages 12–13 of transcript).

the country.[46] At Monash, meanwhile, Legge managed not only to entice Geoffrey Serle (1922–98) and Alan McBriar to join him as senior members of staff, but also several of the brightest honours students from Melbourne.[47] The networks were expanding.

Sydney and Queensland remained largely immune to the Balliol network, favouring if anything the London School of Economics. In 1948, Stephen Roberts was promoted to the vice-chancellorship of the University of Sydney, and the succession lay between two members of his departmental staff, Gordon Greenwood (1913–86) and John Manning Ward (1919–90). Both of their areas of research built upon Sydney's established interests in Asia and the Pacific. Greenwood was the senior of the two. He had taken his doctorate at the London School of Economics in 1939, whereas Ward had not seen overseas experience. In 1948, however, he had published *British Policy in the South Pacific (1786–1893)*, in which his legal expertise enabled him to offer new interpretations about British imperialism in the region. Once again, the selectors went for the younger man and Ward, not yet 30, was appointed to the Challis chair.[48]

Greenwood took himself off to the McCaughey chair of history at the University of Queensland, where for more than 30 years he was a baronial presence. With him, he brought an entrepreneurial energy that during the next decade resulted in a number of initiatives. He edited a history of Australia, which became standard fare for high schools and universities until the 1970s. In 1955, he launched the *Australian Journal of Politics and History*, the title of which indicated a different emphasis to Melbourne's *Historical Studies*.[49] Using his contacts with the Australian Institute of International Affairs, he launched a series of five-year surveys of Australia in international relations, forming a partnership with Norman Harper, and thus bringing the University of Queensland into a closer relationship than hitherto with the University of Melbourne.

---

46 Stretton's role as 'architect builder' and 'pathfinder' is stressed by several of the contributors to the recent history of the Adelaide history department. Prest, *Pasts Present*, 16, 46–7, 192, 210; see also Doug Munro, 'The House that Hugh Built: The Adelaide History Department during the Stretton Era, 1954–1966', *History of Education* 46:5 (2017), 631–52, dx.doi.org/10.1080/0046760X.2017.1318306.
47 John Thompson, *The Patrician and the Bloke: Geoffrey Serle and the Making of Australian History* (Canberra: Pandanus Books, 2006); Anderson, *An Historian's Life*, 347.
48 B.H. Fletcher and D.M. Schreuder, 'John Manning Ward', in Caine et al., *History at Sydney*, 83–7.
49 John A. Moses, 'Fifty Years of the *Australian Journal of Politics and History*', *Australian Journal of Politics and History*, 50:2 (2004), 155–62, doi.org/10.1111/j.1467-8497.2004.00329.x.

At Sydney, Ward tended to explore Australian history as the offshoot of a wider British diaspora, adapting and modifying in response to a new environment, but needing to maintain contact with the metropolitan original. In this he was paralleling the approach of a section of the Department of English at the same university, including Leonie Kramer, but the approach could not satisfy the nationalist thrust embodied in works such as Russel Ward's *Australian Legend* or Manning Clark's *History*. If there was any risk that Sydney might find itself isolated from the mainstream currents of Australian historical thought, this was averted partly through Ward's assiduous participation in such ventures as the *Australian Dictionary of Biography*, and also through the part played by Sydney academics in launching historical associations with specialist interests. In 1956, the Business Archives Council of Australia started its own *Bulletin*, renamed *Business Archives and History* in 1960, transforming into the *Australian Economic History Review* in 1967, and finally its ownership being transferred to the newly founded Economic History Society of Australasia. In the meantime, the Australian Society for the Study of Religious History was set up in 1959 and began publishing the *Journal of Religious History* in 1960, while a Sydney branch of the Australian Society for Labour History was established in 1962. The founding of the society had been discussed in Canberra some two years previously by Keith Hancock and the visiting British historian Asa Briggs, and formally launched in 1961 at the congress of the ANZAAS in Brisbane in May 1961. Its journal, *Labour History*, began publication in 1962.[50]

The appearance of such specialisms, coinciding with the unprecedented expansion in universities and their funding that followed the Murray Report in 1957, raised questions about future networking among historians. The time had now come in the eyes of some for the creation of some umbrella organisation that might serve as a network for all historians and avert fragmentation. During the 1950s, the Social Sciences Research Council and its counterpart in the Humanities, both by-products of the era of postwar reconstruction, had struggled to find a purpose. By the

---

50 Stephen Morgan and Martin Shanahan, 'The Supply of Economic History in Australasia: The *Australian Economic History Review* at 50', *Australian Economic History Review*, 50:3 (2010), 217–39, doi.org/10.1111/j.1467-8446.2010.00303.x; Bruce Mansfield, 'Sydney History and Religion: A Memoir', *Quadrant*, 49:11 (2005), 56–9; Eric Fry, 'The Labour History Society (ASSLH): A Memoir of its First Twenty Years', *Labour History*, 77 (1999), 83–96, doi.org/10.2307/27516671; Melanie Nolan, 'Entwined Associations: Labour History and its People in Canberra', in Melanie Nolan, ed., *Labour History and its People, Twelfth Biennial National Labour History Conference* (Canberra: Australian Society for the Study of Labour History, 2011), 1–15.

later 1960s, it became increasingly certain that both would become learned academies, along the lines of the Australian Academy of Science, and history would be represented in both, but this was hardly a substitute for a body entirely consecrated to history in its various forms.[51]

ANZAAS still provided a regular national meeting place at which seniors in the profession might lay down their notions of future directions for the discipline, juniors might find an audience and all participants exchange ideas and gossip (and who knows how much networking took place in the pubs and restaurants outside the formal hours of meeting?). Some historians enjoyed the opportunity of catching up with important new developments in other social sciences such as anthropology and geography, and saw value in remaining within ANZAAS. Others grew increasingly insistent that there should be a body, probably along the lines of the long-established American Historical Association, that could speak and exercise pressure on behalf of the discipline as a whole. During the later 1960s, the issue was regularly aired at Section E meetings of ANZAAS, among the strongest advocates of a new association being Frank Crowley and George Rudé.

Eventually the decision was taken at the ANZAAS conference in Perth in 1973 to create a new Australian Historical Association. A.G.L. Shaw (1916–2012), professor at Monash University and a historian with links to both the Melbourne and the Sydney schools, was to be the first president. For a few years, the new association would coexist with ANZAAS, with some historians attending both; however, by the 1980s, ANZAAS itself was facing decline because many scientific and medical scholars preferred to support the organisations representing their specialised interests.

The decision to form the Australian Historical Association was taken just in time, in the sense that new sub-branches of the discipline of history were proliferating. A number of women historians – Anne Summers, Beverley Kingston and Miriam Rechter prominent among them – were preparing the first major critiques of the neglected place of women in Australian history, supported by a lively growth of collectives and working parties keen to set the story straight. Environmental history was coming into view. Among younger historians there was a dawning realisation, growing in depth and conviction, that the history of Australia had not

---

51 Stuart Macintyre, *The Poor Relation: A History of Social Sciences in Australia* (Melbourne: Melbourne University Press, 2010).

begun in 1788 and had not subsequently been a story of the peaceful spread of flocks and herds across an empty land. Aboriginal history would have to be accommodated not only as a branch of the discipline but would also need to be integrated into the mainstream historical narratives. The conversations that enabled communication among historians from both the newer and the older fields of historical endeavour could best be conducted under the aegis of the Australian Historical Association. Such during the ensuing 40 years has proved to be the case.

11
Country and Kin Calling? Keith Hancock, the National Dictionary Collaboration, and the Promotion of Life Writing in Australia[1]

Melanie Nolan

Australian historians and *ego-histoire*

In his international comparison of history, historians and autobiography in 2005, Jeremy D. Popkin concluded that Australian historians were early to, and enthusiastic about, the *ego-histoire* movement or the 'setting down [of] one's own story'. Australians anticipated Pierre Nora's collection of essays, *Essais d'ego-histoire*, which was published in 1987.[2] They had already founded 'a series of autobiographical lectures in 1984', which resulted in a number of publications, and Australian historians' memoirs thereafter appeared at a rate of more than one a year.[3] When he considered Australian

---

1   I thank Ann Curthoys and the editors for their comments on an earlier draft.
2   Pierre Nora ed., *Essais d'ego-histoire* (Paris: Gallimard, 1987), 7.
3   Jeremy D. Popkin, *History, Historians, & Autobiography* (Chicago/London: University of Chicago Press, 2005), 74. In '*Ego-histoire* Down Under: Australian Historian-Autobiographers', *Australian Historical Studies*, 38:129 (2007), 110, doi.org/10.1080/10314610708601234, Popkin dates the Australian memoir bulge from 1982 when collective projects including 'a volume of professional women's narratives, *The Half-Open Door*, which appeared in 1982, and the four volumes of essays starting with the Victorian History Institute's 1984 forum in which R.M. Crawford, Manning Clark and Geoffrey Blainey participated'. Patricia Grimshaw and Lynne Strahan, eds, *The Half-Open Door: Sixteen Australian Women Look at Professional Life and Achievement* (Sydney: Hale & Iremonger, 1982);

historians' memoirs more specifically in 2007, Popkin argued that '[o]n a proportional basis, more historians from Australia than from any other country' have written *ego-histoire*: he had identified 'more than three dozen different' Australian historians who had written her or his memoirs compared to just 200 United States historians' published memoirs.[4] Popkin also argued that contemporary Australian historians' memoirs helped to establish 'a tradition of first-person writing, a relatively recent development in their own culture' and that they had greater impact in Australia than groups of other historians elsewhere in other countries. Works by both male and female authors such as Keith Hancock, Kathleen Fitzpatrick, Bernard Smith, Jill Ker Conway, Manning Clark, Ann Moyal and Inga Clendinnen constituted a distinctive strain of historical life writing generally and had become major contributions to the national literature.[5] This creative non-fiction won major mainstream literary prizes, not simply specialist history ones. Australian historians' life writing had a greater impact within society than French or US contemporaries had in theirs, according to Popkin, because of the literary quality of the work and the 'high degree of authorial self-consciousness' in the context of a relatively new sense of Australian cultural identity.

This work has been methodologically important to the profession, too, in two ways. First, historians' personal lives and experience challenged received versions of the national past. Popkin argued:

> Australian historians have used their personal stories to dramatise the issue of Australia's relationship to Britain and Europe, its ability to define a distinctive national personality, the role of gender in that definition and how Australia might come to terms with its troubled relationship to its Aboriginal population.[6]

R.M. Crawford, Manning Clark and Geoffrey Blainey, *Making History* (Melbourne: McPhee Gribble/Penguin, 1985); Bain Attwood, ed., *Boundaries of the Past* (Melbourne: History Institute, 1990); Bain Attwood and Joy Damousi, eds, *Feminist Histories* (Melbourne: History Institute, 1991); Bain Attwood, ed., *Labour Histories* (Melbourne: Monash University Printing Services, 1994).

4 Popkin, '*Ego-histoire* Down Under', 110, 119.

5 W.K. Hancock, *Country and Calling* (London: Faber & Faber, 1954); Hancock, *Professing History* (Sydney: Sydney University Press, 1976); Kathleen Fitzpatrick, *Solid Bluestone Foundations: Memories of an Australian Girlhood* (Ringwood: Penguin, 1983); Jill Ker Conway, *The Road from Coorain* (New York: Knopf, 1989); Manning Clark, *The Puzzles of Childhood* (Ringwood: Viking, 1989); Clark, *The Quest for Grace* (Ringwood: Viking, 1990); Bernard Smith, *The Boy Adeodatus: The Portrait of a Lucky Young Bastard* (Melbourne: Oxford University Press, 1990); Ann Moyal, *Breakfast with Beaverbrook: Memoirs of an Independent Woman* (Sydney: Hale & Iremonger, 1995); Inga Clendinnen, *Tiger's Eye: A Memoir* (Melbourne: Text Publishing, 2000). For instance, Smith's *Adeodatus* won both the Victorian Premier's Literary Award and the National Book Council Prize.

6 Popkin, '*Ego-histoire* Down Under', 123.

Indeed, Indigenous Australian historians' autobiographies, including those of Gordon Briscoe and of the contributors to the recent collection, *Ngapartji Ngapartji*, discussed how these scholars' life histories have impacted on their research on Indigenous Australians and their more general perspectives, just as occurred for women historians earlier.[7] Their experience led them to question the national Australian narratives. Second, autobiographical works also helped to break down the wall or methodological divide between history and autobiography, which had been premised on the view that memoirs were private, subjective and 'beyond the reach of historical investigation' while history was research-based and in accordance with the documentary record.[8] Many others have questioned what is sometimes described as the 'illusion of objectivity',[9] but *ego-histoire* confronted this issue directly in terms of source material.[10] Not only did many memoirists resort to documentary evidence but historians, as well as biographers, used subjective material. As Popkin argued, biographies of historians and their own *ego-histoire* were important factors in the wider reconciliation between history and autobiography.[11]

Popkin singled out the trailblazing importance for Australian historians of W.K. (Keith) Hancock's reflections: his 1954 volume of memoirs, *Country and Calling*, and his 1976 extended autobiographical essay, *Professing History*.[12] Historians regard Hancock as Australia's greatest historian because he displayed an impressive range, quality and volume of work. He also held an impressive range, quality and number of political involvements, appointments and honours.[13] Hancock's biographer, Jim Davidson, notes that 'Hancock's once immense reputation is now hard for Australians to

---

7   Gordon Briscoe, *Racial Folly: A Twentieth Century Aboriginal Family* (Canberra: ANU E Press and Aboriginal History, 2010); Vanessa Castejon, Anna Cole, Oliver Haag and Karen Hughes, eds, *Ngapartji Ngapartji: In Turn, in Turn: Ego-histoire, Europe and Indigenous Australia* (Canberra: ANU Press, 2014).
8   Popkin, *History, Historians, & Autobiography*, 17, 90.
9   Peter Novick, *That Noble Dream: The 'Objectivity Question' and the American Historical Profession* (Cambridge: Cambridge University Press, 1988), doi.org/10.1017/CBO9780511816345.
10   Luisa Passerini and Alexander Geppert, 'Historians in Flux: The Concept, Task, and Challenge of Ego-histoire', *Historein: A Review of the Past and Other Stories*, special issue, European Ego-histoires: Historiography and the Self, 1970–2000, 3 (2001), 7–18.
11   Popkin, *History, Historians, & Autobiography*, 12.
12   Hancock, *Country and Calling*; Hancock, *Professing History*; Popkin 'Ego-histoire Down Under', 109. See also Jaume Aurell, *Theoretical Perspectives on Historians' Autobiographies: From Documentation to Intervention* (New York/London: Routledge, 2015), 485 – together with G.V. Portus's autobiography, *Happy Highways* (Melbourne: Melbourne University Press, 1953); and David McCooey, *Artful Histories: Modern Australian Autobiography* (Cambridge: Cambridge University Press, 1996), doi.org/10.1017/CBO9781139084956.
13   D.A. Low, ed., *Keith Hancock: The legacy of an Historian* (Melbourne: Melbourne University Press, 2001).

grasp: most of it was earned outside Australia, and the Commonwealth context which gave it coherence has virtually collapsed'.[14] Stuart Macintyre famously suggested in 2010 that 'if there were a Nobel Prize for History, Hancock would surely have won it'.[15] Hancock (1898–1988) attained a First in History at Melbourne University (BA Hons, 1920), and was a temporary lecturer at the University of Western Australia before taking up a Rhodes Scholarship to Balliol College, Oxford (BA, 1923; MA, 1930). He secured a prize fellowship at All Souls (1923) and the next year, at the age of 26, he became a 'boy professor' of history at Adelaide University (1924–34). He then held chairs successively at Birmingham (1934–44), Oxford (1944–49), Institute of Commonwealth Studies London (1949–56) and The Australian National University (ANU) (1957–65). He became an ANU Visiting Fellow and founding director of the Australian Academy of the Humanities in 1969 in his 'retirement'. Hancock wrote more than 20 books: most importantly, *Australia* (1930), *Survey of British Commonwealth Affairs* (1937–42), *British War Economy* (with Margaret Gowing, 1949), *Smuts: The Sanguine Years, 1870–1919*, vol. 1 (1962), *Smuts: The Fields of Force, 1919–50*, vol. 2 (1968), and *Discovering Monaro* (1972), as well as his two works of professional memoir and reflection. His British knighthood in 1953 stemmed from his most famous service in managing and editing the 28 volumes of the *British Civil Histories of War*. Hancock was involved in a mission to Uganda on behalf of the British government in 1954. The Italian government appointed him to the Order of Merit of the Republic of Italy in 1961, on the strength of his first, and least known, work on *Ricasoli and the Risorgimento in Tuscany* in 1926, which Mussolini's ascendancy had rendered relevant. The Australian government instigated his Knight Commander of the Order of the British Empire award in 1965 primarily for his role at ANU, with which he had been associated from its foundation in 1946 when he was one of the inaugural four 'academic advisors'.[16]

Australian historians' struggle with the challenge of writing 'their own history' was played out poignantly in Hancock's own biographical practices, negotiating the conflicts of a historian writing his own history

---

14 Jim Davidson, *A Three-Cornered Life: The Historian W. K. Hancock* (Sydney: University of New South Wales Press, 2009), 510.
15 Tom Griffiths, *The Art of Time Travel: Historians and their Craft* (Carlton, Vic.: Black Inc., 2016), 42–60.
16 See, for instance, Robin Gollan, 'Sir (William) Keith Hancock 1898-1988', *Proceedings of the Australian Academy of Humanities*, vol. 14 (Canberra: Australian Academy of the Humanities, 1990), 61–63; and Jim Davidson, 'Hancock, Sir William Keith (1898-1988)', *Australian Dictionary of Biography*, vol. 17 (Melbourne: Melbourne University Press, 2007).

and the separate dilemma of what he called 'country and calling' during the twentieth century. First, Hancock's writings and life abound with tensions arising from his being both an insider and outsider: Davidson describes a three-cornered life in terms of country, while Sandra Holton argues that he never resolved the dilemmas of being an Antipodean-born European.[17] Second, Hancock's two volumes of memoirs epitomise the struggle he had in disentangling the personal and the professional. Reviewers noted that the 'best part' of his first memoir was his childhood reminiscences.[18] While his first wife, Theaden Brocklebank, is deliberately excluded from discussion in the first volume, she does appear in the second volume.[19] He also 'draws a veil' over disagreements he had with other scholars at ANU, observing that 'those stories better not be told'.[20] Hancock, as an Australian historian writing his memoirs, had a lot of work to do in defending his positions on the nation, as well as the extent to which he wrote about his professional and personal life. One aspect of Hancock's engagement with Australian life writing, which Popkin neglects, is Hancock's being the leading figure in the establishment of the *Australian Dictionary of Biography* (*ADB*) at ANU in the late 1950s.[21] Three decades later, there were 306 biographies of historians in the *ADB* for the period between 1788 and 1990; nearly 2.5 per cent of the *ADB*'s 12,500 subjects who died before 1990 are fielded, or indexed, as 'historians'.[22] In this way, Hancock was responsible for the writing of many Australian historians' lives as well as his own.

While Hancock struggled with being himself the subject of a biography, his ambivalence waned over time.[23] He had begun pondering his life in the light of R.G. Collingwood's autobiography. Hancock initially bridled at Davidson's suggestion of a biography on himself. He had after all

---

17 Sandra Stanley Holton, 'The Autobiographies: Country and Calling and Professing History' presented at a 'Sir Keith Hancock Symposium' held in The Australian National University in Canberra in 1998, for the centenary of Hancock's birth and 10 years after his death; and '"History is about Chaps": Professional, National and Gender Identities in Hancock's Autobiographies', in Low, *Keith Hancock*, 271.
18 C.E. Carrington, review of *Country and Calling* by W.K. Hancock, *International Affairs*, 31:2 (1955), 210.
19 O'Brien, review of *A Three-Cornered Life*; Holton, '"History is about Chaps"', 271.
20 Moyal, *Breakfast with Beaverbrook*, 137–49, tells the stories, as does Davidson, *A Three-Cornered Life*, ch. 6.
21 Melanie Nolan and Christine Fernon, eds, *The* ADB*'s Story* (Canberra: ANU E Press, 2013).
22 See *ADB* website, adb.anu.edu.au/facets/?facet=occf, for a breakdown of the distribution among 13 categories: general (188), military (40), religious (15), economic (11), architecture (8), art (7), music (6), medical (5), labour (4), legal (4), political (3), social (3), and literary (2).
23 See Davidson, *A Three-Cornered Life*, 485, for a discussion of his change of mind on this issue.

burned all his and his first wife Theaden's correspondence after her death, although he used extensive 'records I kept at that time of her state of health'.[24] As he warmed to the idea, Hancock teased Davidson by showing him personal diaries and personal papers that he was (literally) not allowed to touch. At the launch of Volume 10 of the *ADB* in 1986, however, Hancock publicly praised Davidson's biography of Dame Nellie Melba as the 'best brief life of a prima donna that anyone has ever written or ever will write'.[25] Melba's article was controversial for its explicit discussion of her facelift as the cause of her death from septicaemia.[26] Hancock opined that *ADB* articles were 'more scholarly' than the British *Dictionary of National Biography* (*DNB*) articles because *ADB* authors had 'delved deep into primary sources' and wrote on a wide variety of subjects. That evening, Davidson said that privately Hancock gave him an 'encoded message of approval' to be his biographer.[27]

In various ways, Hancock was not only central to overcoming a general reluctance towards all forms of life writing in Australia, and by and for historians in particular, but also to influencing the kind of biography written. In leading the way, he was not only party to, but also a subject of, the transition. As Macintyre noted in the 1998 *Companion to Australian History* '[h]istorians have largely dropped their suspicion of the genre of biography'; now, '[t]hose who regard biography as a mere ancillary of their discipline underestimate it'.[28] Popkin, of course, did not consider biographies of historians in his analysis. Indeed, many commentators continue to distinguish between history and biography, and by kinds of life writing, too. While they include autobiographies, they draw the line at memoirs, believing autobiographies to be fuller and documented, while memoirs are mere perspectives based on memory.[29] However, I would argue that this refined distinction is still fraught; at the very least there is a continuum. Jaume Aurell has noted that some historians 'design their autobiographies in the same way as they articulate their historical texts'.

24   Hancock, *Professing History*, 24.
25   W.K. Hancock, speech notes, launch of vol. 10, ADB, Box 116, Q31, ADB Archives (ADBA), Australian National University Archives (ANUA).
26   Jim Davidson, 'Melba, Dame Nellie (1861–1931)', *Australian Dictionary of Biography*, National Centre of Biography, The Australian National University, adb.anu.edu.au/biography/melba-dame-nellie-7551/text13175, published first in hardcopy 1986 (accessed 6 October 2016).
27   Davidson, *A Three-Cornered Life*, x.
28   Graeme Davison, John Hirst and Stuart Macintyre, eds, *The Oxford Companion to Australian History* (Melbourne: Oxford University Press, 1998), 72.
29   Robert Drewe, Seymour Biography Lecture, 17 September 2015, National Library of Australia (NLA), www.nla.gov.au/audio/robert-drewe; McCooey, *Artful Histories*, 5, also distinguishes between history and autobiography.

We can consider some autobiographies as a valid form of history, and one might include some memoirs too.[30] For instance, biographies have increasingly been based, in turn, on rich 'first-person' archival material, diaries and correspondence. Some memoirs are increasingly researched and are referenced. If autobiographies break down the methodological divide between history writing and subjective sources, so too can biographies.

In the face of debates about the differences between primary and secondary life writing, and amidst a current multitude of memoirs by, and biographies about, Australian historians, in this essay I consider the history of biographical practices among those in the Australian academy from the vantage point of Hancock's experience. I chart the history of Australian historians' memoirs and biographies and their changing natures, considering especially the recent emergence of historians' family memoirs. This analysis complements assessments, such as Popkin's, which concentrate on national identity; it seeks to broaden the changes in quantity and kind of life writing over time that we should consider.

Kick-starting Australian biography writing

Hancock and the *ADB* were central to the evolution of Australian biography from the foundation of ANU. When planning for ANU began in earnest at the end of the Second World War, H.C. Coombs was charged with consulting expatriates, such as Hancock, on the shape of the new research university. Hancock, together with medical scientist Sir Howard Florey, physicist Mark Oliphant and anthropologist Raymond Firth made up the Academic Advisory Committee, which met the Interim Council in Canberra over Easter 1948 to discuss the university. The committee invited Hancock to advise it on the proposed school of social sciences. In turn, in preparation, Hancock invited a number of Australian social scientists to report on recent developments in their fields, their opinion on the main directions for future research, and 'the facilities which are necessary for the encouragement of research'. Professor R.M. (Max) Crawford at the University of Melbourne wrote the survey on the discipline of history. He argued generally that social scientists needed to be 'brought together' in Canberra. In terms of history, there were seven great needs: the collection, preservation and cataloguing of documents;

---

30   Jaume Aurell, 'Autobiography as Unconventional History: Constructing the Author', *Rethinking History*, 10:3 (2006), 433–49, doi.org/10.1080/13642520600816213.

public policy history; interpretative histories of Australia (Melbourne was planning a five-volume history of Australia); regional history; histories of private institutions; Pacific history; and biography.

Three of the academic advisors, Mark Oliphant, Keith Hancock and Howard Florey, reviewing proposed sites for ANU, Canberra, Easter 1948

Source: Oliphant Papers, Barr Smith Library, University of Adelaide. Reproduced in Stephen Foster and Margaret Varghese, *The Making of the Australian National University 1946–1996* (St Leonards, NSW: Allen & Unwin, 1996), p. 44. openresearch-repository.anu.edu.au/handle/1885/11333.

Above all, Crawford saw a special role for the ANU historians in a dictionary project: '[t]here is, I believe, more work being done now in Australia biography, a field in which we have in the past done relatively little'. Crawford provided a list of just three dozen biographies of published between 1933 and 1947.[31] Similarly, H.M. Green's survey of biography as part of a more general survey of Australian literature in 1951 argued that the first Australian biographies were akin to 'extended, more considered, and permanent version of the obituary'. Green pointed to just three 'outstanding' Australian biographies before the 1950s: Nettie Palmer's biography of her uncle and High Court Judge, Henry Bournes

---

31 Raymond Maxwell Crawford, 'Present state of historical research in Australia, and comments on main directions which research may take', Research in the Social Sciences in Australia, Reports Prepared at the Request of Professor Keith Hancock, January 1948, tabled in the Minutes, 10 October 1947, p. 3, ANU Council, box 26, series 19, ANUA. This study was subsequently published as *Research in the Social Sciences in Australia: Reports Prepared at the Request of Professor W.K. Hancock* (Canberra: The Australian National University, 1948).

Higgins; M. Barnard Eldershaw's *Phillip of Australia* ('the' author was, in reality, a professional collaboration between Marjorie Barnard and Flora Eldershaw, the subject being Arthur Phillip, the first governor of New South Wales (NSW), 1788–92); and H.V. Evatt's *Australian Labour Leader*, a memoir of William Holman, NSW Premier 1913–20.[32] Crawford distinguished between the historian's and ANU's roles:

> I do not need to labour the point that biographical studies will teach us about much more than the persons studied. This is work for individual scholars. The role of the National University might be the eventual production of an Australian Dictionary of National Biography.[33]

Interim Council meeting with academic advisors, April 1948
Pictured from left, moving clockwise around table (according to writing on back of photograph): Sir Frederic Eggleston, Ernest Clark, Professor D. Copland, R.G. Osborne, Professor R.C. Mills, Dr H.C. Coombs, A.S. Brown, Mr Goodes, Professor R.D. Wright, Mr McDonald, Lord Florey, Professor M. Oliphant, Professor R. Firth, Professor K. Hancock, C.S. Daley and Sir Robert Garran.
Source: Australian official photograph, Department of Information (photographer unknown).

---

32 H.M. Green, *A History of Australian Literature, Pure and Applied: A Critical Review of all Forms of Literature Produced in Australia from the First Books Published After the Arrival of the First Fleet until 1950* (Revised ed.; 2 vols.; Sydney: Angus & Robertson, 1985), II, 1367–92; Nettie Palmer, *Henry Bournes Higgins* (London: Harrap, 1931); M. Barnard Eldershaw, *Phillip of Australia* (London: Harrap, 1938); H.V. Evatt, *Australian Labour Leader: The Story of W.A. Holman and the Labour Movement* (Sydney: Angus & Robertson, 1942).
33 Crawford, 'Present state of historical research in Australia', 3.

This proposal struck a chord with Hancock. The ANU charter was a nation-building one: to encourage, and provide facilities for, research and postgraduate study, both generally and in relation to subjects of national importance to Australia.[34] The dictionary project could play a tangible role in promoting Australian history. Above all, no other Australian university was in a position to develop a dictionary project, and ANU could show intellectual leadership in this regard and develop a national collaboration around the project. Hancock had been slightly involved in the *DNB* in wartime Britain, serving on its national committee. In his biography, Davidson cites Hancock's role in the *DNB*, as do others, observing that he 'rarely thought it worth mentioning'.[35] Perhaps he did not mention it because the *DNB* was not an elaborate organisation at this time: Hancock is thanked in a list of 86 others in the supplementary volume on Britons who died between 1941 and 1950, and is thanked along with 43 others for 'their advice' in the decadal successor of those who died between 1951 and 1960.[36] The project was an 'Oxford project' and Hancock was friends with both editors, L.G. Wickham Legg and Bill Williams; the latter was a co-fellow of Balliol and a Warden of Rhodes House, itself a centre for Commonwealth Studies, Hancock's specialty. The editors did not have a national collaborative network; they were merely adding supplements to Leslie Stephen and Sidney Lee's initial project. Hancock's honing of skills in a large collaborative historical project in Britain arose not from the *DNB* but primarily from the series of histories about the nation at war that he designed and managed for the War Histories Branch, attached to the Cabinet Office. His plan for this undertaking was approved and he appointed 10 historians. He thus became general editor for the next dozen years on the 28 volumes that comprised the Civil Histories of the *History of the Second World War*, his duties involving not only writing the first volume but also managing directly for five years about 40 historians and researchers.[37]

---

34 Hon. John Johnstone Dedman, MP, Minister for Post-War Reconstruction, 'Second Reading Speech – Australian National University Bill 1946', *Hansard*, 19 June 1946.
35 Davidson, *A Three-Cornered Life*, 393.
36 L.G. Wickham Legg and E.T. Williams, eds, *The Dictionary of National Biography, 1941–1950* (Oxford: Oxford University Press, 1959), v.
37 The War Histories Branch of the Cabinet Office staff numbered 122 in 1949, of whom 20 were employed part time. The 28 historians and 48 researchers were divided about equally between military and civil histories of the war. See Jose Harris, 'Thucydides Amongst the Mandarins: Hancock and the World War II Civil Histories', in Low, *Keith Hancock*, 122–48.

Others have narrated the difficulty ANU experienced in appointing Hancock the inaugural director of the Research School of Social Sciences.[38] He did not take up that position up until 1957. Meanwhile, Laurie Fitzhardinge was drumming up support for a dictionary of Australian biography. Fitzhardinge taught classics at the University of Sydney from 1946 to 1950. He was charged with setting up a Sydney University press, which involved his travelling, with his family, to Britain for a year in 1947 to 1948 to visit university printing presses. He was based at the Clarendon Press at Oxford University. He spent a brief afternoon at the *Dictionary of National Biography* with the editor of the supplement, Hancock's friend Wickham Legg, who had been Fitzhardinge's moral tutor in New College, Oxford, from 1931 to 1933. Fitzhardinge thought that a dictionary of biography should be a flagship project for a nascent university press.[39] He loved dictionaries himself; wet Sunday afternoons of his childhood spent reading his way through the *Dictionary of National Biography* in his school library had been 'an endless source of enjoyment … I devised games, dodging about in it, opening a volume at random and then following all the cross references and following up the cross references to that, and so on'.[40] His experience of working at the National Library from 1934 to 1944 and writing Australian biography taught him how 'very difficult' it was 'to get even the most elementary background information about the people, the cast'. Finally, the publication of Percival Serle's two-volume *Dictionary of Australian Biography* in 1949 convinced Fitzhardinge that writing biographical dictionaries was 'no longer a one-man job. It's got to be a team job on the model of the DNB'.[41]

At Oxford, on the advice of R.C. Mills, the chair of the interim council at ANU, Fitzhardinge gave Hancock his report on the resources of the National Library. Hancock was impressed with Fitzhardinge and wanted to employ him as a bibliographical consultant on local materials for the various high-powered heads of schools that he was proposing to bring out to ANU. The Sydney University press project was aborted in 1948. When he was appointed Reader in the Sources of Australian History at ANU

---

38 Davidson, *A Three-Cornered Life*; Gerald Walsh, 'Recording "the Australian Experience": Hancock and the Australian Dictionary of Biography', in Low, *Keith Hancock*, 249–68. See also Nolan and Fernon, *The ADB's Story*, 5–9.
39 Keith Hancock, 'Formation of the Australian Dictionary of Biography', Box 69, Q31, ADBA, ANUA.
40 Laurie Fitzhardinge, Interview by Barbara Ross, 4–26 March 1987, TRC 2159, transcript, NLA, p. 2.
41 Fitzhardinge, interview by Ross, 1987.

on Hancock's recommendation in 1951, Fitzhardinge proposed that the ANU press project produce a dictionary of biography as its flagship. Again he was unsuccessful. He suggested the dictionary idea more widely at the 1951 Australian and New Zealand Association for the Advancement of Science (ANZAAS) Conference, and started a Biographical Register in the history department at ANU in 1954.[42] As Head of History, Fitzhardinge employed Pat Tillyrand and others to work on the card index, 'building up material' for a dictionary.[43] Later, Fitzhardinge described his efforts as 'a typically Fitzhardingian feeble and waffly attempt' to get the dictionary off the ground: 'I'd prepared a plan for the preparation, within our resources more or less, of a dictionary of biography – not to be written by the Department, to be an all-over effort, but not to be attempted all at once'.[44] He envisaged the annual publication of articles contributed by Australian historians, which would build up, over the years, into a dictionary of concise articles organised alphabetically.

Fitzhardinge acknowledged that it was Hancock, however, finally arriving as inaugural professor of history and director of the Research School of Social Sciences (RSSS) in 1957, who seized upon the dictionary idea and 'turned imaginatively a set of cards into a great national achievement of historical scholarship'.[45] He, Fitzhardinge admitted, 'could do things which I would never have been able to do in a month of Sundays'. Drawing on his experience of overseeing the Civil Histories, Hancock set about organising a national collaboration. He wrote to all the professors of history and economic history, and all specialists in Australian history, inviting them to a conference in August 1957, together with non-academic historians (including journalist-historians Malcolm Ellis and Brian Fitzpatrick, Catholic archbishop and historian Dr Eris O'Brien and military historian Gavin Long), to discuss how to 'advance the study of Australian history'.[46] Ellis was one of the few attending who had both written biography and reflected on Australian biographical practice. He had published biographies of pastoralist John Macarthur, Governor

---

42   W. K. H. [Hancock], 'The ADB' (12 April 1962), Box 69, Q31, ADBA, ANUA. 'Excerpt from Statement prepared by Professor Hancock. Formation of the Australian Dictionary of Biography', Box 69, Q31, ADBA, ANUA.
43   George Temperly, Obituary 'Patience (Pat) Australie Wardle nee Tillyard (20 June 1910–22 April 1992)', *Canberra Historical Journal*, no. 30 (September 1992), 5–7.
44   Fitzhardinge, interview by Ross, 1987.
45   'Notes and News, Arrival of Hancock in Canberra', *Historical Studies*, 7:28 (1957), 486–7.
46   Fred A. Alexander, Boyce Gibson, Margaret Gowing and Robin Gollan, 'Hancock: Some Reminiscences', *Historical Studies,* 13:51 (1968), 229–306, doi.org/10.1080/10314616808595379.

Lachlan Macquarie and architect Francis Greenway. He was on record in 1955 as describing most Australian biographies as being like 'licking the cold outside of a champagne bottle on a thirsty day'.[47] Hancock, however, deftly steered the conversation of this first conference, by, and for, Australian historians, towards a dictionary project: by the end, they agreed that a 'Concise Dictionary of Australian Biography' was the single most important priority for stimulating the development of Australian history.[48]

As well as Hancock's first publication in 1926 on Ricasoli as dictator of Tuscany, he had lectured on Machiavelli's morality and expediency, and in the early 1950s he began to research General Jan Christiaan Smuts' biography. He was not hampered in his own biographical projects by lack of knowledge of milieu, but he was aware that some of his colleagues thought the problem of a lack of historiographical context was acting as a governor on the writing of Australian biography. As late as during the 1930s, academics such as Gerry Portus had maintained that 'Australian history was not deserving of being a university subject'.[49] Ernest Scott introduced a course at Melbourne in the early 1930s; in 1946, Clark became the second historian to teach a full-length course in Australian history, and he was soon followed by others.[50] Moreover, Fred Johns, whose 1906 *Johns's Notable Australians* was the precursor of *Who's Who in Australia*, had wanted to stimulate academic biography and bequeathed the sum of £1,500 to the University of Adelaide in 1932 for the purpose of founding 'the Fred Johns Scholarship for Biography' to encourage the writing of biographies on eminent Australians.[51] The scholarly journal *Historical Studies: Australia and New Zealand* had been founded in 1940 and a body of scholarly articles on Australian history was being published. The journal's editor from 1940 to 1949, the historian Gwyn James, had

---

47 Malcolm Henry Ellis, 'The Writing of Australian Biographies', *Historical Studies, Australia and New Zealand*, 6:24 (1955), 432, doi.org/10.1080/10314615508595013.
48 Robin Gollan, 'Canberra History Conference', *Historical Studies, Australia and New Zealand*, 8:29 (1957), 81, doi.org/10.1080/10314615708595099; Ellis, 'The Writing of Australian Biographies', 432. W. K. H. [Hancock], 'The ADB' (12 April 1962), Box 69, Q31, ADBA, ANUA; 'Excerpt from Statement prepared by Professor Hancock. Formation of the Australian Dictionary of Biography', Box 69, Q31, ADBA, ANUA; Stuart Macintyre, 'Biography', in Davison et al., *The Oxford Companion to Australian History*, 72.
49 Mark McKenna, *An Eye for Eternity: The Life of Manning Clark* (Melbourne: Miegunyah Press, 2011), 250.
50 My thanks to Stuart Macintyre for drawing my attention to Scott's pioneering course at Melbourne, email, 9 July 2016.
51 *Johns's Notable Australians* became *Who's Who in Australia*, published in 1927–8, 1933–4, 1935, 1938, 1941, 1944, 1947, 1950 and 1955; and then triennially from 1959 to 1988.

also been appointed director of Melbourne University Press (MUP) and, over the period of his tenure from 1943 to 1962, he began to welcome academic biography.[52] Academic historians began to publish biography, including Margaret Kiddle on Caroline Chishom with MUP in 1957 and others followed such as George Mackaness and Kathleen Fitzpatrick. Fitzhardinge himself seriously began his biography of W. Hughes in 1952 (although volume one did not appear until 1964 and volume two in 1979).[53]

So an Australian dictionary of biography project in the late 1950s was a timely proposal. There was a developing disciplinary infrastructure, as well as a broader historical consciousness. Indeed, writing in 1962, Green noted that Australian history 'stretches out behind its present like a long wake' and was being populated; the developing universities were providing 'biographers with opportunities' but, above all, a large element in Australia 'in the best sense' had become 'literate'.[54] Australia had 6 universities and approximately 10,500 students before 1939; there were 10 universities with 53,000 students by 1960; there were 19 universities with 148,000 students by 1975.[55] The number of historians grew in leaps and bounds.

There was also agreement among those who attended the 1957 conference that the growing sources in Australia would sustain good biography, taking account of human agency and consciousness. Australian historians' intellectual reference point was the English historical philosopher and idealist R.G. Collingwood, who emphasised not how a biographical subject might appear from an external perspective but rather how the person's thought processes could be assessed. Collingwood argued in *The Idea of History* that history consisted of 'recollection' of the 'thinking of historical personages'.[56] This required depth of evidence and the maturity to interpret it. It required biographical understanding, too. Similarly, Wilhelm Dilthey had written on how the past is based on personal memory and the importance of narrative to ideas of subjectivity. He held

---

52   Peter Ryan, *Final Proof: Memoirs of a Publisher* (Sydney: Quadrant Books, 2010).
53   *Argus*, 9 December 1952, 3. Stephen Foster interview of L.F. Fitzhardinge on 5 August 1992, ANU History Project, ANUA 44, Transcripts and tapes of oral history interviews, interview no. 26 by Stephen Foster, 5 August 1992, pp. 14–17, ANU Archives.
54   Green, *A History of Australian Literature, Pure and Applied*, 1355–6.
55   Jim Breen, *Higher Education in Australia: Structure, Policy & Debate* (Melbourne: Monash University, 2002), sections 5.2, 5.3.
56   R.G. Collingwood, *The Idea of History* (Oxford: Clarendon Press, 1946).

that reflective autobiographical material helped understand human and historical life: '[U]nderstanding the meaning of history requires both an inner articulation of the temporal structures of our own experience and the interpretation of the external objectifications of others.' E.H. Carr was to use and popularise Dilthey's ideas in his lectures published in 1961 as *What is History?*.[57] Concerns about the availability of sources that were sufficiently rich to sustain research on an Australian subject's consciousness were assuaged by the developing archives collections. Indeed, Fitzhardinge's job at the Commonwealth National Library from 1934 to 1946 had been Historical Research Officer in charge of Australian collections.[58] Australia's national archives were separated from the National Library in 1954.[59] As collections of papers developed, specialist Australian biographical bibliographies also appeared.[60]

More difficult to overcome, however, was a prejudice against biography. Francis West argued that historians such as Sir Lewis Namier, noted historian of the British Parliament, and the Cambridge historian and Tudor specialist Geoffrey Elton belittled biography. To some extent, West misread both historians' 'opposition' to biography; the point is that they both grappled with the relationship between the individual and human nature.[61] West was right to argue, however, that academic historians had shunned biography; in the twentieth century, biography had been the work of 'non-historians'.[62] The rise of structuralism and social history undermined explanations based on the role of the individual in history. Hancock devoted a chapter of his *Professing History* to these issues, explaining historians' reluctance to write biography and criticising that reluctance. He argued that during the postwar period, historians had been 'unduly subservient to the then fashionable doctrine that history is always made by "impersonal forces, never persons"'. He lamented the popularity of Marxist ideas of history from below, and sociological ideas of statistical

---

57 H.P. Rickman, ed., *Meaning in History: W. Dilthey's Thoughts on History and Society* (London: Allen & Unwin, 1961), 15; E.H. Carr, *What is History?* (New York: Knopf, 1962).
58 Peter Cochrane, *Remarkable Occurrences: The National Library of Australia's First 100 Years* (Canberra: National Library of Australia, 2001), 27.
59 See, for instance, Hilary Golder, *Documenting a Nation: Australian Archives – The First Fifty Years* (Canberra: Australian Government Publishing Service, 1994).
60 See Ulrich Ellis, *Select Bibliography of Australian Political Biography and Autobiography* (Canberra: Ulrich Ellis, 1958).
61 See, for instance, Linda Colley, *Lewis Namier* (London: Weidenfeld & Nicolson, 1989), 72–89.
62 Francis West, *Biography as History: The Annual Lecture delivered to The Australian Academy of the Humanities at its Fourth Annual General Meeting at Canberra on 15 May 1973* (Sydney: Sydney University Press for the Australian Academy of the Humanities, 1973), 1.

averages that had undermined biography.⁶³ More prosaically, Hancock was all too aware of how a dictionary of biography would in turn help to promote biography. As he argued to the ANU council in May 1962, 'when I started work on Smuts, I found good cause to curse the lack of a South African DNB … If a Dictionary had existed, I should have been saved a year or more of finicky work', tracking down references to hundreds of individuals.⁶⁴

As Hancock convinced others it would, the *ADB* was established and proved to be the midwife of much Australian biographical practice. So, initially based on a plan Ellis proposed, with the cooperation of the state universities, and the general public, the *ADB* began. Articles started to be drafted in 1959 and the first two volumes of the *ADB* were published in 1966 and 1967. Retrospectively, delivering in 1973 the annual lecture to the Australian Academy of the Humanities, West credited the 'Past President, Sir Keith Hancock, and his official ancestor as Chairman of the Australian Humanities Research Council, Professor James Auchmuty' for regarding biography as 'the proper concern' of an historian over the objections of some distinguished historians, and for helping turn around attitudes. Instead of resorting to Britain, students were born and bred in Australia. Hancock welcomed the burgeoning of Australian biography under his supervision. For example, 10 per cent of the first 60 PhDs at the ANU were biographies and a number of others were biographical. This was not surprising, given that potential supervisors Fitzhardinge, Hancock and Manning Clark had written and were writing biographies, were involved in the *ADB* project, were writing memoirs and were being interviewed about their lives; in Clark's case in 1967 as part of pioneering series of interviews by the oral historian Hazel de Berg.⁶⁵

---

63 Hancock, 'My Particular Person', in *Professing History*, 43–65.
64 Hancock Notes [towards a history of the ADB], Box 69, Q31, ADBA, ANUA. Hancock's 'prehistory' paper has not survived but his speaking notes for the ANU Council meeting of 11 May 1962 were comprehensive.
65 W.K. Hancock, *Smuts* (2 vols; Cambridge: Cambridge University Press, 1962–8); L.F. Fitzhardinge, *William Morris Hughes: A Political Biography* (2 vols; Sydney: Angus & Robertson, 1964–78). Hazel de Berg interviewed Clark on 25 May 1967, NLA, about his childhood, his work and how he collected his material, and Bernard Smith in 1975. The National Library holds interviews of Clark by a succession of interviewers, including Hazel de Berg, 1967 (DeB 253–54), Don Baker, 1985 (TRC 1187), Neville Meaney, 1986–87 (TRC 2053), Michelle Rowland, 1986 (TRC 2141) and Terry Lane, 1990 (ROH 907.2092 C594). ANU had its own Oral History Program in the 1980s and 1990s, which included Manning Clark (1990 and 1991) and Robin (Bob) Gollan (1993). Other historians who wrote their autobiographies such as John Molony (2008) and John Mulvaney (2010) were included as interviewees in a more recent oral history project focusing on the ANU Emeritus Faculty.

From the outset, the chairs of the working parties across the country were contributing authors: Gregory McMinn (Newcastle), Edwin Tapp (New England), Bede Nairn (NSW), Allan Morrison (Queensland), Harold Finnis (South Australia), Geoffrey Serle (Victoria), Frank Clifton Green (Tasmania) and Frank Crowley (Western Australia), along with many of the working party members. McMinn, Nairn, Morrison and Serle were among the 1 per cent of *ADB* authors who contributed 20 or more articles. Even the publisher, Gwyn James, contributed four *ADB* articles. Many working party and national committee members having written *ADB* articles went on to write full biographies. To give just one example of this much-observed phenomenon, Auchmuty was the first member listed on the *ADB*'s National Committee.[66] In 1966, Auchmuty's *ADB* entry on Governor John Hunter was published, in 1968 he published a full biography on Hunter, and in 1971 he edited a collection of 'ADB colleagues' on Australia's first governors, consisting of himself on Hunter, Margaret Steven on Arthur Phillip, Michael Roe on Philip Gidley King, John Bach on William Bligh, Marjorie Barnard on Lachlan Macquarie and Ruth Teale on Thomas Brisbane.[67] Barnard went on to write 2 *ADB* articles, Auchmuty 3, Bach 4, Steven 24, Roe 33, and Teale 57.[68]

Kick-starting Australian *ego-histoire*: From national to familial tribes

Crawford's survey of 'Australian' biographical works between 1933 and 1947 lists just 35 monographs in 15 years. There followed a tsunami of life writing in Australia. A search of the National Library of Australia catalogue, Trove, in 2013 lists over 13,000 'Australian biographical' works.[69] If one breaks it down by decade, the rising popularity of biography is clear and other patterns can be discerned. Of course, counting is problematic. Crawford's counting was biased, as was Popkin's in arguing for 1983 as a crucial turning point in Australian historians' autobiographical writing, following Nora's work. Popkin's calculations only stand up if we venture

---

66   See, Nolan and Fernon, *The ADB's Story*, 32.
67   J.J. Auchmuty, 'Hunter, John (1737–1821)', *Australian Dictionary of Biography*, Volume 1, (MUP), 1966; *John Hunter* (Melbourne: Oxford University Press 1968); *The First Australian governors* (Melbourne: Oxford University Press, 1971). See also Kenneth R. Dutton, *Auchmuty: The life of James Johnston Auchmuty (1909-1981)* (Brisbane: Boombana Publications, 2000).
68   *ADB* Author Database.
69   Trove, National Library of Australia online catalogue, catalogue.nla.gov.au/Search (accessed 15 December 2013).

judgements by which earlier works can be dismissed as being of poor 'quality'. For example, Francis Patrick Clune (1893–1971) wrote over 60 books, including accounts of Frank Gardiner (1945) and Ben Hall (1947) and, in 1933, an autobiographical work in *Try Anything Once*. A number of historians also wrote autobiographical work long before *egohistoire* popularised the genre: Garnet Vere Portus (1883–1954) wrote his autobiography, *Happy Highways*, in 1953; Alan Moorehead (1910–83) wrote his, *A Late Education: Episodes in Life*, in 1970; and Paul Hasluck (1905–91), *Mucking Around*, in 1977 and so on.[70] Patsy Adam-Smith even published a volume of her autobiography in 1964 before writing history.[71] These all predate Popkin's 'count', but his analysis is based on there being little historians' biography and autobiography before 1983. He was, of course, concentrating on academic historians.

Despite the undercounting, was there a turning point in the 1980s nonetheless? The evidence suggests that there was, but that defining it is not simply a matter of volume. Hermione Lee has observed we can identify the 'popularity of certain kinds of biographies in different countries, periods and cultures ... [which] provides an insight into that society. What does that society value, what does it care about, who are its visible – and invisible – men and women?'[72] In Australia, for instance, radical historians concentrated upon the close relationship between the 'being' of the human finding its essence in the being of place. A wave of work appeared, especially in the 1970s and 1980s on Ned Kelly, Peter Lalor, Henry Lawson and William Lane – bushrangers, militants, poets and socialists.[73] Especially in the wake of transnationalism, subjects have since diversified: there is considerable interest in the recent past but, above all, historians have written family biographies and memoirs as much as topos.

---

70 Francis Patrick Clune, *Try Anything Once: The Autobiography of a Wanderer* (Sydney: Angus & Robertson, 1933); Portus, *Happy Highways*; Alan Moorehead, *A Late Education: Episodes in a Life* (London: Hamish Hamilton, 1970); Paul Hasluck, *Mucking About: An Autobiography* (Melbourne: Melbourne University Press, 1977). Portus was an academic historian, at the University of Adelaide, while the others did not work within the academy.
71 Patsy Adam-Smith, *Hear the Train Blow: An Australian Childhood* (Sydney: Ure Smith, 1964).
72 Hermione Lee, *Biography: A Very Short Introduction* (Oxford: Oxford University Press, 2009), doi.org/10.1093/actrade/9780199533541.001.0001.
73 See Lloyd Ross, *William Lane and the Australian Labour Movement* (Sydney: Forward Press, 1937); John Molony, *I am Ned Kelly* (Ringwood, Melbourne: Allen Lane, 1980); Robin Gollan, *Revolutionaries and Reformists: Communism and the Australian Labour Movement, 1920–1955* (Sydney: Allen & Unwin, 1985); and Bede Nairn, *The 'Big Fella': Jack Lang and the Australian Labor Party 1891–1949* (Melbourne: Melbourne University Press, 1986).

So Australian biography has been characterised by three principal developments of late. First, sometime in the era spanning the end of the twentieth and the beginning of the twenty-first century, the connection with time and place was loosened, with new transnational themes emerging. This was in keeping with wider developments. Whereas Frank Moorhouse's *Grand Days*, the first in a trilogy – about a young Australian, Edith Campbell Berry, at the League of Nations – was excluded from consideration for the Miles Franklin Prize in 1994 because it was deemed not to have sufficient Australian content, this was controversial and his second volume in 2001, *Dark Palace*, won. Similarly, if we survey the National Biography Award (NBA) we can see the question about 'quintessential' Australian biography broadening. Geoffrey Cain agitated for the foundation of the NBA, a biannual award in 1996 and annual since 2000, which the State Library of New South Wales administers. Cain with fellow philanthropist Michael Crouch have provided the funding. 'Australian biography' had been broadly defined:

> The subject of the work is to be an Australian or have made a significant contribution to Australia. Other subjects may be considered if the author is an Australian citizen or permanent resident and the work provides a particularly Australian perspective of the subject.[74]

About half the winners have been unambiguously Australians writing about Australian subjects. Brian Matthews's biography of historian Manning Clark won in 2010.[75] Sheila Fitzpatrick's account of being a Soviet historian working in Soviet archives and teaching and writing in the United States was shortlisted in 2014.[76] Of course, this international dimension is particularly pertinent in a country Europeans settled from 1788; which attracted 2 million migrants between 1945 and 1965; and with a quarter of Australians being 'foreign born' in 2007, and more than 43 per cent of whom were either born overseas themselves or had one

---

74 'National Biography Awards', State Library of New South Wales website, www.sl.nsw.gov.au/about/awards/national_biography (accessed 16 December 2013). See also Melanie Nolan, 'Country and Lives: Australian Biography and its History', in *Cercles: Revue Pluridisciplinaire du Monde Anglophone*, no. 35 (March 2015), 96–117.
75 Brian Matthews, *Manning Clark: A Life* (Sydney: Allen & Unwin, 2008).
76 Sheila Fitzpatrick, *My Father's Daughter: Memories of an Australian Childhood* (Melbourne: Melbourne University Press, 2010); Fitzpatrick, *A Spy in the Archives* (Melbourne: Melbourne University Press, 2013).

parent who was born overseas.[77] So there is increasing acknowledgement of the variety of Australian lives. There is now a growing literature on the relationship between self and nation.[78] As Ros Pesman notes:

> To place Australian experience in a wider framework is not to reject Australian nationality and culture, but to emphasize their connections with the rest of the world, their porous and permeable qualities. Identity and nationality are, like everything else, not fixed structures, but processes in the making. There is no Australian 'identity', only 'identities', and these have been forged abroad as well as at home, in contact and in collision with others, as well as in isolation.[79]

By 2014, the former director of the Art Gallery of New South Wales, Edmund Capon, was declaring that Australia's greatest visual artists, including twentieth-century artists Sidney Nolan, Arthur Boyd and Russell Drysdale, were virtually unknown overseas or else ignored because their work was 'too strongly defined by place'.[80] By contrast, Capon argued, Australian literature had more international impact because cosmopolitan themes were increasingly harnessed to national stories. Transnational biography has become fashionable and had impact starting, as Popkin noted, with Conway's *The Road from Coorain*.[81] The 'system of cultural signification' that makes up the nation is ambivalent precisely because it is in constant flux.

Second, with diversity have come more searching questions about biography itself, notably concerning its gendered character. There have been an increasing number of women historians' memoirs and biographies.[82] Yet just two women, Jessie Webb and Kathleen Fitzpatrick, are among the 10 historians Macintyre and Thomas profiled in their 1995 collection, *The Discovery of Australian History*.[83] Women made up 11 per cent, or 13 of the 118, historians profiled in the 1998 *Oxford Companion to Australian History*. Moreover, women historians such as Alexandra Hasluck, Kathleen Fitzpatrick, Catherine Berndt, Maie

---

77   'Population', Australian Bureau of Statistics, *Migration, Australia, 2008–09* (cat. no. 3412.0).
78   See Suzanne Falkiner, *The Writers' Landscape: Wilderness* (Sydney: Simon & Schuster, 1992).
79   Ros Pesman, *Duty Free: Australian Women Abroad* (Melbourne: Oxford University Press, 1996), 17.
80   *Sydney Morning Herald*, 10 September 2014.
81   Ker Conway, *The Road from Coorain*.
82   See Jane Carey and Patricia Grimshaw, *Women Historians and Women's History: Kathleen Fitzpatrick (1905–1990), Margaret Kiddle (1914–1958), and the Melbourne History School* (Melbourne: Department of History, University of Melbourne, 2001).
83   Stuart Macintyre and Julian Thomas, eds, *The Discovery of Australian History 1890–1939* (Melbourne: Melbourne University Press, 1995).

Casey and Nettie Palmer did not get as much space as the men they were married to, and Ann Blainey, author of five biographies, got none at all – although, to be fair, her award-winning biography on Dame Nellie Melba was written after the companion had been published. The *Encyclopedia of Women and Leadership in Twentieth-Century Australia* lists 73 women historians out of 680 individual entries, about 11 per cent, albeit including living historians.[84] The *ADB* will eventually have perhaps four times as many historians: certainly those who died before 1991 mentioned in the *Companion* are all in the *ADB*. The *Oxford Companion* is revealing because it discusses the schools, groups and ideas as it profiles the 118 historians, in much more detail than the *ADB*. Moreover, a small number have substantial entries and are consequently signalled as more important: C.E.W. Bean (1879–1968), Geoffrey Blainey (1930–), Geoffrey Bolton (1931–2015), Noel Butlin (1921–91), Vere Gordon Childe (1892–1957), Manning Clark (1915–91), Timothy Coghlan (1855–1926), Brian Fitzpatrick (1905–65), Robin Gollan (1917–2007), Keith Hancock (1898–1988), Paul Hasluck (1905–93), John Mulvaney (1925–2016), Stephen Roberts (1901–71), Ernest Scott (1867–1939), and Russel Ward (1914–95). Max Crawford is relegated to a short entry; much of the analysis of him and his 'school of history' was published after 1995.[85] Women, however, lack prominence then and now. Biographies on women do raise unsettling questions about 'the search for identity in Australian biography'. Bill Wilde notes that Matthews, in his biography of Louisa Lawson, female newspaper proprietor and mother of poet Henry Lawson, asks the same questions that Virginia Woolf, author and an experimenter in biographical methodology, asked: the central problem of biography was how to weld together the 'granite-like solidity' of truth or fact and the 'rainbow-like intangibility of personality or character'.[86] Despite all the 'multivocality', Ann Curthoys noted in her Russel Ward

---

84 Australian Women's Archives Project, *The Encyclopedia of Women and Leadership in Twentieth-Century Australia*, www.womenaustralia.info/leaders/about.html (accessed 26 June 2015).

85 Robert Dare, 'Max Crawford and the Study of History', in Macintyre and Thomas, *The Discovery of Australian History*, 174–91; Stuart Macintyre and Peter McPhee, eds, *Max Crawford's School of History* (Melbourne: Department of History, University of Melbourne, 2000); Fay Anderson, *An Historian's Life: Max Crawford and the Politics of Academic Freedom* (Melbourne: Melbourne University Press, 2005); Robert Dare, 'Theory and Method', in Fay Anderson and Stuart Macintyre, eds, *The Life of the Past: The Discipline of History at the University of Melbourne, 1855–2005* (Melbourne: Department of History, University of Melbourne, 2006), 339–53.

86 W.H. (Bill) Wilde, *The Search for Identity in Australian Biography* (The 1990 Colin Roderick Lectures; Townsville, Qld: Foundation for Australian Literary Studies and James Cook University, 1991); Brian Matthews, *Louisa* (Melbourne: McPhee Gribble, 1987); Virginia Woolf, *Granite and Rainbow* (London: Harcourt Brace, 1958), 149.

Annual Lecture in 1992: 'While we might undertake a feminist analysis of the gendered character of the debate about conceptions of the nation, we have not yet been able to redefine what national identity might mean.'[87] In terms of biography, while national identity might not have been redefined, conceptions of appropriate subjects and sources have led to consideration of networks, particularly familial ones, and increasingly this tendency has gender implications.[88]

Indeed, thirdly, the most notable recent pattern is not 'simply' the inclusion of women historians but that, increasingly, male and female historians are both writing about their families as much as themselves. Of course this is part of a wider phenomenon, too. As Hans Render and others have shown, this interest in families is part of the tendency towards interiority (biography) and has been attended by an interest in the social meaning of an individual life.[89] Linda Colley has shown the global significance of the life of Elizabeth Marsh.[90] Family-centred history is another method increasingly used by historians themselves, such as Alison Light in her family account, *Common People*.[91] Frank Vandiver noted the advantages of family biography more generally:

> Theoretically the advantage of a family biography is that it allows a perspective that delves into the 'thick issues of relationships' and which is not slanted by a focus on any one participant (or his or her version of the historical allowing character and personality to more fully emerge. As a result the biographer has more 'clay' from which to interpret meanings, nuances, and appreciations.[92]

Searching 'Australian family biographies' in Trove by decade reveals starkly the trajectory of the popularity of this new genre.[93] As others have noted, the focus of Australian historians' biographies seems to be moving from

---

87 Ann Curthoys, *Australian Legends: Histories, Identities, Geneaologies* (Armidale, NSW: University of New England Union, 1992).
88 See Alison Light, *Common People: The History of an English Family* (London: Fig Tree, 2014), xxvii ff., for a discussion on changing attitudes among professional historians to family history.
89 Hans Renders and Binne de Haan, eds, *Theoretical Discussions of Biography: Approaches from History, Microhistory, and Life Writing* (Lewiston, NY: The Edwin Mellen Press, 2013).
90 Linda Colley, *The Ordeal of Elizabeth Marsh: A Woman in World History* (New York: Pantheon Books, 2007).
91 Light, *Common People*, 34.
92 Frank E. Vandiver, 'Biography as an Agent of Humanism', in Stephen B. Oates, ed., *Biography as High Adventure: Life Writers Speak on their Art* (Amherst: University of Massachusetts Press, 1986).
93 The rate has dramatically increased from 1950–1959 (2,119), 1960–1969 (2,040), 1970–1979 (2,432), 1980–1989 (3,789), 1990–1999 (6,803) to 2000–2009 (135,046), trove.nla.gov.au/result?q=%27Australian+family+biographies%27 (accessed 15 September 2017).

nation to family.[94] Historians, including David Walker, John Rickard and Graeme Davison, are consulting their own personal biochemical archives to produce family histories.[95] When macular degeneration dimmed his eyesight, for instance, Walker turned to family history, something he had previously avoided. He had 'to rethink the kind of history I was able to write. I had to find another, more personal voice and another way of writing. The mix of the historical and the personal seemed promising'. How, he asks, can we reconcile or accommodate the competing claims of the big events of history with the constant flow of small, day-to-day trials and pleasures? He was disconcerted to find that 'the lives, values and preoccupations of most of my forebears had no place in the national story', so he has rewritten the national story. The trend is similar among biographies of historians.[96] And the list of historians writing their 'family memoirs' continues to grow apace: in the last decade, in addition to Walker, Rickard and Davison, there have been Tim Bonyhady, Marjorie Theobald, Sheila Fitzpatrick, Jill Roe, and others such as John Molony and Ann Moyal, writing second instalments.[97] These accounts include female, Chinese, working-class and Irish relatives. Some are intergenerational, and some are about circles and networks. Russel Ward wrote his autobiography, *A Radical Life*; a generation later, his daughter Biff wrote hers.[98] A range of related biographies, such as that by Keith McKenry on John Meredith, have also appeared.[99] Similarly, Don Watson wrote a

---

94   John Rickard, 'Pointers to the Future of Family History', review of *Good Living Street: The Fortunes of my Viennese Family* by Tim Bonyhady, *Australian Historical Studies*, 44:3 (2011), 457–62, doi.org/10.1080/1031461X.2013.817289.
95   David Walker, *Not Dark Yet: A Personal History* (Sydney: Giramondo, 2011); John Rickard, *An Imperial Affair: Portrait of an Australian Marriage* (Melbourne: Monash University Publishing, 2013); Graeme Davison, *Lost Relations: Fortunes of my Family in Australia's Golden Age* (Sydney: Allen & Unwin, 2015).
96   See, for instance, Elizabeth Kleinhenz, *A Brimming Cup. The Life of Kathleen Fitzpatrick* (Melbourne: Melbourne University Press, 2013); Geoffrey Bolton, *Paul Hasluck: A Life* (Perth: UWA Publishing, 2014).
97   Tim Bonyhady, *Good Living Street: The Fortunes of my Viennese Family* (Sydney: Allen & Unwin, 2011); Marjorie Theobald, *'The Wealth Beneath their Feet': A Family on the Castlemaine Goldfields* (Melbourne: Arcadia, 2010); Jill Roe, *Our Fathers Cleared the Bush: Remembering Eyre Peninsula* (Adelaide: Wakefield Press, 2016); John Molony, *Luther's Pine: An Autobiography* (Canberra: Pandanus Books, 2004); Molony, *By Wendouree: Memories 1951–1963* (Ballan, Vic.: Connor Court Publishing, 2010); Ann Moyal, *A Woman of Influence: Science, Men & History* (Perth: UWA Publishing, 2014).
98   Russel Ward, *A Radical Life: The Autobiography of Russel Ward* (South Melbourne: Macmillan, 1988). See, for example, Don Watson, *Brian Fitzpatrick: A Radical Life* (Sydney: Hale & Iremonger, 1979); and Amirah Inglis, *The Hammer & Sickle and the Washing Up: Memories of an Australian Woman Communist* (South Melbourne: Hyland House, 1995). Biff Ward, *In my Mother's Hands: A Disturbing Memoir of Family Life* (Crow's Nest, NSW: Allen and Unwin, 2014).
99   Keith McKenry, *More than a Life. John Meredith and the Fight for Australian Tradition* (Sydney: Rosenberg, 2014).

biography of Brian Fitzpatrick, and there are biographies of and by his first wife and his daughter.[100] Most recently Judith Armstrong has written a biography of Dymphna Lodewyckz, 'wife, mother, research assistant and unofficial editor for her husband', Manning Clark.[101]

Conclusion: Fuller circumstances in which historians construct history

In this essay, I have considered the history of biographical practices of Hancock, the *ADB* and the wider historical community more generally. During the middle years of the twentieth century, many historians did not regard biography as the best practice of history. Hancock argued in 1976 that Collingwood and others were wrong when they said that biography was 'poor history'. He thought that they were overreacting to the excesses of pseudo- and psycho-biographies by Lytton Strachey and others and, more recently, social history perspectives:

> I found rather more perplexing that assertion made by another philosopher R.G. Collingwood that every work of biography is not only non-historical but anti-historical. It seems to me that Collingwood was hitting below the belt, for he also had published an autobiography … I had applauded his contention that the subject-matter of history is past experience re-enacted in the historian's mind; but I parted company from him when he went on to argue that human experience is all mind and no body.[102]

Hancock increasingly became interested in biographical consciousness and, first, topos or locality in Australians' biographies and, second, in family. As noted at the outset, conspicuously early, Hancock himself wrote about his origins from the manse but very little about 'my wife'; there were many more references to his first wife, Theaden, in *Professing History* in 1976. By the time of his death, he gave approval to Davidson to write the biography. The *ADB* has also started to create 'big data' for families and to mediate systematically between families and broader developments, navigating family relations structurally and historically by

---

100 Watson, *Brian Fitzpatrick*; Kathleen Fitzpatrick, *Solid Bluestone Foundations*; Kleinhenz, *A Brimming Cup*; Sheila Fitzpatrick, *My Father's Daughter: Memories of an Australian Childhood* (Melbourne: Melbourne University Press, 2010); and *A Spy in the Archives* (Melbourne: Melbourne University Press, 2013).
101 Judith Armstrong, *Dymphna* (North Melbourne: Australian Scholarly Publishing, 2016).
102 Hancock, *Professing History*, 53–5.

mapping families. Rather than just linking to other family members in its websites, it is naming the relationships between family members (mother, grandfather and so on) in order for complex family trees across multiple generations to be automatically generated as a visualisation and be easily navigated, including of course for historians in the *ADB*. This perspective undermines elitist and unrepresentative approaches.

Hancock might have had a three-cornered life, have been 'neither a founder of history in a new Australian university, and have not spent a career building the subject in a particular institution', but he was instrumental in the foundation of the *ADB* and in promoting life writing in Australia.[103] Over the years, the *ADB* has been itself subject to the same forces of change as those affecting Hancock. It is now commissioning and editing lives that are perilously close to the present, such as those who died between 1991 and 2000. Hancock not only wrote mainly about events in his own lifetime but he also wrote about events in which he was himself involved, for example chairing the Namirembe Conference – which created a new constitutional monarchy for Buganda in 1954 – while writing on the Commonwealth. Hancock began writing his second volume of memoirs with two chapters he had 'left over' from his history of his involvement in protest against the Black Mountain tower in Canberra. He came to see autobiography, and biography, both as part of the task of professing history. It should be noted that in his wake, while there are 306 biographies of historians in the *ADB* for the period between 1788 and 1990, the proportion of historians in the *ADB* overall is more than the proportion of Indigenous Australian subjects, although the *ADB* has a current project to rectify this.[104]

While it is commonplace today to regard biography as just one form of history, many argue that autobiography and memoir can involve history but are, nevertheless, conceptually distinct. Others question these distinctions.[105] Hancock came to see varieties of life writing on a continuum, and this is the position argued in this essay too. He was involved in the events of the time and knew some of the subjects he wrote

---

103 Julian Thomas, 'Keith Hancock: Professing the Profession', in Macintyre and Thomas, *The Discovery of Australian History*, 146.
104 Melanie Nolan, '"Insufficiently Engineered": A Dictionary Designed to Stand the Test of Time?' in Nolan and Fernon, *The ADB's Story*, 26; *Biography Footnotes*, 15 (2015), 5.
105 Aurell, 'Autobiography as Unconventional History'; Robert A. Rosenstone, 'Invitation to Historians: Confessions of a Postmodern (?) Historian', *Rethinking History*, 8:1 (2004), 149–66, doi.org/10.1080/13642520410001649787.

about. He researched his memoirs. Similarly, Australians' public lives are increasingly being placed in their familial and wider contexts. Whatever our view on these debates and approaches, the academic status of both memoir and biography has changed in the last three decades as subjectivity – once swept off the academic stage, particularly with postmodernism decreeing the 'death of the subject' – has now reappeared.[106] While interest in the individual coherent self continues strongly outside the academy, within it historians have returned to this genre in recent years to write about themselves and/or other historians. Some interest in historians' personal and familial circumstances is prurient, some in keeping with a wider genealogical and family consciousness in the history. Much of it is motivated by the thought that how, and in what circumstances in all its fullness, one writes helps to understand the history that a historian constructs.

---

106 Barbara Taylor, AHR Roundtable, 'Separations of Soul: Solitude, Biography, History', *American Historical Review*, 114:3 (2009), 641.

12

Imperial Women: Collective Biography, Gender and Yale-trained Historians

John G. Reid

On 23 May 1931, a reception at Yale University marked the retirement of Charles McLean Andrews from the Department of History. At 68 years of age, Andrews had completed some 42 years as an active historian – at Bryn Mawr College from 1889 to 1907, at Johns Hopkins University from 1907 to 1910, and at Yale thereafter – since receiving his doctorate from Johns Hopkins and publishing his dissertation on *The River Towns of Connecticut: A Study of Wethersfield, Hartford, and Windsor*.[1] Although, as the son of a prominent clergyman of the short-lived Catholic Apostolic Church who lived and made his evangelical base in Wethersfield, Andrews had written a dissertation that was in a sense a local study of his own home territory, his interests as a historian were nevertheless wide-ranging. Much of his early post-dissertation work was in English medieval history, but increasingly he moved into American history of the colonial era. Indeed, as Richard R. Johnson argued some years ago, he can properly be

---

1 Charles McLean Andrews, *The River Towns of Connecticut: A Study of Wethersfield, Hartford, and Windsor*, Johns Hopkins University Studies in History and Political Science, Seventh Series, VII-VIII-IX (Baltimore: Johns Hopkins University, 1889). I am very grateful to my research assistant Samantha Bourgoin for the thorough biographical reconnaissance that was foundational to this essay, and also to Michael Frost and other staff members in Manuscripts and Archives, Yale University Library.

regarded as having defined and originated US colonial history as a historical field.[2] By the time that Andrews was publishing his multivolume work, *The Colonial Period of American History* – the first volume of which won him the 1935 Pulitzer Prize for History – his emphasis on the institutions that bound the colonies to the metropolis had been communicated to many of his graduate students and would lead to his posthumous historiographical designation as the founder and leader of the 'imperial school'.[3] His own view, however, was that his contribution was to colonial rather than imperial history, as he explained in 1926 to one of his recent doctoral graduates:

> Approaching the colonies from the English side, and so seeing them in quite a new light, showed me that they had never been properly studied before and that their history could not be understood when interpreted – as was ordinarily the case – in the American field only. I saw that the 'colonial' aspect had been almost entirely left out and it is that aspect that I have tried to present.[4]

It was thus appropriate that the centrepiece of Andrews's retirement reception was the presentation of a *Festschrift* entitled *Essays in Colonial History Presented to Charles McLean Andrews by his Students*.[5] The book contained 12 essays, nine contributed by Yale PhD graduates. One author, Mary Patterson Clarke of Beaver College in Pennsylvania, was still working on the Yale dissertation she would complete in the following year, while two others were PhD graduates from Johns Hopkins. Nellie Neilson, the Mount Holyoke scholar who was later to become the first woman president of the American Historical Association and who in 1931 could reasonably be seen as Andrews's most distinguished former student, had studied with him at Bryn Mawr in his earlier field of interest and so, 'hopelessly mediaeval by nature', she could 'make no scholarly contribution in his honor to this volume of colonial studies', but instead wrote the Introduction.[6] Of the 12 authors of the substantive essays, four

---

2   Richard R. Johnson, 'Charles McLean Andrews and the Invention of American Colonial History', *William and Mary Quarterly*, 3rd series, 43:4 (October 1986), 519–41. Andrews had also been the subject of an intellectual biography published some 13 years after his death in 1943: A.S. Eisenstadt, *Charles McLean Andrews: A Study in American Historical Writing* (New York: Columbia University Press, 1956).
3   Johnson, 'Charles McLean Andrews', 528–9.
4   Charles McLean Andrews (hereafter CMA) to Hastings Eells (copy), 5 March 1926, Charles McLean Andrews Papers (MS 38), Manuscripts and Archives, Yale University Library (hereafter CMAP), Box 24, Folder 289.
5   *Essays in Colonial History Presented to Charles McLean Andrews by his Students* (New Haven: Yale University Press, 1931; reprinted Freeport, NY: Books for Libraries Press, Inc., 1966). The presentation copy is in CMAP, Box 98, Folder 1035.
6   Nellie Neilson, 'Introduction', in *Essays in Colonial History*, 1.

were women. In addition to Clarke, Viola Florence Barnes of Mount Holyoke College contributed the lead essay, while others were authored by Isabel MacBeath Calder of Wells College and Dora Mae Clark of Wilson College. The proportion of women authors, along with their exclusive concentration in women's colleges, is already suggestive in gender terms. However, for those historians interested in the gender dimensions of the discipline of history, and in the history of academic and professional women in the twentieth-century United States, it is another part of the book that has attracted the greatest attention.

Charles McLean Andrews
Source: Courtesy of Special Collections, Sheridan Libraries, Johns Hopkins University.

Nellie Neilson
Source: Courtesy of Mount Holyoke College Archives and Special Collections.

The four-page Dedication of *Essays in Colonial History* not only affirmed to Andrews that 'for your skill as a teacher and your kindliness and sympathy as a man, your students hold you in the warmest affection', but also – in the reprinted edition of 1966 although not, oddly, in the original edition of 1931 – carried a signature list of 114 names. They comprised 50 women and 64 men.[7] The first to comment on this gender distribution, with some 44 per cent of the former students being women, was Ian K. Steele in a 1984 paper that remained unpublished; two years later, Johnson elaborated by noting that 'the fact that women composed over 40 percent of those who listed themselves as Andrews's students … may have hampered the spread of his message and methods because of the scant opportunities then open to women for teaching at major doctorate-granting schools'.[8] In my own biographical study of Viola Barnes, drawing on Steele and Johnson, I also cited the proportion of women who studied with Andrews as a reason for exploring Barnes's career in the context of her association with the 'imperial school'.[9] Yet, as Johnson correctly pointed out in a footnote, the list of signatories includes a number who 'did not study with Andrews in the field of colonial history'.[10] The list, in reality, is a complex source in many respects. Not all of the signatories had been doctoral students, and some from Bryn Mawr – where Andrews had taught undergraduates, by contrast with his years at Johns Hopkins and Yale when he dealt exclusively with graduate students – had not been graduate students at all. Thus, the women listed were more varied in scholarly terms than the men, of whom 55 (or 86 per cent) had or would attain doctoral degrees compared with 21 of the women (42 per cent). Of the Yale graduate students, women or men, it is difficult in some cases to establish which were actually supervised by Andrews and which may have taken his seminar but were primarily supervised by others, prominently including at Yale his own former students Charles Seymour and Leonard Woods Labaree. The process by which signatories were added to the list also bears examination. It was, of course, a self-selected group, and esteem for Andrews was a precondition. If there were students who, for whatever reason, disapproved of his teaching or scholarship, or did not share in the

---

7   *Essays in Colonial History*, v–viii. The reasons for the omission of the list in 1931 are unknown, but its authenticity is corroborated by the tracing of connections to Andrews on the part of the signatories, as well as in some cases by agreements to make donations to the cost of the volume in CMAP, Box 30, Folders 347–8.
8   Johnson, 'Charles McLean Andrews', 532.
9   John G. Reid, *Viola Florence Barnes, 1885–1979: A Historian's Biography* (Toronto: University of Toronto Press, 2005), xiii, doi.org/10.3138/9781442628076.
10 Johnson, 'Charles McLean Andrews', 542–3, note 41.

affection expressed in the Dedication, then they would by definition be excluded. The only essential qualifications for inclusion, in addition to being well disposed towards Andrews, seem to have been having at some point studied with Andrews and being willing to contribute at least $10 to the production costs of the *Festschrift*. Stanley M. Pargellis, a Yale PhD graduate of 1929 and one of the five-person editorial steering group – which also included Barnes, Helen Taft Manning, Frederick J. Manning and Labaree – was the chief collector, and the criteria he used for deciding who should be approached have not survived.[11]

Nevertheless, this essay will argue that collective biographical analysis based on the list of 114 names in *Essays in Colonial History* – focusing especially on the 50 women and, within that number, on those who in 1931 either had or would attain the PhD degree or in some other way were demonstrably associated with Andrews in a research capacity – can contribute significantly towards our understanding of the career trajectories of women historians in the United States during the twentieth century. As well as illustrating the obstacles that they – along with women in other professional fields – had to face and overcome, the analysis can also indicate the nature of the institutions and networks that lent support to their efforts. Yale was not alone in offering doctoral degrees to women. As well as Bryn Mawr and Radcliffe, Columbia, Cornell and the University of Pennsylvania offered doctoral programs in history by the early twentieth century, as did state universities further west.[12] Nevertheless, the department at Yale, and Andrews's 'imperial school' in particular, offers an opportunity to explore one well-defined group of women scholars and to compare their experiences directly in some respects with those of their male colleagues.

A report drafted for the Yale graduate school during the 1919–20 year, which had clearly been influenced by initiatives led by Viola Barnes on behalf of the women graduate students, claimed that 'Yale has done pioneer work in making the facilities for higher education available to women', but went on to enumerate a series of difficulties that women

---

11   See the correspondence in CMAP, Box 30, Folders 347–8; the editorial group is named in *Essays in Colonial History*, vii.
12   Julie Des Jardins, *Women and the Historical Enterprise in America: Gender, Race, and the Politics of Memory, 1880–1945* (Chapel Hill: University of North Carolina Press, 2003), 34–5. For a valuable contemporary analysis of the availability of PhDs to women in the United States from 1877 to 1927, although with limited differentiation of history as a field, see Emilie J. Hutchinson, *Women and the Ph.D.* (Greensboro: North Carolina College for Women, 1929), esp. 20–7.

graduate students encountered that ranged from dining and residential restrictions to the inaction of the Board of Appointments in finding professional placements for women.[13] With the publication in 1920 of a booklet for which the report had been a precursor, pride in achievement took a higher priority. Andrews himself contributed the section on graduate programs in history, including a biographical directory of the 12 women who to that point had gained PhDs. His analysis, that 'two of the twelve are investigators [researchers], four more are teachers, and the remaining six have withdrawn from all connection with historical work', led to definite conclusions that he believed confirmed what he had learned also at Bryn Mawr:

> With this evidence before us, it is not unreasonable to conclude that the majority of women, whose interest lies in the historical field, should be urged to attempt no more than one or two years of graduate study, for the purpose of familiarizing themselves with graduate methods and the handling of historical materials. The M.A. degree, for which two years are required, is a sufficient qualification for those who have no other aim than to teach ... On the other hand, those with special aptitude and enthusiasm, who are possessed of a fixed determination to make investigation a part of their life-work and have proved themselves competent to do so, may well be encouraged and aided to go on to the Doctor's degree.[14]

In the context of the significant representation of women among Andrews's research students, as shown in the list of signatories to the *Festschrift*, and also of the limitations thus enunciated by Andrews on his own receptiveness to women students, this essay will therefore explore through an analysis of the experience of the signatories the extent to which Yale and the 'imperial school' offered genuine scope for aspiring women historians to advance in their chosen field.

Of the 50 women signatories, 11 were Bryn Mawr students who did not take doctorates at that institution; most had been graduate students or graduate fellows, but two were undergraduates. Among the 11 was Caroline Miles Hill, who was a graduate fellow in history at Bryn Mawr in 1891–92 but took her doctorate in 1892 from the University of

---

13 Draft Report, [1919–20], Graduate School Records, Records of the Dean (RU 948), Manuscripts and Archives, Yale University Library, 2004-A-173, Box 1, Folder on Graduate Women, 1902–1944; the report was almost certainly prepared by Margaret Trumbull Corwin, executive secretary of the Graduate School. On Viola Barnes's advocacy, see Reid, *Viola Florence Barnes*, 34–5.
14 Charles McLean Andrews, 'History', in [Margaret Trumbull Corwin, ed.], *Alumnae Graduate School, Yale University, 1894–1920* (New Haven: Yale University, 1920), 40–1.

Michigan.[15] Six of the signatories, however, were PhD graduates from Bryn Mawr: Eleanor L. Lord (1898), Nellie Neilson (1899), Ellen Deborah Ellis (1905), Marion Parris Smith (1908), Louise Dudley (1910) and Margaret Shove Morriss (1911). Of those whose connection with Andrews was through Yale, 11 were either PhD graduates by 1931 or would later take that degree at Yale: Viola Florence Barnes (1919), Dora Mae Clark (1924), Helen Taft Manning (1924), Isabel MacBeath Calder (1929), Gertrude Ann Jacobsen (1929), Ruth May Bourne (1931), Mildred L. Campbell (1932), Mary Patterson Clarke (1932), Mary Reno Frear (1933), Helen Stuart Garrison (1934) and Maybelle R. Kennedy (1945). Nine were MA graduates from Yale, of whom two are known later to have taken PhD degrees elsewhere: Bessie E. Hoon (University of London, 1934) and Sarah R. Tirrell (Columbia, 1946). A further 10 were registered at some point with the graduate school at Yale, but took no degree; one, Eleanor S. Upton, took a PhD in 1930 from the University of Chicago. There was also one other small but significant subgroup among the 50: three Scottish holders of fellowships at Yale from the Commonwealth Fund,[16] comprising two who already held PhD degrees from the University of St Andrews – Edith E. MacQueen (1926) and Edith E.B. Thomson (1928) – and one – Agnes M. Whitson – who would not take a PhD but became a published author on the basis of her MA thesis from the University of Manchester.[17]

Thus, 21 of the 50 women were graduate students from the United States who, whether before or after they signed the list for Andrews's *Festschrift*, took doctoral degrees. A number of the others, in particular the three holders of Commonwealth Fund fellowships and two of the Yale MA graduates – Florence Cook Fast and Dorothy S. Towle – who continued their interest in research even after marriage had made further academic

---

15 Others who can be identified as graduate students were Mabel Davis, a Canadian who studied at Bryn Mawr during the 1905–06 year after taking a University of Toronto MA, and Katharine Dame, who spent a year at Bryn Mawr after taking her AB at Boston University. In order to avoid burdening of the footnotes to this essay with specific evidence on individual students, the sources used for each person have been gathered, along with essential biographical data, in a document entitled 'Summary of Sources for Biographical Data', posted at: library2.smu.ca/handle/01/25926.

16 Not to be confused with the Commonwealth Scholarships scheme launched in 1959, the Commonwealth Fund was a private, New York-based foundation that existed in part to provide fellowships (analogous in reverse to Rhodes Scholarships) to enable young scholars from the British Commonwealth to study in the United States.

17 For simplicity, the names of the women signatories to Andrews's *Festschrift* are given throughout this essay – even though a few were married names, and other signatories used married names later in life – in the form that is found on the list.

career progress difficult, are also relevant to this essay in a qualitative sense through their correspondence with Andrews. The 21, however, provide a core group for a more basic biographical analysis, even though it must be remembered that because the list itself is far from being a scientific sample, and moreover the numbers are small, any quantification is valuable more for its ability to inform qualitative conclusions than for inherent statistical validity. Initial distinctions can be drawn in age of PhD graduation, both chronologically and in gender terms. Chronologically, the seven PhD graduates associated with Andrews through Bryn Mawr were younger when they gained the degree: 27.6 years on average, with a median of 27, compared to 36.6 with a median of 34 for the 14 women associated with Andrews through Yale. In part, the difference undoubtedly reflects more elaborate requirements for the degree in the later years – the PhD graduations of the Bryn Mawr group spanned the years from 1892 to 1911, the Yale group from 1919 to 1946 – and a comparable age difference is also found among the men, although not so marked: an average of 28.5 with a median of 26.5 (26 and 27) for the six linked with Andrews through Johns Hopkins, compared with 32.6 and a median of 32 for the 49 linked through Yale. Where the gender distinction is clear, according to the numbers given above, is between the Yale-linked women and men, and if only the actual Yale PhD graduates are considered, the difference is even more marked: an average age of 35.2 and a median of 34 for the 11 women, with an average of 31.5 and a median of 31 for the 41 men.[18]

For women, especially during the interwar years – the era during which all but one of the Yale women graduates and all but two of the overall Yale-linked group of women took their degrees – gaining a PhD was an extended, expensive and labour-intensive process. The Bryn Mawr graduates, small in number as they were, had family origins in the professional and business occupations of their fathers (mothers' occupations rarely appearing in surviving documentation): a minister, a lawyer, a YMCA official, merchants in tobacco and coal, and a mining engineer who was one of the founders of Standard Steel in Philadelphia. They also came mainly from the north-eastern United States, the exception being Louise Dudley, a minister's daughter from Kentucky. The Yale-linked graduates were much more diverse, in ways that also help to explain why they took

---

18 Because exact birthdates are not known in all cases, nor are exact graduation dates, age is taken in all cases to be the number of years reached at whatever birthday fell in the year of graduation.

their degrees at a somewhat more advanced age than had their Bryn Mawr predecessors, in that for many of the Yale women a demanding prerequisite was the ability to support themselves. They ranged in social origins from Isabel MacBeath Calder, the daughter of Scottish immigrants whose father worked as a carpenter, to Helen Taft Manning, the occupations of whose father included lawyer, judge and 27th President of the United States. In between were two whose fathers were ministers (Hoon and Jacobsen), two university professors (Frear and Upton), and one each of physician (Clark), engineer (Garrison), small-town newspaper editor (Barnes), farmer (Campbell), liveryman (Clarke), greenhouse manager (Kennedy), shoe factory foreman (Tirrell) and pottery presser (Bourne). While it would be foolish to attempt to construct a firm ranking of these bare, mainly census-derived occupational descriptions in terms of wealth or lack of it, it is clear that – although not, of course, representing the full spectrum of US society at the time – this was no simple cohort of the daughters of affluence. These 14 women also had varied geographical origins. Unsurprisingly, the largest single group consisted of six New Englanders (three from Connecticut, and one each from Massachusetts, Rhode Island and Vermont), while another came from Pennsylvania. The remaining seven were spread from West Virginia and Ohio south to Tennessee, then west to Illinois and Kansas, and north to Nebraska and North Dakota. They had first degrees to match, although with some variations representing family moves during childhood: Bryn Mawr, Mount Holyoke and Smith College were all represented, but in general the 'Seven Sisters' were handsomely outnumbered by state universities – Nebraska, Kansas, Minnesota and others – and other institutions – Northwestern, Maryville College in Tennessee – outside of the north-east.

However, when it came to careers followed after PhD graduation, the Seven Sisters and other women's colleges loomed much larger. Of the seven women connected to Andrews through Bryn Mawr, two (Ellis and Neilson) spent their subsequent careers at Mount Holyoke, one (Smith) at Bryn Mawr, one (Dudley) at Stephens College, Missouri, and another (Morriss) became a long-serving dean at Pembroke College, the associated women's college at Brown University. Of the remaining two, one (Lord) had spells at Smith, the Baltimore Women's College, and Goucher College, while the other (Hill) followed entirely different, non-academic career avenues. The careers of the Yale-linked women were more complex, in that five of the 14 married, including four whose husbands were academics, three of whom were other Yale graduate students. Of those who married, one (Garrison) appears to have had no further formal academic career, while Bessie (later preferring to be known as Elizabeth) Hoon continued to write and undertook later in life an extended visiting professorship at the coeducational Rider College in New Jersey. Another (Frear) had an early appointment at Pennsylvania State College, took a break presumably for child rearing, but after the death of her husband when she was still in her late 40s had brief sojourns at Vassar and Wellesley before spending some 15 years as dean of the faculty at the all-women Hood College in Maryland. A fourth (Kennedy) took her doctorate in 1945, long after she had first attended Yale, and by the time her book was published in 1948 she had an association with the Department of History at Smith College. Helen Taft Manning, meanwhile, had a long and uninterrupted career as an administrator and professor at Bryn Mawr, while her husband taught at nearby Swarthmore College. Of the remaining nine, six had long careers as historians at women's colleges: Barnes at Mount Holyoke, Calder at Wells, Campbell at Vassar, Clark at Wilson College in Pennsylvania, Clarke at Beaver College also in Pennsylvania and Jacobsen – who died relatively early in life, however, in 1942 – at Hunter College. Ruth Bourne had a series of positions at coeducational institutions before completing her career at California Western University, and Sarah Tirrell held administrative positions in admissions offices at Mount Holyoke and the New Jersey College for Women before taking her Columbia PhD in 1946 and taking up a professorship at the Municipal University of Omaha, later part of the University of Nebraska. Finally, Eleanor S. Upton had an earlier career as a social worker, became a librarian first at Brown University and then at Yale in 1921, took her University of Chicago PhD in 1930, and then returned to the library at Yale for the balance of her working life.

Thus, in the most general terms, the women PhDs associated with Andrews – and especially those whose connection was through Yale – present a pattern of relatively diverse social and geographical origins, which were then distilled through graduate study into careers at institutions that were largely though not exclusively specific to women, among which prestigious colleges predominated, although again not exclusively. Yet within this overall configuration lay complex decisions and dilemmas that the women characteristically encountered. The issues centred in two areas – economic and career challenges, and those surrounding marriage and family – while the ability to address them effectively depended not only on the resourcefulness of the individual, along with possible support from Andrews and Yale, but also on the formation of networks to coordinate responses to common problems.

The economic and career issues, although obviously depending on the social background of each individual, began for many of the women even before reaching Yale. Among the reasons for the age – mid-30s – at which women typically took PhD degrees was the necessity of working and saving funds before and frequently during doctoral study and research. Of the Yale-linked women, it was common to have taught high school for a number of years prior to enrolment at Yale: Bourne, Campbell, Frear, Garrison, Hoon and Tirrell are examples. Others already had appointments at colleges, but not necessarily of the elite variety. One who felt the resulting dilemma acutely was Mary Patterson Clarke, the liveryman's daughter from Lawrence, Kansas, who was 53 years old when she took her doctorate in 1932 and had been a student of Andrews at both Bryn Mawr and Yale.[19] Clarke spent most of her career – both before and after PhD graduation – at Beaver College. Although in the early 1920s she entertained thoughts of finding a position at the University of Kansas, her *alma mater*, or at one of the institutions in Philadelphia, she faced a constraint with which she found that the appointments bureaus at either Bryn Mawr or Yale were of no help. Characterising Beaver College as a two-year vocational school where no work at college level was possible, she found her research on the role of colonial Assemblies slow going. She wrote to Andrews in March 1925 that:

> I am supporting myself and working at the same time on my assemblies, and … I have not an oversupply of strength to bear the double burden … After spending so much time and money and effort as I have done on this subject I cannot afford either to give it up or to rush it too much, and it is hard to think of staying in this kind of institution till it is completed and in print if that should ever occur.[20]

---

19   Mary Patterson Clarke to Evangeline W. Andrews (hereafter EWA), 14 September 1943, CMAP, Box 89, Volume I.
20   Mary Patterson Clarke to CMA, 4 March 1925, CMAP, Box 23, Folder 280; see also Clarke to CMA, 17 April 1923, CMAP, Box 22, Folder 267.

By 1927, again casting in vain for alternatives, Clarke was even more direct:

> I am caught in a 'vicious circle.' I can not get the position I want – I mean the kind of position, I have no one in mind – without my degree; I can not get the degree without finishing the book; and I can not finish the book to my satisfaction in this atmosphere.[21]

For Clarke, matters did eventually improve. Although still encountering heavy teaching loads at Beaver College, she conceded by the summer of 1930 that the college had 'improved until I begin to have some hope that I might sometime be less out of sympathy with the way it is managed than I always have been' and, moreover with some pushback on her part on contested points, she gained Andrews's approval of her dissertation in early 1932.[22] Nevertheless, she had set out clearly and accurately the economic pressures that had slowed and threatened to stall her progress.

Ruth Bourne, meanwhile, daughter of an Indiana pottery presser, wrote to Andrews in 1928 from California, where she was teaching high school, that she hoped to apply to Yale but still had debts from working her way through college. A fellowship from the American Association of University Women proved to be a crucial support, and Bourne received her doctorate in 1931.[23] Even so, and after finding employment at Bowling Green State College in Ohio, she still had debts and the pressures of the Great Depression were adding further complications: 'it is not certain yet whether my parents are going to need my assistance soon. They have double liability stock in a defunct loan company!'[24] Bessie Hoon, perhaps from a more financially secure though certainly not wealthy background as a minister's daughter from Illinois, by age 24 had already headed a high school history department and had gained two degrees including a Yale MA. In early 1930, she hoped to find a college or university teaching position prior to turning fully to research. 'I realize,' she commented to Andrews, 'that as a woman competing with men such a position may not be easy to locate; the lack of a PhD perhaps will handicap me, but on the other hand I have absolute confidence in my own ability to fill such a position if it can be located.'[25] Hoon's determination stood her

---

21   Mary Patterson Clarke to CMA, 24 November 1927, CMAP, Box 26, Folder 309.
22   Mary Patterson Clarke to CMA, 19 August 1930, CMAP, Box 29, Folder 340; Clarke to CMA, 6 March 1932, CMAP, Box 31, Folder 359.
23   Ruth Bourne to CMA, 19 November 1928, CMAP, Box 27, Folder 318; Bourne to CMA, 24 February 1929, CMAP, Box 27, Folder 321.
24   Ruth Bourne to CMA, 29 February 1932, CMAP, Box 31, Folder 358.
25   Bessie E. Hoon to CMA, 26 February 1930, CMAP, Box 28, Folder 334.

in good stead, as she found a position for two years at Albany College in Oregon and then began the research that would earn her a University of London PhD. Yet even college employment, as others discovered, did not ensure a smooth path. Dora Mae Clark, a physician's daughter from Vermont, who had lamented after gaining her doctorate in 1924 that 'for the first time in my experience history teachers are a drug on the market', nevertheless found a position at Wilson College, but by 1930 found that her research time was severely limited and a leave of absence difficult to negotiate.[26] Gertrude Ann Jacobsen, meanwhile, was employed at Hunter College in New York as she arranged in 1928 her transfer from the doctoral program at the University of Minnesota to Yale and Andrews, and she too had difficulty obtaining a leave. For Jacobsen, the leave itself was not the problem, but rather her need for half-salary, especially as her father, a minister in Minneapolis, had recently had an accident which 'has rendered my financial status even more precarious'.[27]

While economic issues of this kind were not the concern only of women – Cecil Johnson, for example, who would take his PhD along with Clarke in 1932, wrote to Andrews in early 1928 of having had to pay off a debt load aggravated by his father's serious injury in a car accident – nevertheless, women did not have access to the range of instructorships that were routinely filled through requests sent quietly to Andrews and other senior scholars to recommend 'a man' for any given position.[28] The informality of such dealings was underlined by Leonard Labaree in September 1929. On a leave from Yale and teaching temporarily at Armstrong College, University of Durham (later the University of Newcastle upon Tyne), Labaree was surprised by the elaborate advertising and interview process that in the United Kingdom went into a junior appointment and commented tersely, 'I must say, I am glad that we do not fill our junior vacancies in that way'.[29] Women scholars, generally, did not have access to employment at the genuinely research-oriented institutions, and at women's colleges as well as at the smaller coeducational colleges

---

26   Dora Mae Clark to CMA, 28 August 1924, CMAP, Box 23, Folder 275; Clark to CMA, 27 February 1930, CMAP, Box 28, Folder 334.
27   Gertrude Ann Jacobsen to CMA, 6 April 1928, CMAP, Box 26, Folder 312. For more general discussion of financial stresses on women PhD students of this era, and their health implications, see Hutchinson, *Women and the Ph.D.*, 38–9.
28   Cecil Johnson to CMA, 1 January 1928, CMAP, Box 26, Folder 311; for one example among many of requests for 'a man', see Beverley W. Bond to CMA, 16 October 1929, CMAP, Box 28, Folder 329.
29   Leonard W. Labaree to CMA, 20 September 1929, CMAP, Box 28, Folder 328.

that did hire women heavy teaching duties often precluded systematic research activity.[30] The problem extended, unsurprisingly, into the area of salaries and working conditions, and was compounded not only by the Depression but also by the increasing trend for women's colleges to appoint men to their faculties. A major study of the career trajectories of women holders of doctorates in history noted in 1943 that 'taken as a whole, women taught in smaller and poorer schools … and, presumably, carried heavier teaching loads for leaner salaries'.[31]

The role of Yale, and of Andrews in particular, in enabling women students and graduates to meet economic and career challenges was complex. By the late 1920s, the Bureau of Appointments was active in placing women as well as men, and in one case in 1928 was experiencing difficulty in finding a woman candidate for a position at Wells College in American history, particularly as both Viola Barnes and Dora Mae Clark preferred to stay in their existing positions at, respectively, Mount Holyoke and Wilson College. 'Do you think of any other possibilities,' the Bureau asked R.H. Gabriel of the Department of History, 'if not with the Ph.D. at least fairly well along the way toward it?'[32] Andrews, meanwhile, was tenacious in efforts to secure funding for both male and female graduate students. 'I know I owe this to you,' observed Isabel MacBeath Calder feelingly on receiving an increased fellowship in 1928, 'It is the kindest thing anyone has done for me for years and far more than I deserve. Thank you.'[33] In 1931, Andrews remonstrated vigorously with the Guggenheim Foundation on behalf of Ruth Bourne, a new PhD at the time who had not been offered the Guggenheim Fellowship.[34] And he promoted his graduate students for vacancies at likely institutions, exemplified by Hoon and Calder (unsuccessfully) at Vassar in 1930 and Mildred L. Campbell (successfully) at the same institution in 1932.[35]

---

30   See, for an example, Patricia Palmieri, 'Here Was Fellowship: A Social Portrait of Academic Women at Wellesley College, 1895–1920', *History of Education Quarterly*, 23:2 (1983), esp. 210, doi.org/10.2307/368159.
31   William B. Hesseltine and Louis Kaplan, 'Women Doctors of Philosophy in History: A Series of Comparisons', *Journal of Higher Education*, 14:5 (1943), 256, doi.org/10.2307/1975170; see also Reid, *Viola Florence Barnes*, 76–7.
32   Sarah Menner, Yale University Bureau of Appointments, to R.H. Gabriel, 10 December 1928, History Department Records (RU 591), Manuscripts and Archives, Yale University Library, 1960-A-2002, Box 2, Folder 14.
33   Isabel MacBeath Calder to CMA, 2 October 1928, CMAP, Box 37, Folder 317.
34   CMA to Henry Allen Moe (copy), 21 November 1931, CMAP, Box 31, Folder 355.
35   Eloise Ellery to CMA, 21, 26 February 1930, CMAP, Box 28, Folder 334; Mildred L. Campbell to CMA, 19 May 1932, CMAP, Box 31, Folder 360.

Viola Florence Barnes
Source: Courtesy of Mount Holyoke College Archives and Special Collections.

Nevertheless, Andrews's advancement of the careers of his women students by this and other means could overbalance at times into being controlling. In 1919, when Viola Barnes took her PhD she had a position being held for her at the University of Nebraska. Andrews, however, pressed her to interview with Neilson for a vacancy at Mount Holyoke, and then urged her to reconsider when she informed him that she would rather return to Nebraska. Barnes ultimately relented and spent the rest of her career at Mount Holyoke, but it was a decision about which she always retained deep misgivings.[36] Barnes, although she continued to have a profound

---

36 See Reid, *Viola Florence Barnes*, 39–40.

and almost reverential regard for Andrews and Yale, also had other difficult experiences with her mentor. On one occasion, she believed – with considerable corroborative evidence – that he had used her research findings without acknowledgement. At another time, he seems to have facilitated access to her recently completed dissertation by James Truslow Adams – self-taught as a historian but winner of the 1922 Pulitzer Prize for his account of *The Founding of New England* – who, Barnes was convinced, then proceeded to appropriate her ideas for his next book.[37] Isabel MacBeath Calder's experience was less dramatic but still indicative. She, it must be said, initiated the episode by asking Andrews in 1929 if he could assist in placing essays drawn from her recently completed dissertation on the seventeenth-century New Haven colony in journals that included the *New England Quarterly*, then edited by Samuel Eliot Morison, who also edited the equally estimable *Transactions* of the Colonial Society of Massachusetts. Andrews clearly took seriously what he saw as his task, but by April 1931 Calder had become aware that she had entirely lost control of the process. Her exasperation showed in her concern over the fate of one of the essays. 'I do not think,' she wrote to Andrews, 'that you should offer this short paper to anyone else until Mr. Morison has said definitely that he does not want it for the Colonial Society of Massachusetts. It may be that he thinks he has accepted it.'[38] In the meantime, Gertrude Ann Jacobsen had been pleased to have Andrews encourage her – in a session along with Dora Mae Clark – to present a paper drawn from her dissertation research on the seventeenth-century imperial official William Blathwayt at the annual meeting of the American Historical Association at Duke University in December 1929.

---

37 These episodes are discussed in Reid, *Viola Florence Barnes*, 48–52, and in John G. Reid, 'Viola Barnes, the Gender of History, and the North Atlantic Mind', *Acadiensis*, 33:1 (Autumn 2003), 9–12. Andrews's relationship with James Truslow Adams was odd and complex. Although Adams had no qualifications as a professional historian, and moreover did not let the absence of such restrain him from giving damaging reviews to works published by Andrews's young recent graduate students, nevertheless, Andrews's letters to him were almost deferential in tone, and in 1925 the Yale Graduate School had to quietly turn back an effort on Andrews's part to have Adams appointed to a position at Yale. See, among other items of correspondence in CMAP, Albert S. Cook to CMA, 30 October 1925, CMAP, Box 24, Folder 286.
38 Isabel M. Calder to CMA, 20 August 1929, CMAP, Box 22, Folder 327; Calder to CMA, 4 October 1929, CMAP, Box 28, Folder 328; Calder to CMA, 1 April 1931, CMAP, Box 30, Folder 348; Calder to CMA, 29 April 1931, CMAP, Box 30, Folder 348. The essay eventually appeared in the 1930–1933 *Transactions*, published in 1935; see www.colonialsociety.org/node/520 (accessed 17 September 2017).

Even though managing to retain her good humour, Jacobsen found herself a few days before the meeting rewriting the paper to Andrews's specifications:

> I quite understand your criticisms and I smile now at my conscious efforts to keep the paper on a general plane, feeling that what you wanted was a presentation of the unity of England's policy at this time and of the common tendencies which displayed themselves in all departments. I shall work at it this weekend using Blathwayt and his activities as the key.[39]

While not all of these experiences were as serious as those of Barnes, there is no indication in Andrews's correspondence of similar pressures being placed on male graduate students. Insofar as Barnes's steering to Mount Holyoke is concerned, Andrews may have had specific motives, beyond his stated rationale that Barnes would be better off to stay close to her archival sources in New England and to the ocean crossing to London, that would have included nurturing his close existing relationship (through Neilson, Ellis and another former student who was a medieval historian there, Bertha Putnam) with the college. However, it was consistent with his efforts to find appointments for others of his women graduate students at Seven Sisters institutions. Even though, for many or most, these were positions they were undoubtedly glad to attain, there was no challenge involved to the orthodoxy that women historians should aspire to careers at women's colleges.[40] Another area in which Andrews held decided and conventional views was on the incompatibility of graduate study with the intent to marry. Again, Viola Barnes had early experience along these lines. Meeting with Andrews for the first time, before being accepted for PhD work in 1916, Barnes was surprised when he asked if she was engaged to be married, but clearly recalled many years later his explanation: that 'Yale did not encourage women who expected to marry, because the training was such a waste'.[41] By 1927, his view was unchanged as he expressed surprise at hearing of the marriage of a promising graduate student, Florence M. Cook (Florence Cook Fast on the *Festschrift* list), soon after her MA graduation and remarked to his correspondent, Frank J. Klingberg – also

---

39 Gertrude Ann Jacobsen to CMA, 24 August 1929, CMAP, Box 27, Folder 327; Jacobsen to CMA, 5 October 1929, CMAP, Box 28, Folder 329; Jacobsen to CMA, 12 December 1929, CMAP, Box 28, Folder 331. For evidence of Andrews's orchestration of Clark's paper also, see Dora Mae Clark to CMA, 4 September 1929, CMAP, Box 28, Folder 328.
40 For trenchant comments on the implications of this constraint made by anonymous women PhD history graduates of the era, see Hutchinson, *Women and the Ph.D.*, 182–5.
41 Viola F. Barnes to [Blanche], 20 December 1958, Mount Holyoke College Archives and Special Collections, Viola Florence Barnes Papers, VIII, 9.

a Yale PhD graduate, though before Andrews's time, and a longstanding mentor to Cook from her undergraduate days at UCLA – that 'you were quite right in thinking that she would not have gone back to Yale after her marriage'.[42] Agnes M. Whitson, one of the Commonwealth Fund fellows, wrote to Andrews in 1934 to announce her own impending marriage, and although her tone was playful, the import of her opening anecdote was clear: 'I remember you once saying to me of [one of] your women students "She fell by the wayside, in other words she married."'[43]

In a revealing contrast, Andrews strongly recommended marriage to his male graduate students. Evangeline Walker Andrews recalled, as cited by A.S. Eisenstadt, that her husband had believed 'that productive scholarship could not proceed without a favourably circumstanced domestic life', and so 'he urged bachelor students to marry and married students to free themselves from encumbering responsibilities at home until they had completed their doctoral work'.[44] The large majority of his female doctoral graduates, however, remained single. The reasons, naturally, went far beyond Andrews's own influence. Emilie J. Hutchinson noted in 1929, on the basis of a large survey of women PhD graduates across the disciplines, that three-quarters of her respondents were single, even though she did observe that 'women who take the Ph.D. after marriage are more likely to combine gainful employment than those who take it before' and discerned an increasing trend for women PhDs 'to make this combination of marriage and gainful occupation'.[45] For most, the reality remained that career and marriage could not be combined, and Bonnie G. Smith has argued that professional women in general and women historians in particular resembled 'a third sex', frequently forming – as did Viola Barnes and no doubt others of the Yale group – close personal relationships with other unmarried women.[46] Of the women PhD graduates linked with Andrews, only one appears to have married and then to have had no further academic activity: Helen S. Garrison, who married an earlier Yale PhD graduate in William H. Dunham, Jr, a member of the Department

---

42 CMA to Frank J. Klingberg (copy), 22 September 1927, CMAP, Box 26, Folder 27.
43 Agnes M. Whitson to CMA, 20 December 1934, CMAP, Box 34, Folder 390.
44 Eisenstadt, *Charles McLean Andrews*, 150.
45 Hutchinson, *Women and the Ph.D.*, 17.
46 Bonnie G. Smith, *The Gender of History: Men, Women, and Historical Practice* (Cambridge, MA: Harvard University Press), 189–90.

of History at Yale until 1970. Hoon, Frear and Kennedy – as noted above – continued their academic work in various ways, although none had a continuous formal career.

Helen Taft Manning
Source: Courtesy of Bryn Mawr College Library Special Collections.

The one who, to all appearances, did not allow marriage to impinge on her professional prowess was Helen Taft Manning. Already married to Frederick J. Manning well before they received their respective Yale PhDs in 1924 (Helen) and 1925 (Frederick), she had apparently announced that she was leaving academic employment behind when in 1920 she resigned to get married, after a year – while still well short of her 30th birthday – as acting president of Bryn Mawr.[47] However, she was approached in 1925 by Marion Edwards Park, the new Bryn Mawr president, about taking up a deanship. Pregnant with her second daughter, she accepted. Although her husband later remarked to Andrews that it was a decision 'I cannot regret',[48] and his own appointment at Swarthmore soon followed, he may have had misgivings at the time. Writing while Andrews was on a leave in France, Charles Seymour relayed the news in early 1925:

> Manning wrote me a long letter some weeks ago, to which I replied giving a personal approval of what he and Mrs. Manning had in mind. I think it is well that he should face now the fact that she would probably not be happy until she had tried her hand at the Bryn Mawr Deanship, and I doubt whether she would be contented to stay on in New Haven as the wife of an Instructor or Assistant Professor for a number of years.[49]

Helen Manning represented, in effect, the exception that proved the rule. While it would be unfair and simplistic to attribute her professional success, as shown in her continuous years at Bryn Mawr until becoming professor emeritus in 1957, primarily to her social origins, as she was a gifted historian and a successful administrator who served another term as acting president in 1929–30, nevertheless she was well placed to subvert gender norms regarding marriage and career. Not only carrying the cachet of being a former president's daughter, she also had the resources to hire a live-in child care nurse.[50] She also enjoyed an easy and informal relationship with Andrews, who wrote to Evangeline Andrews in June 1930 – who was travelling at the time but, as usual when absent, exchanged lengthy daily letters with her husband:

---

47 See obituary, 'Helen Manning, Bryn Mawr Dean and Daughter of President Taft', *Philadelphia Inquirer*, 23 February 1987, p. B06.
48 Frederick J. Manning to CMA, 28 November 1927, CMAP, Box 26, Folder 309.
49 Charles Seymour to CMA, 9 February 1925, CMAP, Box 23, Folder 279.
50 See Frederick J. Manning to CMA, 8 September 1924, CMAP, Box 23, Folder 276.

> yesterday Helen Manning blew in for a talk about her dissertation [as revised for publication], which is approaching completion. I thought she looked tired and worn, for she has had a hard spring, what with her father's death and her duties at Bryn Mawr. But she seemed cheerful and full of energy.[51]

Andrews deliberately did not maintain an office at Yale, so as to avoid interruptions to his work, but if a student – 'man or woman', according to Labaree – visited him at home, he was well known for being open to extended conversation.[52] It is likely, however, that few if any of the others, students or graduates, 'blew in' as confidently as did Helen Taft Manning.

Quite different was the experience of two of Andrews's MA graduates, Florence Cook Fast and Dorothy S. Towle, who attempted to maintain their research interests in conjunction with marriage and motherhood. Towle was already married at the time of her MA graduation to Carroll S. Towle, another Yale graduate student who would take his PhD in English in 1933 but had already taken up in 1931 a faculty position at the University of New Hampshire. Dorothy Towle confided to Andrews soon after moving to Durham, NH, that 'you have no idea how much I miss your seminar. It is very difficult to work all alone, but I am doing the best I can until I can put all my [research] problems before you'.[53] However, caring for a frail mother-in-law was a prelude to child-raising with limited assistance from either husband or hired help and, by 1937, Towle noted that 'my summers are one long nightmare of housekeeping'.[54] Although she still hoped to apply for a fellowship to advance her research, she was neither in academic employment nor studying for a doctorate and had no illusions about the resulting disadvantages. Even so, Towle had already built sufficiently on her MA work to publish in 1936 a 595-page scholarly edition of eighteenth-century records of the Rhode Island court of vice-admiralty, with an introduction by Andrews.[55] Later publishing other works of more popular history before her death in 1950 while still

---

51 CMA to EWA, 17 June 1930, CMAP, Box 29, Folder 338.
52 Leonard W. Labaree, 'Charles McLean Andrews: Historian, 1863–1943', *William and Mary Quarterly*, 3rd series, 1:1 (January 1944), 11.
53 Dorothy S. Towle to CMA, 30 October 1931, CMAP, Box 31, Folder 354.
54 Dorothy S. Towle to CMA, 24 November 1931, CMAP, Box 31, Folder 355; Towle to CMA, 5 October 1937, CMAP, Box 37, Folder 417.
55 Dorothy S. Towle, ed., *Records of the Vice-Admiralty Court of Rhode Island, 1716–1752* (Washington, DC: American Historical Association, 1936).

in her early 40s, Dorothy Towle had undoubtedly pushed the limits of combining scholarship with reproductive responsibilities, but had found that the limits were at a certain point unyielding.

Florence Cook Fast, daughter of the proprietor of a Los Angeles poultry hatchery and wife of a printer whose California-based enterprises were sometimes fragile during the years of the Depression, took only a few months after her marriage to observe to Andrews:

> I have been forced to be utterly domestic, learning how to run a house and more especially how to cook … I find myself at times quite homesick for New Haven and particularly for the cordial atmosphere of the Graduate Seminar Room. Miss Calder has promised me a letter full of 'gossip' but so far has been too busy to write it … My marriage, I am afraid, makes it unlikely that I shall return to New Haven for more work.[56]

Almost a year later, she expressed similar feelings about Yale and, working for the time being in the picture department at Gump's art store, she confided the difficulties of finding teaching employment in San Francisco in the face of prejudice against married women. Fast, however, was clear-sighted about her life choice and the costs it involved, and resisted any feelings of regret, especially as she had a husband 'who understands my interest in historical work so that it is not difficult to find time to give to it'.[57] The task would become more complicated with the birth of her son in 1932,[58] but over the years she maintained her research ambitions and also – facilitated by Klingberg, and by her husband's willingness to move to Los Angeles – had short-term teaching positions at UCLA. Studying the logwood trade of British Honduras in the colonial era, and able by late 1932 'to take a few hours a day off from infant care', she had thoughts of pursuing a doctorate at Pomona College – conveniently located close to Los Angeles – with Frank W. Pitman, a Yale PhD graduate of 1914 and another signatory to Andrews's *Festschrift* list.[59] By 1935, she maintained her ambition but was increasingly forced to recognise the difficulties that would ultimately prove insurmountable. 'I am often envious', Fast wrote, 'of the men whom I knew in New Haven who have married and who have been able to pursue their academic interests without interruption. However, after eight years of marriage I cannot honestly say that I would

---

56 Florence Cook Fast to CMA, 16 February 1928, CMAP, Box 26, Folder 311.
57 Florence Cook Fast to CMA, 23 January 1929, CMAP, Box 27, Folder 320.
58 Florence Cook Fast to CMA, 8 February 1932, CMAP, Box 31, Folder 358.
59 Florence Cook Fast to CMA, 14 November 1932, CMAP, Box 32, Folder 367.

have chosen a different course.' She also announced to Andrews – having lacked the courage, she said, to do so hitherto – that she had given her now three-year-old son the middle name 'Andrews', doing so 'as a token of what my two years in New Haven meant to me and as a constant reminder of the things I hope to do in the field to which you introduced me'.[60] Tragically, the child died of leukemia at the age of 10 and, according to Klingberg many years later, Fast had carefully kept Andrews's letters, including 'one written to her on the death of her only son [which] is much treasured by her'.[61]

Andrews's continuing mentorship of both Towle and Fast showed that there were more nuances to his views on women scholars and marriage than might have appeared from his direct statements on the matter. To both he offered ongoing encouragement, and his introduction gave a valuable stamp of approval to Dorothy Towle's book, even though it also gave some reviewers the opportunity to review the introduction rather than the book itself.[62] He continued to regard Florence Fast as an actively promising researcher, facilitating her publication of an article in *North Carolina Historical Review* in 1931 and arranging for transcripts of sources relating to the logwood trade to be sent to her from the Public Record Office in London.[63] Still, in 1938, again in the context of the logwood study, he was 'quite sure that you would be able to write a doctorial [sic] dissertation on the general subject, should you choose to do so'.[64] Yet the constraints imposed by societal convention on married women, like the career limitations that were felt by all aspiring women, went far deeper than mentorship could offset. Networks among women scholars themselves provided some assistance, and Yale scholars were prominent in the most well-organised and effective of all, the Berkshire Conference of Women Historians. Viola Barnes presided over the group from 1933 to 1938, while Mildred Campbell and Helen Taft Manning were also prominent participants.[65] As well as taking action in the interests of smoothing

---

60 Florence Cook Fast to CMA, 2 June 1935, CMAP, Box 35, Folder 396.
61 Frank J. Klingberg to EWA, 14 May 1948, CMAP, Box 46, Folder 500.
62 See *American Historical Review*, 43:2 (January 1938), 403–6, doi.org/10.2307/1839763; *New England Quarterly*, 10:2 (June 1937), 408–9, doi.org/10.2307/360050.
63 Florence Cook, 'Procedure in the North Carolina Colonial Assembly, 1731–1770', *North Carolina Historical Review*, 8:3 (1931), 258–83; A.R. Newsome, North Carolina Historical Commission, to CMA, 11 July 1931, CMAP, Box 30, Folder 351; Florence Cook Fast to CMA, 2 November 1931, CMAP, Box 31, Folder 355.
64 CMA to Florence Cook Fast (copy), 8 November 1938, CMAP, Box 39, Folder 433.
65 See Radcliffe Institute for Advanced Study, Schlesinger Library, Berkshire Conference Papers, passim.

the paths of younger women scholars into scholarly activities, such as conference presentations and promoting exchange plans that would allow women greater freedom of movement between institutions, the Berkshire group also addressed the issues of gender inequality and contemplated, as recommended by Barnes as president, 'a crusade in the interests of equal opportunity for women in professional competition with men'.[66]

Less formal but undoubtedly sustaining was the network of women scholars that grew up among the Yale-linked historians. Men, of course, networked too, and occasionally gender lines would be crossed. Clarence W. Rife, a PhD graduate of 1922, reported to Andrews in early 1929 on the recent American Historical Association meetings: 'among the Yale students of my day who were present were Malone, Hail, Van Slyck and Miss Helen Gray. I had the pleasure of meeting Miss Barnes who spoke ably at the Luncheon Conference on Colonial and Revolutionary American History'.[67] But there was also a clear separation, with the male network relying principally on meals taken with colleagues at conferences or on research sojourns, supplemented by visitations in summer or at other times of family travel that would involve wives and children but were determined essentially by the random crossing of paths.[68] Undoubtedly, as well as professionally related exchanges and general gossip, there were gender-related issues to discuss on these occasions, especially for those of the generation directly affected by the First World War. Frederick Manning expressed to Andrews in 1926 the hope that 'the passing of the war generation of graduate students will do something to stop attempts to combine full time teaching, matrimony, and doctors' theses. It can be done, but at a very high cost'.[69]

The women's network, however, was more proactive, including contacts associated with conferences or research travel but also extending to frequent exchanges of news by letter and to visits for the sake of visiting, sometimes across long distances. Key members were the Scottish women who had been at Yale through the Commonwealth Fund, perhaps because they were accustomed to being geographically mobile. Edith MacQueen,

---

66   Viola Barnes to [Beatrice] Reynolds, 4 May 1937, Mount Holyoke College Archives and Special Collections, Viola Florence Barnes Papers, IV, 47; see also Reid, *Viola Florence Barnes*, 83–6.
67   Clarence W. Rife to CMA, 4 January 1929, CMAP, Box 27, Folder 320.
68   For examples, see Leonard W. Labaree to CMA, 2 August 1925, CMAP, Box 23, Folder 284; Ralph G. Lounsbury to CMA, 7 August 1925, CMAP, Box 23, Folder 284; Cecil Johnson to CMA, 17 February 1930, CMAP, Box 28, Folder 334.
69   Frederick J. Manning to CMA, 14 May 1926, CMAP, Box 24, Folder 291.

in January 1929, was on the point of going to New York to visit Gertrude Ann Jacobsen for a few days.[70] Edith Thomson visited Bessie Hoon in Seattle the following summer.[71] The following year, Ruth Bourne – in London for research – travelled to Oxford to meet Agnes M. Whitson and her sister. Bourne also reported to Andrews that, at the Public Record Office, 'I have met your student Miss Barnes and find her exceptionally charming … She has taken a very kind interest in me on your account'.[72] London was certainly a networking hub, and in 1933 Whitson – who by now had finished her studies at Yale – noted that she was teaching in the Northamptonshire town of Kettering but had been at the Public Record Office during the summer. She had not only lunched daily with Hoon but had also met up with Thomson – who was in London briefly while now living in Malta with her naval officer husband – and another unnamed Yale friend, so that 'we made a Yale quartette several times, at lunch'.[73] Marriages and, later, warfare made meetings more difficult to arrange, but letters continued to carry both professional and personal news and allow exchanges that were sustaining in both of those areas of life.

In summary, the presence of 50 women's names on the Dedication of *Essays in Colonial History* to Charles McLean Andrews was significant and revealing, although its nuances require some explication. Andrews was no radical thinker when it came to gender differentiation, and he held conventional views both on marriage and family and on suitable career placements for women historians. There was also a paternalistic element in his dealings with women graduate students that came occasionally to the fore, as experienced by Barnes and others. Nevertheless, collective biography reveals that Yale did at least provide an intellectual environment where it was a matter of routine for the scholarship of women to be valued and nurtured alongside that of men. Whether on his retirement, on his 80th birthday, in letters to Evangeline Andrews following his death, or for no particular reason, women among his former graduate students repeatedly praised Andrews in this vein. Two of the most poignant tributes were delivered in 1940, one from Dora Mae Clark and the other from Edith MacQueen. MacQueen wrote from a small farm that (following several years of production work with the BBC) she had bought in Essex, where she was doing freelance work on war propaganda broadcasts, participating

---

70 Edith MacQueen to CMA, 23 January 1929, CMAP, Box 27, Folder 320.
71 Bessie E. Hoon to CMA, 5 August 1929, CMAP, Box 27, Folder 327.
72 Ruth Bourne to CMA, 14 August 1930, CMAP, Box 29, Folder 340.
73 Agnes M. Whitson to CMA, 25 September 1933, CMAP, Box 33, Folder 377.

in local defence and awaiting invasion by the Axis powers. 'At this very grim hour in our country's history,' she avowed, 'I feel I cant [sic] let the moment pass without saying in what may perhaps be a goodbye letter, how very much I appreciate all you have done for me in the past. My years at Yale were some of the happiest in my life and to work with you was a great inspiration.'[74] Clark also wrote with apprehensions for the future, though of a different kind. She was finding it difficult to know how to advise the ambitious among her students at Wilson College. 'Many of them,' she explained, 'want careers. Some of them are very capable; but the graduate schools are becoming exceedingly inhospitable to women. I regret that your attitude toward women students is becoming very rare.'[75] Clark's comment was far-sighted, in the context of the austere climate that would be faced by aspiring women scholars following the Second World War. It also recalled the bleak observations of an earlier generation of women historians who had been quoted in Emilie J. Hutchinson's 1929 analysis. According to one, identified only as a college professor who had gained her PhD between 1877 and 1915:

> the problem for history women is to get a good teaching position in college or university after taking the Ph.D. There are not enough positions to go around because there is a prejudice against women on the part of men in co-educational colleges and in men's colleges.[76]

Andrews and Yale could provide no sovereign remedy for problems that would become more entrenched during the late 1940s and 1950s, and begin only gradually to be addressed thereafter. What did develop, however, was a fragile ecology within which the biographies of women historians could begin from social origins that had some admixture, advance through scholarship that could genuinely thrive and – for a significant number – emerge into life patterns that allowed for the balances between employment and research and between career and family to become negotiable, though always within limits.

---

74 Edith MacQueen to CMA, 29 May 1940, CMAP, Box 41, Folder 450.
75 Dora Mae Clark to CMA, 2 January 1940, CMAP, Box 41, Folder 446.
76 Hutchinson, *Women and the Ph.D.*, 182.

13

Concluding Reflections

Barbara Caine

In the last couple of decades, many historians have sought to move beyond the longstanding and probably futile quest to establish the precise place of biography in history and instead explore a number of new ways of thinking about the relationship between history and individual lives. One of these ways focuses on historians themselves and on the different kinds of insights that an exploration of their lives can offer. As one can see in this volume, several different approaches have been taken to this question, with some historians turning to write their own autobiographies, and exploring the broader historical understanding that can be gained from describing and analysing one's own experience, while others have sought rather to see whether a study of the lives of particular historians, either individually or in groups, offers a new understanding of the kinds of history that they wrote and of broader developments within the discipline.

The increasing numbers of historians who have turned their attention to autobiography in recent years has been widely noted, both by other historians and by scholars of biography. Paul John Eakin and Jeremy Popkin have both pointed to the importance of historical training and the sense of being part of a disciplinary community evident in much of this work. Autobiographers with a trained historical consciousness, in Eakin's view, may be uniquely capable of 'explaining what it means to be living in history' and of offering both a personal account of major historical developments and a sense of their impact on particular lives, families and communities.[1] Australian historians, as Popkin points out, have taken to the writing of autobiography with particular enthusiasm.[2] It has offered some, such as David Walker, a way to write a new kind of history in which personal and family memory could be drawn on more extensively as his loss of sight made other kinds of research more difficult, or others, such as Tim Bonyhady and Graeme Davison, a way to explore aspects of a family past that reflected wider historical patterns or placed Australian experiences into an unexpected European or global historical context.[3] Women have been significant players here too, as both Ann Moyal and Sheila Fitzpatrick make clear.[4] Moyal's survey, in this volume, of the Australian women historians who have written autobiography shows both how rich and extensive this literature is.

While one approach of historians to the writing of autobiography has centred on the extra insights their training might offer them in describing the world in which they lived, others have turned their attention rather to questions about the writing of history and whether and how it differs from writing autobiography. For Manning Clark, as Mark McKenna argues in this volume, it was impossible to write history without writing autobiography – although this approach was not one that was well received by his colleagues. But other historians have rather emphasised the challenges that writing autobiography or memoir posed to their understanding of history and to their sense of themselves as writers. This question is addressed by Fitzpatrick in this volume in her engaging discussion of the problems that she encountered as she moved from writing history, in the course of which she had always stressed her objectivity and impartiality, to writing memoir, which sometimes depended on fallible memory – and made her much more aware of herself as a writer and of the kinds of response she sought to produce in her readers. Fitzpatrick's essay also offers a useful reminder of the challenges to once dominant notions of objectivity in history that came to the fore in the 1980s and 1990s, as women and people of colour began insisting not only on

---

1   Paul John Eakin, *Touching the World: Reference in Autobiography* (Princeton: Princeton University Press, 1992), 145–51, doi.org/10.1515/9781400820641.
2   Jeremy D. Popkin, *History, Historians, & Autobiography* (Chicago/London: University of Chicago Press, 2005).
3   David Walker, *Not Dark Yet: A Personal History* (Sydney: Giramondo, 2011); Tim Bonyhady, *Good Living Street: The Fortunes of my Viennese Family* (Sydney: Allen & Unwin, 2011); Graeme Davison, *Lost Relations: Fortunes of my Family in Australia's Golden Age* (Sydney: Allen & Unwin, 2015).
4   Sheila Fitzpatrick, *My Father's Daughter: Memories of an Australian Childhood* (Melbourne: Melbourne University Press, 2010; Ann Moyal, *A Woman of Influence: Science, Men & History* (Perth: UWA Publishing, 2014).

being included as objects of historical inquiry, but on the importance of their perspectives and critiques of forms of objectivity that saw them as insignificant.

One strand of historian's autobiography that has become prominent in some American, British and particularly French historical writing, but is not explored here, centres on autobiography as a way for historians to explain the link between their personal lives and the historical questions they chose to address. It is an approach closely connected to Pierre Nora, who sought to collect autobiographical essays that examined their work within the framework of their lives and beliefs for his collection, *Essais d'ego-histoire*.[5] Not all of those who wrote for Nora accepted his sense that the life and the beliefs and commitments of a historian did, or should, have an impact on their work. However, a number of those who worked with him found the approach to be a very stimulating one and went on to write at much greater length about the close connection between their political experiences and beliefs and their historical writing. Luisa Passerini and Annie Kriegel stand out as historians who have done major work here.[6] Inevitably, this discussion has raised issues related to those dealt with by Fitzpatrick concerning memory and its place in the writing of history.

The sense of exercising a disciplinary training in writing autobiography and memoir, or of writing as a member of a professional or disciplinary group has often meant that historians' autobiographies eschew the intimate or very personal aspects of their lives and concentrate rather on broader social, political and institutional questions. This is not always the case, however. Two of the really outstanding historians' autobiographies, Carolyn Steedman's *Landscape for a Good Woman* (1986) and, more recently, Barbara Taylor's *The Last Asylum* (2014),[7] have both drawn on painful and intimate experiences to explore major social questions: the impact not only of poverty, but also of state agencies on family relationships in Steedman's case, and the end of the asylum and its painful consequences for those with mental illness in Taylor's. These works show very clearly the importance of historical training and understanding in the writing of lives in ways that enable those lives to explore historical

---

5   Pierre Nora, ed., *Essais d'ego-histoire* (Paris: Gallimard, 1987).
6   Luisa Passerini, *Autobiography of a Generation: Italy, 1968* (Hanover, NH: University Press of New England, 1996); Annie Kriegel, *Ce que j'ai cru comprendre* (Paris: Robert Laffont, 1991).
7   Carolyn Steedman, *Landscape for a Good Woman: A Story of Two Lives* (London: Virago, 1986); Barbara Taylor, *The Last Asylum: A Memoir of Madness* (London: Hamish Hamilton, 2014).

subjectivities and central questions in family and personal life as well as to offer insights into particular periods and places in broad social and political terms.

Moving from autobiography to biography, one can see from this volume how large and varied a field it is. A number of prominent historians have been the subject of excellent and expansive biographies that explore their lives, works and personalities. Mark McKenna's prize-winning biography of Manning Clark is a case in point, as is Maxine Berg's wonderful biography of Eileen Power, or Adam Sisman's biographies of A.J.P. Taylor and H.R. Trevor-Roper.[8] All of these biographies in their different ways add significantly to our understanding of the work of their subjects: the reasons why, and the way in which, they chose to study particular periods or problems; the influences exercised on them by teachers, friends or colleagues; the development of their methods and approaches. There is a question here, however, as to whether the biographical treatment provided by historians to their subjects when the subjects are historians is different in kind from the treatment of any other subject whose biography is written by a trained historian. Whether these works are simply good contemporary intellectual biographies, whose subjects simply happen to be historians, rather than something different in kind is difficult to resolve.

At the same time, it is clear that focusing on the lives of historians currently offers a new way of writing the history of history, both as a discipline and as a profession. Rather than focusing on institutions or changing scholarly methods, this new approach via both individual and collective biography is concerned with the impact of particular forms of family life and education, of personal outlook and especially of social networks on the work of historians. This line of enquiry allows ample scope for exploring the very different ways of writing history of near contemporaries – Strachey and Trevelyan, for example – and relating it to their personalities, the way they chose to live and their understanding of what writing history entailed. It does also serve to highlight the links between historians and the wider social and political world they inhabited or which served to furnish their imagination. As several essays in this

---

8   Mark McKenna, *An Eye for Eternity: The Life of Manning Clark* (Melbourne: Miegunyah Press, 2011); Maxine Berg, *A Woman in History: Eileen Power, 1886–1940* (Cambridge: Cambridge University Press, 1996); Adam Sisman, *A.J.P. Taylor: A Biography* (London: Sinclair-Stevenson, 1994); Sisman, *Hugh Trevor-Roper: The Biography* (London: Weidenfeld & Nicolson, 2010).

volume show, a biographical approach often underlines the importance of national stories and of the ways in which individual historians imagined them or imagined themselves in relationship to them.

The fallibility of memory is something that many autobiographers have to deal with. It is, as Sheila Fitzpatrick makes clear, particularly troubling for a historian, accustomed to questioning sources and checking facts, who is seeking in this case to use his or her own memory as an archive. Recognition of this difficulty in recording and writing their own lives, even for the most scrupulous of historians, alongside a much broader interest in the many challenges involved in understanding and writing the lives of others, does seem to have had a significant impact on how historians see their biographical subjects – especially on how they see the various ploys those subjects use to confuse later researchers. Where once the emphasis for the historian writing biography would have been placed squarely on unmasking the lies that a person told about him or herself and on revealing the *truth*, there now seems to be much more interest in how the subject constructed his or her own life, even if the construction was clearly fictitious. The fantasies and the creation of myths by a person have increasingly come to be seen as an important aspect of their lives and as something that needs to be understood, rather than exposed.

In a similar way, the false leads carefully constructed for later biographers by figures as different from each other as Manning Clark and Joseph Stalin become a source of interest and even of amusement. For the historian as writer, interested in the creative process of writing, it is as important to tell the reader how the clue was laid, discovered and then disentangled and what it is intended to hide or overlay, as it is to ascertain the actual truth of an event or a situation. What one begins to see here then is not just, as Fitzpatrick suggests, that the writing of autobiography by historians challenges many common assumptions about the writing of history but also that this wide and ever-growing interest in historians' autobiography and biography will fundamentally change the ways in which we see, think about and write history.

Index

Aboriginal history. *See* Indigenous history
Abramsky, Chimen 180, 183–5
Acton, J.E.E.D., Lord Acton 132–4, 154
Adam-Smith, Patsy 67, 264
Adams, James Truslow 289
Adler, Louise 20–1, 58
Aitken, Max, Lord Beaverbrook 21, 73–4, 78
Albany College (Oregon) 286
Alcock, Henry 229
Alexander, Fred 233, 239, 242
All Souls College, Oxford. *See* University of Oxford
American Historical Association 245, 274, 289, 297
Anderson, Perry 174, 201–2
Andrews, Charles McLean 12, 273–99, *275*
Andrews, Evangeline Walker 291, 293, 298
Angell, Norman 160
Antipodeanism 9, 199–224
Armstrong, Judith 270
Arnold, Matthew 159–60
Arnold, Thomas 147, 153, 162–3, 165–6
Askew, Susan 175
Auchmuty, James 262–3
Aurell, Jaume 2, 252–3

Australasian Association for the Advancement of Science. *See* Australia and New Zealand Association for the Advancement of Science
Australia and New Zealand Association for the Advancement of Science (ANZAAS) 229, 230, 237, 244–5, 258
Australian Broadcasting Commission. *See* Australian Broadcasting Corporation
Australian Broadcasting Corporation (ABC) 82, 92, 233, 238
Australian Dictionary of Biography (*ADB*) 10, 11, 67–8, 74–5, 227, 240–1, 244, 247–72
Australian Historical Association 10, 227, 245–6
Australian Institute of International Affairs 236, 238, 243
Australian Institute of Political Science 236
Australian Labor Party 6, 83, 88–9, 96. *See also* Dismissal
Australian National University (ANU) 1, 11, 81, 99, 240, 250–8 passim, 262
Australian Security Intelligence Organisation (ASIO) 31

Bach, John 263
Balliol College, Oxford. *See* University of Oxford
Baltimore Women's College (Maryland) 282
Banks, Sir Joseph 205–7, 213
Barnard, Marjorie 234, 238–9, 255, 263
Barnes, Viola Florence 275, 277, 278, 280, 282, 283, 287–90 passim, *288*, 291, 296–8 passim
Bassett, Jan 71–2
Beaglehole, J.C. 204
Bean, C.E.W. 267
Beaver College (Pennsylvania) 274, 283, 284–5
Beaverbrook, Lord. *See* Aitken, Max, Lord Beaverbrook
Beilharz, Peter 215
Bennett, Bruce 89
Berg, Maxine 304
Berkshire Conference of Women Historians 296–7
Berlin Wall 81
Berndt, Catherine 266
Bindman, David 203
Blackman, Barbara 217
Blackman, Charles 215–16
Blainey, Ann 267
Blainey, Geoffrey 237, 267
Bliss, Michael 129
Bloomsbury Group 8, 138, 140–1, 143, 149, 167, 170
Blunt, Anthony 201–2, 203, 208
Bolton, Geoffrey v, xi, 10–11, 242, 267
Bonyhady, Tim 269, 302
Bourne, Ruth May 280, 282–5 passim, 287, 298
Bowling Green State College (Ohio) 285
Boyd, Arthur 87, 212, 214, 215, 220, 266
Boyd, Robin 214

Boyer Lectures 82, 208
Brack, Helen 217
Brewin, Andrew 131
Briggs, Asa 244
Briscoe, Gordon 249
British Labour Party (BLP) 125, 178–9, 183, 193, 195. *See also* Oxford Labour Club
British Union of Fascists (BUF) 179–80
Brocklebank, Theaden 251, 252, 270
Brown University 282, 283
Brown, George 120, 124–5
Brown, William Jethro 229
Bruce, James Fawthrop 232, 237
Bryn Mawr College (Pennsylvania) 12, 273, 274, 277–84 passim, 293–4
Burn, Ian 223
Bury, J.B. 138, 153–4, 156, 160, 170
Butler, Rex 223
Butlin, Noel 267
Butt, Dennis 195

Caine, Barbara xi, 12–13
Calder, Isabel MacBeath 275, 280, 282, 283, 287, 289, 295
California Western University 283
Cambridge Apostles 138–9, 140, 149, 151–3, 158. *See also* Bloomsbury Group
Campbell, Mildred L. 280, 282–4 passim, 287, 296
Campbell, Persia 234–5, 236
Campion, Edmund 87–8
Canadian Broadcasting Corporation (CBC) 103
Cannadine, David 8
Capon, Edmund 266
Carey, Peter 84
Carlyle, Thomas 23, 86, 107, 117, 149, 154, 159, 170
Carr, E.H. 261
Casey, Maie 66, 266–7

Cassirer, Ernst 204
Catalyst Club 234
Charteris, Archibald 236
Childe, Vere Gordon 267
Church of England 50–1, 117
Clark, Dora Mae 275, 280, 282, 283, 286, 287, 289, 298, 299
Clark, Dymphna 6–7, 84, 86, 94–5, 97, 99, 270
Clark, Sir Kenneth 203, 214, 217–18
Clark, Manning 6–7, 9, 20, 81–102, 241–2, 244, 248, 259, 262, 265, 267, 270, 302, 304, 305
Clarke, Mary Patterson 274–5, 280, 282, 283, 284–5, 286
Clendinnen, Inga 72–3, 248
Clune, Frank 264
Coghlan, Timothy 267
Cold War 18–19, 26–31, 76–7, 118, 125, 187–93, 197, 208, 214, 215, 217, 220
Colley, Linda 268
Collingwood, R.G. 251, 260, 270
Columbia University 278, 280, 283
Communism. *See* Communist Party of Great Britain; Historians' Group of the Communist Party; Marxism; Soviet Union
Communist Party of Great Britain (CPGB) 174, 178–88, 192–6
Conlon, Alf 239
Conway, Jill Ker 4, 70–1, 78, 248, 266
Conway, John 71
Cook, Florence. *See* Fast, Florence Cook
Cook, George Russell 106–17, 120–1
Cook, James 204–6, 212
Cook, Lillie Ellen 106, 107, 109–11, 114–16
Cook, Ramsay 6–7, 103–34
Cornell University 278
Crawford, R.M. (Max) 10, 232, 234, 239, 242, 253, 254–5, 263, 267

Creighton, Donald 104
Crisp, L.F. (Fin) 239, 241
Crowe, Harry 124–5, 127–8
Crowley, Frank 242, 245, 263
Currey, C.H. 239
Curthoys, Ann 267
Curtin, John 87

Danos, Michael (Misha) 31–6
Dark, Eleanor 238
Davidson, Jim 231, 249–50, 251–2, 256, 270
Davison, Graeme 269, 302
De Berg, Hazel 262
Deakin, Alfred 63, 87
Dening, Greg 210
Deutscher, Isaac 29
Dicey, A.V. 132
Dickinson, Goldsworthy 138, 153
Dictionary of National Biography (*DNB*) 252, 256, 257
Dilthey, Wilhelm 260–1
Dismissal (1975) 89–91
displaced persons (DPs) 30, 31–2, 33, 35–6
Disraeli, Benjamin 138, 167, 168
Drysdale, Russell 212–13, 266
Dudley, Louise 280–2 passim
Dunbabin, Robert 229
Dunham, William H., Jr 291–2
Dutton, Geoffrey 90
Dyason, E.C. 235–6

Eagleton, Terry 138
Eakin, Paul John 301–2
Edel, Leon 143–4, 149
Edele, Mark 31
Eisenstadt, A.S. 291
Eldershaw, Flora 234, 238, 255
Elkington, John 228
Ellis, Ellen Deborah 280, 282, 290
Ellis, Malcolm 74–5, 239, 241, 258–9, 262
Elton, Geoffrey 74, 261

Evatt, H.V. 255
Eyre, Joe 42, 54–5, 61

Fast, Florence Cook 280–1, 290, 294–6
Fernon, Christine 75
Finnis, Harold 263
First World War 24, 44, 51, 71, 74, 127, 132, 139, 151, 160–1, 164, 209, 227, 230, 233, 235, 297
Fitzhardinge, Laurie 240, 257–8, 260–2 passim
Fitzpatrick, Brian 20–5, 30, 31, 32, 34–5, 42–3, 45, 50, 57, 70, 76, 258, 267, 270
Fitzpatrick, Doff 32, 42–3, 45, 48
Fitzpatrick, Kathleen 70, 233, 248, 260, 266, 270
Fitzpatrick, Sheila xi, 2–3, 4, 17–37, 39–63, 76–7, 265, 270, 302–3, 305
Foss, Paul 223
Foster, Leonie 235
Franklin, Miles 212, 238
Frear, Mary Reno 280, 282–4 passim, 292
Fry, Roger 153
Fussell, Paul 164

Gabriel, R.H. 287
Garner, Alice 75–6
Garner, Helen 75
Garrison, Helen Stuart 280, 282–4 passim, 291
Gibbon, Edward 1, 86
Gibson, Frederick 130
Gilmore, Dame Mary 66, 238
Goldsmith, Oliver 7
Gollan, Robin 267
Gordon, Lindsay 200, 202
Gosse, Edmund 24
Goucher College (Maryland) 282
Grant, Jane. *See* Strachey
Grass, Gunter 92

Gray, Geoffrey xii, 3–4
Great Depression 67, 108–9, 209, 285, 287, 295
Great War. *See* First World War
Green, Frank Clifton 263
Green, H.M. 254–5, 260
Green, J.R. 117
Greenwood, Gordon 243
Greer, Germaine 69
Grenville, Kate 88
Griffin, Helga 68
Griffin, Jim 68
Grimshaw, Patricia 68–9

Hall, Hessel Duncan 232–3, 236
Hall, Stuart 191–2
Hancock, Ian 99
Hancock, W.K. (Sir Keith) 11, 74–5, 233, 240–1, 244, 247–72, *254, 255*
Harper, Norman 243
Hartwell, Max 242
Harvard University 71
Hasluck, Alexandra 67–8, 266
Hasluck, Paul 67, 239, 264, 267
Heaman, Elsbeth 105
Hearn, W.E. 228
Hebrew University, Jerusalem 184
Heilbrun, Carolyn 77
Henderson, George 229, 230, 233, 238
Herder, Johann Gottfried 128
Higgins, Esmonde 233
Hill, Caroline Miles 279–80, 282
Hill, Christopher 188, 190
Historians' Group of the Communist Party (HGCP) 174, 187–90
History Workshop 9, 174–6, 197
Hobsbawm, Eric 196
Hofstadter, Richard 125
Hoggart, Richard 55, 61
Holmes, Richard 155
Holroyd, Michael 8, 94
Holt, Stephen 85

Holton, Sandra 251
Hood College (Maryland) 283
Hoon, Bessie E. 280, 282–4 passim, 285–6, 287, 292, 298
Horne, Donald 69, 90
Hughes, Robert 218–19
Hunter College (New York) 283, 286
Hutchinson, Emilie J. 291, 299

Indigenous history: Australia 11, 72–3, 83, 87, 97–8, 205, 208, 238, 246, 248–9, 271; Canada 115, 118, 120
Inglis, Amirah 68
Inglis, Ken 2, 84, 87, 96, 242
Institute of Pacific Relations 236, 238

Jacobsen, Gertrude Ann 280, 282, 283, 286, 289–90, 298
James, Gwyn 259–60, 263
Japanese Canadians 111–13, 131–3
Johns Hopkins University 12, 273, 274, 277, 281
Johns, Fred 259
Johnson, Cecil 286
Johnson, Richard R. 273–4, 277
Johnson, Samuel 7
Jones, Barry 88
Jones, Ken 174–5

Kean, Hilda 175
Keele University 56
Kennedy, Maybelle R. 280, 282, 283, 292
Kerr, Sir John. *See* Dismissal
Keynes, John Maynard 138, 150, 153
Kiddle, Margaret 260
Kingston, Beverley 245
Klingberg, Frank J. 290–1, 295–6
Korean War 125
Kramer, Leonie 244
Kriegel, Annie 303
Kristallnacht 6–7, 97
Ku Klux Klan 116

Labaree, Leonard Woods 277, 278, 286, 294
Labor Party (Australia). *See* Australian Labor Party
Labour Party (United Kingdom). *See* British Labour Party
Lambert, Sheila 74
Lamont, Peter 103, 104, 134
La Nauze, John 241, 242
Lane, Terry 92
Laski, Harold 167, 238
La Trobe University 72
Laurence, Margaret 113, 123
Laurendeau, André 131
Lawson, Henry 82, 87, 264, 267
Lawson, Louisa 267
League of Nations Union 235
Lee, Hermione 104, 264
Legge, John 43, 54, 240, 242–3
Lejeune, Philippe 2–3, 17, 22
Lessing, Doris 81, 88
Levinas, Emmanuel 206
Light, Alison 268
Liversidge, Archibald 229
Lloyd Jones, Richard 173
Lodewyckz, Dymphna. *See* Clark
London School of Economics 235, 237, 238, 243
Long, Gavin 258
Lord, Eleanor L. 280, 282
Lower, Arthur 129–31
Lyceum Club 234

Macalester College (Minnesota) 126
Macaulay, Thomas Babington 86, 141, 144, 151, 154, 157, 159, 170
McAuley, James 41
McBriar, Alan 242–3
McCarthy, Wendy 75
McGill University 131
Macintyre, Stuart 250, 252, 266
Mackaness, George 260
McKay, Ian 105

McKenna, Mark xii, 6–7, 20, 302, 304
McKenry, Keith 269
MacLachlan, Alastair xii, 8
McLachlan, Noel 99
McLuhan, Marshall 122
McMinn, W.G. (Greg) 263
McNaught, Kenneth 124–5, 127–8, 130
McPhee, Peter 75
MacQueen, Edith E. 280, 297, 298–9
McQueen, Humphrey 89, 95, 98, 99
Madgwick, R.B. 237, 239
Magritte, René 103, 104, 134
Malcolm, Janet 98
Manning, Frederick J. 278, 283, 293, 297
Manning, Helen Taft 278, 280, 282, 283, *292*, 293–4, 296
Martin, Allan 87, 240, 242
Marx, Karl 68, 202. *See also* Marxism
Marxism 8–9, 19, 20, 173–5, 182, 187–93, 202, 205, 210, 211, 217, 222–4, 242, 261. *See also* Communist Party of Great Britain; Historians' Group of the Communist Party; New Left; Soviet Union
Maryville College (Tennessee) 282
Matthews, Brian 85, 265, 267
Maxwell, Camilla 22
Melbourne University Press 20, 58, 82, 88, 234, 260
Melbourne University Publishing. *See* Melbourne University Press
Melbourne, Alexander 229
Mill, James 157
Mitchell Library, Sydney 238
Mitchell, W.O. 106, 115, 117
Mitchell, W.T.J. 207
Molesworth, Bevil 233
Molony, John 269

Monash University 40, 43, 51, 54, 242, 243, 245
Moore, G.E. 138–9, 151–2, 156
Moorehead, Alan 78, 264
Moorhouse, Frank 265
Morison, Samuel Eliot 289
Morrison, Allan 263
Morriss, Margaret Shove 280, 282
Mount Holyoke College (Massachusetts) 274, 275, 282, 283, 287, 288, 290
Moyal, Ann xii, 4–5, 73–5, 77–8, 248, 269, 302
Mulvaney, John 267
Municipal University of Omaha 283
Munro, Doug xii–xiii, 3–4

Nagel, Thomas 28, 29
Nairn, Bede 87, 242, 263
Namier, Sir Lewis 261
National Biography Award 265
National Library of Australia 62, 78, 88, 257, 261, 263
Neilson, Nellie 274, *276*, 280, 282, 288, 290
New College, Oxford. *See* University of Oxford
New Jersey College for Women 283
New Left 174, 191–2, 196
Nicolson, Nigel 44
Nolan, Melanie xiii, 11–12, 75
Nolan, Sidney 87, 212, 214, 220, 266
Nora, Pierre 1–2, 247, 263, 303
Northwestern University 282
Novick, Peter 10

objectivity 2, 10, 17–19, 28, 33, 37, 154, 191, 249, 302–3
O'Brien, Eris 258
Orwell, George 55
Oxford Labour Club 190, 193–4
Oxford Movement 163

Palmer, Nettie 212, 254, 267
Palmer, Sheridan xiii, 9
Pargellis, Stanley M. 278
Park, Marion Edwards 293
Passerini, Luisa 303
Pembroke College (Rhode Island) 282
Pennsylvania State College 283
Pesman, Ros 266
Phillips, Peter 242
Pietsch, Tamson 10
Pike, Douglas 241
Pitman, Frank W. 295
Pomona College (California) 295
Popkin, Jeremy 1, 5–6, 63, 247–9, 251, 252–3, 263–4, 266, 301–2
Popular Front 178–9, 186, 187, 196
Portus, G.V. 236, 259, 264
Power, Eileen 304
Pringle, John Douglas 219–20
Public Record Office, London 296–8 passim
Putnam, Bertha 290
Pybus, Cassandra 75

Queen's University (Canada) 104, 128, 129–33
Quiet Revolution 131

Radcliffe College (Massachusetts) 278
Radi, Heather 69
Rechter, Miriam 245
Reid, John G. xiii, 12
Reid, Stewart 124–5, 127–8
Render, Hans 268
Reynolds, 'Josh' 242
Richards, Eric 61–2
Rickard, John 4, 39–63, 87, 269
Rickard, Pearl 41, 45, 47, 50, 52, 58, 59–60
Rickard, Philip 41, 44, 47, 50, 52, 58, 59–60
Rider College (New Jersey) 283
Riemer, Andrew 99

Rife, Clarence W. 297
Roberts, Stephen Henry 237–8, 243, 267
Robertson, Bryan 217–18
Roe, Jill 269
Roe, Michael 263
Rose, William 127
Ross, Sinclair 109
Round Table 235, 238
Rowbotham, Sheila 176, 197
Rudé, George 242, 245
Ruskin College, Oxford 174, 195
Russell, Bertrand 138, 140, 150, 152–3
Russia. *See* Soviet Union
Russian Revolution 77, 81
Ryan, Susan 75, 88–9

Said, Edward 203, 222
St Andrew's College, Saskatoon 108–9, 114, 115
St Antony's College, Oxford. *See* University of Oxford
Salter, James 92–3
Samuel, Barnett 177, 183
Samuel, Minna 177, 182–5
Samuel, Raphael 8–9, 173–97
Sats, Igor 26, 33, 77
Saville, John 177, 181
Schwarz, Bill 187, 188
Scott, Ernest 228, 233, 234, 236–9 passim, 259, 267
Scott, F.R. 131
Scott-Brown, Sophie xiii–xiv, 8–9
Second World War 10, 26, 31, 32, 55, 110–13, 116, 128, 131, 132, 180–1, 184, 209–10, 212, 237, 239–40, 241, 253, 298, 299
Sedgwick, Peter 191
Serle, Geoffrey 243, 263
Serle, Percival 257
Seymour, Charles 277, 293
Shann, Edward 229, 233
Shaw, A.G.L. 245

Simpson, F.A. 169–70
Sisman, Adam 7, 304
Smith College (Massachusetts) 71, 282, 283
Smith, Arthur Lionel 232, 233
Smith, Bernard 9, 199–224, *200*, *221*, 248
Smith, Bonnie G. 291
Smith, Marion Parris 280, 282
Smith, Terry 223
Solzhenitsyn, Alexander 29, 83
Southern, Richard 241
Soviet Union 18–20, 24–33, 76–7, 82, 83, 180–1, 186, 196, 217, 239, 265
Spanish Civil War 179, 180–1, 183
Spence, Catherine Helen 66
Spurr, Barry 158
Stalin, Joseph 19–20, 22, 26, 27–31, 193, 195–6, 305
Steedman, Carolyn 303
Steele, Ian K. 277
Stegner, Wallace 121–2
Steinberg, Jonathan 25
Stephens College (Missouri) 282
Steven, Margaret 263
Strachey, Jane 143
Strachey, Lytton 8, 137–71, 270, 304
Strachey, Sir Richard 142–3, 146
Stretton, Hugh 242
subjectivity 2, 18–19, 33, 37, 260, 272
Suez Crisis 55
Summers, Anne 75, 245
Swarthmore College (Pennsylvania) 283, 293

Tapp, Edwin 263
Taylor, A.J.P. 3, 21, 63, 123, 304
Taylor, Barbara 303
Taylor, Charles 191
Taylor, Paul 223
Teale, Ruth 263
Theobald, Marjorie 269

Thomas, Julian 266
Thompson, E.P. 174
Thomson, Edith E.B. 280, 298
Tillyrand, Pat 258
Tirrell, Sarah R. 280, 282–4 passim
Towle, Carroll S. 294
Towle, Dorothy S. 280–1, 294–5, 296
Trevelyan, George Macaulay 8, 137–71, 304
Trevelyan, George Otto 141, 144–5, 151
Trevelyan, Janet 153
Trevor-Roper, Hugh 7, 304
Trinity College, Cambridge. *See* University of Cambridge
Trotsky, Leon 29
Trudeau, Pierre 131
Tucker, Robert 29
Turner, Ian 68, 242
Twain, Mark 104

United Church of Canada 106, 108–11, 114–15, 117–18
United College, Winnipeg 123–9, 132
University of Adelaide 229, 233, 238, 241, 242–3, 250, 259
University of California, Los Angeles (UCLA) 290, 295
University of Cambridge 8, 138, 127, 149, 151, 158, 170, 171, 230, 238, 261; Trinity College 137, 138, 149, 169. *See also* Cambridge Apostles
University of Chicago 19, 40, 280, 283
University of Durham 286
University of Kansas 282, 284
University of London 127, 280, 286
University of Manchester 280
University of Manitoba 124

University of Melbourne 10–11, 18, 43, 48, 57, 68, 70, 72, 75–6, 85, 228, 233–43 passim, 245, 250, 253–4, 259. *See also* Melbourne University Press
University of Michigan 279–80
University of Minnesota 282, 286
University of Nebraska 282, 283, 288
University of New Hampshire 294
University of Oxford 10, 43, 54, 57, 70, 76, 82, 85, 90, 127, 190–5, 229, 230, 257; All Souls College 233, 250; Balliol College 10, 190, 230–3, 237, 241–3, 250, 256; New College 257; St Antony's College 26–7
University of Pennsylvania 278
University of the Punjab 237
University of Queensland 219, 229, 233, 243
University of St Andrews 280
University of Sydney 53–4, 68–9, 70–1, 73, 75, 228–39 passim, 243–4, 245, 257
University of Tasmania 229
University of Toronto 71, 128, 134
University of Western Australia 67, 229, 233, 241, 242, 250
University of Western Ontario 115
University of York (United Kingdom) 40
Upton, Eleanor S. 280, 282, 283

Vandiver, Frank 268
Vassar College (New York) 283, 287
Victoria University College (New Zealand) 237
Vietnam War 83
Vimy Ridge, Battle of 107, 114
Volkogonov, Dmitri 29

Walker, David 269, 302
Walter, James 89
Walvin, Emma 42, 46, 55, 56, 61

Walvin, James 4, 39–63
Ward, Biff 269
Ward, John Manning 243–4
Ward, Mary 153, 162
Ward, Russel 240, 244, 267, 269
Watson, Don 269–70
Webb, Jessie Stobo 233–4, 266
Wellesley College (Massachusetts) 283
Wells College (New York) 275, 283, 287
West, Francis 261, 262
White Australia Policy 83, 234
White, Patrick 87, 89–90
White, Richard 87, 99
Whitlam, Gough 43, 89. *See also* Dismissal
Whitson, Agnes M. 280, 291, 298
Wilde, W.H. (Bill) 267
Willard, Myra 234–5
Williams, C.M. (Mick) 242
Wilson College (Pennsylvania) 275, 283, 286, 287, 299
Winks, Robin W. 213
Winnipeg General Strike 125, 132
women historians 4–5, 11, 12, 19, 65–78, 233–5, 245, 249, 266–8, 273–99, 302–3
Wood, F.L.W. (Fred) 232, 237
Wood, G. Arnold 228–34 passim, 237
Woodsworth, J.S. 116, 123
Woolf, Leonard 138, 139, 142, 153, 164, 168
Woolf, Virginia 93, 151, 159, 267
Working Men's College, London 149, 152, 153
Wright, Donald xiv, 6–7, 10

Yale University 10, 12, 273–99
York University (Canada) 103, 122

www.ingramcontent.com/pod-product-compliance
Lightning Source LLC
Chambersburg PA
CBHW061255230426
43664CB00033B/2923